Iranian Politics and
Religious Modernism

Iranian Politics and Religious Modernism

THE LIBERATION MOVEMENT OF IRAN UNDER THE SHAH AND KHOMEINI

H. E. CHEHABI

Cornell University Press

ITHACA, NEW YORK

First published 1990 by Cornell University Press.

Library of Congress Cataloging-in-Publication Data

Chehabi, H. E.
   Iranian politics and religious modernism / H. E. Chehabi.
      p.   cm.
   Includes bibliographical references.
   ISBN 0-8014-2416-X (alk. paper)
      1. Nahzat-i Āzādī-i Īrān.   2. Islam and politics—Iran.   3. Iran—Politics
and government—1941–1979.   4. Iran—Politics and government—1979–   I. Title.
DS318.C47   1990
955.05′3—dc20   89-46180

⊚   The paper used in this publication meets the minimum requirements of the American National Standard for Permanence of Paper for Printed Library Materials Z39.48–1984.

Printed in the United States of America

For my parents

Contents

Acknowledgments

Many individuals helped me plan, research, and write this book. First and foremost I thank my parents. Only they and I know how much I owe them. Over a period of six years Mehdi Noorbakhsh provided me with most of my printed primary sources. I could not have undertaken my task had it not been for his constant assistance.

I gathered much information in the course of extensive interviews during four research trips to Europe in the summers of 1981, 1982, 1984, and 1985. The second trip was funded by a grant from the Yale Concilium on International and Area Studies. I thank all those in France and Germany, identified in the footnotes, who patiently answered my questions and shared their insights into Iranian politics. Mariam Salour and Dominique Menu in Paris and Edith Haag, Schapur Ansari, and Biejan Scherwatzke in Germany granted me gracious hospitality on these trips, for which I am grateful.

From the inception of this project Ervand Abrahamian's advice was most helpful. He generously made primary sources available to me and regularly commented in great detail on everything I wrote.

Much of the rewriting of the original version was done during the summers of 1986 and 1987, which I spent with hospitable friends in Berkeley who read my work and commented on it: Farhad Atai and Haleh Sadrzadeh gave both spiritual and culinary nourishment; Michel Chaouli and Marie Deer provided both rhyme and reason.

Ahmad Ashraf, Gerhard Böwering, Cosroe Chaqueri, Amy Colin, Hamid Dabashi, Stanley Hoffmann, Homa Katouzian, Gholamhosein Sadiqi, and Reza Sheikholeslami read parts of the manuscript; David

Apter, Richard Cottam, Robert Dahl, and Kavous Seyed-Emami read all of it. Their comments were most helpful.

Customary academic acknowledgments do not adequately capture the extent of my intellectual and personal indebtedness to Juan Linz. From the very beginning of my graduate studies he was teacher, adviser, guide, critic, and mentor. To Juan and Rocío Linz goes my deep gratitude for all they have given me.

In the course of my work I have sought, and received, the advice of many other friends, teachers, and colleagues. If this book contributes something to our understanding of contemporary Iran, I have them to thank for it.

H. E. Ch.

Cambridge, Massachusetts

A Note on Transliteration
and References

The frequent use of primary sources in this work warrants some explanatory remarks. All Persian words and names have been transliterated according to a simplified system that avoids diacritical marks. In a direct quote, however, the author's transliteration is respected. Arabic words in current Persian usage have been transliterated from Persian. Toponyms that have an accepted English form are not transliterated, such as Qum, Teheran, and Isfahan, instead of Qom, Tehran, and Esfahan. Personal names are transliterated according to the same system, even when the person used a different form himself: hence Mosaddeq instead of Mossadegh. Iranian double family names are not hyphenated.

When a Persian-language work is quoted, the translation is my own. Where English translations of Persian primary sources exist, these have been used. All Qoranic quotes are taken from Arthur J. Arberry's version.[1]

In the second and third parts of this study, the dates of important events are often given both in the Gregorian and in the Iranian (A.H.S.) calendar. Where warranted, the Islamic (A.H.L.) date is given too.

[1]Arthur J. Arberry, *The Koran Interpreted* (1964).

Abbreviations

Ay.	Ayatollah
CR	Council of the Revolution
H.	Hajj
Ho.	Hojjat ol-eslam
ICDFHR	Iranian Committee for the Defense of Freedom and Human Rights
IP	Iran party
IRP	Islamic Republican party
LMI	Liberation Movement of Iran
LMI(a)	Liberation Movement of Iran (abroad)
MPRP	Muslim People's Republican party
MSA	Muslim Student Association
NDF	National Democratic Front
NF	National Front
NF(II)	Second National Front
NF(III)	Third National Front
NRM	National Resistance Movement
PG	Provisional Government
PIN	Party of the Iranian Nation
PIP	Party of the Iranian People
PMOI	People's Mojahedin Organization of Iran
S.	Seyyed
SDFSIP	Society for the Defense of Freedom and the Sovereignty of the Iranian People

Iranian Politics and
Religious Modernism

Introduction

The Iranian revolution of 1979 has focused attention on Iran and the interaction between religion and politics, both in Iran and elsewhere. It has produced a wealth of scholarly works that try to analyze and explain the events and their underlying causes.

As valuable as these contributions are individually, a total picture of the Iranian problematic can emerge only after more monographs on more restricted topics have been written. Exclusive concentration on the revolution and the Shi'ite ulema can make events look inevitable in retrospect, and this retrospective inevitability can lead one to interpret the past in terms of the present. Historians call this the fallacy of *nunc pro tunc*, "the mistaken idea that the proper way to do history is to prune away the dead branches of the past, and to preserve the green buds and twigs which have grown into the dark forest of our contemporary world."[1] Social scientists, by paying attention exclusively to movements, currents of thought, institutions, and ideas that seem important at the time also risk creating a reductionist and incomplete picture of the world. Just as a full understanding of the Bolshevik revolution and subsequent developments in the Soviet Union must take into account the Mensheviks, the Social Revolutionaries, and even the Kadets, recent political developments in Iran can be grasped only if the apparent failure of moderate, secular, leftist, and regionalist groups is analyzed in some depth.

This book seeks to fill one of the gaps in our understanding of

[1]David Hackett Fisher, *Historians' Fallacies: Towards a Logic of Historical Thought* (1970), p. 135.

Iranian politics by focusing on the Nehzat-e azadi-ye Iran, or Liberation Movement of Iran, as party members like to call it in English.[2] Choosing the LMI is justified for a number of reasons. With the exception of the communist Tudeh party, about which we already have excellent monographs, there have been very few true political parties in Iran. Even the LMI is more a group of people who have always aspired to form a political party than an actual political party. Nevertheless, its role in recent Iranian history warrants a study, for the following reasons.

First, next to the Tudeh, the LMI is the oldest *continuously functioning* political grouping in Iran. Its leaders were active in the opposition against the Shah after 1953, carried out parapolitical oppositional activities during the most repressive years of the Shah's dictatorship, 1963–77; took a leading role in the attempted liberalization of 1977–78; negotiated the transition to the Islamic Republic; staffed the ephemeral Provisional Government of 1979; and have led the only tolerated opposition in the Islamic Republic of Iran. Analyzing the interaction of such a group with successive regimes adds to our knowledge of political development in Iran. Also, a monograph on an oppositional party in a nondemocratic setting throws considerable light on our understanding of the transitions between regimes, peaceful or revolutionary.

Second, most studies of nondemocratic countries neglect oppositional groups and concentrate on the institutions, policies, and social bases of the ruling regimes. The opposition groups that have escaped this scholarly neglect are either those whose goals a sizable portion of academia supports, or those that pose a clear threat to the international status quo. Leftist and more recently fundamentalist political movements have thus received much more attention than moderate groups. This overall neglect of oppositional activity in nondemocratic regimes can easily lead to an overestimation of these regimes' stability.

A third reason has to do with the changing role of religion in Iranian society. The sudden eruption of the Islamic Republic on the world scene in the penultimate decade of the twentieth century may lead one to declare religion the independent variable in Iranian history and comb it for hitherto-overlooked events and developments that support such a view. A close look at the LMI can help us to avoid this pitfall. The beginnings of the LMI fall into a period when secularism dominated political life in Iran. The party was then led by moderately religious laymen and based its appeal on religion *among other things*. In the span

---

[2] The actual translation of the Persian words is "Iranian Freedom Movement," which is what many scholarly publications call the LMI.

of less than two decades, society as such became so infused with religious values and sentiments, that the selfsame men who had looked like religious fanatics to some in the early 1960s now are the most secular members of Iran's political class.[3] The evolution of the LMI is at the same time a reflection of, and a contributor to this development. By studying the party's interaction with both the secular political groups and the ulema, we gain insights into how the momentous shift came about.

As already mentioned, the LMI is not really a political party in the common sense of the word, largely because conditions in Iran have seldom allowed for the constitution of parties. Above all the LMI is a group of men gathered around one politician who has put his mark both on Iran's political life and on its intellectual history: Mehdi Bazargan. Many other figures who gained temporary or permanent prominence in recent Iranian history have also been associated with the party to varying degrees: the late Ay. S. Mahmud Taleqani, Ali Shariati, Sadeq Qotbzadeh, and Ebrahim Yazdi, to name the best known. Given the absence of true party structures, the individual activities of these men constitute LMI activity over long periods of time. An emphasis on these personal activities, therefore, is not an expression of a "Great Men" conception of history, but quite simply a recognition of the fact that, to quote Guenther Lewy, "where genuine alternatives exist, the presence or absence of a great man may be crucial."[4]

It is the social scientist's aim to discover wider patterns, to generalize from the particular. Monographic studies can easily lose sight of this goal, for as Sidney Verba remarked, the monographs do not "easily add up."[5] To avoid this danger, I have tried to adopt Verba's remedy, the "disciplined configurative approach."[6] The structure of this book reflects this choice: Part I (especially chapter 1) sets up the "configurations" and by the same token puts the case study in comparative perspective, while Parts II and III analyze the LMI in depth using the analytical tools developed in the first part. Part II deals with the development of religious modernism as a political force under the Shah's regime; Part III focuses on the LMI's role in the Islamic revolution. Comparativists might find Parts II and III marred by longueurs, but I would like to remind them that the development of social theory is an inductive

[3]This excludes all the secular forces who are either silenced, in the underground, or exiled.
[4]G. Lewy, "Historical Data in Comparative Political Analysis," *Comparative Politics* 1 (October 1968), 105.
[5]S. Verba, "Some Dilemmas in Comparative Research," *World Politics* 20 (October 1967), 112.
[6]Ibid., p. 114.

process, and, as Joseph LaPalombara rightly noted, we know very little about the actual politics of many countries.[7]

A final word on methodology. Given the scant attention that moderate opposition movements in nondemocratic states receive in the press, information on their activities is difficult to come by. Also, their own publications are more likely to concentrate on denouncing the regime than on internal workings of the opposition, as these must be surrounded by secrecy. Field research seems to be the only answer.

In my case this was not feasible. I decided on the following strategy. First I made careful readings of all the available sources, both primary and secondary. The primary sources were most often produced by the LMI itself; exclusive reliance on them might have produced a skewed picture. I decided to balance these sources by interviewing Iranian political figures outside Iran who have been in contact with the party during their career. Two of these were founding members of the LMI, and were thus privy to very valuable information.

This method, however, was not without its pitfalls, for sometimes accounts of the same event varied considerably. In such cases I have tried to the best of my ability to relate only those facts on which my sources agreed. Nonetheless, it is quite probable that here or there I got something wrong, and I hope that future studies will correct these errors.

[7] J. LaPalombara, "Macrotheories and Microapplications in Comparative Politics," *Comparative Politics* 1 (October 1968), 62–65.

PART I

RELIGIOUS MODERNISM
AND NATIONALISM
IN A DUAL SOCIETY

CHAPTER 1

The Iranian Polity in
Comparative Perspective

Iran is one of the few Third World states that are not "new," in the sense that they do not owe their present configuration to European colonialism. While Iran's political development certainly lagged behind that of Western Europe, it can still be analyzed in terms of a time-frame roughly similar to that of most European nations. To give but one example, Iran had its constitutional revolution in 1906—only one year after Russia, the European "late-developer" par excellence.

Nations do not develop in isolation and the influence of the international environment is perhaps most significant in the case of old non-Western states such as Iran, for it is often the particular place of such a country in the international system that enabled it to preserve its independence. Nationalist activity is conditioned by external variables, to which it is a response. In studying a political party such as the Liberation Movement of Iran, which has always understood itself as part of the Nationalist tradition in Iranian politics, one therefore has to begin by trying to understand the external factors that impelled the Nationalists to political action.

Old Polities of the Developing World: The Case of Iran

Crisis of Sovereignty

Samuel Huntington has recognized the existence of an intermediary category of nation-states between the new states of the Third World and the old nations of the West and attempted to analyze their politics

7

systematically.[1] Although in many ways brilliant, his analysis tends to minimize the foreign influence on these nations' internal politics. Their sovereignty was forever threatened, as their governments were weakened by internal unrest, by contact with European commerce and finance, by involvement with European politics, or by ignorance and administrative inefficiency which left them helpless in the modern world, whose hegemonic powers would often come to arbitrary agreements as to their destiny. Lenin, who had a clear appreciation of the unequal nature of these countries' relations with the West, called them "semi-colonies" as early as 1915.[2]

The five-crises model of political development elaborated by the Committee on Comparative Politics of the Social Science Research Council was formulated mainly on the basis of the European experience, and fails to take into account the strong external impact on the old polities of the developing world.[3] The impact of external forces can be termed a "crisis of sovereignty."[4] Building on Raymond Grew's scheme, the diagram shown in Figure 1 suggests itself.

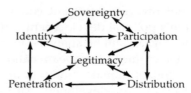

Figure 1. Six crises of political development

Sovereignty is most closely related to legitimacy, as any authority that becomes too subservient to foreign interests is likely to see its legitimacy undermined. The precarious international situation of the weak country may also mean that foreign powers encourage or even foment separatist stirrings, exacerbating the crisis of identity. Conversely, identity may also be fortified by the perception of a foreign threat equally affecting everybody. Another type of crisis of identity may occur if certain population strata are well integrated into international networks of exchange but others are not. External factors may block or encourage (or nullify the results of) participation. And finally, a crisis of sovereign-

[1]Samuel P. Huntington, *Political Order in Changing Societies* (1968), chap. 3, pp. 140–91.
[2]V. I. Lenin, "On the Slogan for the United States of Europe," 1st publ. in *Sotsial-Demokrat*, no. 44, August 23, 1915. *Collected Works*, vol. 21 (1967), pp. 339–43.
[3]See Leonard Binder et al., *Crises and Sequences in Political Development* (1971).
[4]The term is Raymond Grew's. See his "Crises and Sequences," in Grew, ed., *Crises of Political Development in Europe and the United States* (1978), p. 10.

ty may precipitate crises of penetration in the peripheral areas of the weak state.[5]

One important consequence of the role played by exogenous forces in the political development of the old non-Western polities is that modernization was not only a societal process, as in the West, but a policy goal of the rulers, often arrived at as a response to Western challenges. If the integrity of the non-Western polities was to be maintained, they had to emulate the Western societies, so as to master their secrets and thus stand up to them. Since there was no other model, modernization ineluctably also entailed a certain measure of Westernization. The West affected these societies therefore not only by its own agents—diplomatic, religious, or military—but also through the actions of indigenous elites.

Modernization imposed from above affected societies selectively, producing what have been called "post-traditional" societies, in which "development of some institutional or organizational frameworks sharing many characteristics of modern organizations may take place in segregated parts of a still 'traditional' social structure, and their infusion may even reinforce those traditional systems."[6] These pockets of modernization are more susceptible to influence by international factors, and can be the avenues of foreign meddling in states whose sovereignty is under pressure.

Iran's Fragile Sovereignty

Iran owed its persistent independence to its strategic position between the expanding Russian Empire, to which it had lost Caucasian territories in the early nineteenth century, and the British Empire in India.

The administrative reforms that were undertaken in Iran in the second half of the nineteenth century on the model of the Ottoman Tanzimat were half-hearted and brought only partial and disappointing results, and the country's decline accelerated after the assassination of Nasereddin Shah in 1896. Internally the country disintegrated as the authority of the central government weakened. Since Iran was quite close to Europe, Western ideas readily found their way into the country, often via Russia. When Russia was defeated by a non-Western power, Japan, in 1905, nationalist modernizers in Iran, like their counterparts elsewhere in Asia, received a tremendous moral boost,

---

[5]For the other relationships, see ibid., pp. 25–28.

[6]S. N. Eisenstadt, "Post-Traditional Societies and the Continuity and Reconstruction of Tradition," in Eisenstadt, *Post-Traditional Societies* (1974), p. 3.

and in alliance with the ulema and the Bazaar merchants, they wrested a constitution from the monarchy as early as 1906–7.

During these years of instability Russia and Britain intervened more or less openly in Iranian politics, backing conservative and liberal factions vying for power in Teheran, and provincial governors whose subordination to Teheran was often only nominal. The division of Iran was made official in 1907, when Russia and Britain divided Iran into "zones of influence," with the lion's share (including the capital) allotted to Russia. During World War I, although Iran had proclaimed its neutrality, the Allies and the Ottomans fought on Iranian territory; they occupied large regions and caused much hardship for the population. At the Paris Peace Conferences, Iran's participation was blocked by Lord Curzon, who feared that "a Persian delegation, let loose in Paris, would play off the powers one against the other."[7] In 1919, Britain, war-weary but frightened by the prospect of Bolshevik advances in the Middle East, attempted to force a treaty on Iran which in fact would have established a protectorate. The Iranian parliament, however, under the pressure of public opinion, refused to give its consent.

In World War II, Iran again proclaimed its neutrality, and again the Allies needed Iranian territory for their war effort. In 1941 they invaded Iran, forced the country's head of state, Reza Shah Pahlavi, to abdicate, and thus inaugurated a period of relative political pluralism that would last until 1953. In that year Mohammad Reza Pahlavi became effective ruler of the country when the CIA gave decisive backing to a coup that ousted Prime Minister Mohammad Mosaddeq. In terms of our scheme (Figure 1), both interventions precipitated crises of sovereignty, which affected—one positively and one negatively—participation. But the Allied occupation of Iran also had an impact on identity: in 1945 two of the Soviet-occupied provinces, inhabited by ethnic minorities, proclaimed their autonomy and created a major crisis of identity. Although the Soviets did not create the peripheral nationalisms in Azerbaijan and Kurdistan, the separatist enterprise would not have gone as far as it did had not Soviet troops prevented the Iranian army from entering the two provinces. The two autonomist states collapsed mainly because the Soviet Union sacrificed local Iranian communists to its own foreign policy interests.[8]

Twice after the fall of Mosaddeq, in 1960 and 1976, were newly

---

[7]Quoted in John Darwin, *Britain, Egypt, and the Middle East: Imperial Policy in the Aftermath of War, 1918–1922* (1981), p. 157.

[8]For details see Rouhollah K. Ramazani, "The Autonomous Republics of Azerbaijan and Kurdistan: Their Rise and Fall," in Thomas T. Hammond, ed., *The Anatomy of Communist Takeovers* (1975).

elected Democratic administrations in Washington, D.C., perceived as exerting a certain amount of pressure on the Shah to liberalize his regime. Whether the Shah's two attempts at liberalization were in fact due to U.S. pressure or not is still debated, but for the purpose of this book what matters is that "if men define situations as real, they are real in their consequences."[9] For the vast majority of Iranians, the liberalizations of 1960 and 1977 were the Shah's responses to U.S. pressure, and therefore illustrated the extent of American influence over Iran's domestic politics.

The long history of foreign intervention in Iranian affairs helps explain the immense popularity among the Iranian population of the androlepsia of November 1979.[10] The occupation of the U.S. embassy, a "spy nest," was a symbolic ending to almost a century of foreign meddling and produced a catharsis that consecrated the success of the revolution.

This is not the place to analyze Iran's political development in terms of the six crises mentioned earlier. The foregoing discussion is meant only to illustrate the close connection between the international environment and domestic politics in the case of Iran. Any case study of Iranian politics must take this connection into account.

Nationalism in the Old Polities of the Developing World

In countries with continuously unresolved crises of sovereignty, the constellation of political forces reflects this fundamental uncertainty, as some political figures and parties inevitably become identified with one or another of outside powers, while others strive for complete emancipation in international society. In Iran, as in China and Egypt, the sovereignty crisis dragged on for long periods. Therefore the cleavage lines that in Europe gave rise to the party systems[11] were superseded by the issue of sovereignty, and those who stood for the unequivocal establishment of sovereignty became known as "Nationalists": the Kuomintang in China, the Wafd in Egypt, and the more amorphous National Movement in Iran. The paramountcy of the sovereignty issue means that within the Nationalist movements people of varying, and even opposing, ideologies and outlooks had to work together, which sometimes diminished their effectiveness.

[9]Robert Merton, *Social Theory and Social Structure* (1963), p. 421.

[10]"Androlepsia: the seizure by one nation of the citizens or subjects of another to compel the latter to do justice to the former, or to enforce some right claimed by the former against the latter." *Webster's New International Dictionary*, 2d ed.

[11]See Seymour M. Lipset and Stein Rokkan, "Cleavage Structures, Party Systems, and Voter Alignments: An Introduction," in Lipset and Rokkan, eds., *Party Systems and Voter Alignments: Cross-National Perspectives* (1967), pp. 1–64.

In Iran this type of emancipatory nationalism is identified with the figure of Mohammad Mosaddeq and the National Movement (Nehzat-e Melli) that he came to lead. This force can be defined as the political movement that has striven to establish Iran's unequivocal sovereignty within and without; in other words, it means rule of law within, and political independence, coupled with full control over natural resources, without. The organizational embodiment of the National Movement was the National Front (Jebhe-ye Melli). The front, being a coalition, was internally heterogeneous, and included liberals, socialists, ethnonationalists, and religiously inspired reformists. What held them together was their common goal of overcoming Iran's crisis of sovereignty.

Beyond interventions and the structure of political cleavages, what are the wider implications for Iranian politics of this close connection between internal affairs and international politics? Paradoxically, the fact that Iran maintained its formal sovereignty throughout this century aggravated the nefarious results of foreign intervention. In protectorates, such as Morocco, the foreign presence was only the result of an unequal power-constellation. Therefore the indigenous elites still identified with the cause of national independence. In Ethiopia, the emperor became a symbol of national independence after the Italian attack of 1935.

In Iran foreign powers operated directly but also indirectly through their friends in the political class. The occult character of this foreign influence as opposed to its directness elsewhere, meant that in the perception of many politically articulate Iranians the country's political system was, above all else, a xenocracy, with various sets of pro-British, pro-Russian, and later pro-American politicians vying to exercise power. This is perhaps the origin of Iranians' well-known penchant for conspiracy theories.

In this general atmosphere of distrust, the natural give-and-take of politics was impossible. Given the salience of the sovereignty issue and the nature of the National Movement, Iranian politics became highly polarized: politicians were either patriots or traitors. These are absolute terms that preclude compromise, the essence of civilized politics.[12]

It stands to reason that for foreign powers to intervene so easily and consistently in Iranian affairs, Iranian society must have suffered from inherent weaknesses. The (real or assumed) ubiquity of foreign interests distracted many well-meaning and progressive Iranians from an analysis of these weaknesses. Blaming foreigners for *all* ills all too often

---

[12]It is symptomatic that in Persian the word for "compromise," *sazesh*, has come to connote sell-out.

became a comfortable way of evading critical confrontation with domestic problems.

Legitimacy in Iran

Legitimacy, of course, is in the eyes of the beholder, and a certain type of authority may be legitimate in the eyes of some and illegitimate in the eyes of others. Iran in the twentieth century is an example of competing claims to legitimacy.[13]

The Monarchy

Compared to the continuity of European monarchies, whose basic legitimation formulas were not substantially changed after the Carolingians, the monarchy in Iran has undergone a surprising number of mutations. As Otto Hintze has shown, monarchies in the West were limited from the outset by three sets of institutions: (1) the old Germanic principle of reciprocity of obligations between the ruler and ruled; (2) representative bodies of the Roman Empire, as transmitted and modified by the church (principally the provincial diets, or *conciliae*); and (3) the "exemption of certain persons or groups from the direct effects of public authority, and the transfer of public, legal powers to these very persons or groups, the upshot being isolated self-government."[14] Out of these institutions grew the Estates, the forerunners of modern parliaments. Royal absolutism in Europe was therefore only an interlude between a monarchy limited by Estates and one limited by a modern parliament. Such representative, limiting institutions were lacking in the monarchies of the Middle East. The outstanding feature of the monarch's role in Iran was the arbitrariness of his power. This does not mean that it was absolute, as he had to contend with organized groups such as the guilds, the clergy, tribal chieftains, and so on; but checks on his power resulted from power relationships and had no formally institutionalized basis. The ruler answered only to God.

Religion

Although to this day half a dozen religions are represented in Iran, the overall picture of the country is one of religious homogeneity.

[13]The concepts in the following discussion are taken from Max Weber, *Economy and Society,* ed. Guenther Roth and Claus Wittich (1978), pp. 215–16.

[14]See Hintze's essay "The Preconditions of Representative Government in the Context of World History," in *The Historical Essays of Otto Hintze,* ed. Felix Gilbert (1975), pp. 309–11.

Shi'ite Muslims constitute the vast majority of Iran's population. The origins of Shi'ism are well-known and need not be retold here.[15]

When the Safavids established Shi'ism as the official religion of Iran in the sixteenth century, they endowed the religious institution with great wealth, and from the seventeenth century onward the ulema had their own sources of income and were therefore less dependent on the state than in most Sunni lands. The caesaropapistic tendencies of the later Ottoman empire (after the sultan called himself caliph) were thus lacking in Iran, and the country had an independent ulema alongside the monarchy, not unlike the church in the Catholic countries of Europe. In the long period of turmoil that followed the fall of the Safavids in 1722, the Shi'ite ulema of Iran maintained their institutional continuity. The political turmoil therefore had an effect similar to that which the fall of the Roman empire in the West had exerted on the Christian church in Western Europe. By the time the Qajars began their rule in Iran in 1785, the two centers of traditional authority, ruler and ulema, existed independently of each other.

During the nineteenth century doctrinal developments within Iranian Shi'ism led to the ulema assuming a greater role in religious life.[16] Since then a Shi'ite believer has had to choose a source of emulation (*marja'*) from among the *mujtahids*, those members of the ulema qualified to exercise the independent interpretation of laws, *ijtihad*. The Shi'ite ulema's role as intermediaries between believers and revelation perhaps justifies the common use of the term "clergy" to designate them, in spite of the fact that they are not "priests" in the technical sense of the word.[17]

Not all religious life is dominated by the ulema, however. One modern anthropologist, proceeding empirically, identified eleven religious settings, catering to a variety of social needs, of which only four or five normally involve the ulema.[18] Shi'ism, never a monolithic force in Iran, has always contained a variety of intellectual styles and traditions, some of which became the basis of challenges to official orthodoxy.[19] For our purpose it is important to note that religious modernism could arise outside the institutional framework of organized religion and still be part of Iran's religious tradition. To quote Edward Shils, "The standards of rejection are almost always acquired from some marginal

---

[15]For an exhaustive study see Moojan Momen, *An Introduction to Shi'i Islam* (1985).

[16]Abbas Amanat, "In Between the Madrasa and the Marketplace: The Designation of Clerical Leadership in Modern Shi'ism," in *Authority and Political Culture in Shi'ism*, ed. Said Amir Arjomand (1988).

[17]See Weber, *Economy and Society*, p. 440.

[18]Michael M. J. Fischer, *Iran: From Religious Dispute to Revolution* (1980), pp. 136–37.

[19]Mangol Bayat, *Mysticism and Dissent: Socioreligious Thought in Qajar Iran* (1982).

strand of the general constellation of traditions which govern or are available in the society."[20] A powerful clergy almost always also leads to strong anticlericalism, even among many believers. The monopoly the ulema claim on the interpretation of Islamic laws represents a formidable problem for religious modernists, who have often assumed "protestant" positions.

The Aborted Emergence of Legal-Rational Authority

In the Christian West, the rise of strong urban centers and the continued conflicts between temporal and religious authorities led to the gradual emergence of a legal-rational order. In Iran such a development did not take place, perhaps because the intermediate institutions and the system of immunities that obtained in the West were lacking.

Under the Qajars, state and clergy coexisted harmoniously until the end of the nineteenth century. The alliance first showed cracks in 1892, when Nasereddin Shah granted the "tobacco concession" to foreign interests. The reaction came in the form of an alliance between merchants, who resented the intrusion of foreigners on their traditional turf, and the clergy, who were weary of infidel infiltration. The Shah had to cancel the concession, but the prestige of the monarchy was tainted. Under the influence of Western ideas a constitutional movement grew in Iran, borne by an alliance of the ulema with the emerging middle classes.[21] This alliance finally triumphed in the Constitutional Revolution of 1905–6. The primary aim of this coalition was not, however, to establish popular rule, but rather to end the *arbitrariness* of the monarchs' powers, which had created intolerable insecurity.[22] Thus the function of the representative assembly, the Majles, that the Constitutionalists demanded was in the early stages not to legislate, but rather to ensure that the old laws not be broken by the monarch, which, after all, was the original function of European parliaments. It is interesting to note that for the purpose of representation Iranian subjects were divided into six classes during the first Majles,[23] as if Iranian history needed to start with Estates before moving to modern parliaments elected by universal suffrage.

[20]Edward Shils, "Tradition," *Comparative Studies in Society and History* 13 (1971), 145.

[21]See Nikki R. Keddie, "The Origins of the Religious-Radical Alliance in Iran," *Past and Present* 34 (1966), 70–80.

[22]For examples see H. Katouzian, *The Political Economy of Modern Iran* (1981), pp. 24–25; and A. Ashraf and H. Hekmat, "Merchants and Artisans in the Developmental Processes of Nineteenth-Century Iran," in A. L. Udovitch, ed., *The Islamic Middle East, 700–1900: Studies in Economic and Social History* (1981), pp. 727–30.

[23]Ahmad Ashraf, "The Roots of Emerging Dual Class Structure in Nineteenth-Century Iran," *Iranian Studies* 14 (Winter–Spring 1981), 9–11.

After a few years most of the constitutionalist ulema withdrew active support from the Constitutionalist Movement. The monarchy as an institution survived the minority of the last Qajar ruler, Ahmad Shah, and his subsequent long absence from Iran, but it was not a ruling monarchy. When Reza Khan wanted to abolish it and declare a republic, on the Turkish model, the ulema, fearing that outright secularization would follow, agitated against this step and as a result Reza Khan crowned himself Shah and founded a new dynasty in 1925.

The rule of Reza Shah and his son, Mohammad Reza Shah, was not a continuation of the Qajar monarchy. To consolidate their rule and enact the kind of societal reforms they thought necessary for Iran's progress, both Pahlavis attempted to curb the power of the ulema. The equilibrium that had existed between the state and the clergy was radically altered in favor of the former. Concurrently with this deemphasis of Islam, the Pahlavis turned to Iran's pre-Islamic past to legitimize their rule. Iran's monarchical traditions were evoked, and the Pahlavi Shahs presented themselves as heirs to the Achaemenids and Sasanians, rather like Napoleon, who said that he was not the successor of Louis XVI but of Charlemagne. Although this rediscovery of Iran's past was not the work of the Pahlavis and had started in the late nineteenth century, in time it became identified with the Pahlavi monarchy. It was popular with some sectors of the Iranian intelligentsia, but its ideological content did not constitute a "tradition," and was more of an innovation. Thus, paradoxically, the more the Pahlavis emphasized the non-Islamic basis of their kingship, the more they corroded their traditional legitimacy. As early as 1964 Leonard Binder wrote: "It must be noted ... that kingship has usually been justified on the basis of some other good in Iran, and that only now is it justified tautologically. Emphasis upon its traditional basis has meaning only when tradition is passing."[24]

Reza Shah is often compared to Mustafa Kemal Atatürk, the father of modern Turkey. The similarities between the reforms they imposed on their societies divert attention from one fundamental difference between them: Atatürk had saved Turkey from disintegration by driving out foreign occupiers, whereas Reza Khan unified Iran by neutralizing internal competitors, some of whom had nationalistic credentials at least as good as his own.[25] Atatürk's nationalistic credentials were therefore much better grounded, which explains why he could get away with far more than Reza Shah, and why (so far at least) his reforms have been more lasting.

[24]Leonard Binder, *Iran: Political Development in a Changing Society* (1964), p. 65.
[25]See Peter Avery, *Modern Iran* (1965), pp. 210–44.

Since both men saw modernization essentially as Westernization, one also has to keep in mind that in Turkey closer contact with the West as compared to Iran had created a larger domestic constituency for Westernization. In Iran, however, even that limited potential constituency was not fully behind Reza Shah, because his legitimacy was in doubt.

Reza Shah's initial popularity with Iran's intelligentsia also diminished under the impact of his ruthless and despotic political style. His dictatorship in many ways derailed the efforts of the Iranian parliament after the Constitutional Revolution to lay the basis of legal-rational authority in Iran. Although Reza Shah consolidated the contemporary Iranian state, he failed to create a state of law, and under his rule the arbitrariness of political power continued and alienated many sectors of the bourgeoisie, even those that had initially supported him. The patrimonial state, when superficially modernized, became increasingly sultanistic, a type of regime Juan Linz has defined as "based on personal rulership with loyalty to the ruler based not on tradition, or on him embodying an ideology or a unique personal mission, or on charismatic qualities, but on a mixture of fear and rewards to his collaborators."[26] This is another major difference with Atatürk, who was a far more skillful politician and who in the end did create a state of law in Turkey.

The monarchy in Iran was also weakened by the close association between the last Shah and foreign powers. At first this impression was held only by the articulate, Westernized segment of society, but in due course awareness of this link trickled down to the entire population: the monarchy's legitimacy increased with the distance from the capital. An intrinsic element of the state's legitimation formula was thus eroded by the continuing crisis of sovereignty.

The anticlerical policies of the Pahlavi Shahs, carried out with disregard for the sensibilities of the majority of the population, constituted a severe blow to the ulema at first. After Reza Shah's abdication, the clergy regained some of its lost prerogatives in society, but came under renewed attack after 1963.[27] On the defensive, it gained new strength, as it was not discredited by unacceptable exercise of its authority. The ulema's resilience and their ability to resist the government and maintain their institutional integrity and independence was due to the fact that, unlike the Ottoman ulema, who had lost their independence to

[26]Juan J. Linz, "Totalitarian and Authoritarian Regimes," in Nelson Polsby and Fred Greenstein, eds., *Handbook of Political Science*, vol. 3 (1975), p. 259.
[27]Shahrough Akhavi, *Religion and Politics in Contemporary Iran: Clergy-State Relations in the Pahlavi Period* (1980).

the state *before* the secularist reforms of Atatürk,[28] in Iran the undermining of the ulema went hand in hand with secularist reforms.

Theoretically an office's legitimacy does not suffer from the unacceptable behavior of any one incumbent of that office. In the long run, however, the illegitimacy of office-holders taints the legitimacy of the office. In Iran the despotic rule of the Pahlavi monarchs undermined the legitimacy of the monarchy itself.

The Emergence of Charismatic Authority

A significant outcome of this struggle between the state and the clergy, especially after 1963, was that a hitherto minoritarian conception of government gained ground among the clergy. As Amir Arjomand has argued, the very separation of temporal and religious authority in Iran created the possibility of the latter's total rejection of the former.[29] The doctrinal basis of this rejection became the doctrine of *velayat-e faqih*, or rule of the religious jurisprudent. The roots of this doctrine go back to the early nineteenth century and the writings of Molla Ahmad Naraqi,[30] but its popularity and influence in contemporary Iran grew with that of the major *mujtahid* who espoused and elaborated it, Ay. Ruhollah Khomeini. Khomeini's rise to power was not a symptom of the revival of traditional authority, as represented by the ulema, however. His relations with the rest of the ulema were fraught with tensions, and in his writings he often criticized them for their conservatism.

The main carriers of legal-rational authority in a state are the bureaucracy and the army. Although Iranian statesmen in the decades following the Constitutional Revolution made great efforts to rationalize the bureaucracy and create a modern legal order, they were not wholly successful. Both Reza Shah and his son turned increasingly sultanistic in the later stages of their reign; Iran thus never developed a true state of law.

Liberalism and democracy can only flourish on the basis of a legal-rational order. Even if we accept that a state of law and liberal democracy could come into being simultaneously, we have to note that in Iran the bourgeoisie, which in the West led the fight for liberalism,

---

[28]See Richard L. Chambers, "The Ottoman Ulema and the Tanzimat," in Nikki R. Keddie, *Scholars, Saints, and Sufis: Muslim Religious Institutions in the Middle East since 1500* (1972).

[29]Said Amir Arjomand, *The Shadow of God and the Hidden Imam: Religion, Political Order, and Societal Change in Shi'ite Iran from the Beginnings to 1890* (1984), p. 264.

[30]See Hamid Dabashi, "Early Propagation of *Wilayat-i Faqih* and Mulla Ahmad Naraqi," in Seyyed Hossein Nasr, Hamid Dabashi, and Seyyed Vali Reza Nasr, eds., *Expectation of the Millennium: Shi'ism in History* (1989), pp. 287–300.

could not do so for a variety of reasons. Great emphasis is usually put on the peripheral, dependent character of Iran's economy to explain the weakness of the bourgeoisie.[31] The semicolonial situation of Iran did indeed constitute a serious obstacle to the development of a vigorous and self-confident bourgeoisie, a situation not peculiar to Iran. But the foreign impact was not only economical but also political: Iran's domination by outside powers meant that the national bourgeoisie sought above all to restore Iran's sovereignty internationally. Iran's nondependent bourgeoisie was nationalistic first, liberal second.

Also, foreign powers did not favor those elements in Iranian society that would have been the natural carriers of liberal ideas. Where the institutions and structures that facilitated the emergence of legal-rational authority in the West did not exist, they might have been successfully implanted only by elite consensus. In countries without such prior structures, the safest way to initiate constitutional government is for charismatic leaders to forsake the age-old traditions of arbitrary rule. In Iran, such a leader, Mosaddeq, had to confront not only his internal enemies but also the world's superpowers.

After Mosaddeq, Ay. Khomeini became Iran's second charismatic leader in recent history. To sum up, we can say that the consequence of the erosion of the two types of traditional authority in Iran was not a strengthening of legal-rational authority, but rather the birth of a new charismatic authority. To understand the roots of Khomeini's popularity in Iran, we have to turn to the evolution of Iran's social stratification.

A Dual Society

As a result of the close contacts the Iranian elite maintained with the West, and the implicit belief that modernization equaled Westernization, in the late nineteenth century the country's ruling strata became more and more distant psychologically and in the patterns of daily behavior from the vast majority of the population.

It is not unusual for a country developing on the periphery of world capitalism to have a dualistic class structure. As elsewhere, economic factors are often used to define this structure. As Ahmad Ashraf puts it,

> The dynamics of the growing world economy and the development of a
> semicolonial situation in the late nineteenth century put enough pressure

[31]See A. Ashraf and H. Hekmat, "Merchants and Artisans," pp. 732–39; and Ahmad Ashraf, "Historical Obstacles to the Development of a Bourgeoisie in Iran," in M. A. Cook, ed., *Studies in the Economic History of the Middle East from the Rise of Islam to the Present Day* (1978), pp. 321–28.

on the state to force adjustments in the agricultural, commercial, industrial, and administrative institutions. From the beginning, these alterations had the effect of giving rise to a form of capitalism—but it was a distorted hybrid which evolved, differing from the course and nature of development of capitalism in the West.

The [resulting] class structure was marked from its birth by a dualistic course of development, i.e., the emergence and sustained growth of modernizing social forces that developed side by side with the survival and *reproduction* of traditional strata. The newly emerging strata were composed of the patrimonial-bureaucratic staff, the mercantile and industrial entrepreneurs, and the industrial working class. The traditional strata comprised peasants and tribesmen in the rural and tribal communities and the clergy and members of the bazaar community in the urban areas.

A definition of social strata solely on the basis of the organization of production is not satisfactory, however. Ashraf is aware of the insufficiency of the Marxian paradigm when he writes: "Coming from the traditional labor force situated either in the bazaar or in the village and tribal communities, and living together with the religio-bazaari strata in the city quarters, the emerging industrial working class, too, showed an affinity toward the life style and the religiosity of these traditional strata. The affinity seems to have persisted in spite of the differences in the organization of production between these two sectors."[32]

Instead of the organization of production, it is therefore more appropriate to divide the population into a traditional and a modern part, with the independent variable being cultural Westernization. Since the forms of the organization of production, and the resulting *economically defined* "sectors" of society may have explanatory value in other realms of analysis, the traditional and modern sections of Iranian society are called "segments."[33]

The Genesis of the Dual Society

The divisions between the two segments came about gradually. Until the end of the nineteenth century Iranians were united by a common perspective on life, and this traditional Islamic culture, although not monolithic, held society together. At that time, under the impact of contacts with the West (economic, political, intellectual), the world-view of the ruling strata of society began to change. Western secularist ideas

[32]Ashraf, "The Roots," pp. 18 and 23.
[33]My use of the term derives from V. R. Lorwin, "Segmented Pluralism: Ideological Cleavages and Political Cohesion in the Smaller European Democracies," *Comparative Politics* 3 (January 1971), 141–175. The difference in the case of Iran is that the two segments were not formally organized, unlike the cases Lorwin studied.

connected with heterodox traditions (such as Sufism) within Iran, to alienate substantial sectors of the ruling classes from traditional religion. For these strata, nationalism became a more important binding force than religion. Under the influence of Western ideas of enlightenment, religion, at least as practiced in Iran at the time, was deemed responsible for the country's backwardness.[34] The carriers of this new culture were the ruling circles of the capital, the intellectuals, and after Reza Shah's seizure of power they were increasingly members of the government bureaucracy, the army, and entrepreneurs of the modern sector of the economy. As time went on and Iran's political scene became more diverse, the modern segment of society included not only supporters of the Pahlavis but also leftists, Nationalists, liberals, fascists, and regionalists. The majority of the population, however, was not touched by this shift and continued to adhere to the old ways.

The division of Iranian society into two segments, one modern and the other traditional, does not mean that the two segments were internally homogeneous; within each segment were different strata with contradictions and tensions between them. At the height of the Shah's rule in the 1970s, at the top of the modern segment were the entrepreneurs who maintained close contact with international capitalism and who were often closely connected with the Shah's court; the upper echelons of the government apparatus; and the highest leadership of the army. The middle stratum consisted of government employees, professionals, academics. One cannot really talk about a "lower class" among the members of the modern segment, but teachers, and intellectuals who returned from Europe or America in the 1970s only to find that their salaries could hardly pay the rent of a small apartment, were an economically disadvantaged group, especially since their desired patterns of consumption reflected their membership in the modern segment. Perhaps one could also include in this segment the oil-workers of southern Iran, among whom the Tudeh party has been entrenched for many years.

The traditional segment of society included various levels as well. Until the early 1960s tribal leaders and big landowners had been the highest traditional echelon, but by the 1970s they had almost disappeared as a class. At that time the leading traditional figures were the richest Bazaar merchants and some industrialists whose roots were in the Bazaar. Below these were other tradesmen and lesser members of the Bazaar community. The lowest traditional social groups included peasants as well as urban workers, many of whom worked in

[34]The peculiar form that modernization has taken in Iran has been analyzed elsewhere and need not be repeated here. See Katouzian, *Political Economy,* pp. 101–7.

the modern sector of the economy while retaining their traditional outlook. What integrated the various classes, rich and poor, was the clergy, another key element in the traditional segment. Iran's dual social structure as described here can be graphically represented (see Figure 2).

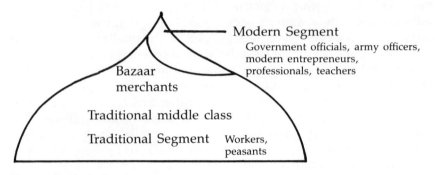

Figure 2. Iran's dual society

What separated the two segments of Iranian society? Outward appearance, certainly, at least in the case of women. Under Reza Shah the government had attempted to impose Western dress on the population, a policy supported by the modern segment. After Reza Shah's abdication in 1941, that policy was relaxed: Wearing Western dress came naturally to the women of the modern segment, while women of traditional background equally naturally continued wearing the veil. It is therefore wrong, as ideologues of both sides are wont to do, to ascribe the sartorial preferences of the Other to "alienation."

Onomastic preferences were another dividing line. With the birth of nationalism in Iran, old Persian names became ever more popular in the modern segment. At the same time the traditional segment continued to use common Islamo-Arabic names.

Most striking, perhaps, is the place religious practice plays in the lives of the two segments' members. Modern Iranians are not necessarily atheists or agnostics; rather, to the extent that they are religious, their religiosity has an ethical and/or mystical coloring while rituals are played down and regarded as signs of backwardness. For traditional Iranians, however, religion gives meaning to everyday experience, and quotidian acts are carried out in accordance with religious rules. It would be wrong to divide Iran into an areligious upper class and a deeply religious populace. Just as the prerevolutionary ruling elite always contained deeply pious individuals, religious practice was quite weak among certain nonelite groups, for instance among the nomadic tribes, although of course they did not belong to the modern segment. What is important is the form of religious expression, the role of religious practice, in individuals' daily lives. Also, the two segments have never been hermetically sealed from one another, and there have always been people with one foot in each of the two segments who are capable of "code-switching" in their everyday activities. Many religious modernists belong to this intermediary group.

Politicization of the Gap between the Two Segments

Naturally the two segments of society did not live in total isolation from one another, and there was some dynamic interaction between them. *Proportionally* the modern segment grew constantly at the expense of the traditional one. As a result of a rising oil income the modern sector of the economy and the state bureaucracy expanded in the 1960s and 1970s, and enjoyed privileged access to the fruits of economic growth. But the two segments moved further apart—even geographically:

> The emergence of *urban* dualism—of a complete sociological division within the urban population—is a product of this period: formerly, the old residential quarters had included families of *all* ranks. . . . This ensured social contact between different classes: the rich were in daily contact with the ordinary, the poor and even the beggars. But all this began to change when new wealth led, in the case of Teheran, to an entirely unplanned movement towards the northern parts of the city, into new houses . . . facilitated by the state's free grants of urban land to army officers and the higher civil servants. . . . The sense of community which, in spite of class differentiation, had always been present in Iranian cities was lost—perhaps for ever.[35]

The contradictions within the modern segment of Iranian society were such that the Shah did not have its wholehearted support, even though the ruling circles of the regime were *all* recruited in the modern segment. As long as traditional Iranians were not politically articulate, the main opposition to the Shah came from the modern segment, and until 1963 the Shah's primary opponents were the Nationalists and the communist Tudeh party. Among traditional Iranians the Shah's authority was still largely perceived as legitimate; any shortcomings were blamed on those who surrounded him.

With the rapid improvement of education and the move of many millions of peasants to the cities, the discrepancy between traditional belief and actual fact became more and more glaring. These newly

[35]Ibid., p. 208. See also Martin Seger, *Teheran: Eine stadtgeographische Studie* (1978), pp. 204–11, for an interesting conceptualization of urban development under dualistic conditions.

articulate city-dwellers could not be socialized into modernity by the leading forces of the political opposition against the Shah, because on the one hand this opposition was not allowed a voice, and on the other, its members had nothing tangible to offer to the masses. The Nationalists' main demand was always that the Shah "reign and not rule," and that is quite an abstract concept, as Bagehot noted long ago.[36] Unlike Victorian England, where the monarchy was accepted on traditional grounds by the masses and on pragmatic grounds by the politically sophisticated elites and thus became the "dignified" part of government, in Iran the monarchy became illegitimate among many members of the elite because of its failure to conform to modern notions of government by law, and among the traditional society because of its more and more visible disregard for the very traditions in which it was supposed to be grounded. For both segments, then, the monarchy's legitimacy was tainted because of the Shah's close association with foreign powers. For the millions of new city-dwellers, religious activities became the main form of socialization. These religious activities were of a new kind, and it was in their course that Ay. Khomeini's name was often invoked.

It would be a mistake to construe the division of Iranian society into two segments and the total domination of the minority segment over the state as the only source of tension in Iranian society. Aside from this important cleavage, it was also significant that the "have's" were found mostly in the modern segment, and the "have-not's" mainly in the traditional segment. It is true that the upper strata of the traditional society benefited from the oil boom, but although they fared well materially in the 1960s and 1970s, Bazaar merchants by and large lost the privileged status in society that they had enjoyed in pre-Pahlavi Iran.[37]

The enormous enrichment of the modern segment and the ostentatious life-styles affected by the nouveau riche led to resentment in the traditional segment. Max Scheler defined resentment as "the repeated experiencing and reliving of a particular emotional response or reaction against someone else."[38] This resentment had different motivations, depending on the group within traditional society. During the late 1960s and early 1970s the resentment of the traditional segment of society overtook the legal, constitutionalist objections of Nationalists, leftists, and liberals, all members of the modern segment, as the main center of opposition against the Shah. At the same time a cultural

[36]Walter Bagehot, *The English Constitution* (1963), p. 241.
[37]See Ashraf, "The Roots," pp. 11–18.
[38]Max Scheler, *Ressentiment*, ed., with intro. by Lewis A. Coser; trans. William W. Holdheim (1972), p. 39.

malaise appeared among significant modern sectors, which became disillusioned with Westernization and experienced a cultural crisis of identity. This malaise facilitated a rapprochement with the traditional Iranians.

The newly articulate masses turned to religion, at least partly because that was the only avenue open to social organization. But it was a new type of religion, born of resentment. As Max Weber has written:

> Resentment is a concomitant of that particular religious ethic of the disprivileged which . . . teaches that the unequal distribution of mundane goods is caused by the sinfulness and the illegality of the privileged, and that sooner or later God's wrath will overtake them. In this theodicy of the disprivileged, the moralistic quest serves as a device for compensating a conscious or unconscious desire for vengeance. This is connected in its origin with the faith in compensation, since once a religious conception of compensation has arisen, suffering may take on the quality of the religiously meritorious, in view of the belief that it brings in its wake great hopes of future compensation.[39]

Ay. Khomeini was the cynosure of this new direction, and in this resentment we find the origin of the charismatic legitimacy he enjoyed in the eyes of the masses. Khomeini's asceticism contrasted favorably with the unrestrained life-styles of the modern segment, whose daily behavior was a constant affront to the sensibilities of the masses. Earlier, until the early 1960s, the Shah's government had been viewed as a xenocracy by many members of the modern segment who did not accept the Pahlavis' claims to traditional authority, and as a traditionally legitimate regime in the eyes of the masses. In the mid-1960s this began to change, as traditional Iranians increasingly came to regard the regime as a pornocracy. This resentment created a fertile ground for the reception of revolutionary ideas.

Many revolutions contain a strong ascetic element.[40] In Iran this ascetic dimension had a clear religious and class basis, confirming Oscar Wilde's aphorism that "morality is simply the attitude we adopt towards people whom we personally dislike."

This explains the direction the Iranian revolution has taken, which has puzzled liberals and leftists alike, but which sparks considerable enthusiasm among politically nondominant Muslims from Yugoslavia to Indonesia. The Islamic revolution in Iran was not only class-based, it was a reversal in the hierarchical order between the two segments of Iranian society. Indeed, when under President Abolhasan Banisadr the

[39]Weber, *Economy and Society,* p. 494.
[40]Bruce Mazlish, *The Revolutionary Ascetic: Evolution of a Political Type* (1976).

modern segment seemed on the verge of a comeback, Ay. Khomeini intervened directly and deposed the first president of the Islamic Republic.

Religious modernists share basic assumptions with both modern and traditional Iranians, and the LMI as a political force has striven to overcome the gap between them by appealing to the better instincts in both segments of Iranian society. This rootedness in tradition, coupled with a critical acceptance of modernity is at the heart of religious modernism.

Religious Modernism

Definition

Religious modernism can be defined as an attempt to reestablish harmony between religion and a changing cultural sociopolitical environment in which the forces of change regard religion as dysfunctional in the process of development. It is essentially an intellectual endeavor to reinterpret religion so that it will no longer contradict the dominant spirit of the times in the more successful societies, and accepted notions of individual rights. Religious modernism always arises when religion is in a position of (perhaps momentary) weakness, for when religion exercises an intellectual and political hegemony over society, it can *define* the norms that rule society.

Religious modernism is thus a *reactive* movement. Typically, it is espoused by individuals who are committed to religion, but are also aware of science and the social problems resulting from technological and economic change. Religious modernists consider the contradiction between religion and science only apparent, and try to prove that *true* religion is by no means opposed or irrelevant to the modern world, that it need not furnish a justification for the maintenance of the social status quo. In 1829 the French Catholic thinker Félicité de Lamennais wrote: "The physical sciences themselves, by their progress—especially geology and physiology—keep putting new weapons in the hands of the defenders of religions, to combat anti-Mosaic hypotheses and materialism."[41]

Religious modernists are not content to accept a fundamental dichotomy between faith and reason. Within the multiple constraints under which they operate, they still try to achieve intellectual coherence by emphasizing the rational and this-worldly aspects of religious tradi-

---

[41]Félicité de La Mennais, *Des progrès de la revolution et de la guerre contre l'église* (1829), p. 279.

tions and by denouncing popular, "irrational," practices as mere accretions. The modernity with which modernists want to reconcile their religion is of course modernity as interpreted by them, through the filters of their religious beliefs. That explains why, as far as the *content* of their thought is concerned, we find great variety among religious modernists. Religious modernism can perhaps best be defined as an attitude, rather than as a body of interconnected principles and beliefs. In Theodor Geiger's terms, modernism is a "mentality" rather than an "ideology."[42]

Modernism may overlap with religious reformism, but it should not be confounded with it. Modernism is the province of people who are close to the religious establishment but outside it, and its motivating force comes from outside. Reformism, by contrast, is an attitude encountered more often among the members of the religious hierarchies, and it is motivated by internal processes of the religion. Its goals are to return to the original meaning of the dominant norms and values, to do away with corruption, and to strengthen the discipline of the religious hierarchy.

Of course modernism is not the only way to confront modernity. While religious modernism tries to come to terms with modernity, another path consists in rejecting it. Arnold Toynbee called the two reactions "Herodian" and "Zealot," defining the former as acting "on the principle that the most effective way to guard against the danger of the unknown is to master its secret," and the latter as taking "refuge from the unknown in the familiar."[43] For the purpose of this book the second attitude is called "fundamentalist."[44]

Religious modernists then face the potential hostility both of nonreligious intellectuals and of the religious authorities themselves. The nonreligious intellectuals are suspicious of the modernists' ulterior motives, sometimes upholding their own positivism with more fanaticism than that of which they accuse the religious intellectuals. On a more sophisticated level they accuse the religious modernists of misunderstanding both modernity and religion, and hence of intellectual incoherence. To the extent that these critics accept a role of religion in

[42]See chapter 2.
[43]Arnold Toynbee, "Islam, the West, and the Future," in *Civilization on Trial* (1948), pp. 193 and 188.
[44]The term *fundamentalist* is in many ways unfortunate, as many so-called fundamentalists are influenced by modernism, while others have a more traditional outlook. What each has in common is that they want to reestablish the Shari'ah as the supreme code of laws. In this sense, the French term *intégriste* is the most appropriate one. Since this study does not deal with fundamentalism, it follows common practice by retaining the term. For a good discussion see François Burgat, "De la difficulté de nommer *intégrisme, fondamentalisme, islamisme*," *Les Temps Modernes* 43 (March 1988).

the modern world that goes beyond ethical generalities, it is often an individual, private mode of religious experience. To the extent that they admit the intrinsic validity of any religious experience, it is often a mystic one.

The religious authorities, on the other hand, resent the criticism leveled against them for not keeping up with the times, and as guardians of a corpus of orthodoxy they criticize the intellectuals for their selective use of religious tenets and sources. At the worst, religious modernists are accused of being instrumentalists who want to make use of religion for worldly purposes.

There is a major difference between religious modernism in the Western and non-Western worlds. In Western Christianity, modernism was a reaction to *internal* developments. Perhaps for this reason the temptation for a "Zealot" reaction was smaller: it was unfeasible to close the doors to modernity, and it was less easy to depict modernity as a foreign aberration. In the colonial and semicolonial world, by contrast, technology, science, and ideas of representative government and individual rights came from the outside, often accompanied by Christian missionaries who had the backing of imperial powers.

Within the non-Western world, the preconditions for a successful reformulation and "updating" of religion vary greatly. For example, modernists face bigger obstacles in Islam,[45] a religion of ethical prophecy, than in Buddhism,[46] which is based on exemplary prophecy.[47] According to S. J. Tambiah,

> It is precisely because Islam legislates on matters social, familial, and jural that reformers feel the need to blast it away when it opposes their remedies, whereas it is precisely because Buddhism is imprecise and scarcely legislates on matters of social ethics that it can act as an umbrella of political identity at the widest level without fear of creating internal cleavages among the believers.[48]

The unambiguous statements and concrete formulations of the sacred texts mean that Islamic modernists can do little *substantive* intellectual work. They can try to awaken the believers and urge them to adopt a this-worldly outlook; but when it comes to giving content to their

---

[45]The fundamental work on Islamic modernism is H. A. R. Gibb, *Modern Trends in Islam* (1972). See also s.v. "Islah," in *Encyclopaedia of Islam* (1978), pp. 141–71.

[46]On Theravada Buddhist modernism the best work is Heinz Bechert, *Buddhismus, Staat und Gesellschaft in den Ländern des Theravada Buddhismus*, vol. 1 (1966), pp. 37–195.

[47]For definitions of ethical and exemplary prophecy see Weber, *Economy and Society*, pp. 447–50.

[48]S. J. Tambiah, "The Persistence and Transformation of Tradition in Southeast Asia, with Special Reference to Thailand," in S. N. Eisenstadt, ed., *Post-Traditional Societies* (1974).

action, most of their work consists in affirming that Islam is not opposed to the modern age, and urging the ulema to do some rethinking. Thus many Sunni modernists have rediscovered the principle of *ijtihad* and have been demanding its application,[49] while Shi'ite modernists point to *ijtihad* as proof that Islam already possesses the necessary instruments for adaptation.

The defensive character of religious modernism is thus more pronounced in the non-Western world. Religious modernism in these countries has an affinity both with Nationalism and with fundamentalism: so long as foreign domination is still present, the three forces usually cooperate. This defensive nature means that religious modernism can easily assume a negative, or "anti" character. Juan Linz has enumerated the "anti" dimensions of fascism,[50] many of which are also present as motivations in religious modernism. The first generation of religious modernists in the Islamic world believed in political democracy, perhaps because they were operating under nondemocratic conditions, and because in the Western countries progress and democracy had gone hand in hand. In later generations this commitment to democracy weakened, largely because other models became available: communism for Islamic socialists, and Zionism for a new kind of fundamentalist. The "anti" dimension as *motivation* became an "anti" dimension of *content*.

In Europe far wider sectors of the population were affected by modernity and had assimilated it, because modernization was primarily a societal process rather than a policy carried out by elites. The church thus had to save what could be saved: while the Syllabus of 1864 still condemned the principles underlying contemporary conceptions of democracy, freedom of speech and the press, and the separation of church and state which the church saw incompatible with its rule, the election of Leo XIII to the papacy in 1878 allowed the Thomistic element to become dominant in Catholic thinking, a factor that ultimately allowed the emergence of Christian Democracy and the reconciliation of the church with the modern world.[51]

[49]Hamid Enayat, *Modern Islamic Political Thought* (1982), pp. 74–76, 82–101.

[50]Juan J. Linz, "Some Notes toward a Comparative Study of Fascism in Sociological Historical Perspective," in Walter Laqueur, ed., *Fascism: A Reader's Guide* (1976), pp. 15–17.

[51]See Pierre Letamendia, *La Démocratie chrétienne* (1977), pp. 11–33. It is interesting that while in the Western tradition political thinking contained simultaneously (and in tension with each other) both Platonic and Aristotelian elements, as exemplified by Augustine and Thomas Aquinas, theoretical political thinking in the Islamic world was much more dominated by the heritage of Plato, and Muslims were not familiar with Aristotle's *Politics*. F. E. Peters, *Aristoteles Arabus* (1968), p. 53. This may explain why in Islam's confrontation with modernity monistic forces seem to outweigh pluralist elements.

Nationalism and Religious Modernism

It is clear that in the old polities of the non-Western world Nationalism and religious modernism share many affinities. Both strive to make the country and its culture an equal among equals: the one in the political sphere, the second in the spiritual sphere. Religious modernists typically perceive themselves as providing a spiritual dimension to Nationalism, especially in countries whose religion constitutes the basis of national identity.

In Sri Lanka, for example, the target of this fusion of religious modernism and Nationalism after independence was the Anglicized elite as represented by the United National Party (UNP); the ideas promoted by religious modernism were then skillfully championed by S.W.R.D. Bandaranaike who integrated them into a basically democratic political system, albeit at the price of antagonizing the Tamil minority. In Thailand, on the other hand, religious modernism and Nationalism worked harmoniously and were not in opposition to the state, a circumstance that explains their relative conservatism. The king's traditional position as protector of the Sangha, the Buddhist order of monks, allowed him to modernize the religious establishment and the state concomitantly. One should also remember that the target of Thai Nationalism was not only foreign domination of the country but also the Chinese minority within it. As for religious modernism, since the state did not pursue aggressively secularizing policies in Thailand, it directed its thrust mostly inward and toward peripheral regions hitherto less penetrated by Buddhism.[52]

In Iran, it is perhaps precisely because of the separation between church and state that the modernizing elites of the early twentieth century chose the path of secularization, unlike, for instance, Thailand or Japan. In Egypt, modernizers worked together with Muhammad Abduh, and from the outset their goals included the modernization of the religious establishment. When religious modernism first appeared on the Iranian scene in the early 1940s, it was a reaction against forces that were believed to be subverting Iranian youth: communism and Baha'ism. Muslim intellectuals felt that they had to provide young Iranians with a vision of "true" Islam, so that they would no longer respond favorably to the lure of communism and Baha'ism. Iranian communists were identified with the Soviet Union, while Baha'is, although adherents of a faith that had originated on Iranian soil, were presented successively as Russian, British, American, and lastly Israeli ("Zionist") agents.[53] The religious modernists were thus confronting

[52]Tambiah, "The Persistence," pp. 62–65 and 69–74.
[53]For a brief discussion of the historical roots of these accusations see Firuz Kazemzadeh,

ideologically the real or imagined local representatives of powers against which all Nationalists were striving: communism, Baha'ism, Zionism. Linz's observation that the "anti" character of fascism can best be understood as anti-international and anticosmopolitan[54] also applies to Iranian Nationalism and religious modernism. Transnational movements such as Baha'ism, communism, and Zionism were seen as elements of the ongoing crisis of sovereignty that characterized the Iranian polity.

Perhaps what kept Nationalism and religious modernism from degenerating immediately into forms and styles of political action akin to fascism was the fact that they were also reacting against a regime that was itself nondemocratic, and whose founder, Reza Shah, had been to some extent influenced by fascist models. Moreover, most of the leaders had been educated in the France of the Third Republic, a fact which also accounts for the absence of an antiparliamentary and antiliberal component in the "anti" dimension. The original "anti" impulse did, however, contribute to the weakening of the commitment to democracy in the anti-Pahlavi opposition.

Politically, the religious modernists were latecomers to the Iranian scene. It was the coup of 1953 that triggered their entry into Iranian politics as they took a leading role in the founding of the underground National Resistance Movement (NRM). By that time Iran already had parties identifying with communism, socialism, fascism, ethnonationalism, and liberalism. The communists were excluded from the National Movement on account of their close ties with the Soviet Union, but the National Movement did comprise socialists, liberals, conservatives, and extreme nationalists. The LMI became a new component of this coalition after 1961.

Nationalism is Iran enjoyed a brief period of ascendency in 1951–53, and religious modernists formed a government for a few months in 1979. Other than that, both forces have always been in the opposition.

Religious Modernism in Iran

Islamic modernism displays a certain paradox in Iran. The man usually considered the founder of Islamic modernism, Seyyed Jamaleddin Asadabadi (al-Afghani) was an Iranian, but he did his best to hide his origins (probably so that his Shi'ite background would not affect his effectiveness in the Sunni world) and had a more lasting impact on Egypt and the Ottoman Empire than on the country of his birth. From

---

"The Terror Facing the Bahais," *New York Review of Books*, May 13, 1982, pp. 43–44.

[54]Linz, "Some Notes," p. 16.

the late nineteenth to the early twentieth century the Shi'ite clergy were the most politically active ulema in the Islamic world,[55] the independence of the clergy from the state enabling them to play that role. Yet with few exceptions it would be wrong to call the ulema who were active in the Constitutional Movement "modernists": They were above all concerned with establishing the rule of law, of Islamic law, not with harmonizing Islam and the prevailing spirit of the times. Modernist tendencies, as defined earlier, appeared relatively late among Iranian Muslims, probably because, compared to India and the Arab Middle East, the foreign impact was less dramatic in Iran. Also, religious modernists in Iran have tended to be of lay background, which has limited their effectiveness among the religious masses, which look to the clergy for guidance. Let us not forget that in Egypt a Muhammad Abduh became Grand Mufti and head of the al-Azhar establishment; he thus had the means and the authority to apply at least some of his ideas. In Iran, by contrast, even the clerical members of the modernist movement were regarded with considerable suspicion by the ulema. In response the modernists became quite anti-clerical, some of them going so far as to evoke wistfully the Protestant Reformation. The existence of a powerful clergy in Iran also explains why the most important modernist movement of the nineteenth century, Babism, when faced with the hostility of the ulema, came to reject certain fundamental tenets of Islam and became in effect first a reformist movement and then evolved into a separate religion, the Baha'i Faith.

The most outstanding representatives of Shi'ite modernism in Iran are H. S. Mahmud Taleqani (1912–79), Mehdi Bazargan (b. 1907), and Ay. S. Morteza Motahhari (d. 1979).[56] Their first activities consisted in the founding of associations for Muslims, a pattern congruent with religious modernists elsewhere.[57] Only in 1961 did Bazargan and Taleqani found the Liberation Movement of Iran, a party with an ideology and program explicitly based on Islam. For most of its history, this party has been in opposition to the ruling regimes in Iran; the dynamics of regime-opposition relations must therefore be explored in greater detail.

Government and Opposition in Iran

Throughout its history, Iran very seldom enjoyed an open political system that would have allowed societal cleavages to be reflected in the

---

[55]For that they were admired even by Sunni modernists who were doctrinally critical of Shi'ism: cf. Enayat, *Modern Islamic Political Thought*, p. 77.

[56]For an overview see William G. Millward, "Aspects of Modernism in Shi'a Islam," *Studia Islamica* 37 (1973), 111–28.

[57]Cf. Gibb, *Modern Trends*, p. 55, and Bechert, *Buddhismus*, pp. 47–58.

democratic interplay between government and opposition. The LMI has been an oppositional force most of the time, and this raises the analytical problem of how to conceptualize the role of oppositions in nondemocratic regimes.

Oppositions in Authoritarian Settings

Nondemocratic regimes vary in their degree of repression, and often oppositional tendencies in monistic systems manifest themselves inside the regime.[58] Few such systems allow structured oppositional movements to emerge, and it is therefore understandable that most studies of oppositions in nondemocratic polities center on functional, or interest-based oppositions, rather than would-be opposition parties.[59] In authoritarian regimes with limited pluralism, there may also appear "semi-oppositions," which Linz defines as "those groups that are not dominant or represented in the governing group but that are willing to participate in power without fundamentally challenging the system."[60] Such truly oppositional movements as try to maintain a societal presence in the face of oppression receive relatively little attention. Moreover, most of these opposition movements become active only in periods of transition, when an authoritarian system is undergoing internal reformulation or even breakdown.

In countries that have a constitutionally anchored one-party system, oppositions are likely to emerge either within the party or from interest groups. Not all authoritarian systems are institutionalized to such a degree, however. Many are closely allied to the West, and in the wake of fascism's decisive defeat in World War II the Western, pluralistic model is the only legitimate one for emulation. Hence the proliferation of dictatorships that at regular intervals organize "elections" at which pseudo-oppositions, regime-sponsored groups with no autonomous volition of their own, take part and regularly lose. In many cases such regimes also display strong sultanistic tendencies. The existence of pseudo-oppositions reflects a degree of cynical manipulation by the government of the whole political process which lessens the likelihood of the appearance of any semi-opposition. We can affirm that the stronger sultanistic tendencies are, the less likely is there going to be a semi-opposition.

The problematic of oppositions in nondemocratic systems leads logically to the question of democratization. This means that we have

[58]For a classification see Juan J. Linz, "Opposition in an Authoritarian Regime: The Case of Spain," in Robert Dahl, ed., *Regimes and Oppositions* (1973), pp. 184–99.

[59]See for instance the articles by Barghoorn, Skilling, and Foltz in the Dahl volume cited in note 58.

[60]Linz, "Opposition," p. 191.

to address the fundamental distinction between democratic and nondemocratic oppositions to nondemocratic systems. Given that the opposition to nondemocratic regimes needs the goodwill of world public opinion, most oppositions to dictatorships base their public appeal on their promise to reestablish democracy if they succeed in overthrowing the existing regime. Even political movements that orient themselves ideologically on established nondemocratic regimes (for example, pro-Soviet Communist parties) tend publicly to advocate the installation of democracy. In fact we find, however, that the breakdown of nondemocratic regimes leads more often than not to the establishment of another dictatorship rather than to a transition to democracy.

Any group claiming to fight for democracy against an authoritarian or totalitarian regime can count on a considerable reservoir of goodwill and sympathy from outside observers who, in borderline cases, are often willing to give it the benefit of the doubt: not to do so would be tantamount to supporting the existing regime. How then is one to ascertain whether a certain opposition movement's claims to be democratic are sincere?

One obvious way, which is unfortunately overlooked very often by social scientists, is to *read* the programmatic statements and ideological writings of the movements one studies. The contents of such texts should be accorded at least as much importance as pronouncements made for the consumption of foreign correspondents. Closely related to this is the relevance of foreign models. If the programmatic and ideological texts, even newsletters or leaflets, praise nondemocratic regimes and reserve their criticism for established democracies, it stands to reason that the group's commitment to democracy is not very deep.

Another method is to study the internal workings and decision-making processes of the movements. Presumably, if the leaders practice democracy and toleration in their dealings with each other, they are more likely to opt for democracy once they come to power.

Yet another indicator of opposition movements' commitment to democracy consists in their attitudes toward each other. If they spend more time criticizing and slandering each other than working and cooperating for the overthrow of the nondemocratic regime, the prospects for democracy would seem to be bleak. Such internecine disputes often center around the issue of representativity, as various groups claim to speak for "the people" and deny that others might do so too. The trouble is that there is no unequivocal indicator for the representativeness of any one group. Any group can claim to be the most popular one, since there are neither elections nor polls.

Matters are further complicated by exile politics. They often receive a lot of attention abroad but have only a limited audience at home. Moreover, the leadership of the opposition in exile often ends up at odds with the internal leadership. Frequently the external leadership ages while there is generational renewal inside the country. In Iran, however, because of the considerable numbers of students abroad, the leadership of the external opposition has tended to be younger.

As we noted earlier, opposition movements to nondemocratic regimes tend to become prominent in times of crisis, when the regime is unable to maintain its repressive rule, or when the price for doing so is perceived as too high. It is then that a nondemocratic regime faces a crisis of participation.

Crisis of Participation in Nondemocratic Polities

Crises of participation have different effects on politics depending on whether they occur in a developing society in which a growing number of people are becoming politically articulate, or in more or less institutionalized nondemocratic regimes. The first case applies to Western Europe, where recurring crises of participation accompanied the emergence of constitutional and later liberal governments, resulted in an ever-widening suffrage, and ultimately led to the emergence of modern democracy. In the second case, the situation is more explosive, especially if the society has little previous experience with democracy. The idea of "rule by the people" is sufficiently rooted nowadays that oppositional forces in nondemocratic systems never ask for a simple extension of the demos. Individuals may be co-opted into a ruling group, but if they have any followers, these are unlikely to follow. Crises of participation in nondemocratic systems are therefore the borderline case of Robert Dahl's model of democratization: a massive increase in the demand for participation without previous increase in contestation.[61] The longer a nondemocratic regime has been in power, and the more distant the memory of democracy is, the less likely it becomes that a crisis of participation will result in a democratization. Mass mobilization by the opposition is a mixed blessing for the cause of democracy: on the one hand a nondemocratic regime is less likely to relinquish its authoritarian governance if there is no mass mobilization, but on the other hand too much mass mobilization by the opposition may result either in bloody repression or in a total victory by the opposition which diminishes the chances for the introduction of democratic procedures. Once "the people" have voted with their feet, there is no overwhelming incentive to make the citizenry vote with their

[61]See Robert Dahl, *Polyarchy* (1971), p. 7.

heads. The breakdown of a nondemocratic regime is more likely to lead to democratization if the regime change is transacted by "transfer of power" rather than "seizure of power."[62]

There can be no democratization without liberalization, but it is in the nature of liberalization that it will be looked upon with suspicion by the opposition. At this point we should define two terms. Following Alfred Stepan, we define "liberalization" as "a mix of policy and social changes, such as less censorship of the media, somewhat greater room for the organization of autonomous working class activities, the reintroduction of some legal safeguards such as *habeas corpus* for individuals, the releasing of most political prisoners, the return of political exiles, possibly measures for improving the distribution of income, and, most important, the toleration of political opposition." "Democratization," goes beyond liberalization and is a more specifically political concept. It "requires open contestation for the right to win control of the government, and this in turn requires free elections, the result of which determines who governs."[63]

The problem of democratization is particularly thorny in regimes that maintain a parliamentary façade. Established one-party systems can open up politically by allowing one or more opposition parties to take part in real elections. That was the path chosen by Turkey in 1948 and Senegal in 1976. In Spain, while the single party of the Franco era was dissolved, the transition to democracy was carried out in an orderly fashion that allowed politicians associated with the previous regime to participate in the competitive politics of the new democracy. In all these cases there was no crisis of sovereignty involved, and whatever the opposition thought of the previous political establishment, it did not accuse it of treason. In terms of Alfred Stepan's classification of paths to redemocratization, there was "redemocratization initiated from within the authoritarian regime."[64]

Regimes that maintain parliamentary institutions as window-dressing, presumably to assuage the guilty conscience of their outside allies, are in a more difficult position. Sometimes during liberalization the "party system" can acquire a life of its own and become the embryo of a real multiparty system. Brazil in the late 1970s and early 1980s is a case in point. But where these pseudo-parliamentary regimes display strong sultanistic tendencies (as in prerevolutionary Iran and Nicaragua, the

[62] My translation of Rainer Lepsius's *machtübergabe* and *Machtergreifung*, as used in his "Zur Strategie des Regimewechsels," in Hans Albert, ed., *Sozialtheorie und soziale Praxis. Eduard Baumgarten zum 70. Geburtstag* (1971), pp. 156–73.

[63] Alfred Stepan, *Rethinking Military Politics: Brazil and the Southern Cone* (1988), p. 6.

[64] Alfred Stepan, "Paths towards Redemocratization: Theoretical and Comparative Considerations," in Guillermo O'Donnell, Philippe Schmitter, and Lawrence Whitehead, eds., *Transitions from Authoritarian Rule: Comparative Perspectives* (1986), p. 72.

Philippines), the very existence of these "party systems" makes democratization more difficult. Opposition leaders may accept a liberalization offered by the regime which later turns out to have been insincere, resulting in a loss of face that prevents them from going along with a later liberalization that *is* sincere. "Free elections" are no longer a clear break with the authoritarian past, as the government that holds the elections will claim that elections have always been free, whereas any group that loses in these elections will maintain that they have been as farcical as previous ones. Also, the opposition might allege that the entire state apparatus is too corrupt to be able to oversee free elections. When ruling clique, government, and state are closely interwoven, it bodes ill for democratization.

The manipulation of democratic institutions and procedures by an authoritarian regime (often in the form of holding plebiscites) allows the nondemocratic opposition to equate the democratic opposition with the pseudo-opposition and thus to undermine its credibility. In response the democratic opposition must become more and more radical or become irrelevant. This is particularly important if the crisis of participation is accompanied by mass mobilization: the nondemocratic opposition is almost by its very nature more adept at bringing out the people into the streets than its democratic counterpart. Even if the democratic leadership radicalizes its positions as the crisis drags on, it tends to lose the initiative and merely follow events. All of this lessens the likelihood of a democratization.

Pressure for liberalization often comes from outside and is often the direct result of policy changes in outside powers which have a certain leverage on the smaller country. This is even true of the Soviet Union's relations with its satellites, as the Polish and Hungarian crises of 1956, which came after Khrushchev's de-Stalinization, illustrate. If the pressured nondemocratic regime has a popular base, it is likely to use the external pressure to shore up its legitimacy by arousing its followers' patriotism. The foreign pressure also means that those oppositional elements that try to take advantage of it by lessening an outside power's commitment to the nondemocratic regime are liable to lose some of their legitimacy by associating too closely with outsiders.

The Dynamics of Regime Change in Iran

Given the history of foreign meddling in Iranian affairs, the links between crises of sovereignty, of legitimacy, and of participation are very close. The usual pattern is that political pressure from without delegitimizes the existing regime or allows doubts about the regime's legitimacy to be aired openly. This is the liberalization phase. As a result of this, oppositional forces are moved to become active, challenging the regime to prove its legitimacy by allowing free elections: where the regime wanted to weather the storm by granting a liberalization, the opposition *outside* the regime demands a full democratization. The semi-opposition might have gone along with a liberalization, but the intransigence of the opposition limits the scope of its actions.

In 1941 the Allies invaded Iran. Reza Shah left his country and political life opened up, creating a system often called "incomplete democracy." During this period of open politics, the National Movement under the charismatic leadership of Mosaddeq came into being. The National Movement's ascendency was cut short by the coup of 1953, which established the Shah's personal rule. While the coup of 1953 put an end to the open political activity of Nationalists and communists, it also provoked others to enter the political arena. The creation of the National Resistance Movement was an attempt to carry on the struggle of Nationalism when the new political situation did not allow the established parties of the National Front (NF) to be active. Religious modernists played a dominant role in the NRM; it is therefore fair to say that the political activism of the religious modernists was a direct outcome of the 1953 crisis of sovereignty.

After 1960, the Kennedy administration's insistence on reforms in Iran emboldened the semi-opposition to raise its head: the result was the reformist administration of Ali Amini. But to have a modicum of credibility, the liberalization of 1960 also had to allow the Nationalists to resurface. It was in the course of this Nationalist revival that Mehdi Bazargan and S. Mahmud Taleqani, veterans of the Islamic modernist movement, founded a new political party, the Liberation Movement of Iran.

Partly because of the Shah's unwillingness to share power, and partly because the general climate of suspicion reigning in Iran, the Amini experiment failed, and with it the liberalization. In January 1963 the entire leadership of the National Movement once again went to prison. This liberalization thus ended abruptly and the Shah's regime reconsolidated itself.

Every reaffirmation of absolutist rule and consequent neutralization of the opposition results in the emergence of more radical opposition forces which, at least implicitly, put some of the blame for the opposition's lack of success on the shoulders of previous, more moderate leaders, in a phenomenon not unlike Duverger's notion of *sinistrisme*, inadequately translated as "Leftism."[65] In 1953 the coup and jailing of

[65]Maurice Duverger, *Political Parties*, trans. Barbara North and Robert North (1959), p. 235.

the National Front leadership had resulted in the birth of the more radical NRM. Ten years later, the failure of the Nationalists, both of the National Front and of the LMI, to wrest a democratization from the Shah, brought Ayatollah Khomeini and a little later the radical Mojahedin to the foreground of oppositional politics. The reconsolidation of the Pahlavi regime thus twice resulted in a radicalization of the opposition. The second time it meant a radical reformulation of the opposition's demands, as new social strata belonging to the traditional segment were mobilized by the opposition. True to its principles, the moderate opposition, both secular and religious, demanded above all the establishment of the rule of law, and during both liberalizations it tried as far as possible to operate legally and use existing laws. These options were rejected by the new radical opposition in 1978–79.

The years 1963–77 are characterized by an increase in sultanistic characteristics of the regime, facilitated by the lavish oil income the Shah had at his disposal.[66] At the outset of this period the Shah tried to create a new power base for himself by relying on young, presumably progressive, technocrats. The assassination of the prime minister who embodied this policy, Hasan-Ali Mansur, in 1965, put an end to this and heralded increased sultanism. The evolution of the rule of the Shah here parallels that of his father, who in the first phase of his rule had enjoyed the support of Iran's progressive forces, but increasingly dispensed with them after the assassination in 1933 of Abdolhosein Teimurtash, the energetic minister of the court.[67]

Until 1975 Iran nominally had a two-party system, with the Iran-Novin (New Iran) party as "government party" and the Mardom (People's) party as "opposition." In terms of our scheme, the Mardom was a pseudo-opposition. We have to look very hard to find any evidence for a semi-opposition in that period. The closest case was the ultranationalist Pan-Iranist party, whose existence allowed the Shah to depict his own ethno-nationalism as moderate. When in 1974 the leader of the Mardom party began playing the role of an opposition leader and stepped up his attacks on the prime minister, whom he accused of not carrying out the Shah's policies forcefully enough, he was first demoted from the party leadership and then died when his jeep collided with a cow. A few years earlier, in 1971, the leadership of the Pan-Iranist party had been jailed for opposing the Iranian government's assent to the independence of Bahrain.

These very limited outbursts of activity by the pseudo- and the semi-opposition may have been a factor in the Shah's sudden an-

---

[66]Homa Katouzian has called this regime "petrolic despotism." *Political Economy,* pp. 234–74.
[67]Ervand Abrahamian, *Iran between Two Revolutions* (1982), pp. 118–65.

nouncement in 1975 that Iran would have a single party, membership in which was obligatory. Like King Carol of Romania before him, he called it the "Resurgence party," Rastakhiz. A single party only fulfills a purpose if membership in it is selective and offers rewards to the members. This was not the case with the Resurgence party, and the nature of the Shah regime was not seriously affected by it. The Shah's early announcements that membership in the party would be compulsory were not followed up, although for a while the prospect of such a membership drive created a lot of resentment on the part of those citizens who had wished to stay out of politics.

When in 1977 the Shah attempted again to liberalize his regime somewhat, this new policy was greeted with more skepticism than the previous attempt in 1960, and for reasons that are likely to be discussed for a long time hence, led to a revolutionary overthrow of his regime. A "transfer of power" was prevented in extremis and instead a provisional government was established by "seizure of power."

This provisional government was headed by Mehdi Bazargan, the leader of the LMI, and consisted of Nationalists and religious modernists. In the face of attacks from religious fundamentalists and leftists the government disintegrated. First the Nationalists left, then, in the wake of the U.S. hostage crisis of November 1979, the religious modernists. The "rule of the moderates," to use Brinton's terminology, was over.[68]

The elements that came to power and created the Islamic government of Iran are internally too heterogeneous to form a monolithic regime. The Islamic Republican party (IRP), played a notable role until about 1982, but was dissolved in the spring of 1987. Inside the Islamic regime are semi-oppositions, groups identified with more or less government interference in economic life, more or less land reform, to name but two examples. The secular Nationalists were excluded from any political activity by 1981, whereas the LMI has tried to play the role of a loyal opposition.

Juan Linz has shown how in such countries as Belgium and the Netherlands the existence of strong Christian parties made it more difficult for fascist parties to gain great popularity.[69] Had the LMI been allowed to represent religious sensibilities on the Iranian political scene, chances are that the fundamentalists would not have gained such a vast following. The comparison with Shi'ite politics in Lebanon is instructive here: in that country's open, and recently chaotic, political system, the Amal movement, which ideologically is very close to

[68]Crane Brinton, *Anatomy of Revolution* (1965), pp. 121–47.
[69]Linz, "Some Notes," p. 85.

the LMI, occupied the space of Shi'ite activism on the political scene. Consequently, Shi'ite fundamentalists, backed by the revolutionary Iranian regime, find it more difficult to gain a monopoly over Shi'ite political activism. Since the LMI was not allowed under Iran's authoritarian regime to occupy this niche effectively, the struggle between modernists and fundamentalists has so far been much more unequal in Iran than in Lebanon.

As an old polity on the periphery of world economic development, Iran's sovereignty has been fragile for more than a century. The unresolved crisis of sovereignty affected the traditional structures of legitimacy on which the state was based. During our century Iranian society lost its consensus as to what constitutes legitimate authority. This lack of consensus in Iran's post-traditional society was at the same time a contributor and a consequence of the division of Iranian society into two segments, one traditional, one modern. As a result, Iran's ongoing crisis of participation was particularly intractable.

CHAPTER 2

Ideological Content and Social
Identity of Shi'ite Modernism

It is not easy to give a coherent account of the ideology of the Liberation Movement of Iran. The background of that ideology is Islamic modernism in its Iranian, Shi'ite variety, yet not all Shi'ite modernists have been members or sympathizers of the LMI. Since this book's focus is that party, it excludes the intellectual contributions of such important figures as Ay. S. Morteza Motahhari and Abolhasan Banisadr (b. 1933).[1]

Another difficulty lies in the occasional discrepancies between what LMI figures have written as religious activists, and what they have said as politicians representing a political force in the political arena. The former pronouncements belong to the corpus of religious modernism, whereas the latter constitute the LMI's ideology *strictu sensu*. Given our primary interest in politics rather than religious life, our discussion of religious modernism will concentrate on those ideas that have a direct bearing on politics.

The final difficulty concerns the problematic place of Ali Shariati within the LMI. His heritage is claimed by many political groupings in Iran, therefore his inclusion in a study of the LMI may be questioned. The fact is that his years of greatest intellectual output fell into the period in which no political parties were allowed to function in Iran, and he died before they reappeared on the scene. The links between Shariati and the LMI are important enough to include him in this analysis.[2] What is certain is that he came out of the tradition created by

---

[1]For a summary of Banisadr's thought see Yann Richard's section in Nikki R. Keddie, *Roots of Revolution* (1981), pp. 202–30.

[2]See chapter 5 for more detail.

Bazargan and Taleqani, although his ideas then developed along lines that diverged considerably from those of his predecessors. Rather than attempt an artificial synthesis, this book concentrates on the thought of Bazargan and Taleqani, while analyzing some of Shariati's modifications of the modernist canon. This deemphasis of Shariati is further justified for two reasons: the greater relevance of Bazargan and Taleqani for the LMI, and the considerable secondary literature that has already been devoted to Shariati.

Precursors and Sources of Inspiration

One of the distinguishing traits of religious modernists is that they are eclectic in what they incorporate into their thinking. To Jorge Luis Borges we owe the insight that writers create their own precursors.[3] The same is true for ideologues: the intellectual lineages that come together in the work of one thinker do not necessarily cohere with each other. This section attempts to untangle the skein of ideas, intellectual movements, sources of inspiration, and influences that have come together to produce the thought, and beyond that, the distinct *forma mentis* of the LMI's major producers of ideology.

Precursors

The historical antecedents for the LMI in Iran have to be sought in the action of the constitutionalist clergy in the early years of our century. After the Iranian revolution of 1905–6 had resulted in the election of a parliament, secular liberals came to dominate the assembly at the expense of the clergy, whose mobilizing capacity had been a crucial factor in the success of the revolutionary movement. As a result of the liberals' domination a split occurred in the ranks of the ulema. One faction, led by Sheikh Fazlollah Nuri, parted ways with the Constitutionalists and henceforth agitated against it, declaring the Constitution to be incompatible with Islam. Another faction, however, was ready to compromise with the liberals. For them, Article 2 of the Supplementary Fundamental Law, providing for a number of ulema to be members of the Majles so as to oversee legislation, was sufficient to ensure the Islamic character of Iran's postrevolutionary political system. The most prominent leaders of this faction were S. Mohammad Tabataba'i, S. Abdollah Behbahani, and Ay. Mirza Mohammad-Hosein Na'ini. The latter left a coherent exposition of his ideas.

[3]See his essay "Kafka and His Precursors," in Borges, *Other Inquisitions* (1965), pp. 106–8.

Ay. Mirza Mohammad-Hosein Na'ini (1860–1936)

Na'ini was one of the major *mujtahids* of the early twentieth century. He lived in Najaf, Iraq, until 1920, when he was expelled by the British and went to Qum. Na'ini called his treatise on constitutionalism *Tanbih ul-ummah wa tanzih ul-millah*, "The Admonition of the Community and the Refinement of the Nation." This book was a systematic refutation of Sheikh Fazlollah Nuri's theses and in due course became very popular among Muslim liberals.[4] Na'ini was above all concerned with ending the despotism of the Qajar Shahs. He was heavily inspired by S. Abdurrahman al-Kawakibi, who in turn had directly borrowed his arguments from Vittorio Alfieri,[5] an admirer of Montesquieu and the author of *Della Tirrannide*.[6]

It appears that Na'ini, like most other constitutionalist ulema, was confused as to the meaning and implications of Western-style parliamentarism. He wanted total ulema control over the judiciary and legislative branches of government and would not admit complete equality of Muslim and non-Muslim subjects, positions not compatible with our modern notions of democracy; he nevertheless argued that a constitutional government with an elected assembly was preferable to a despotic regime. According to Na'ini a despotic regime usurped the legitimate rights of God, the Twelfth Imam, and the people, whereas a constitutional regime usurped only the rights of the Imam, who, being in transtemporal occultation, cannot exercise his rightful dominion anyway.[7] And with the ulema's control over the judiciary and legislative branches even the Imam's rights would not be usurped, since the ulema represent him.

Na'ini soon became disappointed with the course of events in Iran and, faced with the continued hostility of large sectors of the ulema, decided to withdraw his book. It nevertheless remained popular, and in 1955 a new edition appeared for the first time in more than thirty years, edited, annotated, and with an introduction by Ay. Taleqani. As the Shah's personal dictatorship took shape after the 1953 coup, and given the support that his regime enjoyed among the ulema, this book very naturally became a major source of inspiration for religiously oriented Nationalists. In the defense Bazargan submitted to the mili-

---

[4]On Nai'ini and his book see Abdul-Hadi Hairi, *Shi'ism and Constitutionalism in Iran* (1977). An English translation of the book's central thesis can be found in John J. Donohue and John L. Esposito, eds., *Islam in Transition: Muslim Perspectives* (1982), pp. 287–91.

[5]Hairi, *Shi'ism and Constitutionalism*, pp. 160–64. For the link between al-Kawakibi and Alfieri see Sylvia Haim, "Alfieri and al-Kawakibi," *Oriente Moderno* 34 (1954), 321–34.

[6]*Of Tyranny*, trans. Julius A. Molinaro and Beatrice Corrigan (1961).

[7]Mirza Mohammad-Hosein Na'ini, *Tanbih ul-ummah wa tanzih ul-millah* (1955), p. 47.

tary court that tried him in 1963, he made frequent use of Na'ini's arguments,[8] and after the fundamentalists' take-over in 1981, LMI leaders would again turn to the text and quote passages condemning religious despotism. These same passages were also quoted by Shariati in his attacks on the clergy.[9]

S. Jamaleddin Asadabadi (1838–1897)

The second major source of inspiration for religiously oriented Nationalism in Iran was Seyyed Jamaleddin Asadabadi, known in the West as al-Afghani.[10] Al-Afghani cannot be called an outspoken advocate of Western constitutionalism, but his influence resides in that he was an advocate of Muslim peoples' rising up to the challenge of the West and putting their own house in order so as to eliminate the sources of weakness that made them easy targets for Western imperialism. He is celebrated throughout the Islamic world for having provided the initial impetus for reform and modernization. On the whole, his impact in Iran was less striking than that in Egypt and the Ottoman Empire, but toward the end of his life he decisively influenced the course of events in Iran by giving one of his followers the green light to assassinate Nasereddin Shah, in 1896.

New studies have shown that al-Afghani was not a religious person by orthodox standards, but this fact is overlooked by (or unknown to) most Islamic modernists (including Bazargan and Shariati), who have accepted the mystifications that surround him.[11]

S. Hasan Modarres (1858–1938)

If Na'ini and al-Afghani influenced contemporary religious modernism in Iran on an intellectual level (the former by providing content, the latter by giving the initial impetus), Modarres provided an exemplary model for religiously inspired political action.[12] As a young cleric he had been a leading constitutionalist activist during the revolution of 1906 in his native Isfahan, and went on to become a member of a clerical triumvirate that drafted the compromise Article 35 of the Supplementary Fundamental Law which got around the sticky issue of

---

[8]Mehdi Bazargan, *Modafe'at dar dadgah-e gheir-e saleh-e tajdid-e nazar-e nezami* (Defenses in the illegitimate Military Court of Appeals) (1971), pp. 294–96, 305.

[9]See for instance his *Fatemeh Fatemeh ast* (Fatima is Fatima) (1977), p. 29.

[10]On al-Afghani see Nikki Keddie, *An Islamic Response to Imperialism: The Political and Religious Writings of Sayyid Jamal-al-Din "al-Afghani"* (1983).

[11]On this mystification see Elie Kedouri, *Afghani and 'Abduh* (1966).

[12]On Modarres's life see Ebrahim Khajehnuri, *Bazigaran-e asr-e tala'i: Seyyed Hasan-e Modarres* (Actors of the Golden Age: Seyyed Hasan Modarres) (1979). Interesting information can also be gleaned from Mohammad-Ebrahim Bastani Parizi, *Talash-e azadi* (The struggle for freedom) (1977).

sovereignty by stipulating that it was a "divine gift entrusted by the people to the Shah."[13]

After the ulema had more or less withdrawn from politics early in this century, Modarres remained a member of parliament. A skillful parliamentarian, he maneuvered to stop anybody from acquiring too much power. As a parliamentarian he had also helped drafting Iran's first civil code by ensuring that it conformed to the Shari'ah, which made it acceptable to the reluctant clergy. This compromise code was later abolished by Reza Shah in 1927.[14]

Modarres also constantly opposed foreign intervention in Iranian affairs. During World War I he became a member of the nationalist and pro-Central Powers provisional government that fled Teheran before the advancing Russian troops, and after the war his house became one of the main meeting places for opponents of the 1919 treaty. All this brought him the cordial hatred of the Western diplomats stationed in Teheran, who were weary of his influence on the populace.[15]

In domestic politics, he successively opposed Reza Khan's nomination as prime minister, the abolition of the monarchy, and Reza Khan's accession to the throne. Modarres's opposition to Reza Shah finally cost him his life, as the new Shah had him arrested in 1929, then assassinated in 1938.

Modarres was a religious person who took political action in defense of Iran and Islam. He wrote: "Our religion is the same as our politics, and our politics is the same as our religion. . . . The source of our politics is our religion."[16] Modarres's life thus foreshadows the very raison d'être of the LMI.

Other Iranians' words, thoughts, and actions have contributed to the LMI's intellectual basis, but it is fair to assume that these three men were the most representative.

External Influences

The exogenous influences on Islamic modernism deserve more attention than they have received. Bazargan, and even Taleqani, view the West with far more serenity than does the generation of Iranians that followed them. Bazargan likes to point out that in the early years of Islam the Arabs borrowed freely from the Persians and Byzantines

---

[13]Shahrough Akhavi, *Religion and Politics in Contemporary Iran* (1980), p. 26.
[14]Bastani Parizi, *Talash,* pp. 507–8.
[15]For interesting details see Ahmad Mahrad, *Iran unter der Herrschaft Reza Schahs* (1977), pp. 48–51.
[16]Quoted in Abolhasan Banisadr, *Vaz'iyat-e Iran va naqsh-e Modarres* (Iran's situation and the role of Modarres) (1977), pp. 124–25.

those aspects of the latters' cultures that were not incompatible with their new religion, as a result of which Islamic civilization flourished. Bazargan has written both on what he considers positive features of the West[17] and on those aspects that he deems negative.[18] Taleqani, for his part, pointed out that "one cannot deny that constitutional government first reached Islamic lands from abroad."[19] Shariati, finally, liked to distinguish between the West that Westernized Iranians imitated, which was not the true one, and the West that valued intellectual inquiry and moral righteousness, which was worth emulating.[20]

Having studied there in the 1930s, France is the Western country Bazargan knows best. It is no surprise that among Western intellectuals French writers have had the greatest impact on him. Three decades later, Shariati also spent a few years in Paris. Two now almost forgotten French intellectuals have left traces in much modernist Shi'ite writing: Alexis Carrel and his one-time disciple, Pierre Lecomte de Noüy.

Alexis Carrel (1873–1944)

Born into a provincial, Catholic, upper-class family in Lyons, Carrel became a prominent intellectual of the interwar years.[21] He combined a highly distinguished career as a surgeon and scientist (in 1912 he won the Nobel Prize in Medicine for his work on the suturing of blood vessels and transplantation of organs) with an active interest in spiritual and religious matters and phenomena. From 1906 to 1936 he worked intermittently for the Rockefeller Institute for Medical Research in New York City, where he was given his own laboratory for highly original and pioneering research on blood vessels, organ transplants, and the culture of organs. For a while he closely collaborated with Charles Lindbergh, who constructed an artificial heart pump for him.[22]

In 1933 Carrel wrote his best-known book, *L'Homme, cet inconnu*, which became a tremendous publishing success and was translated into nineteen languages.[23] This book contained a good summary of the state of knowledge of human physiology and medicine as it existed in the mid-1930s. It was also a plea for scientists to devote more attention to the study of the human mind. Carrel had witnessed miraculous

---

[17]See Bazargan's *Modafe'at*, pp. 42–66.

[18]See for instance M. Bazargan, *Mazhab dar Orupa* (Religion in Europe), 3d ed., ed. and notes by M. Khosroshahi (n.d.).

[19]See Taleqani's introduction to Na'ini, *Tanbih*, p. 4.

[20]See for instance Shariati's *Fatemeh*, pp. 55–58.

[21]Biographical information on Carrel is taken from W. Sterling Edwards and Peter D. Edwards, *Alexis Carrel: Visionary Surgeon* (1974).

[22]For a contemporary account of their collaboration and a critical review of Carrel's most famous book, see *Time* July 1, 1935, pp. 41–42, and September 16, 1935, pp. 40–43.

[23]An English translation came out soon after the original: *Man the Unknown* (1935).

healings on his annual pilgrimages to Lourdes,[24] and he endeavored to integrate his findings into a general picture of man. His relations with the Catholic Church were quite problematic, however. He had a generally low opinion of the clergy, and his endorsement of eugenics was condemned by the church. Like so many intellectuals in the interwar period he viewed certain aspects of fascism and Nazism quite favorably.

The appeal of *Man the Unknown* to Islamic apologists is not difficult to understand. Here was a well-known, widely respected scientist who upheld his religious faith defiantly, criticized the materialism of the West, and devoted much time to achieving a synthesis between the natural sciences and religious beliefs. At a time when Middle Eastern governments were pushing for secularization in the name of progress, Carrel was living proof that the progress of civilization was not incompatible with belief in phenomena that science could *not yet* explain but that were congruent with religious beliefs. In addition, the book contained views with which a Muslim could easily agree: Carrel's views on women and sex were conservative even by the standards of his own time, and he believed in the preeminent role of an intellectual elite that would have to lead the rest of society.[25]

After *Man the Unknown*, Carrel wrote a series of articles for *Reader's Digest*, including one that eventually became an opusculum on the human need for and the efficiency of prayer.[26] In 1939, upon his retirement, he left New York for France, where he seems to have collaborated with Vichy and even the Germans. He died in 1944, before he could stand trial.

Bazargan quotes Carrel often in his writings, and Shariati started his career as a writer in 1948, when, at the early age of fifteen, he translated Carrel's *Prayer* into Persian.[27] In a later book, he mentioned Carrel first in a list of "star intellectuals" of the twentieth century.[28]

Pierre Lecomte de Noüy (1883–1947)
Scion of an artistically inclined family of minor aristocracy, Pierre

---

[24]For details, see Edwards and Edwards, *Alexis Carrel*, pp. 57 and 105.
[25]For a summary of the book and a glimpse of contemporary reactions to it, see ibid., pp. 97–103.
[26]Alexis Carrel, *Prayer*, trans. Dulcie de Ste. Croix Wright (1949).
[27]A. Shariati, *Niayesh* (1948).
[28]The others on the list are Frantz Fanon, Amar Mawlud, Albert Einstein, Max Planck, Kateb Yasin, Omar Ozgan, Karl Jaspers, Martin Heidegger, Josué de Castro, René Guénon, and Chandel. Ali Shariati, *Man and Islam*, trans. Fatollah Marjani (1981), p. 80. The fact that as confirmed a Eurocentric as Carrel and militantly anti-Western "Third Worldist" such as Fanon head the list, illustrates the wisdom of Borges's insight on precursors.

Lecomte de Noüy was born in 1883 in Paris.[29] He started his adult life as a playboy, actor, and playwright. In 1915, as an officer in the French Army, he met Alexis Carrel, who was also serving in his country's armed forces. Through Carrel he became interested in biology, and in 1917 he found a mathematical expression of the process of healing of wounds, the first time mathematics had been successfully applied to a biological problem. Lecomte de Noüy collaborated closely with Carrel, especially from 1920 to 1927, when he was an associate member of the Rockefeller Institute in New York City. He fell out with Carrel over the latter's positive attitude toward Vichy, and escaped to the United States in 1942, where he died in 1947.

Lecomte de Noüy's major contribution to religious apologetic literature is his book *Human Destiny*.[30] Grossly simplified, his thesis runs as follows. The Second Law of Thermodynamics states that inanimate matter tends toward entropy. Scientific evidence shows, however, that this law does not apply to organic matter. Besides, the evolution of living beings shows that they have constantly moved toward more complicated and higher states, rather than in the direction of entropy. The highest form so far reached is the human brain. Chance alone cannot explain its apparition at the end of the long process of evolution, therefore evolution must have been willed and directed toward a goal. This is Lecomte de Noüy's theory of "telefinalism." The logical consequences of this theory are, first, the philosophical necessity of humanity's complete liberty, and second,

> the necessity of revivifying religion by a return to its source, to the fundamental principles of Christianity and of fighting against the superstitions which creep into the doctrine and menace its future. It is certain that the additions to the Christian religion, and the human interpretations which started in the third century, together with the disregard for scientific truths, supplied the strongest arguments to the materialists and atheists in their fight against religion.[31]

Substituting "Islam" for "Christianity," this could be the summary of any Islamic modernist's agenda.

The prominence of such writers as Carrel and Lecomte de Noüy for the Islamic modernists has two explanations. On the one hand it is in

---

[29]The only account of his life is due to the somewhat hagiographic pen of his wife, Marie Lecomte de Noüy, *The Road to "Human Destiny": A Life of Pierre Lecomte de Noüy* (1955).

[30]P. Lecomte de Noüy, *Human Destiny* (1947).

[31]Ibid., p. 238. For a summary of "telefinalism" and its consequences, see pp. 223–45. The fallacy of this theory is that the Second Law of Thermodynamics applies to closed systems, whereas the earth constantly receives energy from the sun.

the very nature of a thought grounded in a cultural synthesis that it should take recourse to a wide variety of sources, and on the other hand Islamic modernists living in Iran share certain limitations that affect intellectuals in most peripheral countries. There are no good libraries, many books are not available, some are not available in languages the local intellectuals can read, and above all hangs the constant threat of official censorship. This explains the sudden fame of certain texts that would be considered quite secondary in their home countries (such as Carrel), but that, having been translated into Persian, become central to intellectual discourse and are mined for suitable quotations.

Interpretative Principles

The principles that Shi'ite modernists in Iran apply to their reinterpretation of Islam are the same as the ones used by their Sunni counterparts elsewhere.[32] Two stand out: the return to the Qoran and a preoccupation with science.

Return to the Sources of the Faith

Like their Sunni colleagues before them, Shi'ite modernists have tried to prove that "true" Islam was deformed by the accretions of later times (although less so than Christianity and Judaism) and that one must return to the sources of the religion to find its pristine qualities. These sources are the traditions of the Prophet (known as *hadith*); the book *Nahj ul-Balaghah*, which Shi'ites attribute to Imam Ali; and above all else, the Qoran itself.

The exegesis of the Qoran (*tafsir*) had fallen in neglect among the orthodox Shi'ite ulema in the nineteenth century: although individual ulema practiced it, it was no longer an obligatory subject matter in the religious schools, where *feqh*, or Islamic jurisprudence, clearly dominated the curriculum. In the 1920s Ay. Aqa Mirza Khalil Kamareh'i revived *tafsir* at the newly reconstituted *howzeh-ye elmiyeh* (center for religious learning) in Qum. When S. Mahmud Taleqani studied there, Ay. Kamareh'i became one of his favorite teachers.[33] After Taleqani founded his Islamic Society, a large part of its activities consisted in interpreting the Qoran in contemporary language. Bazargan attended many of these activities. But Bazargan has also been inspired by French critical works on the Qoran, such as Blachère's *Introduction au Coran*.[34] When

---

[32]S.v. "Islah," in *Encyclopaedia of Islam*, especially pp. 145–47.

[33]Bahram Afrasiabi and Sa'id Dehqan, *Taleqani va tarikh* (Taleqani and history) (1981), p. 29.

[34]Régis Blachère, *Introduction au Coran* (1959).

one survey's Bazargan's writings chronologically, one notices that Qoranic quotations become ever more frequent, no doubt a reflection of Bazargan's personal growth as an Islamicist.[35]

Taleqani wrote a multivolume interpretation of the Qoran that enjoys great popularity among lay Muslim activists but does not meet with much respect from the ulema, who deem it intellectually inferior to the contemporary twenty-volume work of Allameh Tabataba'i.

For Bazargan, accounts of the Prophet's life by Western scholars have also been valuable, as they have helped him demystify the historical figure of Muhammad, thereby enabling him to make his example relevant to the modern age. Such works include Emile Dermenghem's *La Vie de Mahomet*,[36] Régis Blachère's *Le Problème de Mahomet*,[37] and Montgomery Watt's *Muhammad: Prophet and Statesman*.[38]

Science

As early as the 1870s Muslim apologists tried to prove that the absence of a scientific spirit of inquiry in the Islamic world was a recent phenomenon, that the West had acquired its science from the Muslims, and that, if modern Muslims learned science afresh from the West, they would be recovering their own past and fulfill the neglected commandments of Islam.[39]

In 1883 Ernest Renan had given a lecture on Islam and Science at the Sorbonne, in which he had attributed the backwardness of Muslims solely to their religion. This drew a reply from al-Afghani, who was residing in Paris at the time. Although the latter actually *agreed* with Renan, and even went further by suggesting that *all* religions stifle the spirit of scientific inquiry, Muslim modernists in general believe that al-Afghani *defended* Islam against Renan's accusations.[40] It seems as if Muslim modernists, at least in Iran, had never ceased trying to prove Renan wrong.

Bazargan, as a French-trained engineer, was in a particularly favorable position to set out proving that Islamic precepts are grounded in science, which is the twentieth-century variety of what all religious rationalists, from Avicenna and Thomas of Aquinas to our own day,

---

[35]This technique is on occasion carried quite far. After the disgrace of the Tudeh party, the LMI in 1983 published an article titled "The Tudeh from the Point of View of the Qoran."

[36]Available in English as *The Life of Mahomet*, trans. Arabella Yorke (1930).

[37]Régis Blachère, *Le Probleme de Mahomet* (1952).

[38]W. Montgomery Watt, *Muhammad: Prophet and Statesman* (1974). I owe this list to a written personal communication from Mehdi Bazargan, January 4, 1988.

[39]Fazlur Rahman, *Islam and Modernity: Transformation of an Intellectual Tradition* (1982), pp. 50–51.

[40]For details on this exchange and the mystifications to which it gave rise, see Kedourie, *Afghani and 'Abduh*, pp. 41–46.

have tried to do, namely to prove the oneness of reason and religion. In his essay on religion in Europe, Bazargan wrote that in the West religion had not come to terms with science, as a result of which Christians emphasized *faith*, whereas Islam always talked about *knowledge*.[41] One of his first articles upon his return to Iran was titled "The Thermodynamics of Love." Earlier Alexis Carrel had suggested that "as much importance should be given to feelings as to thermodynamics."[42]

Bazargan's attitude toward evolution is also instructive of his frame of mind. Like Christian defenders of Darwinism before him,[43] Bazargan reconciles scientific evidence for evolution and his belief in creation by reading a "design" or "purpose" into history. He backs up his synthesis by quotes from the Qoran and references to General Systems Theory and to Lecomte de Noüy's theory of telefinalism.[44] Bazargan states that more important than the evolution of the species is the evolution of humankind toward higher planes.[45] It is interesting to note that he does not mention the Iranian philosopher Molla Sadra, who elaborated on the spiritual side of this theme in the seventeenth century.[46] The two aspects, return to the source and science, come together in Bazargan's book *Seir-e tahavvol-e tadriji-ye Qor'an* (The gradual evolution of the Qoran), in which he attempts to prove the revelatory nature of the book by analyzing its contents with the help of analogies drawn from the natural sciences.

Major Themes

Among all Shi'ite modernists in Iran, Bazargan, being a politician, gave the most detailed attention to political questions. This discussion of political concepts concentrates on his work, whereas on economic matters we will present the views of both him and Taleqani. A consideration of the ideology of the LMI as a political party will close this section.

[41]Bazargan, *Mazhab dar Orupa*, p. 46.

[42]Carrel, *Man the Unknown*, p. 279.

[43]For the earliest example of these see Asa Gray, *Darwiniana: Essays and Reviews Pertaining to Darwinism*, ed. A. Hunter Dupree (1963).

[44]Mehdi Bazargan, *Tabi'at, takamol, towhid* (Nature, evolution, and monotheism) (1977). Lecomte de Noüy's idea is mentioned on p. 40.

[45]Ibid., pp. 29ff.

[46]For Henri Corbin "the mobility of Molla Sadra's universe ... is not that of a world in *evolution*, but that of a world in *ascension*." "La place de Molla Sadra Shirazi dans la philosophie iranienne," *Studia Islamica* 18 (1963), 106.

Political Aspects

Bazargan's political thought is pluralist, but he is opposed to the secularist foundations of classical liberalism; "Islamic liberalism" thus describes his thinking best. Taleqani's views are more problematic.

Iran's and Islam's Position in the World

Given the defensive nature of religious modernism noted earlier, it is not surprising that modernists in Iran have devoted considerable attention to the problem of Iranians' collective identity. The early modernizers of the late nineteenth century had rediscovered Iran's pre-Islamic past but had not repudiated the country's Islamic heritage. Under Reza Shah's rule the Islamic ingredient was definitely de-emphasized. Bazargan's conceptions of what constitutes the Iranian identity must be seen in this context: coming from a religious background he could not accept the marginalization of Islam, but growing up under Reza Shah, he internalized many of the topoi of secular nationalism, such as the notion of an "Aryan race."

For Bazargan and for the LMI, Islam is indissolubly linked with Iran, and is the *major*, albeit not the *only* ingredient of Iranian identity. Iran's obvious decline is therefore both part of the wider decline of the Islamic world, and due to specific, national, circumstances.

Bazargan analyzes the sources of Islamic countries' relative under-development, and, significantly, comes to the conclusion that this underdevelopment predates the rise of the West, and that the West therefore should not be blamed for everything that is wrong in the Islamic world. The main source of Muslims' plight is that very early in their history religion withdrew from public affairs; pious people concentrated on practicing their religion and left the conduct of social and political affairs to those not committed to Islamic values. One result of this divorce was the emergence of a class of religious men totally oblivious to practical concerns.[47]

Unlike fundamentalists, who tend to be more pan-Islamic and downplay the national differences among Islamic peoples, modernists admit the distinctiveness of their nation but refuse to draw chauvinistic conclusions from it. Bazargan has written a great deal about the factors that explain the present makeup of the Iranian nation and its national character. He gave the most coherent statement of these ideas in a

---

[47]Mehdi Bazargan, "The Causes of the Decline and Decadence of Islamic Nations," *Islamic Review* 23 (6) (1951), 8–12. In this text, which later appeared in an augmented Persian version as *Serr-e aqab-oftadegi-ye melal-e mosalman,* Bazargan's anticlericalism is quite blunt and foreshadows future elaborations by Ali Shariati.

supplementary chapter he wrote for the Persian translation of Siegfried's *L'Ame des peuples*.[48] To "Latin realism," "French ingenuity," "English tenacity," "German discipline," "Russian mysticism," and "American dynamism," to quote Siegfried's chapter headings, Bazargan added "Iranian adaptability." Bazargan begins by refuting the notion of racial purity so dear to some secular Iranian nationalists, but reveals his own ethnic pride when he notes that Iranians are the outcome of mixtures between "peaceful and tolerant Aryans" and "aggressive and violent" peoples such as the Assyrians, Chaldeans, Ummayyad and Abbasid Arabs, Mongols, and Tatars. Iranians have never resisted their invaders actively, but rather assimilated them over time, which is why they survived as a nation.

According to Bazargan, the immense majority of Iranians have always engaged in agriculture, and the Iranian genius has always flowed from the countryside to the culturally sterile cities. Agriculture demands less precision than commerce or artisan activity, and the fruit of human work is always ultimately dependent on elements over which one has no control. The result is that Iranians are fatalistic and indifferent to precision. Persian literature prizes exaggeration at the expense of realism, and

> unfortunately we have to admit that neatly ironed trousers, punctual arrival at the work place, finishing one's job or one's talking on time, respect for strict guidelines in the remuneration and promotion of employees, and thousands of other principles and criteria that today are the undisputed necessities of civilized life, all came to our country from Europe.[49]

The fact that the inhabitable areas on the Iranian plateau are so far apart led to extreme individualism, an inability to cooperate on larger projects, and the weakness of a national consciousness among Iranians at the mass level. Bazargan also states that Iranians have a tendency to be hypocritical, making constant professions of piety while "lying and cheating have perhaps been more common in Iran than in any other country."[50] In politics, this has meant that Iranians are prone to use force to implement their goals, and want everything immediately, having no patience for careful planning and systematic changes. To-

---

[48]André Siegfried, *L'Ame des peuples* (1950). Translated by Edward Fitzgerald, it became *The Character of Peoples* (1952) in Britain and *Nations Have Souls* (1952) in the United States. For his additional chapter, Bazargan was influenced by René Grousset's *La Face de l'Asie* (1955), which includes a chapter called "L'Iran et son role historique." Personal written communication from Mehdi Bazargan, January 4, 1988.

[49]Mehdi Bazargan, *Sazegari-ye Irani*, 2d ed. (1978), p. 30.

[50]Ibid., p. 46.

ward the end of the book he writes, somewhat prophetically as it turned out: "Many of our revolutionaries are equally impatient, and it is obvious that with haste and without careful calculations nothing can be improved."[51]

Bazargan's views of Iran and Iranians are interesting for three reasons. First, they show him to be critically seeking the roots of Iran's travails inside Iran, which contrasts favorably with so many others who blame outside forces, especially the West, for every problem. Second, it sets the agenda for his political and social action, whose common denominator is the quest for the diffusion of legal-rational authority in Iranian society. And third, it shows him to be a nationalist, in that his analyses focus on and aim for the improvement of Iran. This combination of religious modernism and moderate nationalism is not peculiar to Iran, as earlier Arab Islamic modernists such as Muhammad Abduh in Egypt and al-Kawakibi in Syria also combined both elements.[52] In all cases this nationalism is justified by the *hadith* "hubb al-watan min al-iman" (the love of the motherland is part of religion). Although an ethnic component is not absent from this nationalism, it is above all patriotic in nature. It is indicative of Bazargan's conception of nationalism, and the place of religion in it, that in a book he wrote on the nationalist struggle of India he expresses his admiration for M. Gandhi and J. Nehru and faults M. A. Jinnah and the Muslim League for their separatism.[53]

In the case of Bazargan, his nationalism would lead to disagreements with Khomeini after the revolution, when Bazargan wrote that he had wanted "Islam for Iran," whereas Khomeini had wanted "Iran for Islam."[54] Earlier, in 1966, he had written that "since the clergy do not have strong links with Iran's society, history, and cultural heritage, their national and patriotic sentiments have at times weakened."[55]

The Need for Political Action

Like other Muslim reformers before him, Bazargan starts from the premise that if Muslims want to improve their lot they must take their destiny in their own hands. He repeatedly quotes a Qoranic verse dear to all Islamic activists: "God changes not what is in a people, until they change what is in themselves" (13:12). Having established that Muslims

[51]Ibid., p. 67.
[52]See Albert Hourani, *Arabic Thought in the Liberal Age* (1983), pp. 156–60 and 271–73.
[53]Mehdi Bazargan, *Azadi-ye Hend* (The liberation of India) (1977), pp. 178–96.
[54]He develops the theme in "Iran va eslam" (Iran and Islam), in *Bazyabi-ye arzeshha* (The recovery of values), vol. 2 (1982).
[55]Mehdi Bazargan, *Be'sat va ideolozhi* (Designation of the Prophet and ideology) (1976), p. 230.

have to give up their fatalistic attitude toward the course of events and act, Bazargan outlines the direction this action must take.

Bazargan's thought developed under conditions in which the state was largely in secular hands. This explains its originally *defensive* aspects. In his article "The Borderline between Religion and Social Affairs," Bazargan writes that as long as the state was not yet developed, as under the Qajars, any pious person could expect to be left alone by the state to practice religion in exchange for total political abstinence. But with the development of the state in recent times, such a "pact of nonaggression" was no longer possible, for the state now actively interfered with people's lives, making it difficult for them to be good Muslims.[56]

One way to assure a Muslim presence in society is to create associations in which Muslims could come together and further their interests. Here Bazargan admits the influence of his experiences in France,[57] which inspired his support for Islamic associations of students, engineers, teachers, and others.

Bazargan also called for less quietism on the part of the ulema. If one remembers that the clergy's attitude to the Shah's government was not altogether hostile in 1953–61, one understands why before the revolution Bazargan repeatedly urged the ulema to lend their support to the Nationalists and become politically active.[58] Ultimately, the necessity of a Muslim presence in politics led to the founding of the LMI, its opposition to the Shah, and most recently Bazargan's and the LMI's refusal to go into exile and their determination to wage their opposition inside Iran.

Islamic Government

What is this Muslim presence in social and political life to achieve? It is here that the potential for conflict arises between, on the one hand, the absolute nature of a religion like Islam, which does not a priori separate the temporal from the religious realm, and, on the other hand, the professed liberalism of Bazargan's political views. Bazargan's solution is that religious affairs and sociopolitical matters are separate, but that their separation is asymmetrical: while politics must never interfere with religion, religion should inspire and inform all acts social and political.

---

[56]Mehdi Bazargan, *Marz-e mian-e din va omur-e ejtema'i* (The borderline between religion and social affairs) (1976), pp. 6–7.

[57]The *Modafe'at*, pp. 54–58, contains a very Tocquevillean discussion of the beneficial effects of associations on society.

[58]See, for example, A. K. S. Lambton, "A Reconsideration of the Position of the *Marja Al-Taqlid* and the Religious Institution," *Studia Islamica* 20 (1964), 122–23.

Religion must not be used by politicians for their partisan aims, nor may the clergy assume that their privileged religious status gives them ipso facto the right to interfere in politics. For Bazargan, the prominence of Islamic jurisprudence (*feqh*), and consequently the Islamic jurisprudents (*foqaha*), is a result of the general decadence of Islamic societies that set in soon after the death of the Prophet.[59] As a result of this exclusive preoccupation with *feqh*, other aspects of Islam—especially its ethical injunctions—have been consistently neglected.[60]

For Bazargan, the basic rules that govern the workings of society are contained in the Qoran and in Islam, but the application of these rules to everyday life constitutes the legislative activity of parliaments.[61] In the absence of the Prophet and the Imams, it is the people themselves who must ensure Islamic government. They themselves choose their rulers, and the government can only handle those matters that the people have placed in its care. That, for Bazargan, is the meaning of *velayat*.[62]

Moreover, all citizens must participate in the choice of a government. One cannot deny some citizens the right to participate because they are ignorant, for who is to define the membership of the enlightened and pious minority? Besides, Bazargan argues, all usurping minorities have claimed to represent the best of their societies.[63] The Qoranic injunction to "take counsel with them in the affairs" (3:159), and the principles of "enjoining what is good and preventing what is evil" can be understood as a plea for wide-ranging participation of the citizenry and accountability of the rulers vis-à-vis the ruled. Islam provides general outlines for the governance of society but leaves the details to be worked out by believers according to the needs of the times.[64]

The Means of Political Action

A liberal attitude in politics, regardless of the *contents* of one's beliefs or opinions, entails a particular attention to methods and the acceptance of the principle that ends do not justify means. The question arises as to how Bazargan proposes to achieve his Islamic order. Among the various verses of the Qoran and the body of *hadith* dealing with the imposition of Islam, Bazargan constantly quotes "No compulsion is there in Religion" (2:256). Bazargan also repeatedly asserts that

[59]Bazargan, "The Causes...," p. 10.
[60]In his *Marz-e mian-e din va omur-e ejtema'i*, on pp. 17–18, Bazargan, quoting the French orientalist Jules La Beaume, gives a breakdown of the pages of the Qoran according to subjects. Ethics occupies 184 pages, while the Shari'ah gets only 14 pages.
[61]Bazargan, *Be'sat*, pp. 98–99.
[62]Ibid., pp. 115–16.
[63]Ibid., p. 159.
[64]M. Bazargan, *Marz*, pp. 29–30.

man is free, and should therefore have the choice of embracing Islam or rejecting it.[65]

Bazargan explicitly rejects the opinion of those who argue that although democracy is a valid ideal, it is unworkable in an underdeveloped country since corrupt elements will take advantage of the ignorance of the majority and prevent its development. One must grant freedom of speech even to opponents, as the Qoran explicitly says "...and reason with them in the better way" (16:125). Those who argue that erroneous opinions should not be allowed freedom of expression are applying double standards, lack confidence that their own ideas could gain acceptance by the majority of the population, and may be cowards who have an axe to grind.[66]

Since Islamic precepts are for Muslims, any political ideology based on Islam has to come to terms with the fact that there will be citizens who do not order their lives according to that religion, whether they be irreligious persons of Muslim background, "people of the book," atheists, or adherents of religions not recognized by Muslims as divinely inspired. There is no getting around the fact that Islam differentiates between Muslims and non-Muslims, and does not confer the same rights on everybody. This raises the question of how an Islamic liberal proposes to achieve legal equality for all citizens, in our time a sine qua non for a parliamentary democracy.

In his most recent writings, Bazargan often refers to the "Abrahamic *umma*" or to the "people-of-the-book *umma*," signifying that he considers the rights and duties of Iranian citizens under Islamic rule to be the same for all, Muslim or non-Muslim.

Bazargan, like other modernists, stresses the *rationalistic* character of Islam. Mere *faith* is played down as a manifestation of an earlier (although in its time fully justified) form of religiosity, which Islam has transcended. God created man free. Open debate, meaningful only under conditions of free speech, is therefore in the long run the most efficient way to bring about voluntary compliance with Islam. On the topic of the Islamic veil, for instance, Bazargan said after the revolution: "The *chador* and scarf which are imposed by force and threats on women's heads are a hundred times worse than going uncovered."[67]

In one of his books Bazargan considers the Universal Declaration of Human Rights, and argues point by point that Islam goes beyond it. He concludes that when the Prophet declared on the day he took

---

[65]Bazargan, *Be'sat*, p. 95.
[66]Ibid., pp. 124 and 137–39.
[67]In his funeral oration for Ay. Taleqani at Teheran University, on September 11, 1980. The text is reprinted in Abdolali Bazargan, ed., *Masa'el va moshkelat-e nakhostin sal-e enqelab* (The problems and difficulties of the first year of the revolution) (1983), p. 334.

Mecca that "the dearest to God were those who were most virtuous," this transcends all later pleas for equality between nations, the sexes, races, and religions.[68] To believe that, obviously, one has to indulge to a considerable extent in eisegesis. Less optimistic writers, such as Hamid Enayat, have argued that Islam is in fact incompatible with certain key assumptions of liberal democracy.[69] One conceivable solution to this problem would be to declare that liberal democracy, with all it entails, is only a temporary form of government, which will be superseded by a purely Islamic state as soon as this can be done without coercion. If such a view contains the implicit understanding that the temporary period is quite long, that it takes time to convince people, and if therefore the advent of the Islamic state is tacitly deferred *usque ad kalendas Graecas*, the incompatibility of Islam with these key assumptions of liberal democracy is of only academic interest.

This discussion may seen pedantic, but it is not. Let us not forget that Islamic liberalism was elaborated under a secular dictatorship, which means that Islam could only benefit from a liberalization of political mores. It requires far more ingenuity theoretically to justify liberalism under conditions where Islam's triumph in Iran seems complete. In the years since his resignation as prime minister in 1979, Bazargan has taken up this challenge. He spelled out his fundamental differences with the current leadership of the Islamic Republic in a series of articles, most of them based on lectures, which have been collected and published under the title *The Recovery of Values*.[70] In the introduction he observes that the Islamic Republic was more demanding of its citizens than God had been of the prophets, or the prophets of their communities.[71] After adducing ample evidence from the Qoran, he concludes that "freedom is a divine gift that God has bestowed on Man, his vicar. Whoever takes away freedom commits the greatest treachery against Man."[72] In another article, Bazargan writes that those verses of the Qoran that command violence against infidels, concentrated in the sura of "Repentance" and constantly invoked by the leadership of Iran, apply only to those infidels who have broken their peace agreements with Muslims.[73] In an oblique reference to the treatment of Baha'is in Iran, he admits that in Islam apostasy is punishable by death, but observes that apostasy is very hard to prove

[68]Bazargan, *Rah-e teyy shodeh* (The completed path) (1977), pp. 113–17.
[69]H. Enayat, *Modern Islamic Political Thought* (1982), pp. 125–39.
[70]M. Bazargan, *Bazyabi-ye arzeshha*, 3 vols. (1982–83).
[71]Ibid., vol. 1, p. 13.
[72]"Din va azadi" (Religion and freedom), in ibid., vol. 1, pp. 68–69.
[73]"Iran va eslam," ibid., vol. 2, pp. 143–44. He might have added that this sura is the only one in the Qoran which does not start with "In the Name of God, the Merciful, the Compassionate," a fact that for many underscores its exceptional character.

and applies only to those who deny the oneness of God, not to those who merely contest principles such as prayers and fasting.[74] On the law of the talion, which was introduced in Iran in 1981, Bazargan wrote that those verses of the Qoran that deal with retribution were revealed so as to limit and attenuate pre-Islamic Arab practices of vengeance.[75] Here Bazargan's argument follows Fazlur Rahman's view that in interpreting a Qoranic injunction one has to keep in mind the historical conditions that prevailed at the time of the revelation, to distinguish between the intended thrust of the injunction and its concrete contents.[76] Finally, in a 1983 work, Bazargan interprets medieval Christianity and the Inquisition in light of the first sura of the Qoran, and by implication condemns the methods used by the Iranian regime to impose religion.[77]

Taleqani did not address the problem of the ideal political system explicitly. In his major work, *Islam and Ownership*, references abound to an "Islamic ruler." The powers Taleqani ascribes to him far exceed those of a democratic chief executive. Later in his life, perhaps under the influence of his leftist children, Taleqani increasingly stressed "rule of the people," which he wanted to enshrine in a vast network of "councils." Toward the end of his life, he told foreign reporters:

> From an Islamic point of view Western democracy is not government by the people, nor does it benefit the people. What is Western has a colonialist face. It rules over the whole people and deceives them with its false propaganda. The colonialist governments that had dragged people through blood and debased them derive from the same democracy. Moreover, I see clearly that the prostitution and loose morals that prevail in the West, especially America, will destroy them before long.[78]

Taleqani clearly opposed one-man rule, both political and religious. He also favored popular participation. But from his writings it is impossible to infer that his ideal political system was a liberal democracy.

Economic Aspects

Maxime Rodinson has shown that historically Islam has not evolved a particular economic system; moreover, "the precepts of Islam have not seriously hindered the capitalist orientation taken by the Muslims world during the last hundred years, and nothing in them is really

---

[74]"Din va azadi," p. 78.
[75]*Mizan*, December 13, 1980 (Azar 22, 1359), p. 4.
[76]Rahman, *Islam and Modernity*, pp. 17–19.
[77]M. Bazargan, *Gomrahan* (The misled) (1983).
[78]Afrasiabi and Dehqan, *Taleqani va tarikh*, p. 419.

opposed to a socialist orientation."[79] This, of course, need not discourage a Shi'ite modernist, as for him the true precepts of Islam have never been applied in the Muslim world, except for the time of the Prophet and the brief effective rule of Ali.

The Shi'ite writers who have given Islamic economics most detailed attention have not been directly linked to the LMI. In Iraq, Ay. S. Muhammad Baqir Sadr (1930–80), hardly a modernist, wrote a lengthy treatise on the subject. In Iran, Abolhasan Banisadr, who has some university training in economics, has written prescriptively about it.[80] The LMI leaders have not developed a coherent set of integrated ideas and policies on economic matters, perhaps because in Iran political questions have always had more urgency. The most important work to come from the pen of a modernist associated with the LMI is Ay. Taleqani's *Eslam va malekiyyat* (Islam and Ownership).

Taleqani's analysis centers, as the book's title indicates, on the question of property, and is not intended as a systematic exposition of Islamic economics. The book's gestation coincided with the Shah's efforts to carry out an agrarian reform. Its final version, published in 1965, was an attempt to confront the agrarian reforms critically. As a socially conscious person, Taleqani was unable to oppose agrarian reform as such, but as a cleric and oppositional politician he could not condone the ways in which it was carried out by the Shah. Hence his efforts to dissect the very notion of "ownership":

> Ownership is relative and limited. Ownership means the authority and power of possession. As human power and authority are limited, no person should consider himself the absolute owner and complete possessor. Absolute power and complete possession belong only to God who has created man and all other creatures and has them constantly in his possession. Man's ownership is limited to whatever God has wisely willed and to the capacity of his intellect, authority, and freedom granted to him.[81]

As far as the question of landownership is concerned, Taleqani maintained that:

> since the rights of individuals to possess and distribute resources differ depending on the commodities, they are not defined legally in perpetuity.

[79]Maxime Rodinson, *Islam and Capitalism*, trans. Brian Pearce (1978), p. 186.

[80]For a critical appraisal of both writers see Homa Katouzian, "Shi'ism and Islamic Economics: Sadr and Bani Sadr," in Nikki R. Keddie, *Religion and Politics in Iran* (1983), pp. 145–65.

[81]Seyyed Mahmood Taleqani, *Islam and Ownership*, trans. Ahmad Jabbari and Farhang Rajaee (1983), p. 88.

> That is, the right of possession and revitalization of unexploited lands is
> established to the extent that the act of revitalization has been carried out
> and will last for as long as the land is properly exploited. Among resources
> such as pastures and forests as well as surface waters the right to
> exploitation is established by the person only to the extent he keeps it
> productive.[82]

For Taleqani, therefore, property was not sacred, as some of his
conservative colleagues maintained, but this did not mean that the
government had the right to rearrange property relationships as it
pleased. The implications of these principles for a modern industrial
and service economy are not spelled out, which is not remarkable,
given the essentially agrarian nature of Iran's economy in the 1950s
and early 1960s. Indeed, Taleqani chides Iranian economists for basing
their theories and prescriptions exclusively on the reality of the advance industrialized countries.

Economic considerations do not form an important part of Bazargan's
thought. His book *Kar dar eslam* (Labor in Islam) is more an analysis of
the Islamic work ethic than a discussion of the social problems of
labor.[83] Scattered in his writings, however, we do find some indica-
tions of his ideas on economic life. Bazargan is aware of the necessity
for Iranians (and Third World people in general) to overcome their
dependency on the advanced nations. The necessary precondition for
independence is to make do with little, to accept a lower standard of
living. He cites the example of Gandhi approvingly.[84] In his writings
he often laments the fact that Iran uses its oil income for current
expenditures rather than for capital investment.

Insofar as the role of the state in the regulation of the country's
economic life is concerned, Bazargan urges caution. Before the Islamic
revolution he warned that "the nationalization of economic activities
can only be of benefit if the appropriating state itself is not anti-
national. If not, nationalizations will only boost the state's income,
which it will use to increase repression. Before nationalizing industries,
it is necessary to nationalize the state!"[85] After the revolution he
repeatedly warned against an overblown state apparatus, because the
bureaucracy was already too large. Nationalization of industry is therefore no panacea in Bazargan's view.[86]

---

[82]Ibid., p. 136.
[83]Mehdi Bazargan, *Work in Islam*, trans. M. Yasfi, Ali A. Behzadnia, and Najpu Denny
(1979).
[84]See Bazargan, *Serr* (1977), pp. 51–52.
[85]Bazargan, *Be'sat*, p. 228.
[86]See for instance Bazargan's message on the occasion of the nationalization of big
industries in 1979, which he accepted only grudgingly. This text can be found in A.
Bazargan, ed., *Masa'el*, pp. 197–201.

Bazargan approves of private enterprise, as long as it is productive and contributes to the creation of wealth. Moreover, employers must pay their workers decent wages, sufficient to cover their basic needs.[87] After the revolution, when Western development models were under attack, he maintained that exaggerated anticonsumerism was itself an import from the West.[88]

In the context of an ideology that claims Islamic inspiration it does not take much effort to justify liberal ideas on economic matters. Maxime Rodinson has pointed out that "the Koran has nothing against private property, since it lays down rules for inheritance, for example. It even advises that inequalities be not challenged, contenting itself with denouncing the habitual impiety of rich men." Rodinson concluded that the Koran "looks with favor upon commercial activity, confining itself to condemning fraudulent practices."[89] The burden of proof is therefore on those who opine that socialist principles inhere in Islam.

And yet, Bazargan's approval of private enterprise is not absolute and admits exceptions. Moreover, his approval must be understood in the general context of his thought. In a society ruled by Islamic ethics the quest for justice that characterizes Muslims will prevent the Islamic entrepreneur from exploiting his work-force. The fact that no historical precedent exists for this state of affairs does not mean much, since true Islam has never been applied in the past. One may find this view naive; yet one has no right to call it hypocritical. Bazargan is a truly religious man: as such he has an eschatological view of human history. We are continuously advancing on the path to perfection: therefore the fact that benign capitalism does not exist now does not preclude its coming into existence once righteous, well-meaning, and competent Muslims have come to dominate social life. The ideal is some sort of mixed economy.

It would be hard to prove that Taleqani and Bazargan actually contradict each other, because they address different sets of problems. Both essentially argue that things would be better if people were good, if they ordered their lives according to the precepts of true Islam. But beyond this quasi tautology, Taleqani is more concerned with achieving justice, whereas Bazargan aims at enabling people to go about their business. These different emphases perhaps reflect their social backgrounds, discussed in the next chapter.

The two authors' attitude to socialism is instructive. Bazargan warns against religiously oriented people's adoption of a vocabulary, style, argumentation, and sets of symbols alien to their tradition, for they

[87]M. Bazargan, *Be'sat*, pp. 219 and 221–23.
[88]A. Bazargan, *Masa'el*, p. 314.
[89]Rodinson,, *Islam and Capitalism*, p. 14.

may lose sight of what is essential, namely religion. As examples he offers two shibboleths of the revolutionary movement in Iran, *este'mar* (colonialism) and *estesmar* (exploitation). An overuse of the term *colonialism* causes the revolutionary movement in Iran to be identified with communism in Western eyes, thus lessening its chance of success. Insistence on the idea of "exploitation" inevitably entails class warfare and acceptance of an ineluctable and ascriptive membership of every individual in a certain social class, which heightens the potential for internal conflict.[90]

Bazargan's rejection of Third World socialist themes can be contrasted with Taleqani, who appropriated one of the slogans of socialism for Islam: "The phrase 'from each according to his ability and to each according to his need' is the first slogan of Islam and the last one of socialism. From the totality of Islamic injunctions and teachings on ownership, this principle can be seen to be of certain validity."[91] Not content to state a convergence between Islam and socialism, Taleqani goes on to say that the phrase is more representative of Islam than of socialism, because its "second part . . . 'to each according to his need' does not conform to the labor theory of value. . . . The socialists had to use this slogan even though it is based on human value and not economic surplus."[92]

In economic matters Islamic modernism clearly faces the same problems as Christian Democracy and Catholic social doctrine. From a religious and ethical point of view, capitalism is amoral at best and immoral most of the time, while socialism puts too many constraints on the individual. For Islamic modernism, the ideal does not lie somewhere in the middle, but rather on a different plane altogether. Capitalism and socialism both share materialist assumptions, and it is these that Islamic economics strives to overcome.

The Ideology of the LMI

The ideology of a political party is different from that of an intellectual current. A party has to operate in a political arena and formulate concrete policy options. When the party has to operate under the constant threat of government repression, it is very constrained in what it can advocate.

In the case of the LMI, it is important to remember that it was founded as a component of the National Movement, whose leader was the secular-minded Mosaddeq. The formation of a new party had to be

---

[90]Mehdi Bazargan, *Afat-e towhid* (The bane of monotheism) (1978), pp. 60 and 62–63.
[91]Taleqani, *Islam and Ownership*, p. 124.
[92]Ibid., p. 130n.

justified. In the view of the founders of the LMI, the various National-ist parties—liberal, pan-Iranist, and socialist—united in the National Front could mobilize Muslims momentarily around specific goals such as the nationalization of oil, but were ill-equipped, given the masses' commitment to Islam above all else, to lead to an overall improvement in society.[93] Committed Muslims themselves, therefore, had to become a force in politics.[94]

In Bazargan's view, his brand of politically active Islamic modernism had to confront three forces: the communists of the Tudeh party, whose growing influence on Iranian campuses was the main reason for the founding of the Muslim Student Associations; the traditional clergy, whose obscurantism was driving the youth away and straight into the arms of antireligious materialism; and, after 1953, the dictatorship of the Shah, whose unjust rule threatened to ruin the country and made it difficult for Muslims to live their lives in accordance with their faith.

The religious orientation did not meet with unanimity in the LMI party. Many of its initial founders, although by no means opposed to religion, were reluctant to give the LMI's actions a religious content. This heterogeneity was a source of weakness for the party. But on the whole it can be said that the LMI in its first period of activity (1961–63) constituted the most religious wing of the National Movement. At its founding meeting, the LMI was defined as "Muslim, Nationalist, constitutionalist, and Mosaddeqist." It's immediate aim was to struggle against despotism and corruption. At the time, the dominant political culture of Iran was secular, and the clergy by and large kept out of politics.

This changed in the fifteen years between the Shah's crackdown on the opposition in 1963 and the beginning of the revolution in 1978. In these years the LMI could not function as a party in Iran. With the onset of the revolution, the intellectual and political climate had changed, and as the revolutionary movement progressed, religion became ever more important in Iranian politics. Concomitantly, the religious colora-tion of the LMI also became more pronounced, and the party became in effect the moderate, modernist wing of the Islamic movement. Firmly entrenched in the opposition to the fundamentalist *government* since 1981 while loyal to the Islamic *regime*, the LMI has now become the standard-bearer of Nationalism in a system that excoriates *all*

---

[93]Bazargan, *Modafe'at*, p. 207.

[94]A cogent statement of the role of religious motivation in party politics, the underpinning of the LMI, was given in "Mobarezat-e siasi va mobarezat-e mazhabi" (Political struggles and religious struggles), *Safehati az tarikh-e mo'aser-e Iran: Asnad-e nehzat-e azadi-ye Iran* (Some pages from contemporary Iranian history: The documents of the Liberation movement of Iran), vol. 1 (1982), pp. 229–59. For a fuller discussion of this text see chapter 4.

varieties of nationalism as un-Islamic. Now, as in the years 1961–63, its major demands are free elections, and an end to the dictatorial rule of the regime.

On the crucial question of *velayat-e faqih*, the LMI's position is that it accepts the concept as enshrined in the Constitution of 1979, because the Constitution was ratified by a popular vote. This acceptance is therefore procedural, and does not entail philosophical agreement. Consequently, the party unambiguously rejected the new *velayat-e motlaqeh-ye faqih*, that is, the absolute rule of the jurisprudent, which was introduced in early 1988 (see chapter 8).

Throughout its history, both under the monarchy and under the Islamic Republic, the LMI's modus operandi has essentially remained the same: to work within the system, and to invite the regime truly to respect the Constitution under whose rules it claims to operate. Therefor, the LMI is still Muslim, Nationalist, and constitutionalist (although the Constitution has changed), and it still claims the heritage of Mosaddeq. Now as under the Shah, its primary goal has been to curb the personalistic tendencies in the regime, to create a coherent order in society, and to base policies, institutions, and development programs on rational principles.

The discussion of democratization in chapter 1 leads us to ask whether the LMI has been a democratic party, whether it has striven to implant democracy in Iran. The answer is a cautious "yes." Democracy has not been the overriding aim of all members of the LMI: like the rest of the National Movement, it has placed Nationalism before liberalism. This becomes clear when one looks at the LMI's foreign sympathies: after its foundation in 1961 LMI statements were enthusiastic about Nasser, who had ended Egypt's liberal regime, but were hostile to the democratically elected government of Adnan Menderes in Turkey. The fact that Menderes's government had been freely elected meant less to the LMI than its generally pro-American stance. On the other hand, India has always been an example for the LMI, and LMI publications often argue that it is from its practice of democracy that India has derived the strength to pursue a policy of genuine nonalignment.

Although Bazargan is clearly the towering figure of the LMI, the LMI is not a vehicle for his personal ambitions, and its programs do not automatically reflect Bazargan's preferences. There is discussion inside the party, and on occasion Bazargan is overruled. On economic questions, for example, the party includes both free-market advocates and advocates of state intervention in the economy.

From Religious Ideology to the Ideologization of Religion

Ideologization of religion refers to the act or process of deriving normative statements about social, political, and economic relationships among the people from the ethical or metaphysical commandments of religion, or, in Ali Merad's words, "to formulate the 'content' of Islam in terms of norms and values of socio-political order."[95] Bazargan's main aim as an Islamic activist has always been to show the reasonableness of Islam's tenets, and to bring out its ethical content. Islamic activists who adhere to the idea of Islam as ideology often say that Bazargan started a trend, and created a craving for an Islamic ideology that he was not able to satisfy.

In 1966, after he was freed from prison, Bazargan gave a talk at a celebration of the Islamic Association of Engineers, in which he set out the basis of an Islamic ideology. He first posited that "the development of the advanced societies shows that so long as the people do not believe in an ideology or a national political philosophy, success will not be achieved. In the civilized world a nation or a state without an ideology is henceforth unimaginable." And yet, when he spelled out what this ideology would be, he came up mostly with general principles that should guide the political and economic life of Iran, as discussed previously. Moreover, near the end of the speech, he acknowledged that "Islam has not specified strict formulas for dealing with the economy and with the state, because there are no absolute and unchanging criteria on which to base economic policy in all places and all times."[96]

Did Bazargan create an Islamic ideology? At one level of analysis, all empirically unverifiable statements with a normative dimension are "ideology," but such an ultrapositivistic stance makes it extremely difficult, if not impossible, to say anything meaningful about the history of ideas. The difficulty, of course, resides in the manifold meanings of the term *ideology*. Paraphrasing Geiger's narrow definition, one can define ideology as "a system of ideas about social reality that is articulated with internal consistency and elaborated logically on the basis of initial assumptions, and that forms a well-defined written corpus, independent of peoples' minds, to which one can refer and that can form the basis of exegesis, comment, and indoctrination."[97]

Taken together, the writings of Bazargan and Taleqani and the policy

[95]See Ali Merad, "The Ideologization of Islam in the Contemporary Muslim World," in Alexander S. Cudsi and Ali E. Hillal Dessouki, eds., *Islam and Power* (1981), p. 37.
[96]M. Bazargan, *Be'sat*, pp. 66 and 227.
[97]See Theodor Geiger, *Die soziale Schichtung des deutschen Volkes* (1932), pp. 77–78.

statements of the LMI do not amount to an ideology thus defined. One of the hallmarks of an ideology is its reductionist nature. Although Bazargan, as an engineer, is very fond of expressing complex relationships with the help of pseudo-mathematical formulas and geometric figures, he does not attempt to squeeze the totality of political, social, economic, religious, and cultural relationships into a set of rigid normative statements.

In the early years of the LMI Bazargan did use the term *ideology* but it referred more to a party program or a general outlook on the world, a general framework for addressing problems. Referring to the LMI, Bazargan would speak of "an Islamic ideology" (presumably one of many conceivable ones), or an "ideology based on and inspired by Islam." His outlook is much more a mentality, which, again paraphrasing Geiger, one might define as "the spiritual disposition of an individual caused by the influences of his social environment on him and oriented by his life experience."[98]

The ideologization of the strain of thought created by Bazargan and Taleqani was carried out by Ali Shariati, who modified it considerably. Although the place of Shariati in the LMI is problematic, since his ideological origins lie in Bazargan's type of modernism, the development that Bazargan's liberal ideas underwent in the hands of Shariati sheds considerable light on the fate of Islamic liberalism.

The Place of Shariati

Shariati set out between 1965 and 1977 to prove that Islam itself, or rather his, correct, interpretation of it, was an ideology capable of providing solutions to all problems. The centerpiece of his ideologization of Shi'ism is his formulation of an ideal "Alavi" Shi'ism, which he contrasts with the actual "Safavi" Shi'ism. The former was dynamic, liberating, and embodied by the Imam Ali, whereas the latter is sterile, exploitative, and represented by the ulema ever since Shi'ism became Iran's state religion under the Safavids.[99]

This leads us to ask how Bazargan and Shariati regarded each other's work. On the personal level, there is little doubt that, in spite of disagreements, their relationship was characterized by mutual esteem. On an intellectual level, Shariati often acknowledged his debt to Bazargan,[100] although he found his gradualist, reformist approach

---

[98]Ibid.

[99]For a summary of Shariati's formulations see Akhavi, *Religion and Politics*, pp. 149–50, and 231–33. For a critique of Shariati's concepts see Esma'il Nuri Ala', *Jame'eh shenasi-ye siasi-ye tashayyo'-e esna-ashari* (The political sociology of Twelver Shi'ism) (1978), pp. 75–80.

[100]In a lecture delivered on October 24, 1972, Shariati likened Bazargan's discoveries

doomed in advance. Admitting that reformism was better than conservatism or a sudden break with the past, Shariati added: "But most of the time this gradual reformism has the disadvantage that during its long period of implementation negative elements, reactionary powers, and the hands of internal and external enemies can divert the reformist movement from its course or bring it to a complete halt."[101]

Bazargan himself accepted the risk of alienating the young by distancing himself from Shariati. On December 4, 1977 (Azar 13, 1356), a few months after Shariati's death, he cosigned a text prepared by Ay. Motahhari, which became a joint communiqué in which they clarified their position vis-à-vis the teachings of Shariati. The nuances of this text are worth pondering:

> In the Name of God, the Merciful and Compassionate. Considering that problems pertaining to the late Dr. Ali Shariati have for quite some time been creating commotion, and [that they have] wasted the time of various strata [of the population] and thus distracted them from our fundamental and vital problems, [and that this] has been used by interested people and the Establishment, [we] deemed it necessary to exchange views on the matter and after a series of meetings came to the conclusion that we agree to a large extent. Since the vast majority of those who are troubled by the problem are seekers of truth, we considered it our religious duty to make public our common views on it, so as to free [the people] from this perplexity and rebuild unity and love among Muslims, for this will please the Lord. Concerning the rumors about [Shariati] and his leanings, interpretations, and opinions about Islamic problems as reflected in his writings, [we], who are not only familiar with his works but also knew him personally, believe that accusations of Sunnism and Wahhabism are unfounded. In none of the principles of Islam, from the Unity of God to Prophethood, Resurrection, Divine Justice and the Imamate, did he sway from Islam. However, since his education was Western, he had not found enough time to devote himself to the acquisition of the Islamic body of knowledge, to the point where he would sometimes be ignorant of certain basic truths of the Qoran, the Sunna, Islamic Studies, and Jurisprudence. Although he was, with great effort, gradually adding to his knowledge on these matters, he committed many errors on Islamic problems, even on questions of principle. It would be wrong to remain silent on these. Therefore, considering the enormous success and attention that his books have encountered among the young, and considering that he himself, at the end of his life, having become aware of his errors through the intervention of disinterested persons and a general rise in the level of his readings,

---

concerning the Qoran (discussed earlier) to Newton's discoveries of the laws governing the movements of the planets. See his "Shi'eh, yek hezb-e tamam" (Shi'a, a total party), reprinted in *Shi'eh* (Shi'a) (1979), p. 80.

[101]Shariati, *Fatemeh*, p. 39.

gave one of his relatives full authority to correct his errors, [we] decided to make our views on the contents of his books public in a frank way. We recognize and honor his personality and his efforts and services in driving the young generation toward Islam, but we will not hide the truth or pay undue attention to the feelings of his most enthusiastic supporters or interested enemies. We seek the help of God and thank all those disinterested people who will help us by putting their reasoned comments at our disposal.[102]

Nothing came of this, but the mere fact that Bazargan considered the corpus of Shariati's ideas as a coherent whole independent of Shariati is indirect proof that he considered it an ideology.

Bazargan had been educated in the France of the 1930s, and when he started to write on social, political, and religious problems his main aim was to make Iran an equal among equals on the international scene. Shariati lived in Paris during the early 1960s, years marked by the Algerian War of Liberation, the rise of Fidel Castro, and the beginning escalation of the Vietnam War. He saw Iran as part of the Third World, and in addition to the Western influences that reached him through Bazargan (Carrel, for example), he came under the spell of the ideologues of Third World emancipation such as Frantz Fanon and Aimé Césaire. Bazargan had tried to formulate an alternative to secularism, which is more a mentality than an ideology, but Shariati reacted directly to Marxism, an ideology par excellence. Shariati thus self-consciously set out to create an ideology, which he regarded as indispensable for struggle.[103] Amir Arjomand has argued that he was above all influenced by Durkheim, and that what he called "ideology" corresponded to Durkheim's collective consciousness.[104]

Shariati's social thought and his theories are reductionist, even more so than Marxism. For instance, he accepts that class struggle has characterized human history since the creation of humankind, but sees evidence for this not in the various socioeconomic stages but in the parable of Cain and Abel; Cain represents agriculturists and all exploiting classes in general, and Abel stands for the "primitive communism" of the pastoralists, and all exploited classes in general.

> The story of Cain and Abel depicts the first day in the life of the sons of Adam on this earth . . . as being identical with the beginning of contradic-

---

[102]Bazargan and Motahhari regretted this letter hours after they had given out a few copies of it, and tried to retrieve them. SAVAK, however, got hold of one copy and distributed further copies of it widely.

[103]For a reconstruction of his conception of ideology and the impact of Marxism on it, see Daryush Shayegan, *Qu'est-ce qu'une revolution religieuse?* (1982), pp. 204–31.

[104]Said Amir Arjomand, "*A la recherche de la conscience collective:* Durkheim's Ideological Impact in Turkey and Iran," *American Sociologist* 17 (1982), 98.

tion, conflict and ultimately warfare and fratricide. This confirms the scientific fact that life, society and history are based on contradiction and struggle, and that contrary to the belief of the idealists, the fundamental factors in all three are economics and sexuality, which come to predominate over religious faith, brotherly ties, truth and morality.[105]

Contrary to what Shariati's translator claims,[106] he based this theory not on folk traditions concerning Adam's two sons, but on René Guénon, whom, as we saw earlier, he considered one of this century's major intellectuals.[107] For Shariati, Abel symbolizes *towhid*, monotheism, and Cain *sherk*, pluralism; Shariati's rejection of the latter is blunt. Like many Third World intellectuals of his generation, Shariati was ambivalent about democracy.

Only two years after Bazargan had stated that democracy with universal suffrage is the best form of government even for underdeveloped nations,[108] Shariati said in 1968 that democracy is at best appropriate for societies that must be administered, but is totally dysfunctional for societies that need to be reformed and improved. In a talk at the Hoseiniyeh Ershad Institute he had this to say about India, a country for whose political system the LMI had traditionally expressed admiration:

> Today the problem that India faces is that they have over 300 languages and even more religions. Therefore their government has two choices. Either they have to accept majority-rule, in which case they have to keep 300 languages. Or they can try to change the people and improve their lives, economy, and culture. But then the government would have to force one common language on all of them... in which case it would lose two-thirds of their votes, for people worship their own gods, their own languages, their own life-styles. Thus a government that has come to power on the basis of the people's vote must preserve everything that the people want, and if it tries to move the people towards what they should be, it loses their consent.... That is why we see that in all societies those who have progressive ideas do not attract the majority of the population. Democracy is therefore incompatible with revolutionary progress and change.[109]

But even in the advanced industrialized countries politics fell short of the ideals of democracy. For example, the French Resistance hero

---

[105]Ali Shariati, *On the Sociology of Islam*, trans. Hamid Algar (1979), p. 104. Shariati develops the same theme in *Man and Islam*, trans. Fatollah Marjani (1981), pp. 17–22.
[106]Shariati, *On the Sociology of Islam*, p. 98n.
[107]Cf. René Guénon, *The Reign of Quantity and the Signs of the Times*, trans. Lord Northbourne (1953), pp. 177–83.
[108]In Bazargan's *Be'sat va ideolozhi*, as analyzed earlier.
[109]Ali Shariati, *Emmat va emamat* (The umma and imamhood) (1977), pp. 161–62.

Vercors lived in a tiny dilapidated apartment and had no part at all in the leadership of France. What is worse, the presidents of France and the United States and the prime minister of Great Britain had to "sycophantically address problems that will convince bankers, big capitalists, even Jews, even the owners of cabarets and gambling casinos and racists of their political mission." Even Robert Kennedy had to pander to the "filthy-rich New York Jews who run America with the help of the Mafia."[110]

The ideal leader, then, is the Imam, whose intrinsic qualities distinguish him from the masses, and who has to lead them not necessarily in a manner that would maximize their happiness, but rather with their reform and improvement in mind. It is the Imam's task to lead people from "what they are" to "what they should be."[111] Whether the founders of the Islamic Republic were influenced by Shariati's elaborations a decade earlier is difficult to say. What is clear is that Shariati, perhaps unwittingly, provided the blueprint of the Islamic Republic.

Another feature of Shi'ism that lends itself to ideological interpretation is the story of Husein, the third Imam who was martyred at Kerbala in 680 A.D. The modernists' handling of that event is instructive. Taleqani, as early as 1963, began using its commemorations in the month of Muharram for political anti-Shah purposes by weaving anachronistic references to current events of his own time into his sermon.[112] Shariati also took up the Kerbala story and used it to illustrate his "Alavi" Shi'ism. The reductionist nature of the ideologizing enterprise can be seen in the following passage:

> Our masses lovingly weep, for only with tears can they express their deeply felt bond with this beloved house that is a true Pantheon, a real Olympus, and in which real idols dwell. . . .
> No other religion, history, or nation has such a family, a family in which the father is Ali, the mother Fatima, the son Husein, and the daughter Zeinab.[113]

This passage is revealing in that it omits one important family member: Imam Hasan, the second Shi'ite Imam, who made peace with the caliph. This omission betrays a deliberate attempt to make martyrdom and struggle the only truly Islamic attitude. The constant reference to Husein by Islamic activists of all stripes after the revolution provoked

[110]Ibid., pp. 168–73.
[111]Ibid., pp. 62–63.
[112]See his "Jihad and Martyrdom," in *Society and Economics in Islam: Writings and Declarations of Ayatullah Sayyid Mahmud Taleqhani*, trans. R. Campbell (1982), pp. 75–104.
[113]Shariati, *Fatemeh*, p. 16.

Bazargan to emphasize that Imam Hasan was as Shi'ite as his younger brother, and that readiness for peace must be as much part of the Islamic movement's repertoire of policies as the readiness for war.[114] In recent years he has criticized the overemphasis of the notion of martyrdom, for which he deems Shariati responsible.[115]

Bazargan's opposition to the excessive ideologization of Islam is apparent in his postrevolutionary writings. In a recent work he derides those who have popularized the idea that a Muslim must serve Islam, since in reality it is God who has to be served, not Islam. He concludes:

> The line of serving Islam is in itself an ideology (*maktab*) . . . , thus it bears a certain resemblance . . . to the European philosophical "isms" of recent centuries, such as Nationalism, Socialism, and Marxism. Its supporters call themselves *maktabi*, and single themselves out. The ideology has to be implemented in the country and in the government, and among the organizational methods used by contemporary political and philosophical ideologies are the monopolization of power and party discipline.[116]

The ideologization of religion is a reaction to the secularization of society, but ironically it is also an expression of that very process. It represents a deliberate downplaying of the sacred, metaphysical aspects of religion in favor of a this-worldly set of a priori solutions to socioeconomic problems.

The Rhetoric of Apologetic Thought

So far we have presented the ideas only of Bazargan, Taleqani, and Shariati. This section analyzes the ways in which they articulate their arguments, the distinctive *style* of modernism, its "rhetoric" in the original sense of the word. Only then can we hope to explain modernism's intellectual strengths and weaknesses, and perhaps account for the fact that the effect of some of these ideas on society seems quite independent of their intellectual validity.

The problem is not new. Gibb sensed it when he wrote:

> However much we may sympathize with the objectives of the reformers . . . it has to be admitted that much of these essays surprise and sometimes shock us by their methods of argument and treatment of facts. We feel a strain somewhere, a dislocation between the outward argument and the inner train of reasoning. We are all of us familiar with books in our own

---

[114]*Mizan*, November 29, 1980 (Azar 8, 1359), p. 4.
[115]"Iran va eslam," p. 126. For Shariati's formulations see *Jihad and Shahadat: Struggle and Martyrdom in Islam*, ed. Mehdi Abedi and Gary Legenhausen (1986), pp. 153–264.
[116]"Iran va eslam," p. 125.

language which leave us with the feeling that either the author is incapable of handling his materials or his treatment of them is vitiated by *writing to a predetermined conclusion*. That we should have something of the same feeling about these modernist writings is only natural, when we reflect that modernism involves a revolution in the very concept of knowledge itself.[117] (Emphasis added)

Not all of Bazargan's, Taleqani's, and Shariati's writings are apologetic in character, but naturally most of the ideology is embodied in those that are. This apologetic function is the key to explaining the "dislocation between the outward argument and the inner train of reasoning," as Gibb calls it. The apologists' rhetorical structures and stylistic devices shed light on these dislocations.

The semiological structures of modern myths, as defined by Roland Barthes,[118] provide an adequate means for analyzing the apologetic functions of the ideological writings of modernists. These texts contain two semiological systems: (1) a linguistic system, that is, all apparent statements about facts and ideas, and (2) an apologetic system, analogous to Barthes's "myth."[119] What the apologists *say* may or may not be true or accurate, but what they *mean* is that Islam is viable, even superior to all other systems. This superimposition of the two semiological systems takes various forms, each corresponding to a different function. What follows is an attempt to identify and interpret some of the rhetorical figures as signifiers of the apologetic system.

Neithernorism
Barthes defines "neithernorism" as the "mythological figure which consists in stating two opposites and balancing the one by the other so as to reject them both."[120] Islamic modernists are so fond of this figure that their discourse often assumes a similar structure; Taleqani's *Islam and Ownership* is the most obvious example. This rejection of "thesis" and "antithesis" does not result in a "synthesis," however, but in "something-altogether-superior": Islam. Barthes's ironical observation about the neither-nor critics as "adepts of a bi-partite universe where they... represent divine transcendence"[121] applies quite literally to the Islamic modernists.

Modernists apply neithernorism to a number of themes. True religion, for instance, is neither the set of practices and rituals preached by the obscurantist clergy, nor the inherently worthless corpus of ideas

---

[117]Gibb, *Modern Trends*, p. 64.
[118]See R. Barthes, *Mythologies*, trans. Annette Lavers (1975).
[119]Ibid., pp. 114–15.
[120]Ibid., p. 153.
[121]Ibid., p. 83.

secularists want to eradicate. True religion is the modernist interpretation of Islam. Here they reveal their inability to distinguish clearly between *normative* Islam and *historical* Islam.[122] Yet neithernorism may also lead to a reasonable golden mean, for instance when both outright rejection of the West and indiscriminate borrowing from it are passed over in favor of a critical attitude, or when both racial chauvinism and the negation of national distinctions are rejected in favor of a moderate national consciousness. But modernists employ neithernorism most consistently to establish the superiority of Islam over both Marxism and liberal capitalism. The comparisons that serve to discredit the two dominant ideologies of the (Western) world are not always rigorous. Taleqani's book illustrates this point.

Taleqani tries to be fair to both capitalism and Marxism, but his analysis is not immune to the logical fallacy to which most ideologues fall victim and which consists in comparing the reality of the systems one rejects with the ideals of the system one endeavors to promote. Taleqani compares the *reality* of capitalist and communist countries with the *ideals* of Islam, as sorted out by himself. The resulting contradictions ultimately weaken his claims concerning Islam. When speaking of the Western systems, Taleqani first states that "these two opposing theories, 'absolute individual freedom and private ownership,' and 'constraint on individuals and a communal and social ownership,' have irreconcilably and distinctly confronted each other since the end of the eighteenth century."[123] Later, however, he suggests the opposite, as the two theories seem to converge:

> Capitalism and communism in practice dispense with their general theories. The capitalist countries which practice the principles of unlimited individual freedom have transgressed these principles and constantly try to "muzzle and fetter" this unbridled horse of capitalism through nationalization of large productive enterprises and factories. On the other side are the principles of theoretical collectivism—with all their rigidities—which in practice have allowed for individual ownership of housing and farms. . . .
>
> There are obvious violations of their respective principles because these two schools of thought are not applicable to the realities of life. Rather they are by-products of recent Western industrial economic fluctuations.[124]

According to Taleqani, neither capitalist, nor communist, nor Muslim countries apply the social and economic theories of capitalism, Marxism, or Islam. But he implies that the reality of capitalist and communist societies leaves something to be desired, because the theories

---

[122]As analyzed by Fazlur Rahman in his *Islam and Modernity*, p. 141.
[123]Taleqani, *Islam and Ownership*, p. 28.
[124]Ibid., pp. 131–32.

cannot be applied, whereas the sorry state of Islamic countries is due to the fact that Islam *is not* applied. Moreover, Taleqani asserts that the Western theories' demonstrated capacity to adapt to new realities is a sign of their inherent weakness, whereas when speaking of Islam Taleqani praises its supposed ability to adapt to changing circumstances; indeed "the duty of a Muslim scholar and thinker is . . . to discover and to adapt."[125] These kinds of double standards weaken the persuasiveness of the arguments for the reader who is not persuaded already.

Where Bazargan discusses socioeconomic systems, he also tries to refute both classical liberal capitalism and communism, although one cannot help feeling that his refutation of the latter is more passionate:

> Under the protection of freedom and democracy, civilization, the economy, science, and welfare can develop freely. Work and money become the chief pastimes and the highest values. . . . But this [high level of] production results in the enslavement of those who earn less and are unsuccessful . . . which leads the dissatisfied and the intellectuals to say that the [dominant] order and its laws should not be based on freedom. . . . Society must become the individual's god and the individual must become society's servant and be sacrificed to it. . . . In these schools of thought [i.e., socialism] they speak about freedom, equality, human rights, and humanism, but in practice we see that they can hold on to power only by the use of force (the dictatorship of the proletariat.)[126]

Shariati, too, made copious use of neithernorism. In fact, his first book, *The Median School* (1955), written when he was just over twenty years old, was an effort to prove that Islam had all the advantages and none of the disadvantages of both capitalism and communism.

As these examples show, neithernorism is one of the essential features of contemporary Shi'ite modernism. The defensive nature of Islamic modernism confers upon it the "anti" dimension that finds its expression in the rejection of all existing systems. It would be wrong to single out Islamic modernism for its refusal to choose "between two evils": to some extent structural neithernorism is inevitable in latecomer ideologies. We find it in Christian Democracy, in the Social Doctrine of the church,[127] in fascism, and in many nationalistic ideologies. It is also quite common in the Third World, whose very name is a neithernorism. Consider the following double neithernorism by Julius

---

[125]Ibid., p. 148.

[126]Bazargan, *Afat-e towhid*, pp. 39–40.

[127]Cf. the encyclical *Rerum Novarum* of 1891 with its vehement repudiation of liberal capitalism and socialism. See M.-D. Chenu, *La "Doctrine sociale" de l'église comme idéologie* (1979), esp. pp. 39–55.

Nyerere: "We don't need to read Karl Marx or Adam Smith to find out that neither the land nor the hoe actually produces wealth."[128] Fundamentalism in Iran inherited this "anti" tendency from religious modernism.

In his postrevolutionary writings, Bazargan eschews neithernorism. Perhaps because the supremacy of Islam need no longer be justified, and also because of the deepening of his own knowledge of Islam, he derives direct meaning from the sources of the religion.

Quotations

Modernist ideologues love to quote, but the quotations' function in their discourse is not limited to their semantic content, to what they add to the meaning of the texts.

Qoranic quotations are needed to convince the religious audience. A statement's plausibility can be advanced more firmly if some verse from the Qoran, or a *hadith*, corroborates it.[129] To the outside reader these quotations' relevance to the subject matter of the text is not always clear, but that hardly matters: the texts are not addressed to outsiders. For the targeted audience the fact that God Himself is being quoted means more than the relevance of the quotation. Moreover, according to an old belief, the meaning of the Qoran is inexhaustible. Occam's Razor need not be wielded.

As *modernists* our ideologues also have a proclivity to quote Westerners, even Western orientalists. Books by Western authors dealing with the Islamic world fulfill a special function. Most immediately, of course, they lend the prestige of Western learning to favorable treatments of Islam. The hidden agenda behind the use of such materials, however, is the need to preempt possible criticisms of domestic secularizers. The argument, never made explicit, would go something like this: "We all know that Westerners do not have our best interests at heart and tend to look down on us. Therefore, when such a Westerner admits the greatness of our civilization, chances are that he is not engaging in wishful thinking. If it elicits his grudging respect, it stands to reason that our cultural heritage be worth more than our secularizers would care to admit."

Historicism

Historicism is to some extent inherent in a religious frame of mind. Even Marxism partakes of what Eliade calls "the old Asianico-

---

[128]"Ujamaa—The Basis of African Socialism," in Julius K. Nyerere, *Ujamaa—Essays on Socialism* (1968), p. 4.

[129]This technique has a long history in the Muslim world. See Roy Mottahedeh, "The Shu'ubiyah Controversy and the Social History of Early Islamic Iran," *International Journal of Middle East Studies* 7 (1976).

Mediterranean myth structure" that informs the eschatological content of Judaism, Christianity, and Islam.[130] To some extent, then, a historicist approach to the human condition is part of any religious outlook, and must be seen as a question of content, rather than rhetorical structure.[131] Bazargan starts many of his books with a brief summary of the history of humankind. The eschatological plot he superimposes on history is expressed in evolutionary terms, thus giving it a scientific veneer.

But historicist passages in modernist texts assume an additional function. Modernists employ the language of historicism to explain the current situation and reassure their audience about the future. In Barthes's terms, the inevitability of both the present situation and the desired future developments are the signified of the apologetic system of the texts. To prove their points, modernists use historical facts selectively. Like many ideologues, they are voracious readers and attempt to integrate those parts of their readings that corroborate their views, or that can serve to make their views more attractive to the targeted audiences, into their writings. The resulting eclecticism is not always felicitous. For example, in his book *Rah-e teyy shodeh*,[132] which many of his followers think is his best work, Bazargan gives an interpretative outline of human history. He tries to prove that human history proceeded along the lines predicted by the prophets, although most people were not aware of this. For his historical data Bazargan cites such diverse sources as the Qoran, the Belgian symbolist poet Maurice Maeterlinck's book *Le Grand Secret*, and one Major Owrang's opus *Yekta-parasti dar Iran-e bastan* (Monotheism in ancient Iran). The references in Shariati's works are even more eclectic.

Yet these juxtapositions do not diminish the texts' attractiveness or credibility for two reasons: first, their readers are unlikely to be serious students of history; and second, as Roland Barthes has noted, fact cannot be distinguished from fiction by any element inherent in historical discourse, as "historical facts" do not exist independently of it.[133]

A more recent example of this use of historicism is Bazargan's postrevolutionary tendency to combine the National Movement under Mosaddeq with the Islamic Movement of Khomeini, and to speak of a "National and Islamic movement."[134] Though it is true that both movements represented moments in Iran's struggle for emancipation,

---

[130]Mircea Eliade, *Myth and Reality*, trans. Willard R. Trask (1963), pp. 183–84.

[131]For a critique of historicist historiography see David Hackett Fischer, *Historians' Fallacies* (1970), pp. 155–57.

[132]See note 68.

[133]Roland Barthes, "Le Discours de l'histoire," *Social Science Information* 6 (August 1967), 65–75.

[134]For instance in Bazargan's *Showra-ye enqelab va dowlat-e movaqqat* (The Council of the Revolution and the Provisional Government) (1982), pp. 7–18.

their goals, leaders, methods, and relevant social forces were very different.

Tautology

The use of tautologies is one of the most elusive features of modernist writing, and very difficult to document. Outright tautologies as defined by Barthes are very rare.[135] There is of course Shariati's *Fatima Is Fatima*, a book ostensibly about the position of women in Islam but, as is typical for Shariati, containing many ideas and tidbits of information that happened to cross his mind when he composed it. The title, which is also the book's last sentence, does not suggest the myth of common sense, but the uniqueness of Fatima.

We do encounter tautologies under another form in many modernist texts, but they are logical flaws in the argument rather than figures of an apologetic system. The trick consists in planting an axiom; in other words, in not distinguishing clearly between assumptions and *demonstranda*. One example: modernists often like to point out that Islam accords with nature, which is one of the proofs of its superiority to other religions (the celibacy of Catholic priests is often mentioned as a counterexample). But since the modernists' faith conditions their definition of "nature," or "human nature," the accordance of "nature" and Islam is a foregone conclusion. Taleqani's comparison of socioeconomic systems, again, provides another example of tautology. He assumes that, because of Islam's divine origin, it is superior to Western, man-made, ideologies—but this superiority is precisely what he set out to prove in the first place. Gibb's remark about the modernists "writing to a predetermined conclusion" captures the circularity of much modernist reasoning.

This circularity no longer exists in Bazargan's postrevolutionary writings. He now writes for a Muslim audience, or at least one that takes Islam and its relevance to contemporary Iran for granted. The logical rigor of his writings has thereby been enhanced.

Repetition

Modernist texts from Iran strike the reader by their sheer amount of repetition. To some extent this is attributable to their origin as lectures; they were not all meant to be cumulative. Still, the impression remains that the authors often bring up subjects well known to their audience, and proceed to draw a moral from them with which all the audience agrees. The aim of these repetitive passages is therefore not to communicate something new to the listeners/readers, but to create and uphold

[135]Barthes, *Mythologies*, pp. 152–53.

a climate of mutual understanding and intellectual communion between speaker/writer and audience: their function is phatic.[136]

Two examples illustrate this point. In Bazargan's, and later in Shariati's
writings, one constantly comes across derogatory remarks about the
Catholic Church in the Middle Ages. Gibb noted that an obsession
with Christianity, and an urge to prove its inferiority to Islam, was a
constant theme in the Arab modernists he studied.[137] In their case this
was easy to explain, for Christian missionaries in Arabic countries
under European domination could be seen as a threat to the spiritual
integrity of Muslim society. By the time Bazargan and Shariati were
writing, however, there was no such threat in Iran. Why then this
obsession with the Catholic Church of the Middle Ages, with the
terribly reactionary popes who oppressed the Christians?

There are probably a number of reasons. The first is to make the
listeners/readers comfortable about their own religion. The second
reason, made explicit in the texts, is to prove that secularism as it
appeared in the Renaissance was to some extent justified—or at least
understandable—in Europe, given the obscurantism of the medieval
church, which was opposed to science (remember Galileo!). But since
Islam does not oppose progress and abhors oppression, secularist ideas
in Iran are a foreign import unsuited to Iranian society. The logical
fallacy of this argument, of course, is that, as was noted earlier,
historical Christianity is being compared to *ideal* Islam. Sometimes,
however, the arguments are more subtle and avoid this fallacy. The
authors then aver that since Christianity had no sociopolitical ideology
and was merely an ethical system, reformers had to turn against it:
hence secularism. Islam, by contrast, has all the ingredients for a
successful ideology, which makes secularism superfluous. A third
reason for this obsession with the medieval church can be only suspected
in prerevolutionary writings, but is quite obvious in one of Bazargan's
postrevolutionary books: the parallel between the Shi'ite clergy and a
dominant Catholic clergy is so obvious that a denunciation of the latter
amounts to a thinly veiled attack on the former. Shariati went so far as
to call for a veritable "protestant reformation" of Islam.[138]

A second theme, more related to internal affairs of Iran, is the
constant denunciation of the Iranian bourgeoisie. In the writings of
Shariati, Iranians who have struck it rich under the Shah are forever
aping the worst habits of the West, are forever traveling to Europe to
gamble away the surplus value extracted from "the people," to dance

[136]On the phatic function see Pierre Guiraud, *La Sémiologie* (1971), pp. 12–13.
[137]Gibb, *Modern Trends*, p. 68.
[138]See his lecture *From Where Shall We Begin*, trans. Fatollah Marjani (1980), pp. 30–31.

in nightclubs, and to waste their time and money in "cabarets." The Persian word *Kabareh* has become a favorite of Islamic ideologues: more than a place where people go and have fun, it serves to focus all the ascetic tendencies of the religious counterelite, or, to quote Clifford Geertz, it is a trope that mediates "more complex meanings than its literal meaning suggests."[139] Here is an example: to illustrate his point that under liberal democracy people cannot be reformed, not even by a charismatic leader, Shariati relates how de Gaulle suggested that the "very ugly and very obscene" dancers in French cabarets put on a *cache-sexe* during their performance. But the liberals protested that this would limit the freedom of the dancers to do as they pleased.[140]

What are the functions of these repeated references? Again, they do not communicate anything to the audience that it would not already know. In the first place, it is natural that pious people should disapprove of other people's sins. But a merely pious person is more likely to feel sorry for sinners and to attempt to guide them back to the righteous path rather than vituperate against them. The second reason, and here the phatic function comes in, is to create a bond among the elect, who can define themselves and acquire a collective identity by being what the Others, those in power, are not, namely "good." Righteousness, when ideologized, becomes self-righteousness. This strikes a chord with a natural tendency of most intellectuals, religious or secular, which is to presume to tell others how to live their lives and how to spend their free time. A third reason for this obsession with the alleged *Kabareh* culture of the Iranian bourgeoisie is plain resentment. Iran's dual society was discussed in chapter 1; the repeated accusations against the Westernized elite are an expression of the resentment felt in the traditional segment, articulated by its most intellectual circles, against the modern segment.[141] For the traditional segment of Iranian society, the very fabric of Iranian culture seemed under attack when a popular nightclub such as *Shekufeh Now* was located in the traditional southern area of the capital.

The Islamic Republic has gone far beyond the closure of cabarets in its efforts to reform Iranians; consequently, since the revolution, Islamic modernists have been more severe toward the excesses of the Islamic regime than with the life-style of the remnants of the modern segment.

---

[139]C. Geertz, "Ideology as a Cultural System," in *The Interpretation of Cultures* (1973), p. 210.

[140]A. Shariati, *Emmat va emamat*, p. 166.

[141]In the case of Shariati, more personal motives may have been present, as his sojourn in Paris was marked by severe financial difficulties. Testimony of close friends of his in Paris, who wish to remain anonymous.

Irony

Irony is a favorite device of Bazargan's, which he uses in political statements and writings but not in his religious texts. Personal temperament aside, external factors easily explain this recourse to irony: during most of his political career, Bazargan has had to operate on the very borders of what successive Iranian regimes tolerated. One form of irony, apophasis, consists in seemingly saying the opposite of what one means. When what one wants to say would be too offensive to the regime, apophasis can indeed be an elegant way out.

As a rhetorical device, irony presupposes a certain degree of subtlety in the audience. This may be one of the factors explaining Bazargan's lesser success during the revolution, a period of mass mobilization, compared to the period 1961–63, when the politically articulate strata were more limited. As Joseph Conrad put it in *Under Western Eyes,* "Revolutionists hate irony, which is the negation of all saving instincts, of all faith, of all devotion, of all action." If this is true, it would fit in with the ascetic component of revolutions mentioned in chapter 1, an ascetic component that has caused many postrevolutionary societies, whatever their ideology, to become so unspeakably antithalian after the initial period of creative euphoria is over.

Taleqani was always more direct in his approach, saying things more bluntly; his style was often angrily polemical. Shariati also used irony a great deal, but with him irony became sarcasm more often than not. Its function changed: while Bazargan used it to get away with saying what he wanted to say, Shariati employed it to discredit the arguments of his adversaries. One of Shariati's favorite rhetorical devices was to present the arguments he wished to refute under their most extreme and caricatural form, which obviously made his task easier. Here sarcasm can become an auxiliary to neithernorism.

Irony is far less in evidence in Bazargan's post-revolutionary writings, probably because the suffering in Iran has reached levels that would make irony frivolous.

In his writings Bazargan often complains about Iranians' propensity to exaggerate. Perhaps as a conscious reaction to these perceived national traits, he practices self-restraint, even at times understatement. There is a certain sober quality to his writings that makes them unsuitable for revolutionaries. Also, Bazargan's writings strike the reader as being fair-minded and balanced, and that, too, is not a revolutionary trait. Shariati, by contrast, had no such inhibitions and could blow up the smallest news item to gigantic proportions to derive propagandistic benefit from it.

Modernism's Legacy to Fundamentalism

As Fazlur Rahman has pointed out, modernism and fundamentalism have many features in common,[142] such as a dissatisfaction with the present and a return to the sources of the religion. Yet modernism and fundamentalism are, as we saw earlier, two different responses to the challenge of the West. What is the link between the two?

Beyond its ethical exhortations, Bazargan's type of modernism, in which the core of religious beliefs remained orthodox, provided a framework for analysis, not a set of solutions. The solutions were elaborated by Shariati and the Mojahedin on the left, and by the fundamentalists on the right. The main legacy of modernism to fundamentalism is a certain *type* of discourse, or, to put it in semiological terms, an idiolect.[143] This discourse is common to both modernists and fundamentalists, and quite different from that of such traditionalists as Khomeini, who do not care about comparing Islam with Marxism and capitalism or proving its scientificity. Traditionalists have in recent years actually accused Bazargan of being *elmzadeh*, "science-struck," a new term coined on the model of *gharbzadeh*, "West-struck."

To supplant modernism, fundamentalism borrowed its rhetorical structures. Shariati, by ideologizing the religious and political thought of Bazargan, and by adding some Third Worldist topoi to it, created a type of discourse that was then taken over by the fundamentalists and used in the service of different ideas. A few examples will suffice.

The traditional neutralist position in foreign policy that the Nationalists advocated under Mosaddeq and which they called "negative equilibrium," became the neithernorist *nah gharb, nah sharq*, "neither West nor East." The formula derived from the following verse:

> God is the light of the heavens and the earth; the likeness of His Light is a niche wherein is a lamp (the lamp in a glass, the glass as it were a glittering star) kindled from a Blessed Tree, an olive that is neither of the East nor of the West whose oil wellnigh would shine, even if no fire touched it (24:35).[144]

Thus the omnipresence of God, becomes ideologized into a metaphor for Iran's equidistance from and the transcendence of two political and

[142]Rahman, *Islam and Modernity*, p. 142.

[143]As defined in Roland Barthes, *Elements of Semiology*, trans. Annette Lavers and Colin Smith (1985), p. 21.

[144]This is one of the most complex and profound verses of the Qoran, and has given rise to many commentaries by orthodox ulema, mystics, and modernists. The most celebrated commentary is Al Ghazali's *Mishkat ul-anwar*, trans. with intro. W. H. T. Gairdner (1924).

ideological blocs. And in Persian too, "neither West nor East" makes for a better and more shoutable slogan than "Negative Equilibrium." The repeated denunciations of the West, meant as *corrective* to the Shah's indiscriminate Westernization, acquired a life of their own and led to a xenophobic frame of mind in which the West became the root of all evils.

The never-ending attacks on the *Kabareh* culture, and the construction of the irreligious, philistine, fat, rich, and hedonistic bourgeois as a countertype produced, when popularized, a negative attitude toward all refinement, all subtlety, values for which Iranian culture has been known traditionally. The ideologization of religion is thus a veritable debasement of religion, as it deprives it of its spiritual dimension and disregards centuries of learning.[145]

Unlike other modernist precursors of fundamentalism in the Middle East, Bazargan has lived to witness the growth and triumph of fundamentalism and has been able to criticize both from a liberal-modernist point of view. The rhetoric of his writings has changed somewhat: before the revolution his focus was on defending Islam against disbelievers and doubters, now he must defend it against the guardians of its orthodoxy. Finally able to take Islamic assumptions for granted, his writings are no longer marred by apologetics, and have acquired great internal coherence. His antiwar pamphlets of 1986 and 1987 (see chapter 8) combine unimpeachable Islamic learning with irrefutable common sense, and move the reader by their tragic urgency and dignified eloquence. They rank among the most powerful political texts produced in recent Iranian history, and have won their author new respect, both among the secular intelligentsia and among the ulema, who have not been able to respond.

Bazargan and his friends have never tired of trying to engage their adversaries in dialogue, yet most of the time the response has been violence. This type of reaction is not new, and Jean-Jacques Rousseau's words gain a new meaning when read in the context of contemporary Iran:

> In ancient times, when persuasion played the role of public force, eloquence was necessary. Of what use would it be today, when public force has replaced persuasion. . . . What sort of discourse remains? Sermons.[146]

---

[145]This point is forcefully made by Fazlur Rahman in "Islam: Legacy and Contemporary Challenge," in C. K. Pullapilly, ed., *Islam in the Contemporary World* (1980).

[146]Jean-Jacques Rousseau, "Essay on the Origin of Languages," in *On the Origin of Languages*, trans. with afterword John H. Moran and Alexander Gode (1986), p. 72.

Parallels with Christian Democracy

The similarities between the institutional Shi'ism of Iran and Roman Catholicism were pointed out in chapter 1. It is perhaps not surprising, then, that Bazargan's and Taleqani's thought also displays some parallels with Christian Democracy.

Taleqani's dissection of the notion of ownership is not very different from the church's teaching on the issue as contained in the Social Doctrine, and Bazargan's formulation of the asymmetrical relationship between religion and sociopolitical affairs bears a certain resemblance to the church's position as formulated at Vatican II: "...in every temporal affair [the faithful] must be guided by a Christian conscience. For even in secular affairs there is no human activity which can be withdrawn from God's dominion."[147] And "there are, indeed, close links between earthly affairs and those aspects of man's condition which transcend this world. The Church...does not lodge her hope in privileges conferred by civil authority."[148]

Bazargan had some contacts with Catholic activists in France, and Catholic lay writers have exercised some influence on him, yet this line of thought should not be carried too far. The Iranian modernists' insistence that the Catholic Church has no ideology betrays their ignorance of the Social Doctrine,[149] and what similarities do exist can be explained by the fact that the problematic of reconciling the absolute nature of monotheistic faith with the relativism of liberal democracy allows for only a limited set of solutions.

To continue our comparison on the social level, it is striking that Bazargan and Taleqani began their efforts without the explicit encouragement or support of the ulema, rather like Dom Sturzo in Italy or Karl Lueger in Austria. Furthermore, the radical transformation of their thought, as undertaken by Shariati, finds a parallel in the Theology of Liberation.

All this should not blind us to the basic differences between Shi'ism and Catholicism, which reflect Christianity's and Islam's fundamentally different attitudes toward political power. The moderating role the Catholic Church played in Poland during the 1979–81 crisis illustrates the difference best.

---

[147]*The Documents of Vatican II* (1966), p. 63.

[148]Ibid., p. 289.

[149]Mehdi Bazargan confirmed to me that he was not familiar with the Social Doctrine and the encyclicals of Pope Leo XIII. Personal written communication, January 4, 1988.

Social Identity of the LMI

In the absence of a free press, public opinion polls, or survey data, what is said here about the social bases of Islamic modernism and the kinds of people with whom Bazargan is popular must remain impressionistic. The results of the 1980 legislative elections, in which a number of party members and sympathizers were elected to the Majles, are of little use. The widespread irregularities that characterized those elections and Iran's peculiar electoral system[150] render any attempt at psephological analysis meaningless. This section first looks at the background of the LMI leadership, then examines the party's ties to the Bazaar, and concludes with a few remarks about the social bases of the party's support in the Iranian population.

Background of the LMI Leadership

The changing fortunes of the LMI throughout its history make it difficult to define a "leadership." Given the impossibility of mass action throughout much of recent Iranian history, it might seem as if the LMI leadership consisted only of Mehdi Bazargan, and secondarily a few of his relatives. Ay. Taleqani, Bazargan's close friend and political ally, was formally a leader of the party only in 1961–63. And yet, the LMI has never been a mere vehicle for the political ambitions of Bazargan; it does possess an identity of its own.

Since the party's reorganization in the early 1980s, it has been ruled by a council of about thirty people, whose identity was not available to the author. The matter is further complicated by the fact that over time many once-important figures have become, for various reasons, estranged from the party. Under these circumstances, it seems best to compile a list of all those men who *at one point or another* have been prominent figures in the LMI. The list would include the twelve founding members of the LMI, those members who were tried and jailed in 1963, leaders of the LMI's external wing, party members who held cabinet rank posts in the Provisional Government, members of the Islamic Republic's first parliament, and a few figures identified by elite respondents. The founders of the Mojahedin, although notable activists in the early LMI, were not included, as they are identified primarily with the Mojahedin. Detailed biographical data are provided for prominent LMI leaders in Part II at points where they become key figures in events; Table 1 summarizes the information for the wider

[150]For details see chapter 8.

Name	Origin	Life-Span	Class	Education	Left LMI
Mehdi Bazargan	Teheran	1907–	Bazaar	Engineering	—
Mahmud Taleqani	Taleqan	1912–79	Clerical	Religious	1970s
Yadollah Sahabi	Teheran	190?–	Middle	Geology	—
Mansur Ata'i	Teheran	19??–83	Upper Middle	Agriculture	1963
M.-Rahim Ata'i	Teheran	1920–77	Upper Middle	Law	—
Hasan Nazih	Tabriz	1921–	Bazaar	Law	1979
Abbas Radnia	Teheran	19??–82	Bazaar	High School	—
Abbas Sami'i	Teheran	?	Bazaar	?	1979
{ Ahmad Sadr Hajj-Seyyed-Javadi	Qazvin	1921–	Clerical	Law	—
Ahmad Alibaba'i	Teheran	1925–	Bazaar	High School	1977
Ezzatollah Sahabi	Teheran	1932–	Middle	Engineering	1980
M.-Mehdi Ja'fari	Bushire	1940–	Peasant?	Teachers' Co.	1980
Abbas Sheibani	Teheran	1931–	Upper Middle	Medicine	1964
Mohammad Moqaddam	Teheran	193?–	?	Engineering	?
Ebrahim Yazdi	Qazvin	1931–	Bazaar	Pharmaceutics	—
Ali Shariati	Mashad	1933–77	Clerical	Humanities	—
Sadeq Qotbzadeh	Isfahan	1936–81	Bazaar	High School	1978
Hashem Sabbaghian	Teheran	1937–	Bazaar	Engineering	—
Reza Sadr	Qum	1932–	Clerical	Rel., Chem., Bus. Adm.	—
Mohammad Tavassoli	Teheran	193?–	Bazaar	Engineering	—
Mostafa Chamran	Teheran	1933–81	Lower Middle	Engineering	—
M.-Ali Raja'i	Qazvin	1933–81	Lower	Mathematics	1979
Abbas Amir-Entezam	Teheran	193?–	Bazaar	Engineering	—
Abdolali Espahbodi	Mashad	1939–	Middle	Economics	1980
Hosein Baniasadi	Arak	193?–	?	Engineering	—
Mahmud Ahmadzadeh	Mashad	1935–	?	Engineering	—
Yusef Taheri	Qum	1930–	Middle	Engineering	?
Abdolali Bazargan	Teheran	1941–	Middle	Engineering	—
Abolfazl Bazargan	Teheran	?	Middle	?	—
Abolfazl Hakimi	Mashad	193?–	Bazaar	Engineering	—
Hasan Arabzadeh	Mashad	1935–	Bazaar	Engineering	1980
[?] Asayesh	Mashad	19??–68	Middle	?	—
Moham. Bastehnegar	?	1941–	Bazaar	?	1980–85
Mostafa Mofidi	Teheran	194?–	Bazaar	Medicine	?
Shahriar Rowhani	Teheran	195?–	?	Physics	—

Table 1. Social background of LMI leaders

group. There is no evidence that this group is actually representative of the broad support that the LMI enjoys in Iranian society.

The table shows that most LMI leaders have a Bazaar background, and thus have their family origin in the traditional segment of society. This origin is very important and will be analyzed later, but we should keep it in mind as we look at the other data. One significant fact that cannot be shown in Table 1 is the close family ties between the core group of the party around Mehdi Bazargan (see Figure 3). Such family ties are common in the traditional segment of Iranian society, both in

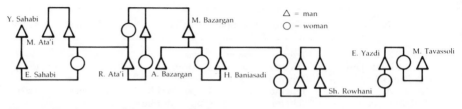

Figure 3: Kinship ties of the LMI leadership

the Bazaar,[151] and among the ulema.[152] In the case of the LMI leadership, such connections have certainly contributed to the maintenance of the party as an aggregate throughout the years when it could not function openly, as kinship ties allowed Bazargan to maintain close contact with his political associates. Kinship ties have not prevented one prominent and very active early member (E. Sahabi) from leaving the party, but even in that case the break was devoid of hostility.

With very few exceptions, the party leaders come from the northern provinces of Iran. Most of Iran's population lives in the northern half of the country, but the geographical distribution of party leaders is nonetheless telling. The main centers of economic activity are situated in the north. Thus, the Bazaar has played a greater role in the north than in the south. In the period 1941–53, with its relatively free elections, the south was always a bastion of conservatives (except for Khuzistan, where the Tudeh party was influential among oil workers),[153] although these did include Nationalists (the ruling family of the Qashqa'i tribe is a case in point).

More important, perhaps, is the north's greater exposure to the West (Khuzistan excepted), which includes the Soviet Union. As we saw earlier, religious modernism in Iran was a response to the perceived threats of communism, secularism, and Baha'ism. Communism, in particular, has had a powerful impact in the north of Iran, for the obvious reason of the long border with the Soviet Union.[154] Among the founders of the LMI, Bazargan was profoundly shaken by the Tudeh's influence among university students in Iran, and Taleqani was deeply affected by the aftermath of the autonomist episode in Azerbaijan. Some years later this development would be paralleled in Lebanon, where under the leadership of Musa al-Sadr, Shi'ites organized politically as a response to communist inroads among the Shi'ite youth.

[151]Gustav Thaiss, "The Bazaar as a Case Study of Religious and Social Change," in Ehsan Yar-Shater, ed., *Iran Faces the Seventies* (1971), p. 199.

[152]Michael M. J. Fischer, *Iran: From Religious Dispute to Revolution* (1980), pp. 89–95.

[153]See Ervand Abrahamian, *Iran between Two Revolutions* (1982), pp. 186–224.

[154]The oil-workers of Abadan are an exception to this rule.

Turning to education, we notice a marked preponderance of engineers and scientists (see Table 1). To some extent this is due to Bazargan's personal influence and his key role in the founding of the Engineers Association and later the Islamic Association of Engineers, and his influence as dean of the Faculty of Engineering at Teheran University. The latter, in particular, became a key recruiting ground for party cadres and a meeting place for like-minded men in the years when the LMI was not able to function. In the years since the revolution the association has been something of a sister organization of the LMI, and many association members held cabinet posts in the Provisional Government.

The preponderance of engineers and scientists among LMI figures is not only a consequence of the chosen profession of the party's leader, however. Both their religious background and their social roots predisposed these men to eschew the humanities, the arts, law, architecture, the military, and the social sciences in favor of engineering, the sciences, and medicine. A military career was probably ruled out on account of the close association between the army and the Pahlavi regime. Merchants are practical men, and for them the purpose of an education is to make a living. Their cultural level is also somewhat lower than that of the aristocracy and landowners, which would make more intellectual, not to speak of artistic, careers seem essentially useless and unproductive to them.

When we look at the secular component of the National Movement, we find far more nonscientists: Mosaddeq himself had studied law and political science, and law was also the career choice of Karim Sanjabi, Ali Shayegan, Abdollah Mo'azzami, Mozaffar Baqa'i, Shamseddin Amir-Ala'i, and Hedayatollah Matin-Daftari. Hosein Fatemi was a journalist, Baqer Kazemi and Allahyar Saleh were high-ranking civil servants, while Gholamhosein Sadiqi is a sociologist.[155]

In a post-traditional society, religious people seem to be attracted to the exact sciences more than to the humanities. The old dichotomy between science and religion seems to have given way to a new one which opposes the certainties provided by positivistic science (*pace* Heisenberg) and religious revelation to the vagaries and relativism of the humanities, the arts, and the social sciences. In the sciences one might run into such problems as evolution, which could contradict basic religious tenets for some, but very little in engineering will shake one's faith. Engineers are also prominent in religiopolitical activist

---

[155]The data on the secular Nationalists are taken from Abrahamian, *Iran*, pp. 190–99 and 232. It should be noted that the National Front had its share of engineers and the LMI has included a few lawyers.

circles elsewhere in the Middle East, as in Egypt.[156] This affinity between religion and the exact sciences almost naturally leads to religious modernism, which is, as we saw earlier, an attempt to reformulate eternal religious truths in the light of the scientific knowledge of the day.

On the relationship between nationalism and professionals, such as engineers, David Apter has observed that "the earliest claims to authority... were made by professionals who demanded equal treatment for all qualified men. Technical training was thus a point of entry into the power and prestige hierarchy at a time when the superordinate roles were monopolized by expatriates operating under a colonial mandate."[157] The engineers of the LMI fit this description, for as founder of the Engineers Association Bazargan was a leader of a nationwide strike in 1943 in which engineers, later joined by other professionals, gained access to influential positions of decision making. Later Bazargan oversaw the transfer of power from the British to Iranians at the head of the National Iranian Oil Company. Moreover, Apter notes, in modernizing societies engineers have a predisposition to view themselves as part of the political elite, as they "have the capacity to build positions of authority into their technical roles that are converted to all-purpose symbolic roles."[158] In one of his most recent writings, Bazargan confirms this when, looking back on his long and active life, he says that "for someone who has been among the people and in public service administrations and whose profession is engineering, which amounts to building and managing, the only aim is serving his country."[159]

One final remark on the educational background of LMI figures: an astonishingly high number received their secondary education at Dar ol-Fonun. This school had been founded in the nineteenth century by the state to train cadres for its military and civil bureaucracies, but was transformed into a high school at the end of the century.[160] It always retained its prestige as the oldest *Iranian*-run modern school in Iran. Although it furnished many members of the post–World War II Iranian political elite, it was increasingly rivaled by Alborz High School, which had been founded as a college by Presbyterian missionaries but transformed into an Iranian high school in 1940. Alborz recruited its

---

[156]Saad Eddin Ibrahim, "Anatomy of Egypt's Militant Islamic Groups," *International Journal of Middle East Studies* 12 (1980), 439–40.

[157]David Apter, *The Politics of Modernization* (1965), pp. 219–20.

[158]Ibid., p. 220.

[159]"Iran va eslam" (Iran and Islam), in *Bazyabi-ye arzeshha* (The recovery of values), vol. 2 (1982), p. 119.

[160]For information on the Dar ol-Fonun, see A. Reza Arasteh, *Education and Social Awakening in Iran 1850–1968*, 2d ed. (1969), pp. 28–32.

pupils among the aristocracy and the ruling elite, and by the 1950s and 1960s was the most prestigious school for members of the modern segment of society, while Dar ol-Fonun continued to cater to the traditional segment. Many of the Alborz graduates who were so prominent in Iran's ruling elite of the Pahlavi years had received their education while the "College" was still run by missionaries.[161] This fact, and later on the high tuition charged by Alborz, may have predisposed middle-class religious people to send their sons to Dar ol-Fonun. The waning overall prestige of the latter may then have induced some of its graduates to challenge the system and become politically active. Even later, in the 1960s and 1970s, pious individuals endowed an academically demanding but religiously rigorous high school, the Alavi School, which educated the future fundamentalist cadres of the Islamic Republic.

We can now turn our attention to the LMI leadership's social background in the Bazaar. Bazargan's father had been a major figure in the Bazaar of Teheran (which found a reflection in his choice of a family name) and president of the Bazaar Merchants Association, and most other founders of the party also had roots in the Bazaar. This does not mean that the LMI is or ever was a party of merchants: although the vast majority of its founders and leaders came from Bazaar families, very few (notably A. Radnia and A. Alibaba'i) were active as merchants. Bazargan and Y. Sahabi were university professors and entrepreneurs; H. Nazih and Ahmad Sadr Hajj-Seyyed-Javadi are lawyers. Their connection with the Bazaar and their relative affluence made them independent of the state, which allowed them to take bigger risks in opposing the government. When Bazargan was expelled from the university, he devoted himself to his business and continued his work as writer and animator of associations. But before examining the significance of the tie between the LMI and the Bazaar, we need to elucidate the role of the Bazaar in Iranian society and recent history.

Excursus on the Bazaar

The Bazaar as a Social Force

Bazaars are the central marketplaces in the Middle East. The urban domination of Middle Eastern societies confers great importance on the commercial hearts of the cities. Thus a bazaar is not merely a place where goods are bought and sold but, in Thaiss's words, "a multi-faceted entity comprising religious, commercial, political, and broadly

---

[161]Marvin Zonis, *The Political Elite of Iran* (1971), pp. 168–69; and Clarence Hendershot, *Politics, Polemics, and Pedagogs* (1975), pp. 14–15.

social elements . . . [and] religion is the cement that binds this structure together."[162] Sociologically speaking, the Bazaar connotes a community with a hierarchy of "merchants at the top of the order, the masters of artisans, and shopkeepers of well over 100 guild-like associations at the middle level, and the masses of workers and apprentices at the bottom, with some marginal elements such as peddlers and beggars at the lowest level," in a description quoted by A. Ashraf.[163] As Weber has pointed out, the social status of merchants and the degree of their commitment to religion has varied greatly across societies and ages.[164] In Islamic societies traders and merchants have traditionally enjoyed great esteem: the Prophet himself was a merchant. In nineteenth-century Iran, merchants and the leaders of the guilds were well-respected members of society. They were closely allied to the ulema, for a variety of reasons. The bazaars occupied the centers of cities, an area that also included the mosques and *madrasah*s (Islamic seminaries); merchants and ulema were thus in daily contact. This close contact helped them in their relations with the government: the ulema needed the bazaaris as a mass basis to put pressure on the government, while the bazaaris needed the ulema's protection against the arbitrary government bureaucracy. In addition, the merchants were also a prominent source of financial support for the religious institutions and their activities.

The alliance between the Bazaar and the ulema crystallized in the face of foreign encroachments on Iranian sovereignty. The ulema feared infidel penetration of Islamic society, while the merchants' prosperity was endangered by Western competition.[165] This alliance won a major victory during the Tobacco Rebellion of 1892, and again in 1905–6 during the Constitutional Revolution, this time together with liberal intellectuals.[166] In the first Majles, elected on a corporate basis, twenty-nine seats were reserved for the guilds, and twenty-eight seats for the merchants. Together, Bazaar representatives made up one-third of that body's total membership. In parliamentary debates the Bazaar deputies spoke out for Iranian sovereignty, against foreign loans, and

[162]Thaiss, "The Bazaar," p. 193.

[163]Ahmad Ashraf in "The Roots of Emerging Dual Class Structure in Nineteenth-Century Iran," *Iranian Studies* 14 (1981), 9. See also Michael Fischer, "Persian Society: Transformation and Strain," in Hossein Amirsadeghi, ed., *Twentieth Century Iran* (1977), p. 180.

[164]Max Weber, *Economy and Society*, ed. Guenther Roth and Claus Wittich (1978), pp. 477–80.

[165]See Kamran Ekbal, "Der politische Einfluss des persischen Kaufmannsstandes in der frühen Kadscharenzeit, dargestellt am Beispiel von Haǧǧi Halil Khan Qazwini Maliku't-Tuǧǧar," *Der Islam* 57 (1980). See also Abrahamian, *Iran*, pp. 58–61.

[166]For details about the Bazaar's involvement in the Constitutional Revolution see Abrahamian, *Iran*, pp. 81–85.

in favor of governmental responsibility.[167] The Bazaar also contributed more than any other force to the defeat of Mohammad Ali Shah when he attempted to reestablish the absolute rule his father had given up. Withal, the Bazaar lost its corporate representation in parliament when the electorate was unified in 1909. From then on the guilds and the merchants of the Bazaar played only a minor role in the politics of Iran.[168] This loss of influence thus paralleled the decline in the overall role of the ulema, which led to their retrenchment and caused many *mujtahids* to break with the Constitutionalists.

The Bazaar in Pahlavi Iran

After Reza Shah came to power, the Bazaar suffered a fate similar to that of the ulema in that the centralizing state put tight controls on it and attempted to end its autonomy.[169] The statist economic policies of Reza Shah hurt the old business communities and destroyed handicraft workshops. The abolition of guild taxes deprived the guild elders of the power to determine how much each guild member paid in taxes, paving the way for the weakening of Bazaar organizations.[170] And the new commercial thoroughfares threatened to dilute the spatial concentration of mercantile activity in central Teheran, and were therefore opposed by the traditional merchants.[171]

The Bazaar revived in the years 1941–53, and generally supported the National Movement and Mosaddeq. In the years 1953–60 it was the organizational backbone of the newly formed National Resistance Movement (NRM). During the liberalization of the early 1960s the Bazaar again supported the Nationalists by closing shops at various points. In the years after the showdown of June 1963, which began outside the Teheran Bazaar, the bazaaris partook of the general growth of the Iranian economy. This growth, incidentally, also benefited the ulema, to which the Bazaar merchants paid their religious taxes. Politically, however, the Bazaar community lost most of its influence, as the regime gradually severed its ties with society's traditional segment. At the same time, Bazaar merchants had some cause to have a sense of relative deprivation.

As an Iranian economist has noted, the Iranian state, committed to capitalism but having tremendous oil income at its disposal, tended to

---

[167]Ahmad Ashraf, *Mavane'-e tarikhi-ye roshd-e sarmayehdari dar Iran: dowreh-ye Qajariyeh* (Historical obstacles to the growth of capitalism in Iran: The Qajar Period) (1980), pp. 118–22.

[168]W. M. Floor, "The Guilds in Iran: An Overview from the Earliest Beginnings till 1972," *Zeitschrift der Deutschen Morgenländischen Gesellschaft* 125 (1975), 109.

[169]Ibid., pp. 109–10.

[170]Abrahamian, *Iran*, p. 151.

[171]Avery, *Modern Iran*, pp. 359–60.

make these financial resources available to the private sector by distributing generous credits through the modern banking system. These credits were thus more readily available to modern entrepreneurs, who could socialize with the bankers in the company of their wives during cocktail parties, than to traditional Bazaar merchants who would not drink (in public) and whose wives lacked Westernized social graces.[172]

The Bazaar community became restless again in the mid-1970s. The bazaaris resented the creation of the Rastakhiz party, whose totalitarian tentacles threatened to reach into the farthest corners of civil society and take away the last vestiges of Bazaar autonomy. In 1976 the party was used by the regime when, in an attempt to stifle inflation, it began an antiprofiteering campaign and imposed price controls. Many respected merchants—but also some modern entrepreneurs—were fined, jailed, or exiled to inhospitable places in the south. The bazaaris interpreted the creation of the party and the antiprofiteering campaign as a declaration of war, and many hitherto apolitical bazaaris were driven into the ranks of the opposition. Their anger and hostility contributed greatly to the close cooperation between the Bazaar and Khomeini during the years that led up to the revolution.[173]

Although not immune to change, the Bazaar remained an essentially traditional force in society. In the 1960s and 1970s the most eminent merchants were still of a generation that had received a traditional education. Regular interaction with the ulema continued at the weekly meetings of religious associations, bazaaris still maintained traditional ways of conflict resolution, eschewing the modern courts of law, associated in their minds with corruption and bribery, in favor of arbitration by trusted ulema according to Islamic guidelines.[174] After his fall, the Shah openly discussed his dislike for the Bazaar:

> Bazaars are a major social and commercial institution throughout the Mideast. But it remains my conviction that their time is past. The bazaar consists of a cluster of small shops. There is usually little sunshine or ventilation so that they are basically unhealthy environs. The bazaaris are a fanatic lot, highly resistant to change because their locations afforded a lucrative monopoly. I could not stop building supermarkets. I wanted a modern country. Moving against the bazaars was typical of the political and social risk I had to take in my drive for modernization.[175]

[172]Djavad Salehi-Isfahani, "The Political Economy of Credit Subsidy in Iran, 1973–1978," *International Journal of Middle East Studies* 21 (1989).

[173]See Ervand Abrahamian's interview with Ahmad Ashraf, "Bazaar and Mosque in Iran's Revolution," *MERIP Reports* (March–April 1983), 16–18.

[174]Thaiss, "The Bazaar," p. 190; and Fischer, "Persian Society," pp. 180–81.

[175]Mohammad Reza Pahlavi, *Answer to History* (1980), p. 156.

The Shah's opinion of the Bazaar is highly instructive. In the first place, it is factually inaccurate, as the Bazaar did adapt, *to some extent*, to socioeconomic changes. For example, with the development of new shopping areas in the modern parts of the city the Bazaar's retail function diminished, while its wholesale functions developed considerably.[176] But the Shah's statement also illustrates his curious conception of modernity: he undermined his country's main centers of social and economic activity to build supermarkets, many of which were opened by the Bazaar merchants themselves. His plan did not work: in 1984 Iran's national conference of mayors decided to change existing zoning laws so as to ban all large-scale development of shopping facilities outside the bazaars.[177]

The LMI and the Bazaar

Table 1 shows the preponderance of Bazaar families in the LMI leadership. This background is in sharp contrast with the top leadership of the more secular National Front, whose origins were often aristocratic.[178] This may explain the relative radicalism of the LMI's politics in the 1960s as compared to the National Front, which had closer connections to the traditional power structure and whose leaders were more likely to belong to the modern segment of society (a paradox only if we forget that in Iran modernization came from above). Upon occasion Bazargan has complained that traditionally a gentleman was recognized by his asceticism and distinguished bearing, while activism was considered somewhat vulgar.[179] The traditional elite of Iran does look down on bazaaris, and part of the tension between the NF and the LMI may have been due to latent class antagonism.

In the period 1953–63 the NRM/LMI had its base mostly in the Bazaar and among the students. The students were attracted to the political radicalism of Bazargan and his friends, and he had a good reputation as a professor at Teheran University. As for the Bazaar, in spite of the fact that the Nationalist Bazaar leaders shared a common social background with the founders of the LMI and had cooperated with them in the NRM, when the split occurred in the National Movement, the bazaaris preferred to cooperate with the more cautious, statesmanlike, and secular leaders of the National Front, most of which were of upper middle if not aristocratic background. Such men as H. S. Mahmud Manian and H. Hasan Qasemiyeh were members of the NF's Central

---

[176]For details on the ways the Teheran Bazaar adapted to the changing times see Martin Seger, *Teheran: Eine Stadtgeographische Studie* (1978), pp. 155–69.

[177]*Iran Times*, August 3, 1984, p. 4.

[178]See Abrahamian, *Iran*, pp. 190–91 and 232.

[179]Mehdi Bazargan, *Pragmatizm dar Eslam* (Pragmatism in Islam) (1976), p. 25.

Council to the end, and the LMI did not manage to co-opt any of them.[180] Inside the National Front, the Bazaar leaders deferred to the secular leadership, which occupied a higher social position.

Bazargan and his friends' enterprise can be interpreted as an emancipatory movement of the traditional middle class. They came from a traditional Bazaar background, a milieu that had lost much of its social prestige and political influence, and yet educationally they were on a par with both the ruling elite of the Pahlavi regime and the leadership of the NF. Many, especially the younger members (Shariati, Yazdi) had done very well in high school but had initially been denied state scholarships to study abroad because of their political activism, a discrimination they resented. The same state that marginalized them was also attempting to take away the independence of their social class, and here the link with the Bazaar is crucial. Neither Bazargan nor Taleqani have ever made specific reference to the declining role of the Bazaar, perhaps because they were not personally affected. But not so their supporters—in March 1962 the Student Organization of the LMI published a pamphlet titled "The University's Destiny and Its Role in the Past and Future." One page two we read the following assessment of the Bazaar's decline:

> The truth is [the regime] . . . does not want the university to reopen. . . . The university is the focal point of the nation's hopes . . . and has to some extent replaced the old religious sanctuaries (*bastgah*).
>
> Formerly the Teheran Bazaar, supported and led by the ulema, was the convening point of demonstrations and Nationalist reactions [to government policies]. The Bazaar had a certain independence and a bazaari could earn his living independently of the state apparatus. With his modest savings he could afford to close shop for a few days. But for a long time now the banks, the monopolies, and the [government] files on the one hand, and the difficulty of earning a living, coupled with police threats on the other hand, have deprived the bazaari of his freedom and prevent him from speaking out. In the strike that followed [the 1953 coup] they destroyed the roofs of the Bazaar and let them fall in.[181]

This middle-class Bazaar orientation also explains the party's rather moderate economic program, with its insistence on the creation of a political climate in which people could go about their business.[182]

---

[180]A leading Nationalist bazaari told me about Bazargan's role in the early 1960s: "He had not done any political work, and had only been active under repressive conditions. Although selfless, he and his friends were immature and too emotional. The National Front, however, thought politically." H. Abolhasan Lebaschi, personal interview, Créteil, July 1982.

[181]*Safehati az tarikh-e mo'aser-e Iran: Asnad-e nehzat-e azadi-ye Iran,* vol. 1 (1982), p. 114.

[182]See the party program of 1961 in Appendix A.

In the years 1963–77 the LMI did not exist as an organized party, and its founders pursued apparently nonpolitical activities in religious and educational fields. By the time political activity became possible again in 1977, two developments had taken place. Those students opposed to the regime had become radicalized and had no use for either the LMI or the National Front, and the ulema had reentered the political scene under the leadership of Ay. Khomeini. The Bazaar thus dealt directly with the ulema, over the heads of the politicians. It was only since the fall of the Provisional Government and the limited reactivation of the LMI that Bazargan and others have sought to rebuild the alliance with the Bazaar, appealing to the economic self-interest of bazaaris and contrasting their technocratic skills with the incompetency of the ruling fundamentalists.

Social Bases of LMI Support

As Iran's educational system expanded in the 1950s and 1960s, even wider groups of traditional middle-class people gained access to the country's universities. Confronted with institutions dominated by the older, Westernized elites, these newcomers to academia felt an urgent need to justify their continued adherence to Islam to themselves. they joined the Muslim Student Associations where Bazargan and others like him would assure them (and offer a living example) that Islamic faith and the modern world were indeed compatible.

The student support for Bazargan in the early 1960s was not distributed evenly across all disciplines. For reasons speculated on earlier, the students of traditional background tended to flock to the technical and engineering faculties whose graduates had a reasonable chance of earning a decent living. Competition was toughest for these disciplines, and sons of middle-class or lower-middle-class members of the traditional segment of society usually did better, perhaps because they were less distracted by what constitutes an affluent modern young person's normal social life. Muslim Student Associations were notoriously more entrenched in the technical and scientific faculties than in the humanities or social sciences, where the mood was more apolitical or leftist. This preference of the more religious students for engineering and the sciences and of the more secular students for the humanities and the social sciences still held for the radical offshoots of the LMI and the National Front, the Mojahedin and the Fada'iyan (discussed in chapter 5).

Upon entering professional life, the new engineers often joined the Islamic Association of Engineers, also founded by Bazargan. This associational network constituted the real organized social support for

Bazargan and Islamic modernism, in contrast to a political party such as the LMI, which was allowed to function freely for just over two years before the revolution.

Herein lies one weakness of Bazargan and his Islamic modernism. A nation's counterelite cannot consist of only engineers, with just a sprinkling of physicians and scientists. Bazargan likes to see himself and his party as bridging the gap between Iran's intelligentsia and its religious heritage. In terms of our scheme of the dual society, Bazargan has attempted to overcome the duality of society by gently encouraging the traditional elements to enter the modern age (or certain aspects of it), and by dispelling the modern segment's misgivings about Islam.

His success has at best been partial. Few intellectuals in Iran, writers, essayists, artists, university professors outside the technical faculties, were seduced by Bazargan's apologetic writings of the 1950s and 1960s, although many respected him for his political courage. The main appeal of Bazargan and his friends was to people who needed to have their religious traditions confirmed, not to those who had already lost them. This limitation is shared with other Muslim modernists. Noting that modernists direct their apologetics toward Muslim doubters, Hamilton Gibb explains that "the object of the apologetic is to prove the divinely inspired origins of the Islamic religion and way of life, in order to establish and strengthen the foundation of an ethic which would otherwise stand exposed and helpless before the subtle assaults of secularism."[183] This aim limited the impact of Bazargan, Taleqani, and Shariati on the country's intellectual life. They may have been extraordinarily well educated and cultured by the standards of the milieu from which they came, but in comparison to Iran's intelligentsia they were amateurs. Bazargan may be an excellent engineer and a competent Islamicist, but as a historian he is a dilettante.[184] Shariati may have been a gifted writer, but his sociology is often confused. Ay. Taleqani may have possessed great courage and was certainly more cultured than his peers, but his contributions to economics have been vastly exaggerated by his admirers, far beyond his own modest claims. All three produced more critical writing than most secular intellectuals (Shariati's collected works fill more than forty volumes), but quantity cannot substitute for quality. These men thus appealed mainly to those people who had no access to anything better, who were often the first generation in their families to read books.

[183]Gibb, *Modern Trends*, p. 53.
[184]In fairness to Bazargan, he has never claimed to be a historian. The fact remains that many Islamic activists got their first (and perhaps only) exposure to history from his writings and those of other nonprofessional historians.

Moreover, Bazargan's and Taleqani's appeal was not necessarily based on their liberality of mind or their advocacy of parliamentary democracy. More persuasive was the way they gave the rising members of the traditional middle class a sense of dignity, which allowed them to affirm their identity in a society politically dominated by what they saw as a Godless, Westernized, and corrupt elite: the modern segment, as it is called in this book.

Having achieved this goal, the population thus awakened by Bazargan and his friends naturally looked for substantive solutions to the growing problems of Iran. Liberalism, be it Islamic liberalism, may have many attractions, but it does *not* provide for ready-made solutions to social and economic problems. At the same time Bazargan, deprived of his teaching position at Teheran University, no longer had daily contact with the younger generation. So it came to pass that the high school students who had flocked to hear Bazargan and Taleqani speak in the Muslim Student Associations or at the Hedayat Mosque, as they matured in the 1960s and 1970s—a period when the LMI was not allowed to function and Bazargan could do little more than give inconspicuous talks in mosques while Taleqani was isolated in his exile most of the time—began to look for solutions elsewhere. Some of these "solutions" came from within the LMI, but from its second-generation members.

Shariati developed Bazargan's methods and ideas in a distinctly radical and totalitarian way, and became one of the main fathers of the Islamic revolution. This radicalism drew large audiences, even from among the modern segment of society, in while many people had become aware of their "alienation." Shariati based his appeal on the necessity to end foreign domination, a goal with which many people in the modern segment agreed. Relatively uneducated people were also drawn to him, because, more than Bazargan, he was able to articulate the resentments of the disadvantaged. Although Shariati's writings were a more direct influence on the revolution than Bazargan's, his heritage is systematically played down in the Islamic Republic, while Bazargan continues to write. The truly pious in Iran have more confidence in Bazargan's commitment to Islam than they had in Shariati's. Ultimately Shariati's thought is much closer to that of the Mojahedin than to the political reformism of Bazargan and the LMI.

In contrast to Shariati, Ebrahim Yazdi's influence was closer to Khomeini's movement. Yazdi has not contributed much explicitly doctrinal writing, but an analysis of the newspaper he edited in the 1970s and which was read mainly by the membership of the Muslim Student Associations in the United States shows little continuity with the generosity of Bazargan.[185] Many cadres of the Islamic Republic are former members of these MSAs.

Bazargan tried to socialize the traditional segment into politics, but events overtook him. By the time the revolution broke out, Bazargan was a well-to-do businessman, and his appeal to the masses was limited. It is significant that after the revolution the LMI set up headquarters in the north of the city, while the IRP chose a run-down neighborhood in the poor south of Teheran as its seat.

This chapter presented the arguments and ideas of Shi'ite modernism, as articulated by the main figures of the Liberation Movement of Iran. These ideas represent attempts by men grounded in tradition and religion to come to grips with modernity. Given the novelty of this enterprise in the Iranian context, it is not remarkable that at times the modernist elaborations strike us as intellectually gauche or inconsistent. Unlike Western theological efforts to adapt faith to secularization,[186] the Shi'ite modernists have operated in a milieu still largely permeated by traditional religion. The necessity of a rigorous intellectual rethinking of Islam was not deemed vital. Yet one need not hold their occasional inconsistencies against them, for, as Leszek Kolakowski has put it: "Total consistency is tantamount in practice to fanaticism, while inconsistency is the source of tolerance."[187]

---

[185]See chapter 5.

[186]See for instance Harvey Cox, *The Secular City: Secularization and Urbanization in Theological Perspective* (1966).

[187]Leszek Kolakowski, "In Praise of Inconsistency," in *Marxism and Beyond: On Historical Understanding and Individual Responsibility,* trans. Jane Zielonko Peel (1969), p. 233.

PART II

THE LIBERATION MOVEMENT OF IRAN UNDER THE SHAH

CHAPTER 3

On the Sidelines:
The Early Years

The LMI is the brainchild of three men who were and are closely related by ties of friendship and kinship. The late Ay. Taleqani, Mehdi Bazargan, and Yadollah Sahabi all belong to the generation whose childhood coincided with the instability that plagued Iran after the 1905–6 Constitutional Revolution. Their adolescence and early adulthood witnessed the rise to power of Reza Khan, Reza Shah after 1925, and the attempts of a small band of Majles deputies, including Modarres and Mosaddeq, to oppose this rise.

After Reza Shah's forced abdication in 1941, political activity once again became possible in Iran. During the period 1941–53 the communist Tudeh party became a powerful force, especially in those parts of the country that had been occupied by Soviet troops.[1] An irreligious regime, which in its final years had become openly antireligious, had given way to a situation in which an atheist party was becoming ever more influential among the youth, the intelligentsia, and the young industrial proletariat. Baha'ism offered a religious alternative to Islam. This course of events could not fail to produce considerable anxiety among the more lucid elements of society who were still attached to Islam as a way of life.

Formative Years

Ay. S. Mahmud Taleqani

Ay. S. Mahmud Taleqani was born on March 6, 1912 (Esfand 15,

[1] See Sepehr Zabih, *The Communist Movement in Iran* (1966), pp. 71–84.

1290), in Taleqan, a mountain valley northwest of Teheran.[2] He was the oldest son of Ho. S. Abolhasan Taleqani, a scion of a local Taleqan ulema family. S. Mahmud's childhood was spent in an atmosphere of frugality and defiance to Reza Shah's regime. Unlike many mullas who were notoriously venal and led quite comfortable lives, S. Abolhasan had a reputation for incorruptible honesty. In Najaf, Iraq, where he had studied as a young man, he had learned the craft of watchmaking. After he moved to Teheran, he refused to live off tithes, although part of the religious taxes are traditionally designated for the upkeep of mullas. Instead, he eked out a meager income repairing watches.

Although Ho. Abolhasan Taleqani was a friend and supporter of Modarres, his activities were on the whole more religious than political: he organized debates between Muslims and members—and in some cases proselytizers—of other religious communities, both recognized (Christians, Jews), and unrecognized (Baha'is). At least one of these debates took place in the house of his good friend, H. Abbasqoli Bazargan, Mehdi Bazargan's father.[3] The perceived threat posed by the existence of these non-Islamic religious groups led some better-educated Muslims to think rationally about their religion, which was a first step toward religious modernism.

Ho. Abolhasan Taleqani regarded the modernizing state's authority with great suspicion. Thus he refused to obtain identity cards for his children, would not allow a number-plate to be affixed to his house-door, and, like many other *mujtahids*, he opposed his young relatives' military service.[4]

S. Mahmud Taleqani spent his childhood in Taleqan and Teheran, where he received his early education in a traditional *maktab*. When he was ten, he was sent to Qum where Ay. S. Abdolkarim Ha'eri Yazdi had revived the *howzeh-ye elmiyeh* only two years earlier, after a century of neglect.[5] S. Mahmud chose to study at the Feizieh School, where early on he made the acquaintance of a fellow student, Ruhollah Khomeini. At the school, he attached himself more particularly to Ay. Ha'eri Yazdi.

Ay. Ha'eri Yazdi was something of a reformer, although his ideas were often frustrated by the conservative inertia of his environment. In the 1920s he had suggested sending some young *tollab* to Europe to learn foreign languages and introduce Islam abroad, but his plans came

---

[2]Unless otherwise indicated, all biographical data for the late Ay. Taleqani are taken from Bahram Afrasiabi and Sa'id Dehqan, *Taleqani va tarikh* (Taleqani and history) (1981).

[3]Mehdi Bazargan, *Modafe'at dar dadgah-e gheir-e saleh-e tajdid-e nazar-e nezami* (Defenses in the illegitimate Military Court of Appeals) (1971), p. 75.

[4]For the motivations behind the ulema's opposition to conscription, see Shahrough Akhavi, *Religion and Politics in Contemporary Iran* (1980), pp. 37–38.

[5]Michael M. J. Fischer, *Iran: From Religious Dispute to Revolution* (1980), p. 109.

to naught when Teheran bazaaris threatened to cut off their payment of the tithes if he went ahead with his plan to send youngsters to learn *kafer* (unbeliever) ways.[6] Ha'eri Yazdi was also the first to suggest that, given the growing complexity of the problems a modern-day believer faces, the leading *mujtahids* establish some sort of specialization and division of labor among themselves, because the totality of all these problems, he said, is beyond the grasp of any one individual.[7]

After the elder Taleqani died in 1931, Teheran's ulema, in keeping with custom, offered to appoint S. Mahmud to his father's position of *emam-e jama'at* of the mosque. He declined, left the position to his sister's husband, and returned to Qum to pursue his studies. During this period he clandestinely crossed the border to Najaf, the major center of Shi'ite devotion and learning, and studied there as an extern with Ay. S. Abolhasan Esfahani and Ay. Aqa Zia'eddin Eraqi, the two *maraje'* of that time. After receiving his *ijazah* from the former, he returned to Iran and got another *ijazah* from Ay. Ha'eri Yazdi. His mentor in Qum died in 1935, and thenceforth Taleqani went to Teheran more often, finally settling there in 1939. He took up his father's activity of organizing religious meetings to discuss current problems.

The anticlerical tendencies of Reza Shah's reign had intensified after 1935. Thus, the modern dress-codes of 1928 were stiffened: women were forced (after a while, *manu militari*) to unveil, and men were ordered to wear brimmed hats, which the clergy interpreted as an attempt to make it impossible for men to touch the ground with their foreheads during public prayers. Members of the ulema were given permission to continue wearing the turban, but had to carry the appropriate government-issued license with them at all times.[8]

One day in 1939, Hojjat ol-Eslam Taleqani, as he was now called, was arrested for not having his license with him. He was sentenced to three months' imprisonment, a sojourn that was to mark him: he got a firsthand knowledge of the dictatorship's ways, and, sharing a cell with a member of the "group of 53," men who had been arrested in 1937 for communist activity and who were to become the nucleus of the Tudeh party,[9] he became acquainted with Marxist views. Long discussions followed, and from this experience dated his grudging respect for leftists, against whom he would from now on advocate free debate and the power of persuasion rather than coercion.

Reza Shah's rule had a profound impact on Taleqani. Recalling that it

[6]Ibid., p. 85.

[7]Ibid., p. 164.

[8]On the dress-codes, see Sh. Akhavi, *Religion and Politics*, pp. 42–44, and Fischer, *Iran*, p. 98.

[9]Cf. Zabih, *The Communist Movement*, pp. 64–70, and Ervand Abrahamian, *Iran between Two Revolutions* (1982), pp. 155–62.

had been the ulema who had persuaded Reza Khan to become Shah rather than declare a republic, as had been his original intention, Taleqani wrote in 1955, in his introduction to Ay. Na'ini's *Tanbih ul-ummah:*

> From the day I became aware of the society I was living in, I have always seen the people of this land under the whips and boots of self-centered despots. At home, every evening, we would be waiting for some bad news: what had happened that day, who had been arrested, exiled, or killed? What decisions had been taken for the people? From the moment my father, who was one of the well-known ulema, left our house in the morning, until his return in the evening, we little children and our poor mother would be worrying that something might have happened to him.

Taleqani characterized the time he spent studying in Qum as

> days when the people of this country were subjected to all the pressures of despotism. They were afraid of one another. Their lives, property, and honor, even the turban of the ulema and the kerchief of the women were not safe from the grab of despotism's henchmen. . . . I began to reflect: was it not that the ultimate aim of all these erudite scholarly debates about the branches (*foru'*) and principles (*ahkam*) [of Islam] consisted in the improvement of the lot of the individual and of society? Could a people which was so blatantly lorded over by an individual or a group ever see happiness and righteousness? Would it not be appropriate to concentrate one's thought and action on the creation of a wholesome environment and the prevention of egocentric wills?

He continued,

> I saw that some men in religious habit had hoisted a self-centered man onto the back of the people while reciting the Qoran and the *hadiths*, . . . that others had ratified this act by their silence and circumspection, only to start praying and asking God for a speedy return of the absent Imam after [the despot] had firmly established himself . . . and crushed everything under his feet.

It was "this policy of some religious leaders, this dark environment, these psychological pressures," that led Taleqani "to study more deeply the Qoran . . . and the history of the Prophet and the Imams. . . . It was given to me to meet certain eminent teachers and ulema, and little by little I found my world brightening up. I got to know the roots of religion, my heart knew certainty, and I recognized the goals and ends of my social duties."[10]

[10]S. Mahmud Taleqani, introduction to Ay. Mohammad-Hosein Na'ini, *Tanbih ul-ummah*

Between 1939 and 1941 Taleqani began to organize Qoran-interpretation sessions. For this he was attacked by some of the traditional ulema, who argued that ordinary people should merely recite the Holy Book.[11] Immediately after the demise of Reza Shah, Taleqani, joining others, founded the Kanun-e eslami, Islamic Society.

Mehdi Bazargan

Mehdi Bazargan was born in 1907 (1286) into a pious family of Bazaar merchants.[12] His father was Hajj Abbasqoli Bazargan, a wealthy merchant from Azerbaijan who had established himself in Teheran. His father's personal integrity and religiosity is often mentioned by Mehdi Bazargan as one of the chief influences on his life.

Young Mehdi received his elementary education in the Madreseh-ye soltani, a traditional school, and his secondary education in the Dar-ol mo'allemin-e markazi, one of the country's earliest modern schools. Its director, Abolhasan Forughi, gave also classes in philosophy and the interpretation of the Qoran, Bazargan's first introduction to this activity. In his adolescence he began the habit of reading the Qoran every day.[13]

In 1928 he was one of the Iranian students who were selected by competition to be sent abroad to pursue their studies. Sometime in September 1928 Reza Shah granted an audience to the chosen students, and of all the things he said, the following words were to engrave themselves on Mehdi Bazargan's memory:

> You must be wondering why we are sending you to a country whose regime differs from ours. There, they have freedom and a republic, but they are also patriots. What you will bring back when you return is not only arts and sciences, but also patriotism.[14]

Europe made a profound impression on Bazargan, who had "never stepped on a paved road and had learnt to bind a tie in the great hall of the Iranian Ministry of Education."[15] He stayed in France for close to

---

wa tanzih ul-millah, ya hokumat az nazar-e eslam (1955), pp. 4–6. Taleqani's text adumbrates themes that would later preoccupy the LMI: the responsibility of the clergy, a return to the sources of religion, and opposition to despotism.

[11]S. Mahmud Taleqani, speech given at the Hoseiniyeh Ershad in 1979 on the occasion of the assassination of Ay. Morteza Motahhari, as quoted in an LMI declaration commemorating the second anniversary of Taleqani's death, p. 2.

[12]All biographical information on Bazargan is taken, unless otherwise indicated, from Bazargan, *Modafe'at*.

[13]Personal written communication from Mehdi Bazargan, January 4, 1988.

[14]Bazargan, *Modafe'at*, p. 38.

[15]Ibid., p. 42.

seven years. First he went to Nantes, where he attended the *classes préparatoires* for the *grandes écoles* at the Lycée Clemenceau. A classmate was Abdollah Riazi, the longtime speaker of parliament under the Shah; Riazi was executed by a revolutionary tribunal in 1979.

In the *Defenses* Bazargan enumerates the seven impressions or lessons with which the stay in Nantes left him:[16]

1. Although the French were advanced and civilized, they had not given up religion. On his first short visit to Paris, before he was sent to Nantes, he was struck by the picture of well-dressed people filling the naves of Notre Dame Cathedral in devout prayer. And for the Iranians of those days, Paris was a summary of the world.

2. The French were patriots. The anecdote illustrating this lesson concerns a vice-minister of the interior who refused to evacuate his office, as ordered by his minister, when German troops were believed to be within shooting range of Paris in World War I. He was awarded the legion of honor by Clemenceau, while his superior resigned.

3. Westerners build things to last, and take seriously whatever they do. He compares this attitude to Iranian sloppiness.[17] The wiring and plumbing of his Nantes dormitory, executed as if serving a palace, illustrated this.

4. The French have a sense of national solidarity. Some volunteers selling antituberculosis stamps in the streets of Nantes prompted this insight.

5. The French are honest: a classmate once lost a glove in a store, and the store-owner immediately had it sent back to the *lycée*.

6. The French are not prone to jealousy. After the first three months at the *lycée*, exams were held. Riazi came first in mathematics, Bazargan in physics. They expected to be treated by their French classmates as provincial Iranians in Teheran would have been treated by their Teherani comrades, with abuse and derision, yet the French carried on business as usual and remained friendly with the Iranians.

7. The French are moderates. In Iranian schools there had been two clearly distinct sets of students: those who were hard-working, religious, and well mannered, and those who were irreligious, lazy, and ill-mouthed. In the French *lycée*, by contrast, students would get drunk and have a good time on weekends, while studying hard during the week. They were, to quote Bazargan, *"ni bête, ni ange."*

At the end of his first year in Nantes he participated in the preliminary *concours* for the Ecole centrale des arts et manufactures, and

---

[16]Whether these seven lessons were actually learned during his stay in Nantes, as he implies in the book, or represent a later ex post facto condensation of his experience there, is immaterial for our purposes. Whatever the case may be, their formulation sheds considerable light on his relationship with the West.

[17]Cf. discussion of his writings on the national character of Iranians, chapter 2 of this book.

became the first Iranian ever to pass an entry examination to a *grande école*. After an additional year in Nantes, he again took part in entry competitions for the elite schools. This time he was definitively admitted both to the Ecole centrale, and the Ecole des mines. For a foreigner this was quite an accomplishment, for both schools count among France's best. He chose to become a *centralien* and studied at the school for four years. After graduation another year was spent on work-training in various factories around France.

The lessons of his Parisian period were threefold:[18]

1. The French were not leader-oriented, but honored the ordinary individual. Their dignitaries put wreaths on the tomb of the Unknown Solider rather than on some military hero's grave. In their public places, they placed statues not only of kings and military leaders, but also of discoverers, inventors, and scientists.
2. The French had voluntary associations for everything. In Iran, by contrast, one *had* to become a member of whatever state-sponsored associations there were. He recalls that in his country there had been only one truly voluntary association functioning free from government interference, and that was the Bazaar Merchants Association. His father had been its chairman for a while, but it was dissolved when Reza Khan came to power.[19]
3. There are significant resemblances between machines and democracy. In a machine, all the various components, nuts, and bolts work together according to a plan. Similarly, in a society that wants to progress, all members must cooperate and work toward the common good. Society can only succeed if the individual members go about their tasks willingly and know what they are doing and why they are doing it. The machine had created democracy in the West. Conversely, without democracy, modern-scale development and industrial production was not possible.

The Ecole centrale, like many other *grandes écoles*, recruited students mainly from the elite of French society, and its atmosphere was therefore more Catholic than the dominant *laïc* culture of Third Republic France. Bazargan reports that fully 68 percent of the school's students were card-carrying and dues-paying members of Catholic student associations. It is only natural, therefore, that after two years spent in traditionally Catholic Brittany, and four years of studying in a Catholic enclave in Paris, Bazargan came away with an exaggerated sense of the importance of religion in pre–World War II France.

In 1935 Bazargan decided to leave Europe. With Yadollah Sahabi and

[18]Bazargan, *Modafe'at*, pp. 52–61.
[19]Ibid., p. 56.

some others he drove to Iran in a car. Barely inside Iran, they were immediately confronted with the ill-mannered behavior and harassment of government officials.

For Bazargan, a year of military service followed. He spent it first shifting pebbles in the courtyard of his barracks (much to his outrage, given his qualifications), and then translating technical articles from French. Then came a variety of jobs, some held simultaneously. He joined the Faculty of Engineering of Teheran University, founded, with some friends, a multipurpose company called Union of Iranian Engineers, and then, in 1940 (1319) became the director of the Construction Bureau (in charge of building new branches, updating old installations, and so on) of the Bank Melli Iran, Iran's national bank.

There, one day in 1941, two young men came and asked to see him. It turned out that they were members of the Islamic Society. They presented him with a copy of the society's organ, *Danesh-amuz*, and asked him to contribute an article. On the masthead of the newspaper Bazargan saw a name that had a familiar ring: S. Mahmud Taleqani.

Yadollah Sahabi

Yadollah Sahabi was born in 1906 (1285) in Teheran into a family of artisans. Here, he received his education in a variety of traditional and modern schools, including Dar ol-Fonun, Iran's oldest modern high school, until he entered the capital's newly founded Teachers Training College in 1928. He graduated in 1931, ranking first in his class. After a year of teaching in a Teheran high school, he was sent to France with a government scholarship. He enrolled at the University of Lille, whence he was graduated in 1936 with a doctorate in geology. In 1931 he had met Mehdi Bazargan, whose closest personal friend and political ally he would be in later years. Upon his return from France he joined the faculty of Teheran University, where he was to teach for twenty-six years. On the whole, Sahabi is a less outgoing and more dour man than Bazargan, to whom he has always played second fiddle.

Years of Turmoil: 1941–1953

In 1941 (1320) Reza Shah was succeeded by his young son, Mohammad Reza Shah (henceforth referred to as "the Shah"). After an authoritarian interlude of sixteen years, civil society once more became active in Iran. Ervand Abrahamian summarized the effects of Reza Shah's abdication:

In rupturing the autocracy, the Anglo-Soviet invasion of August 1941 unleashed the pent-up social grievances of the previous sixteen years. As officers fled to the capital and conscripts absconded to their villages, tribal chiefs, many of whom had given up hope of better days, escaped from police surveillance in Teheran and rushed home to their tribal warriors. Veteran politicians who had been nursing their wounds in forced retirement hurried back into public life. Religious leaders, emerging from seminary libraries, resumed the exhortative stance of pulpit preachers. Intellectuals, many of them too young to remember the difficulties of 1907–1925, plunged enthusiastically into politics, editing newspapers, publishing pamphlets, and forming political parties with the goal of building a new Iran. Even the obsequious deputies and sycophantic bureaucrats suddenly found the courage to declare their political independence and denounce their former master. The reign of silence was superseded by the clamor of flamboyant deputies, lively journalists, outspoken party leaders, and discontented demonstrators.[20]

Economically, the Allied occupation and the general problems caused by the war created great hardship for Iranians. Internal trade was disrupted by the use of the Trans-Iranian Railroad mainly to send supplies to the Soviet Union. The demand created by the presence of Allied troops fueled inflation, which was aggravated by the activities of speculators. A particularly bad harvest in 1942 brought famine to many areas. As the government took little action to remedy the situation, discontent grew.[21] There were plenty of challenges for young, European-trained technocrats.

The first crisis Iran faced after the war was the continued presence of Soviet troops in the northwest of the country and the existence of separatist governments under their protection in Kurdistan and Azerbaijan. In 1946 this problem was solved, Soviet troops left the country, and the central government reestablished its sovereignty over the northwest. The years 1949–53 were characterized by the struggle for the nationalization of oil and the power struggle between Mosaddeq and the Shah, leading to the coup of 1953. It is against the background of the political and religious life of this period that the early activities, both political and religious, of the future founders of the LMI have to be understood.

Political Forces

The aim of the following exposition is not to give an account of Iranian politics in the twelve years of relative freedom that followed

---

[20]Abrahamian, *Iran*, pp. 169–70.
[21]Cf. Nikki Keddie, *Roots of Revolution* (1981), p. 114.

Reza Shah's abdication. Rather, our aim is to introduce the dramatis personae of the country's political life in this period, for many adversary relationships, alliances, and affinities crystallized in these years. With the general revival of civil society after 1941, several major currents emerged in Iranian politics.

The first, and most organizationally sophisticated, of these currents was the communist left. In September 1941 the survivors of the "group of 53" were released from prison. Joining others, they formed the Tudeh party in late 1941. Given the measure of widespread discontent that was developing in Iran, and its initially moderate party program, the Tudeh managed to get a considerable amount of support from all walks of society. Its success was initially greater in the north, which had a long-standing radical tradition and which was also under Soviet occupation until 1946. But after 1944 Tudeh's support also spread to the center and south of the country, where important oil fields and textile mills are located. In the elections of 1943–44, although the Tudeh contested only a few seats, its candidates received 70 percent of the votes cast in their constituencies.[22] The trade union movement was by and large dominated by the Tudeh,[23] and the party also had the support of many of Iran's intellectuals, writers, and thinkers. After 1946 the party was repressed by the government, but could nevertheless continue its activities semiclandestinely. Tudeh's attitude toward the National Movement led by Mosaddeq was unsteady: at first the party attacked Mosaddeq for being allegedly pro-American, only to rally to his government after enough ill feeling had been created between the two sides to make any genuine cooperation impossible. Mosaddeq's last act as prime minister was to unleash the security forces on Tudeh-led demonstrations demanding the declaration of a republic after the Shah had left Iran in August 1953.

The second force that arose after 1941 was composed of conservative elements such as the big landowners, tribal chieftains, many members of the clergy, and some Bazaar merchants. The primary leaders of this establishment were S. Zia'eddin Tabataba'i, Reza Shah's erstwhile ally and later rival; Ahmad Qavam, who became prime minister a number of times; and General Ali Razmara, who preceded Mosaddeq as prime minister in 1951. These men were torn by internal rivalries, and oftentimes entered tactical alliances with other political currents. Some were pro-Shah, others, like Qavam, opposed the Shah's personal

---

[22]Abrahamian, *Iran*, p. 292.

[23]For the history of the trade union movement in this period see Ervand Abrahamian, "The Strengths and Weaknesses of the Labor Movement in Iran, 1941–1953," in Michael E. Bonine and Nikki Keddie, eds., *Continuity and Change in Modern Iran* (1981), pp. 181–203; and Habib Ladjevardi, *Labor Unions and Autocracy in Iran* (1985), pp. 28–192.

political ambitions. They were generally supported by Western powers, which, together with their conservative leanings on socioeconomic issues, disqualified them in the eyes of most intellectuals and Nationalists.

The third significant force was the National Movement led by Mohammad Mosaddeq. Its dual aim of reasserting Iran's national sovereignty both inside the country and in the conduct of its foreign relations found widespread support among politically aware Iranians; therefore it is not surprising that it contained widely divergent ideologies, from ethno-nationalist Pan-Iranists to socialists.

Mosaddeq himself, a European-educated aristocrat who had spent part of Reza Shah's reign in prison, reentered politics in 1941. Early in his career he had joined the Moderate party (E'tedaliyun), but after 1941, considering himself a national leader, he never joined, nor founded, any political party, and took some pride in being an independent.

The main political grouping in the National Movement was the Iran party, which was founded on the eve of the elections to the fourteenth Majles in 1943 by members of the Engineers Association, which had been founded two years earlier; the Party of Patriots (Hezb-e mihanparastan); and some other smaller groups.[24] The new party's membership consisted of young, often foreign-educated technocrats and professionals with vaguely socialist leanings, government employees, and students. As early as 1943 the party more or less consistently supported Mosaddeq, who, together with five candidates of the party, was elected to the parliament in the 1943–44 elections.

In 1946 the Iran party, against the wishes of Mosaddeq, entered an electoral coalition with the Tudeh party, causing many members to leave it. The Iran party, however, soon left the coalition and when the National Front was formed in 1949, the IP became the most important political party in this new alliance of parties, personalities, associations, and religious leaders.[25]

A second element in the National Front were the progressive Muslims usually associated with the name of Mohammad Nakhshab. In a sense Nakhshab was the first Iranian to attempt to form a party based on modernist Islam, and since his endeavors foreshadowed (and later paralleled) those of Bazargan and Taleqani, his activities deserve some attention.

Born in Rasht in 1923 (1302), Nakhshab joined the Iran party in 1944, then left it in 1946 over the party's coalition with the Tudeh. In 1944

[24]For the founding of the Iran party and an interesting discussion of the social bases of early party leaders, see Abrahamian, *Iran*, pp. 188–92. Cf. Leonard Binder, *Iran: Political Development in a Changing Society* (1962), pp. 209–11.

[25]For an account of the founding of the National Front, see Abrahamian, *Iran*, pp. 251–57.

(1323), with a few others he founded the Society of God-Worshipping Socialists (Nehzat-e khodaparastan-e sosialist). In 1949 (1328) together with some other members of the society he rejoined the Iran party. Soon after, however, he again left the IP with his followers.[26] This split in the IP was prompted to some extent by the Nakhshab group's greater emphasis on religion (they advocated what they called a "spiritual socialism"), but also by tactical differences with the IP leadership, which the younger people around Nakhshab considered too conservative.[27] In 1952 (1331) Nakhshab's group contacted Bazargan and proposed the founding of a large, openly Islamic party.[28] Given Bazargan's objections to the IP (discussed later), which resembled Nakhshab's, it is puzzling that he did not accept the offer. Perhaps Bazargan's pronounced Bazaar background made him somewhat suspicious of Nakhshab's socialism. Also, in those years Bazargan did not see himself as a politician, and one must also bear in mind the generational gap between the two—Nakhshab was considerably younger. After Nakhshab left the Iran party, he founded the Society for the Freedom of the People of Iran (Jam'iyat-e azadi-ye mardom-e Iran), which in 1953 (1332) finally became the Party of the Iranian People (Hezb-e mardom-e Iran).

The third ideologically distinct element within the National Movement was Pan-Iranism. Composed of anti-Arab and pro-German ultranationalists, this current was weakened by successive splits, some siding with Mosaddeq, others with the Shah. The numerical strength of the Pan-Iranists was never great. They concentrated their activities in high schools and universities, specializing in brawling with Tudeh sympathizers. Thus they managed to maintain a presence far out of proportion with their real weight.[29] The pro-Mosaddeq faction of the Pan-Iranists was organized by Dariush Foruhar into the Party of the Iranian Nation (Hezb-e mellat-e Iran).

The fourth element in the National Movement was its left wing, as represented by the Toilers party (Hezb-e zahmatkeshan) of Mozaffar Baqa'i and Khalil Maleki, the latter a renegade Tudeh leader. The Toilers party split in 1952: Baqa'i left the National Front, while Khalil Maleki

[26]Bazargan, in his chronology of the Islamic movement in Iran in *Showra-ye enqelab va dowlat-e movaqqat va sima-ye dowlat-e movaqqat as valadat ta rahlat* (The Council of the Revolution and the Provisional Government, and the Provisional Government from its birth to its death) (1982), p. 9, gives 1950 as the year Nakhshab left the IP; while Richard Cottam, in *Nationalism in Iran* (1978), p. 266, gives the year 1952.

[27]Cottam, *Nationalism*, pp. 265–66.

[28]*Yadnameh-ye bistomin salgard-e Nehzat-e Azadi-ye Iran* (Commemorative publication for the twentieth anniversary of the Liberation Movement of Iran), May 21, 1981 (Ordibehesht 31, 1360), p. 5.

[29]On the Pan-Iranists, see L. Binder, *Iran,* pp. 216–20, and Mehdi Mozafari, *L'Iran* (1978), pp. 162–64.

formed the Third Force (Niru-ye sevvom), a party of vaguely "Titoist" sensibility which attracted many a leftist intellectual.[30]

To these four elements in the National Front one must add the "independent personalities," collaborators of Mosaddeq who were not affiliated with any party. The dichotomy between parties and personalities was a source of constant friction. The National Front had its moments of glory from March 1951 to August 1953, the years of Mosaddeq's prime-ministership and the struggle for the nationalization of oil. Although led by liberals, the National Front appealed above all to Nationalist sentiment in Iran.

The Religious Community

After 1941, the clergy revived after the humiliations inflicted upon it by Reza Shah. In 1945, at the deaths of S. Abolhasan Esfahani in Najaf and H. Hosein Qomi, the leadership of the Qum *howzeh-ye elmiyeh* passed to Ay. Borujerdi, a scholarly man with no political ambitions. The highest leader of Iranian Shi'ism now resided inside Iran. Under Borujerdi's leadership (he soon became the sole *marja'*) the bulk of the ulema stayed out of politics. Ay. Borujerdi applied himself to rebuilding the religious networks in Iran and strengthening the institutions of religious learning.[31] Some of the ulema supported conservative groups, such as S. Zia'eddin Tabataba'i's National Will party.[32] But among those who engaged in autonomous political activity, two groups stand out.

The first is the movement associated with Ay. S. Abolqasem Kashani. An early foe of British influence in the Middle East (he had participated in the largely Shi'ite anti-English rebellion in Iraq in 1920), he was interned by the British occupiers in 1942 and spent the rest of World War II in jail. Kashani was not a *marja'*, and the traditional clergy felt uneasy about his activities. His relations with Ay. Borujerdi were cool.[33] After the war, he became associated with an organization called the Warriors of Islam (Mojahedin-e eslam). This group had been founded by a cleric named Shams Qanatabadi, but it soon came under the leadership of Kashani. With it, he became a useful ally of Mosaddeq, and his services as a skillful rabble-rouser soon proved to be very valuable to the National Movement, whose educated, often aristocratic,

[30]The main contemporary exegete of Khalil Maleki's Third Force is Homa Katouzian. See his introduction to Khalil Maleki, *Khaterat-e siasi* (Political memoirs) (1979), pp. 9–248.
[31]See Shahrough Akhavi, *Religion and Politics*, pp. 65–91, and Hamid Algar, "The Oppositional Role of the Ulema in Twentieth Century Iran," in Nikki R. Keddie, ed., *Scholars, Saints, and Sufis: Muslim Religious Institutions since 1500* (1972), pp. 242–44.
[32]Nikki Keddie, *Roots*, p. 117.
[33]On Kashani's place within the ulema see Sh. Akhavi, *Religion and Politics*, pp. 61–69.

secular leaders had no such inclinations or talents. But this alliance was based on common aims (the nationalization of oil and the general curtailment of foreign influence in Iran) rather than on common ideological grounds, and it is no surprise that the relations between Mosaddeq and his secular followers on the one hand, and Kashani on the other, were marked by strains from the very beginning.

The first open signs of this rift appeared in the wake of the elections to the seventeenth Majles in early 1952. Mosaddeq and his minister of the interior, Allahyar Saleh, had vowed that they would be the first truly open and free elections in Iran's history.

In Tabriz the National Front presented two slates of candidates for the nine available seats. An active campaign was waged between moderate intellectual figures associated with the Iran party and religious figures supported by Kashani. The result was a stunning victory for the latter. The Iran party, thoroughly alarmed, called for the Tabriz elections to be abrogated. (They were not.) In an editorial that with hindsight can be called prophetic, the organ of the party stated: "We are in turn threatened by the possibility of military dictatorship and the rule of the clergy."[34] Faced with the possibility of not gaining a decisive majority in the elections, Mosaddeq stopped any further balloting after the necessary quorum of deputies had been reached.[35]

In July 1952 (Tir 1331), Mosaddeq resigned from the premiership after the Shah had refused him the right to name his own defense minister. It now appears that the street riots that brought Mosaddeq's triumphant return to power (July 21, 1952/Tir 30, 1331) were largely the work of Kashani. For all this cooperation, Kashani demanded a price; namely, a bigger say in the running of the country. When Mosaddeq refused this, Kashani parted ways with him. It is a sign of Mosaddeq's charismatic hold on public opinion and popular emotion that in spite of Kashani's great personal popularity before the split, the overwhelming majority of the National Movement, *including* its religious sector (such as the deputies from Tabriz), sided with Mosaddeq, while Kashani faded into obscurity. He died in 1962.[36]

Most observers associated Kashani with a small traditionalist group of religious activists who called themselves the Devotees of Islam (Fada'iyan-e eslam). It appears that Kashani skillfully manipulated them, but was not their leader. The group was founded in 1945 by a

---

[34]*Jebhe-ye azadi*, February 20, 1952. As quoted in Cottam, *Nationalism*, pp. 153–54.

[35]For a full account of these elections, far too complicated to detail here, see Cottam, *Nationalism*, pp. 274–77.

[36]Yann Richard, "Ayatollah Kashani: Precursor of the Islamic Republic?" in Nikki Keddie, ed., *Religion and Politics in Iran: Shi'ism from Quietism to Revolution* (1983).

young cleric, Navvab Safavi.[37] At the time they were seen as the Iranian, Shi'ite, counterpart to the Muslim Brotherhood. Although never a mass movement, they were a notable force in Iranian politics in the late 1940s. It now appears that the Devotees had early contacts with Ruhollah Khomeini, who was a second-rank *mujtahid* in Qum, and who had attacked the Pahlavi regime as early as 1943. In 1944 Khomeini had written a tract against Ahmad Kasravi, the historian, nationalist essayist, and anticlerical thinker. The Devotees interpreted Khomeini's pronouncement to mean that Kasravi's life was free for a Muslim to take, and consequently a Fada'i assassin murdered Kasravi in 1946.[38] In March 1951 another member of the organization assassinated the prime minister, General Ali Razmara, who was believed to be in collusion with the British. Shortly after the murder of Razmara, Kashani broke with the organization. The strengthening of the secular arm of government and the refusal to take guidance from the religious leadership which accompanied Mosaddeq's rise quickly threw the Devotees into opposition. A year after Razmara's death, a Devotee gunman wounded Hosein Fatemi, a leading anticlerical Mosaddeqist, and then admitted that the prime minister had been his first target.[39] At this point, at the latest, the Devotees of Islam became anathema to the secular elements in the National Front, and began to be accused of connivance with the court.

Early Activities

After 1941 the rise of the Tudeh was perceived as a great danger by Bazargan and Taleqani and propelled them to action. For them the struggle against the Tudeh had taken three forms in Iran. First was repression. This method was used by some of the conservative groups, such as S. Zia'eddin Tabataba'i's National Will party, in the years of open politics 1941–53, when they would occasionally burn Tudeh party offices in the south of Iran; repression was also used by various governments, especially after 1953. The second method was political, national, and governmental action. This was the way of the National Movement. The third, and, for Bazargan and Taleqani, the most efficient and correct way, was to confront Tudeh on the ideological

---

[37]See Farhad Kazemi, "The Fada'iyan-e Islam: Fanaticism, Politics, and Terror," in Said Amir Arjomand, ed., *From Nationalism to Revolutionary Islam* (1984).

[38]On Kasravi's brand of nationalism, see Ervand Abrahamian, "Kasravi: The Integrative Nationalist of Iran," in Elie Kedourie and Sylvia G. Haim, eds., *Towards a Modern Iran* (1980), pp. 96–131.

[39]Cottam, *Nationalism*, p. 151.

level. They wanted to offer Iran's youth an alternative to the communists, who seemed to have history's dynamics on their side.

As they saw it, the conservatives were backed by the West (then chiefly Britain), and Tudeh benefited from Russian support. The clergy, hopelessly out of touch with the political situation and the spirit of the times, unwittingly contributed to the massive defection of Iran's youth from religion. The National Movement was certainly worthy of whole-hearted support, but such support was not enough.

Bazargan and Taleqani perceived Tudeh's impact on society in many ways, and their responses to the communist challenge must be seen against this background. Bazargan had become a professor at the Faculty of Engineering at Teheran University, and in 1945 (1324) was elected its dean. He was to hold that post for six years, serving with distinction. This is how he summed up Tudeh's influence on campus in the late 1940s:

> In those days it was not easy to administer a faculty. More difficult than all educational, technical, administrative, financial, and human problems was the struggle against the Tudeh members. The Tudeh party had made the university its main bastion. Tudeh activities reached their peak in the years 1324–1330 [1945–51].... We were besieged from all sides—by students, professors, clerical workers, janitors. The communist students had taken over the university clubs, held their meetings in classrooms, ordered employees and workers to strike, and claimed they had a right to interfere with the curriculum. They had no discipline and committed all sorts of outrages and insults. Administrative and educational activities had totally broken down. These were truly dark days. One day they besieged the University Council and imprisoned the professors...[40]

Taleqani maintained that the greatest challenge confronting "religion and the people" after August 1941 was "the rapid spread of Marxist and materialist principles and the founding of the Tudeh Party." He pointed out that "Iran's rulers have always made the mistake of trying to destroy any ideology or way of thinking that they deem harmful to their interests by pressure, force, jail, and killing." But "beliefs and thoughts can not be wiped out in this fashion, and even if they are forced underground, will reappear under a new guise at the first opportunity."[41]

The events following the reoccupation of Azerbaijan and Kurdistan by the forces of the central government in 1946 confirmed Taleqani in his views. He had been delegated by the ulema to accompany the

---

[40]Bazargan, *Modafe'at*, p. 116.
[41]Quoted in Afrasiabi and Dehqan, *Taleqani*, p. 64.

troops, and to prepare a report on the affair afterward. He went as a loyal supporter of the central government, addressing the officers and troops, praying for their success. After the rebels were routed, it became clear to him, however, that the lines between good and evil were not clearly drawn. The separatists had enjoyed a certain measure of popular support, had managed to limit corruption, and carried out useful reforms. They only lost popular support when they turned against religion. The behavior of the government troops, on the other hand, was far from exemplary. He remembers:

> They had told us that the Democrats [the separatists] had cut heads and looted people's property. They had conditioned us to believe that nothing remained of the city of Tabriz. But when we arrived there, we saw that although the Democrats had done such things to their enemies, most savage acts, including plunder and rape, had been perpetrated by the [Iranian] Army.[42]

For Taleqani and Bazargan the lesson of this state of affairs was that for the struggle against the Tudeh to be efficient it had to take three forms: founding associations to counter Tudeh's influence, preparing an ideological alternative to Tudeh's attractive materialism, and supporting Mosaddeq's National Movement. Three associations in which the future founders of the LMI were involved stand out: the Islamic Society, the Engineers Association, and the Muslim Student Associations.

The Islamic Society
Sometime in late 1941 Taleqani founded the Kanun-e eslami, or Islamic Society. Its headquarters was on Amiriyeh Street, then a middle-class neighborhood of Teheran. The aims of the society were to discover, teach, and spread religious truth. It grew out of the regular religious meetings that Taleqani had organized as a continuation of his father's efforts. Soon, however, what with the hardship caused by the Allied occupation, the society also undertook welfare activities on a modest level.[43] Toward the end of 1941 the Islamic Society published its own journal, *Danesh-amuz* (Seeker of Knowledge).

As noted earlier, Bazargan was approached by the editors of this journal to contribute an article. The piece he wrote—it appeared in 1942—he called "Religion in Europe." It was to be his first article after his return to Iran; he recalls its genesis as follows:

> Next to my professional activities I considered my most important task making my compatriots understand that the civilized, developed, real

[42]Quoted in ibid., p. 79.
[43]Ibid., p. 64.

Europe [was] not the Europe of the novels and the cinema. Europe had not become Europe because of the men's ties and the women's lipstick. Europe had spirituality, religion, and ideals. It [was] dynamic, had the will to sacrifice, and [was imbued with] righteousness and social spirit.... In those days Europe was the model for all Iranians.[44]

Bazargan's article was critical both of the West and of Iran. For example, he wrote that Europeans were clean although their religion had discouraged cleanliness in the Middle Ages, whereas Muslims were obsessed with ritual hygiene and yet lived in filth.[45]

The year 1942 also marks the beginning of Bazargan's and Sahabi's close collaboration with the Islamic Society when they attended Taleqani's Qoran-interpretation sessions. It was during these meetings that Bazargan first began reflecting deeply on the congruence between modern science and Islamic tenets; tenets that were accepted as a matter of course by believers and ridiculed as superstition by secular modernists. In 1943 (1322) Bazargan published his first study on the matter, in which he set out to prove with mathematical formulas and the laws of chemistry and physics that Islamic prescriptions for ablution and personal cleanliness (*motahharat*), an important chapter in Islamic jurisprudence, were grounded in science, specifically the principles of biochemical filtration.[46]

Parallel to Taleqani's activities in Teheran, Mohammad-Taqi Shariati (d. 1987), Ali Shariati's father, was pursuing similar aims in Mashad (Iran's other "religious capital" and, unlike Qum, a city of consequence in its own right) with his Center for the Propagation of Islamic Truth (Kanun-e nashr-e haqayeq-e eslami), founded in 1941.

The Engineers Association

While in France, Bazargan had frequented the meetings of the Societé des ingénieurs civils de France, the professional association of French engineers.[47] In 1942 he became one of the leading figures in the founding of the Iranian equivalent of that association, the Kanun-e mohandesin, which was joined by the overwhelming majority of Iranian engineers.

The Engineers Association first attracted attention in April 1943, when it called a strike throughout Iran, soon joined by professionals in other fields. The slogan of the strike was "Entrust tasks to the qualified," for as the association saw it, the older generation of bureaucrats

---

[44]Bazargan, *Modafe'at*, pp. 73 and 77.
[45]*Mazhab dar Orupa* (Religion in Europe), ed. and ann. Hadi Khosrowshahi (1961), p. 53.
[46]Bazargan, *Modafe'at*, p. 78.
[47]Ibid., p. 57.

was preventing younger and more skilled professionals from exercising authority and responsibility in their areas of expertise. The strike was called off after a few weeks, having brought about a considerable shakeup of bureaucratic procedure. Engineers and other skilled personnel were appointed to key positions in government agencies and on the administrative boards of educational establishments. Moreover, Teheran University gained its independence, and every faculty gained the right to send two elected representatives to the University Council.

Tudeh had jumped on the band-wagon of the strike, and actually organized most of the supportive action elsewhere. A few months after the victory, Tudeh sympathizers within the association seceded from it. Accusing the association's leadership of working too closely with the Iran Party, they formed their own Syndicate of Engineers and Technicians, affiliated with the Tudeh-dominated trade union movement. The syndicate soon overtook the Engineers Association in terms of membership, and by 1946 was the main representative body of engineers.[48] After the split the Engineers Association's activities were more scientific and its political role diminished, largely because the Iran party was now available as a vehicle for political action.

The Engineers Association Central Council, reelected annually, practiced political pluralism and from its very inception Bazargan always belonged to it. A number of times he was elected its president. His popularity among his peers can be gauged by the fact that he received his highest personal score in the elections of 1964, when he was in prison. More particularly, Bazargan was entrusted with two tasks: presiding over the association's loan fund, and editing its organ, *San'at* (Industry), for which he also regularly wrote technical articles.[49] In later years Bazargan also founded the Islamic Association of Engineers and the Alumni Association of the Faculty of Engineering of Teheran University. The first, founded in 1957, was meant as a service organization for engineers who had been members of the Muslim Student Associations and it also did charitable work.

Muslim Student Associations

From the very beginning, Tudeh concentrated a substantial part of its propaganda efforts on the country's student body. Even after 1946, when the party had to operate semiclandestinely, the government tolerated Tudeh activities among students.[50] In April 1943 Tudeh began

[48]After 1953, however, the Tudeh and all the organizations it had spawned were outlawed, whereas the Engineers Association has never ceased functioning.
[49]Information on the Engineers Association is taken from Bazargan, *Modafe'at.* pp. 102–4, and Abrahamian, *Iran,* pp. 329–31.
[50]Bazargan, *Modafe'at,* pp. 117–22.

its activities on the campus of Teheran University, then the country's only university. That month, the party's youth organization, formed a month earlier, opened a club near the Faculty of Medicine, and established a student union. By February 1945 the union won recognition from university authorities as the official representative of medical students.[51] Although Tudeh publications tried to avoid direct attacks on religion, the organized presence of so many communist or procommunist students on campus was resented by other students, mostly from the provinces, who were believers and found it difficult to have to perform their daily prayers in secret. In addition Baha'is were actively proselytizing among the students. To stem this tide of what Muslims perceived to be antireligious propaganda, some medical students founded the first Muslim Student Association (MSA) at the university's Faculty of Medicine in 1944.[52]

The association's main aim was to disseminate religious propaganda to counteract the Tudeh and the Baha'i efforts. Its statute spelled out four objectives:

1. To reform society on the basis of Islamic precepts
2. To foster friendship and unity among Muslims, especially the young intellectuals
3. To publicize Islamic truth by means of propaganda centers and written publications
4. To struggle against superstitions

The program's preamble said that the MSA was founded because society's leaders had not ensured that Islamic laws and practice were respected in the country.[53]

The MSA quickly spread to other educational establishments. Ezzatollah Sahabi, Yadollah Sahabi's son, became an early member of the Faculty of Engineering MSA, and was the editor of the two MSA publications: first, until 1950 (1329) *Forugh-e elm* (The Light of Science), and then *Ganj-e shayegan* (The Bountiful Treasure).[54] The associations solicited the cooperation of Bazargan, Sahabi, and Taleqani, who responded favorably. The titles of some of Bazargan's talks at the association ("Islam or Communism," "Pragmatism in Islam," "Labor in Islam"), which were then printed in the association's publications, reflect the

---

[51]Abrahamian, *Iran*, p. 331.

[52]This date is given by E. Sahabi in Naser Hariri, *Mosahebeh ba tarikhsazan-e Iran* (Interviews with makers of Iranian history) (1979), pp. 173–74; and by Afrasiabi and Dehqan, *Taleqani*, p. 75. M. Bazargan, however, gives 1942 as the founding date of the Muslim Student Association. Cf. Bazargan, *Modafe'at*, p. 78.

[53]Quoted from Bazargan, *Modafe'at*, pp. 78–81.

[54]*Modafe'at-e mohandes Ezzatollah Sahabi dar bidadgah-e tajdid-e nazar-e nezami* (The defenses of Engineer Ezzatollah Sahabi in the Military Court of Appeals) (1976), pp. 5–6.

preoccupation with communism. Taleqani's major contribution was a talk titled "Ownership in Islam," which in later years was to become a major source of inspiration for Islamic economics, as explained in the last chapter. These early talks by Bazargan, Sahabi, and Taleqani became the seeds of the LMI's ideological canon.

The activities of the Muslim Student Associations, mostly held on Fridays, were essentially religious and its members shunned political involvement, at least until 1951 (1330), when Mosaddeq's struggle for the nationalization of oil began in earnest. At that point many MSA members became active in the National Movement, but never qua MSA members.

However novel the concept of intellectuals forming Islamic associations may have been in 1941–53, the general atmosphere among Iran's intelligentsia in those years was secular. Thus, the real influence and impact on society of the Muslim Student Associations was negligible in the years before the coup.[55] Their importance lay in the fact that they were seedbeds for a new generation of activists who entered politics after the 1953 coup, when many members joined the National Resistance Movement, and when, unlike political parties, the MSAs could continue functioning openly (although they had to restrict their activities). While it is true that Sahabi, Bazargan, and Taleqani cooperated closely with the associations, many others, whose political options would later diverge considerably from the LMI, did also. Thus, the MSAs also provided the structure where some future fundamentalist leaders would receive their first organizational experience.

Islamic Teachers Associations and even Physicians Associations were also founded, but they failed to gain any importance. Although many of the clergy looked askance at these associations, since they undermined their monopoly on religious teaching, the MSAs organized regular trips to Qum, where members could come together with young *tollab* for discussion and exchange of ideas.

Religious Activities

In the wider sense of the term, Bazargan's, Sahabi's, and Taleqani's involvement with the Islamic Society and the Muslim Student Association was of course religious. But here we are concerned specifically with Taleqani the cleric, for his understanding of his role as a cleric was rather atypical for his time.

Taleqani had multiple activities. He taught at the Sepahsalar School, Teheran's main center of religious learning. In 1948 (1327) he became the *emam-e jama'at* of the Hedayat Mosque, located on Istanbul Avenue

---

[55]This is admitted by Ezzatollah Sahabi in Hariri, *Mosahebeh*, p. 173.

in what was then Teheran's modern business district. In due time this mosque became a vital and much-frequented gathering place for religious Mosaddeqists. Taleqani's Thursday evening sermons and talks, often discussed at the meetings of the MSAs on the morrow of the Hedayat Mosque gatherings, earned him a modest notoriety in Nationalist circles.

But Taleqani's major contribution to spreading the Islamic message was his innovative and daring use of the mass media. In early 1947 (Bahman 1325) the Internal Propaganda Office of the Ministry of Labor and Propaganda invited "the distinguished orator" S. Mahmud Taleqani to contribute articles which could be read over the radio. The ulema had always shunned the airwaves, arguing that they spread corruption (that is, music). Taleqani's response was characteristic of him:

> There are two reasons why I found it difficult to accept [the radio invitation]. First there are the reservations many believers have about the radio. Second there are my own occupations and activities. However, upon consulting certain ulema and religious (*feqh*) sources, I see no more obstacles. For although this mysterious apparatus is also used for corruption (*lahv*), it was not invented for that purpose; and the definition of an instrument of corruption (*alat-e lahv*) demands that it be invented for that purpose, not merely used for it!
>
> In spite of all their purity and virtue, the righteous ulema have to be faulted for their negative attitude, as a result of which they have deprived themselves of all means of propaganda (*tabligh*) and education, leaving the field free for the ignorant. . . . Jihad, in its general sense, and "enjoining what is good and preventing what is evil" by all available means are among the obvious commandments of the living religion of Islam.[56]

In his weekly radio talks Taleqani dealt with topics of general interest, illustrating his points with episodes from the life of the Prophet. Having noticed that the Arabic *hadith* and suras he included in his articles were often mispronounced, he started giving only their content in Persian. The general style of these pieces, where the Prophet and other leading figures of early Islam were talked about in everyday language, was also rather unorthodox. Taleqani's aim was to derive exemplary significance from events which, until then, had been shrouded in ritual and myth.[57] This method of making Islamic history "relevant," increasingly adopted by others in later years, would become an indispensable element in the rhetoric of the Islamic Movement of the 1960s and 1970s. The radio talks were discontinued by the government after a while.

[56] As quoted in Afrasiabi and Dehqan, *Taleqani*, pp. 84–85.
[57] Examples of these articles can be found in ibid., pp. 86–101.

Political Activities

Politically speaking, Bazargan was more active than Taleqani, but it would be wrong to call him a politician in this period. Although a founding member and leader of the Engineers Association, he never became a card-carrying member of the Iran party. Bazargan saw this party as Nationalist, socialist, and modernist, but lacking a veritable ideology. Its members, in his judgment, were well-meaning, reformist individuals who thought that for the country's ills to be cured it was enough for qualified and honest individuals to occupy key positions in politics and administration. Unlike Tudeh members, they did not believe in the necessity of deep ideological, social, and political change to reform society. He did not become a member of the Iran Party because he felt no disposition for party politics and because he was more interested in ideas, spiritual renewal, and self-improvement.[58]

This did not prevent Bazargan from having many friends in the Iran party, occasionally attending their meetings, and giving a number of talks. Two of these were later published: "The Coefficient of Conversion between Material and Spiritual Matters" and "Swearing and Ritual Courtesy in Iran." In the first talk he tried to convey the point that spiritual values and morality were not only worthwhile from a religious or humanistic point of view, but also for the pursuit of mundane matters in everyday life. Therefore political reform programs should not neglect them. If nothing else, a higher degree of public morality would lead to savings in the budgets for the police and the judiciary, as many preventive measures, taken in anticipation of infractions, would become superfluous. In the second article Bazargan pointed out that the florid conventions of the Persian language and its ritualized courtesy formulas (*ta'arof*), favored artificiality and thereby predisposed its speakers to insincerity. Iranians, therefore, had to make extra efforts to be honest.[59]

The founding of the National Front in 1949 was greeted with relief by Bazargan. He acknowledges that he and his friends had failed to win the hearts of the young at Teheran University and that the MSA had not managed to weaken the Tudeh's grip on the student body.[60] The struggle for the nationalization of the oil industry had finally provided

---

[58]This view of the Iran party is given in *Modafe'at*, pp. 109–12. It has to be taken *cum grano salis*, however. Let us not forget that this book was written *after* the events of the early 1960s. There was a lot of bitterness then between the leadership of the LMI and the secular leaders of the National Front. Bazargan may be projecting back in time his pessimistic 1964 view of the Iran party.

[59]Ibid., p. 110. Cf. his views on the national character of Iranians, as described in chapter 2.

[60]*Modafe'at*, pp. 123–24.

a counterattraction to the lure of communism. For the first time Nationalist candidates opposed Tudeh candidates in student elections and won. The élan of Tudeh's penetration of the university was broken.

After Mosaddeq became prime minister in March 1951, his minister of education, Karim Sanjabi, a leading figure of the Iran Party, invited Bazargan to become his deputy. He accepted reluctantly. After only three weeks, however, Bazargan was called upon to perform far more momentous tasks. He was chosen by Mosaddeq to become chairman of the Provisional Board of Directors of the newly founded National Iranian Oil Company, in charge of overseeing the transfer of operations from the British to Iranians. When Kazem Hasibi brought him Mosaddeq's offer, Bazargan went to Taleqani's Hedayat Mosque, performed a Qoranic bibliomancy, and then accepted. Although successful in his delicate mission, personal disagreements with other members of the board (including Hasan Makki) induced him to resign after ten months and to return to his Thermodynamics Laboratory. Academia could not hold him, however, for soon the head of the Plan Organization, Ahmad Zanganeh, also a leading Iran Party member, asked him to oversee the installation of Teheran's water-supply network as director of the Teheran Water Authority. He was busy with this task when General F. Zahedi's coup ousted Mosaddeq.

As we have seen, Bazargan had no political ambitions in the years 1941–53. He did not belong to Mosaddeq's inner circle then, but the prime minister had a high opinion of his managerial capabilities. As a result, Mosaddeq would have liked Bazargan to accept a cabinet post, such as the Ministry of Post, Telegraph, and Telephone.[61] Bazargan consistently refused. It is said that he secretly coveted the Ministry of Education. But this Mosaddeq, who, although not antireligious, was "religiously unmusical," to use Weber's felicitous term, would not give him, arguing that Bazargan wanted to "put kerchiefs on the heads of school girls."[62] The story may be apocryphal, but it is not implausible.

Taleqani's activities in those years were mostly religious, as we have seen. He was in contact both with religious politicians, such as the Devotees of Islam and Kashani, and secular politicians of the National Front; and his main goal was to bridge the gap between the two currents. He warned Kashani not to break with Mosaddeq, but when the break occurred, like most politically active clerics, he sided with Mosaddeq. In 1979, in a speech at Mosaddeq's tomb commemorating the anniversary of his death, Taleqani spoke of the split between

---

[61]Ibid, p. 162.
[62]Convergent testimonies of personalities linked to the National Front, as interviewed in Paris, July 1982.

Mosaddeq and the Devotees and blamed it on the agents of foreign powers.[63] Noting that the period of unity between religious and secular forces had seen great accomplishments (the nationalization of oil), he lamented the breakdown of this understanding, which he explained as follows:

> They [spies, agents of despotism, etc.] told the Devotees that it had been they who had advanced the Movement. To that, the Devotees replied that they wanted full Islamic government. They told them that Mosaddeq was irreligious and will not heed your wishes. To Mosaddeq they said that the Devotees were fanatic young terrorists and that he should shun them. I wanted to create understanding between the two, but that was impossible. Mosaddeq would say that he neither pretended to be working towards Islamic government, nor intended to remain prime minister forever. He asked them for time to finish the oil business. The Devotees insisted that he act according to their wishes. That is how they separated that wing [from the Movement]. Then they went to Kashani. Spies whom I knew personally surrounded him and separated him from Mosaddeq.[64]

Taleqani's most visible political activity came in early 1952, when he became a Nationalist candidate in the Caspian provinces for the elections to the seventeenth Majles. The initiative to invite him to become a candidate seems to have come from the large immigrant population of people from the Taleqan Valley in the north. His opponents represented the Tudeh and the conservative landed interests. Taleqani's candidacy was warmly endorsed by Ay. Kashani. He appears to have waged an active campaign, but we cannot tell whether he could have become a deputy, because the northern constituencies were among those where Mosaddeq halted the election process after the quorum of ninety-seven elected members had been reached for the seventeenth Majles.[65] Incidentally, the same fate was reserved for Mohammad-Taqi Shariati's candidacy in Mashad. There various religious organizations had presented a common slate of candidates, among them Shariati (another candidate was Sheikh Halabi, founder of the ultraconservative, anti-Baha'i Hojjatiyeh society).[66]

Summarizing Bazargan's and Taleqani's political involvement in the twelve years of open politics that preceded the 1953 coup, we can say that their activities stayed at a relatively low level, that neither was particularly close to the charismatic leader of the National Movement, and that the main sphere of their activities was the as yet small world

---

[63]He was right, as we now know. See Mark Gasiorowski, "The 1953 *Coup d'Etat* in Iran," *International Journal of Middle East Studies* 19 (1987).

[64]Quoted in Afrasiabi and Dehqan, *Taleqani*, pp. 139–40.

[65]Ibid., pp. 142–44.

[66]Interview with H. Mohammad Shanehchi, Paris, July 1982.

of modernist Shi'ism. As we have seen, the National Movement of Mosaddeq was torn by strife between secular and religious elements. Until his break with Mosaddeq, Kashani had been the pole around which religious Nationalists congregated. Had the National Front been allowed to function openly, in due course Bazargan and Taleqani might have taken Kashani's place at the center of a reconstituted and reformulated religious wing of the National Front. But there was not enough time for such a development to take place.

It bears emphasizing that at all critical moments in the life of the National Front the future founders of the LMI sided with Mosaddeq, and by implication, the secular forces. They were Nationalists who happened to be good Muslims. Their relative obscurity before the coup was to be both an asset and a handicap in the next stage, namely the formation of the National Resistance Movement.

The National Resistance Movement

On August 19, 1953 (Mordad 28, 1332), the Iranian army, under the leadership of General Fazlollah Zahedi and with generous help from the CIA, toppled Mosaddeq and called back the Shah from his temporary exile in Rome.[67] The Shah named Zahedi prime minister.

Barely a few days after the coup, in late August or early September, a few low-ranking Mosaddeqists established contacts among themselves to try to set up some sort of clandestine organization that might keep the flame of Nationalism alive. Most of them had religious inclinations. Mosaddeq's close secular collaborators were in prison, and even had they not been, it is unlikely that they would have had a taste for secret political work.

On August 29, 1953 (Shahrivar 7, 1332), the Mosaddeqists issued a statement declaring "nehzat edameh darad" (the movement goes on), of which 2,000 copies were distributed in Teheran. The statement defined the goals of the movement as follows: (1) to continue the National Movement and to establish Iran's independence and national sovereignty, (2) to fight against all foreign colonialisms and (3) to struggle against all dependent governments in Iran and the agents of corruption.[68] They also established contact with Hosein Fatemi, who had gone into hiding after the coup.

Roughly a month after the coup, Ay. S. Reza Zanjani, a leading

[67]For an account of this coup see Gasiorowski, "The 1953 *Coup d'Etat* in Iran."

[68]*Safehati az tarikh-e mo'aser-e Iran: Asnad nehzat-e moqavemat-e melli-ye Iran* (Some pages from contemporary Iranian history: Documents of the National Resistance Movement of Iran), vol. 5 (1984), p. 257.

Mosaddeqist cleric from Teheran, convened a first meeting. The initiative was shared by Abdollah Mo'azzami (d. 1972), who had replaced Ay. Kashani as speaker of the Majles after the latter's break with Mosaddeq. Present at this meeting were Ay. S. Reza Zanjani, Mo'azzami, Abbas Sami'i, Mohammad-Rahim Ata'i, Mansur Ata'i, Abbas Radnia, Mehdi Bazargan, and Shah-Hoseini. These men, plus Hasan Nazih, who joined a few weeks later, became the Central Council (Kadr-e Markazi) of the National Resistance Movement.[69]

The lack of previous visibility of the founders of the NRM meant that the newly installed government took relatively little notice of their activities, a fact that facilitated their moves. This does not mean, however, that the government did not suspect anything: Ay. Zanjani's house was under constant surveillance, and Bazargan was told that although his activities were known, the prime minister wanted him to finish his job of bringing drinking water to the inhabitants of Teheran.[70]

A New Force in Iranian Politics

Composition of the National Resistance Movement

Most initial members of the NRM came from a religious Bazaar background. Abbas Radnia, Abbas Sami'i, and Hasan Nazih, a lawyer who had left the Iran Party after the 1946 alliance with the Tudeh, had secular views, but their Bazaar background gave them a certain affinity with Bazargan and Zanjani. Mansur Ata'i had been minister of agriculture in one of Mosaddeq's cabinets and was a member of the Engineers Association. His (and Bazargan's) nephew, Mohammad-Rahim Ata'i (1920–77), had studied at Dar ol-Fonun High School in Teheran and then read law and political science at Teheran University, joined the Iran Party, and left it in 1946. He then worked for the State Railway Company, and soon became the head of its accounting division. Here he started a drive against corruption and bad management and produced the first profit in the history of the company. As a high-ranking employee of the company his task was complicated by the activities of the Tudeh-led unions.[71] Rahim Ata'i was one of the key leaders of the NRM and authored many of its tracts, particularly those on international affairs. His brother-in-law, Ezzatollah Sahabi, long active in the MSAs, was also a major figure in the NRM.

They were soon joined by Mohammad Nakhshab and his Party of the Iranian People (PIP), whose younger members were often active in

---

[69]Hasan Nazih in an interview, July 18, 1982, Paris.

[70]Bazargan, *Modafe'at*, pp. 145–49.

[71]Biographical information for Rahim Ata'i is taken from *Payam-e Mujahid*, Mehr 1356 (September 1977), p. 3.

the Muslim Student Associations. In Mashad the NRM was led by Taher Ahmadzadeh. Here, many of the members of the circle around Mohammad-Taqi Shariati, including his son Ali Shariati, were also active. Ali Shariati and many of the young PIP members (such as Kazem Sami, who would rise to a certain prominence in later years) were also members of Nakhshab's Society of God-Worshipping Socialists. Nakhshab himself, however, left Iran for New York City in the mid-1950s and took a Ph.D. in public administration at New York University.

In Teheran most of the activists of the NRM came from the university or the Bazaar. The university students tended to be members of the Muslim Student Association, which means that many had probably Bazaar connections.

The NRM did include some secular intellectuals, however. After the coup, Khalil Maleki, the leader and founder of the Third Force party, had been arrested and jailed in Luristan. With his arrest, the party, which had never been very big, went underground. Three weeks later, two other leaders of the Third Force, Mohammad-Ali Khonji (d. 1972) and Mas'ud Hejazi, accused Maleki of being a traitor, because he had visited the Shah once.[72] A split ensued, and the faction that followed Khonji and Hejazi was admitted to the NRM. Khalil Maleki and his faction accused their opponents of, among other things, having had dealings with the Tudeh.[73] The Iran Party, on the other hand, joined the NRM only for a short period. Initially most of its leaders were in jail or abroad anyway. After some time, however, the IP was admitted to the NRM, together with Foruhar's Party of the Iranian Nation (PIN).

After July 21, 1954, when the planned demonstrations of the NRM had failed, the participation of the parties in the NRM declined. Some activists unaffiliated with parties claimed that the party activists were not under the NRM's control, and therefore less reliable.[74] And early in 1955 disagreements arose within the NRM leadership. The secular intellectuals of the IP and the PIN argued that the new regime was consolidating itself, and that opposition to it should be cautious. Leading opposition figures, such as Karim Sanjabi and Allahyar Saleh, attacked only the government in their statements, sparing the Shah himself. The original members of the NRM, by contrast, insisted on identifying the Shah as the main element of the regime. These tactical differences explain why the people around Bazargan and Taleqani became emotional radicals in the eyes of the more politically prudent

---

[72]The information on the Third Force comes from H. Katouzian's introduction to Khalil Maleki, *Khaterat*, pp. 114–23, and M. Mozafari, *L'Iran*, pp. 176–79.

[73]*Safehat*, 5, p. 59.

[74]Ibid., pp. 263–66.

leadership of what had been the National Front. Later in 1955 the IP and the PIN left the NRM.[75] The IP leader who was most active in the NRM was Shapur Bakhtiar, a deputy minister of labor in Mosaddeq's last cabinet, who had some experience in clandestine work since he had been active in the French Resistance during World War II.[76]

Organization

From the outset, organizational matters were given much consideration, since many Nationalists felt that the National Movement had failed because of its insufficient organizational capacity. Unlike the Tudeh elements who had returned to the underground after the coup, none of the founders of the NRM had any experience in clandestine organization: they had to improvise. Initial plans had called for a very elaborate structure, with a great many committees, commissions, and subcommissions at the top, and small cells of three to five members at the grass-roots level.[77] To maintain maximum secrecy, the members of one such cell would not know the identity of the other cells' members. Such cells were also formed outside Teheran. In Qazvin, Ahmad Sadr Hajj-Seyyed-Javadi was active. Tabriz, Kermanshah, and the Caspian provinces also saw some activity, but the outstanding center outside Teheran was Mashad, as described earlier. One member of each cell maintained contact with the Central Council. This contact was far from perfect, however, for the decisions of the leadership often did not reach the membership.[78] The Central Council of the NRM met at irregular intervals in the houses of its members, usually when responses had to be formulated to particular policy initiatives of the Shah.[79]

From the outset, the Bazaar played a strong role in the organization of the National Resistance Movement. In September of 1953 Bazaar merchants were said to have constituted a secret committee with a capital of 40 million rials to help bring back Mosaddeq.[80] The NRM's own expenses did not amount to much. Membership dues were 20 rials per month for students and workers, and 50 rials for all others.[81] Considerable financial contributions were made by prominent bazaaris such as H. Hasan Shamshiri, owner of a famous restaurant in the Bazaar; H. Hasan Qasemiyeh, a wealthy cotton merchant; and Taqi Anvari, a wholesale textile merchant. This involvement of the Bazaar also meant that declarations, pamphlets, newsletters, and other docu-

---

[75]E. Sahabi, as quoted in Hariri, *Mosahebeh*, pp. 174–77.
[76]Chapour Bakhtiar, *Ma fidélité* (1982).
[77]See *Safehat*, 5, pp. 12–27.
[78]Ibid., p. 117.
[79]Interview with Hasan Nazih, July 18, 1982, Paris.
[80]Edouard Sablier, "L'Extravagant en pyjama," *Le Monde*, September 18, 1953.
[81]*Safehat*, 5, p. 76.

ments could easily be disseminated throughout Iran concealed in the constant flow of merchandise.[82] In Teheran, Taleqani's Hedayat Mosque also provided a relatively safe place for religiously oriented Nationalists to come together and discuss the issues of the day.

The NRM attempted to put out a regular publication, *Rah-e Mosaddeq* (Mosaddeq's Way). Given the regime's vigilance, it could only appear sporadically and few issues saw the light of day. Another publication was *Hashiyeh bi hashiyeh* (With and Without Annotation) devoted to developments on the international scene for which Rahim Ata'i did most of the work. Ata'i and a young NRM activist named Abbas Amir-Entezam were also in contact with an American graduate student, Richard Cottam, whose research in Iran led to his study of Iranian nationalism.

Relations with Other Groups

One of the most debated issues inside the NRM was the relationship with the underground Tudeh, which had proposed the establishment of an anti-imperialist united front with the Nationalists. It appears that students in the university favored such a coalition, whereas the leadership was split on the matter.[83]

Relations with the clergy were not very close, and very few members of it became active in the NRM; the most important was Ay. S. Reza Zanjani. Ay. Borujerdi, then Shi'ism's main *marja'*, had congratulated the Shah upon his return to Iran. We now know that under the direction of Ay. Behbahani, a pro-court cleric, letters with forged Tudeh signatures were sent to all major mullas in Iran, threatening that they would be "hanged by their own turbans from the lamp-posts of Iran's streets." Many were thus hoodwinked into believing that a communist take-over was imminent, which led them to support the coup.[84] Besides, in those years most ulema were supporting the Shah anyway.

In May 1954, the NRM sent an open letter to Ay. Borujerdi. It stated that the Constitutionalists had put the ulema in charge of guarding over the application of the Constitution until the Parousia of the Twelfth Imam, and that therefore it was incumbent upon them to use their influence over the Muslim masses of Iran to help rid the country of its illegitimate government.[85]

---

[82]Interview with Ali-Asghar Hajj-Seyyed-Javadi, July 1982, Paris.

[83]From the extensive correspondence between the NRM and the Tudeh, and the internal documents of the NRM published in *Safehat*, 5, it is not possible to establish who was actually in favor of collaboration with the communists and who was against it.

[84]The revelations were made by Taher Ahmadzadeh in a section he contributed to Afrasiabi and Dehqan, *Taleqani*, p. 121.

[85]*Hadis-e Moqavemat: Asnad-e nehzat-e moqavemat-e melli-ye Iran* (The saga of resistance: Documents of the National Resistance Movement), vol. 1 (1986), pp. 135–38.

Taleqani, despite having sided with Mosaddeq after the Devotees of Islam had fallen out with the prime minister, extended his help to the terrorist organization and sheltered Navvab Safavi on a few occasions. Taleqani was arrested a number of times. Encouraged by Bazargan, he unearthed an old copy of Ay. Na'ini's *Tanbih ul-ummah wa tanzih ul-millah, ya hokumat as nazar-e eslam*, the major Shi'ite treatise on constitutionalism, discussed in chapter 2. He wrote an introduction (in which allusion is made to "Dr. S. and Eng. B."), and published an annotated version of it in 1955.

On the whole, relations between the Shah's regime and the ulema were courteous and positive in the 1950s. The Shah managed to buy a certain amount of goodwill by instituting an anti-Baha'i campaign, and the ulema quietly acquiesced in the crushing of the Devotees of Islam: Navvab Safavi was executed in 1955.

The NRM had sympathizers in the armed forces, and for a while the Central Command of Officers affiliated with the NRM operated inside the military. This unit supplied the NRM with information on rivalries within the army, and on the struggle between allegedly pro-British and pro-American factions.[86]

Activities of the National Resistance Movement

The Trial of Mosaddeq

The first open act of defiance against Prime Minister Zahedi's regime sponsored by the NRM took place on October 8, 1953 (Mehr 16, 1332). The Bazaar shut down and about 2,000 students demonstrated in two locations in central Teheran, shouting "Death or Mosaddeq" and demanding Mosaddeq's release from prison.

Mosaddeq's trial began on November 8 (Aban 17), and the NRM decided to center its activities on it. The NRM managed to maintain contact with Mosaddeq, and obtained the text of his defense in court, which it printed and distributed widely.[87] After much internal debate, the leaders of the movement agreed to collaborate with the Tudeh in the organization of a general strike. It was planned that on November 12 (Aban 21) the Nationalists would close down the Bazaar, the university, schools, and offices, while busses and factories would be paralyzed by the communists. According to NRM sources, the Tudeh reneged on its promise, while the NRM did close down the university and the Bazaar. A mass demonstration was held in front of the Bazaar.

Repression was harsh: thousands were arrested and exiled, including prominent Bazaar leaders and a few members of the ulema. To add

[86]Ibid., pp. 24 and 128.
[87]*Safehat*, 5, pp. 269–71.

insult to injury, the government destroyed parts of the Bazaar's ceiling, not merely an act of random destruction but one imbued with great symbolic significance in Iran.

The Nixon Visit

A few weeks after these events it was announced that the vice-president of the United States, Richard Nixon, was to visit Iran. Also, Iran reestablished diplomatic relations with Britain, which Mosaddeq had broken. The NRM planned further mass actions to protest against these, as they saw it, acts of treachery. The university organization was put in charge of organizing the Nationalists' response. On December 5 (Azar 14) unrest began, as activists gave speeches in classrooms, which then led to demonstrations all over the campus of Teheran University. To forestall further action, the government took the offensive and on the morning of December 7, 1953 (Azar 16, 1332), the day Nixon was due to arrive, security forces attacked the Faculty of Engineering of Teheran University. Three students were killed by machine-gun fire.[88] The events of December 7 still held great significance in recent Iranian history, and the day has since been Iran's unofficial "University Day."[89] For Nixon and the Shah this visit marked the beginning of a lifelong friendship.

The 1954 Elections

In early 1954 the Shah and Zahedi tried to institutionalize the regime by holding elections to the Senate and to the lower house. The Nationalist parties had not been officially outlawed, and therefore those Nationalists who had not been arrested became active, hoping either to gain seats or to prove that the elections were rigged.

Bazargan was told that his political activism was incompatible with his position as director of the Teheran Water Authority; accordingly, he tendered his resignation on January 31, 1954 (Bahman 11, 1332). On that same day, a group of Nationalists sent an open letter to various authorities arguing that according to a law passed on January 23, 1951 (Bahman 3, 1329), it was unlawful for the government to maintain martial law during an election. They asked that martial law be lifted to guarantee free elections.[90] This the government had no intention of doing.

Elections to the Senate began in February. The NRM issued a number of declarations, providing details of how and where and by whom the

[88]They were named Bozorgnia, Qandchi, and Shari'at Razavi. The latter's sister later married Ali Shariati.
[89]*Safehat*, 5, pp. 273–76.
[90]*Hadis*, pp. 41–42.

elections had been rigged. In an open letter to the judicial authorities it declared that the corruption at the polls was unprecedented, and had not been seen even under Reza Shah's dictatorship.[91] The elections to the lower house (the eighteenth Majles) began in the provinces and were also held in February. This is how *Time* summarized them:

> Item: a constituency near Kerman beat up the man Zahedi sent there to be elected; Zahedi suspended the balloting. Item: a former Iranian ambassador to the U.S. [Allahyar Saleh] announced himself as a pro-Mossadegh candidate from Kashan; Zahedi forced him to remain in Teheran. Item: the powerful Zolfaghari tribe in the northwest rigged the election of two pro-Mossadegh deputies; Zahedi arrested the chiefs for using "undue force" on the voters. Moral: nobody in Iran save Fazlollah Zahedi is allowed to use undue force on voters.[92]

Even Kashani came out against the government, declaring that the government did not have the support of the people and protesting against the rigging of the elections and the official censorship that accompanied the voting.[93]

The crucial elections for Teheran's twelve deputies came last. Nationalists published the following list of candidates: Ahmad Razavi, Abdollah Mo'azzami, Allahyar Saleh, S. Ali Shayegan, Kazem Hasibi, Mohammad-Ali Angaji, Mahmud Nariman, Karim Sanjabi, S. Baqer Jalali Musavi, Asghar Parsa, Ahmad Akhgar, Ahmad Zirakzadeh. Angaji and Jalali Musavi were clerics. In March the NRM put all its efforts into the electoral campaign of these men, of whom some were in hiding. It produced a letter bearing the signatures of its leading members to protest against the lack of democratic freedom surrounding the elections. To distribute the letter among the people of Teheran, at one point Bazargan and Bakhtiar had to take a taxi and drive around Teheran, throwing copies out of the windows and speaking in French to conceal their identity and purpose from the driver.[94] This episode shows how weak the organizational capacities of the NRM were: whatever sympathy it may have commanded in the population, it could not rely on a vast network of activists.

The elections were held on March 9 and 10. Bazargan himself led a group of about 2,000 voters in the direction of the Sepahsalar Mosque.[95] But there and elsewhere in the city security forces, *chaqukesh* bands led by Sha'ban Ja'fari, and members of fascist parties (for example the

---

[91]Ibid., pp. 46–47, 65.
[92]*Time*, February 15, 1954, p. 27.
[93]*Le Monde*, February 20, 1954, p. 3.
[94]Shapur Bakhtiar, personal interview, Suresnes, August 19, 1983.
[95]*Hadis*, p. 103.

pro-Nazi SUMKA) combined to prevent suspected Nationalists from casting their ballots. The NRM publicized the irregularities widely and gave detailed accounts of events at all major polling stations.[96] The *New York Times* also covered the elections extensively, wrapping up its report with the following anecdote: A voter, after doing his electoral duty, bowed three times in the direction of the ballot box. When asked why, he said: "I am merely making my obeisance to the magic box. When one drops in a ballot for Mohammad [Mosaddeq], lo, when the ballot is opened it is transformed into a vote for Fazlollah" [Zahedi].[97]

After the elections the NRM published a short statement about its activities, and declared that "his Majesty the Shah has transgressed his constitutional powers by deposing Dr. Mosaddeq as prime minister."[98] The wide coverage that the NRM gave to the rigging of the election to the eighteenth Majles ultimately did not achieve much. Even a slate of candidates led by Mozaffar Baqa'i and supported by Kashani was barely tolerated by Zahedi, and in Teheran all twelve pro-Shah candidates were declared elected. They were led by Ja'far Behbahani, a nephew of the pro-court Ay. Behbahani. As a nod to civil society, the government also gave a Teheran seat to Mohammad Derakhshesh, the chairman of the Teachers Association. In spite of the NRM's failure to change the course of events, its vigilance contributed to the regime's failure to legitimize itself through elections.

The NRM and the 1954 Oil Agreement

In the spring of 1954, the Iranian government began negotiations concerning a new oil agreement with Western companies. The NRM publicized these efforts, and lost no time denouncing Zahedi for intending to go back on Mosaddeq's nationalization. On May 19 (Ordibehesht 29) the NRM sent a letter to the Iranian negotiators, including Ali Amini, warning them not to accept a mission that would force them to sign an agreement that opposed the spirit of the nationalization.[99]

Before the 1954 oil agreement was submitted to the newly "elected" parliament, an open letter bearing the signature of more than seventy public figures was sent to the Majles, asking it not to ratify the agreement. Among the signatories were such NRM leaders as Ay. Zanjani, Bazargan, Mo'azzami (who initiated the move), Ata'i, Y. Sahabi, but also many nonmembers. Of these, the most famous were Khalil Maleki; Ay. Firuzabadi, a prominent cleric, former member of

---

[96]Ibid., pp. 75–84.
[97]*New York Times*, March 12, 1954, p. 2.
[98]*Hadis*, p. 114.
[99]Ibid., p. 155.

parliament, and philanthropist; and Ali-Akbar Dehkhoda, Iran's leading man of letters at the time. The group included twelve university professors, who were then suspended from the university: the prime minister had told the president of Teheran University to fire professors who "took money from the government and then attacked it."[100] To earn a living, eleven of them, including Bazargan, founded a company which they called Yad, the Persian acronym for "eleven university professors." The private sector thus provided a safe space for many top NRM activists in which to survive materially.

The End of the NRM

On July 21, 1954 (Tir 30, 1333), the NRM had planned to organize wide demonstrations to commemorate the day Mosaddeq had swept back to power in 1952. These demonstrations failed, and the NRM later blamed insufficient secrecy and its weak organizational structure for the failure.[101]

On November 10, 1954 (Aban 19, 1333), Hosein Fatemi, Mosaddeq's foreign minister and arguably the most radical of Iranian leaders under the rule of the Nationalists, was executed. The NRM widely publicized first his arrest (during which he had been stabbed by a *chaqukesh*), and then his travails in prison, and finally his final speech which he gave to a group of army officers.[102]

In April 1955 Hosein Ala' replaced General Zahedi as prime minister. He held negotiations with some Nationalist leaders, and reportedly offered the Ministry of Justice to Allahyar Saleh, the leader of the Iran party. The NRM had always stated that the participation of Nationalists in any unelected government would be an admission of defeat,[103] and it now set out to prevent a rapprochement between the Nationalist leadership and Ala'. Its party paper published an article titled "The Danger Threatening Us," warning that the foreign masters of the country wanted to entice Iranians to cooperate with the regime by substituting new goals for the Nationalist demands: a fight against corruption instead of a fight against foreign domination, redistribution of wealth and land reform instead of democratic freedoms, and an increase in living standards instead of popular sovereignty.[104] Nothing came of the new prime minister's scheme. The NRM claimed the credit of having thwarted his efforts thus saving the honor of the Nationalists,[105]

[100]*Safehat*, 5, p. 102.
[101]Ibid., p. 282.
[102]*Hadis*, pp. 331–35.
[103]*Safehat*, 5, p. 49.
[104]Ibid., p. 129.
[105]Ibid., p. 289.

but it is difficult to say to what extent it was the sharp warning of the NRM that deterred Saleh and other Nationalists from cooperating with the Shah's prime minister.

Perhaps as a result of the foregoing events, Bazargan was arrested in the spring of 1955 for the first time, only a few months after having been reinstated in his position at Teheran University in September 1954, the beginning of the academic year. Ezzatollah Sahabi was arrested too, and they were kept in jail for five months, during which Bazargan wrote a book called *Love and Adoration, or the Thermodynamics of Man*, in which he set out to prove the importance of love. He also came to the conclusion that after 2,500 years of despotism, Iranians had lost the capacity to work together. Therefore, before any meaningful political action could be attempted, it was necessary to educate Iranians for democracy by teaching them to practice tolerance, compromise, and cooperation. These thoughts later became the material for a talk he gave at the Muslim Student Association of the Faculty of Agriculture in Karaj. He was released from prison just as the new academic year began, and was teaching again in the autumn of 1955.[106] When they were freed, Bazargan and E. Sahabi found that the IP had left the NRM, and that from among the top-level organizers of the NRM only Rahim Ata'i and Yadollah Sahabi were left.[107]

By now the security apparatus of the Shah regime had become more and more efficient (SAVAK, the secret police, was founded in 1957), and it became increasingly difficult to engage in any sort of activity against the dictatorship. The last important acts of the NRM were the dissemination, in 1957, of two long open letters. The first commented on the change in Iran's Constitution in 1957,[108] the other was based on foreign press reports and was a reflection upon the economic and political consequences of the 1954 oil agreement.[109] Both letters were written by Hasan Nazih, and apparently caused a certain amount of displeasure among the country's ruling circles.[110]

In 1957 the Mashad branch of the NRM was discovered. Mohammad-Taqi Shariati, his son Ali Shariati, Taher Ahmadzadeh, and the eleven other members of the Khorasan provincial committee of the NRM were arrested, brought to Teheran, and jailed in the capital. According to Ay.

[106]This account of Bazargan's personal trajectory after the coup is based on his *Modafe'at*, pp. 148–64.

[107]E. Sahabi, as quoted in Hariri, *Mosahebeh*, p. 175.

[108]See Mozafari, *L'Iran*, p. 82.

[109]On this agreement see Katouzian, *Political Economy*, p. 202. For an exhaustive treatment see Chamseddine Amiralai, *Les Régimes politiques et le consortium du pétrole en Iran (1953–1962)* (1963), pp. 89–126.

[110]Khalil Maleki had written a similar letter. See H. Katouzian's introduction to Maleki, *Khaterat*, p. 122.

Reza Zanjani, the pressures exerted on the arrested Mashad activists led to the uncovering of the Teheran organization.[111] In 1957 Taleqani, Zanjani, Bazargan, E. Sahabi, Y. Sahabi, R. Ata'i, and some others were arrested. This meant the definite end of the NRM as an active resistance force against the Shah. The top leadership of the NRM were imprisoned for eight months. The harshness with which the regime treated its Nationalist prisoners was so unprecedented in recent times that even the pro-court member of parliament S. Ja'far Behbahani questioned the prime minister, Manuchehr Eqbal, about it in parliament. Eqbal replied that "these people in Teheran and Mashad have again followed Mosaddeq's thesis."[112] The regime thus effectively crushed the NRM in 1957.

The prisoners were freed eight months after their arrest. The NRM no longer had any public activity, but its leaders still met informally. The liberalization of the early 1960s allowed them and other Nationalists to broaden the scope of their political activity.

In conclusion, it can safely be said that in spite of the occasional participation of certain secular elements, the NRM was essentially a movement of religious Mosaddeqists. At this stage of Iran's history, however, the leaders of the National Resistance Movement kept religion and politics apart. While their action may or may not have been religiously motivated, they did not attempt to give any explicitly religious content to it. The beliefs of its principal leaders notwithstanding, the NRM's main function was to keep alive Nationalism, not to advance Islam. Their Islamic activism had been motivated by their fear of communist and Baha'i inroads into Iranian youth, and this religious activism gradually converged with their political involvement in the National Movement to produce the LMI.

In terms of our scheme of chapter 1, the crisis of sovereignty of 1953 propelled a new group of men into political action, people who had been socially concerned and active but who by and large had remained outside politics. Their political aims were more radical than those of their predecessors in the National Movement. These aims would lead to tension and mistrust between the two groups, as we shall see in the next chapter.

[111]See his interview in Hariri, *Mosahebeh*, p. 273.
[112]*Keyhan*, September 29, 1957 (Mehr 7, 1336).

CHAPTER 4

The Liberalization of the Early 1960s

After they regained their freedom, the erstwhile NRM activists, like other Nationalists, looked for ways to end the post-1953 dictatorship. The hope that the Shah's regime might be only an unpleasant interlude was not absurd, for at that point it was only four years old. The leader of the National Movement, Mosaddeq, who had lost a considerable amount of support before the coup, regained his popularity after his courageous defense during his trial of 1953.[1]

Since the regime was well entrenched, two possibilities suggested themselves. One was for Nationalists to start some sort of rapprochement with liberal elements within the regime. It must be remembered that Mosaddeq had had internal enemies, that the Shah regime was not quite monolithic between 1953 and 1963, and that therefore some politicians played roles of their own. This path to liberalization, however, proved to be unfeasible. For one thing, the Shah did not allow any independent figure to develop enough initiative to help bring about such a scenario. The other reason was that for most Nationalists the Shah and many of his lieutenants were little more than foreign agents. Under such circumstances, compromise was extremely difficult.

The alternative path to liberalization followed from this view of the situation. Since the Shah regime was seen by Nationalist opinion as entirely foreign-based, Nationalists were convinced that any change in the degree of repression could come about only as a result of U.S. pressure. American attitudes toward the Shah regime were of crucial importance to the Nationalists. The more moderate elements, such as

[1]Richard W. Cottam, *Nationalism in Iran* (1978), p. 288.

the Iran party, hoped to convey the message to the U.S. government that the Nationalists would not necessarily threaten the vital interests of America. The more radical former NRM members, by contrast, hoped that U.S. pressures on the Shah to liberalize his regime could be used to block a retreat into a more dictatorial stance and that the climate of liberty thus created could be used to wrest a true democratization from the regime.

Whatever the strategy, Nationalists were paradoxically hampered by the fact that Mosaddeq was still alive. No Nationalist leader could speak for the National Movement and be accepted by all Nationalists. Mosaddeq himself was in jail until 1956, and then under house arrest at his estate in Ahmadabad until his death in 1967. Communication with him was therefore difficult and sporadic; this explains why part of the argument between moderates and radicals was about who really represented Mosaddeq's thought.

Nationalist activity surfaced again in 1960–63, while the Shah attempted to liberalize his regime. Usually the Kennedy administration is credited with this liberalization, during which the LMI constituted itself. If we look carefully, however, we find that in the United States signs of impatience with the Shah were already visible as early as 1956.

American Dissatisfaction

The immediate reason for U.S. disenchantment with the Shah's post-1953 regime was its incapacity to improve the country's economy and to alleviate social tensions.

When the 1953 coup occurred, Iran's treasury was empty. This crisis was largely due to the international boycott imposed on Iranian oil by Britain after the Iranian oil industry had been nationalized by Mosaddeq. To keep the country afloat, the U.S. government gave generous help to Iran, help that did not achieve the desired results. This failure led to a series of hearings in the U.S. House of Representatives in mid-1956.[2] The resulting report, published in January 1957, showed that the United States had given Iran about a quarter of a billion dollars between 1951 and 1956, that the "aid and technical-assistance programs in Iran . . . were administered in a loose, slipshod, and unbusinesslike manner," and that "Iranian budget deficits increased rather than decreased during this period."[3] But on the whole the report was more critical of the way U.S. organizations had handled the aid,

[2] U.S. Congress, House Committee on Government Operations, *United States Aid Operations in Iran* (1957).
[3] Ibid., pp. 3–5.

and it abstained from any criticism of the Shah himself. Moreover, the criticisms addressed to the Iranian government centered on its technical incompetence rather than on its dictatorial nature.

When in early 1958 the chief of Iran's Army Intelligence, General Valiollah Qarani, was arrested on charges of having planned a coup, and when he was condemned to only three years, the light punishment led many to believe that he had enjoyed at least some American support. In the U.S. Senate, William Fulbright, John F. Kennedy, and others were critical of the Republican administration's attitude toward corrupt Third World regimes in general and the Shah's in particular.[4] The government in Iran was as corrupt as ever, and Prime Minister Eqbal's much-fanfared attempts at combating corruption in high places quickly became a public joke. At the same time the general economic situation was deteriorating. There were widespread strikes, prominent Bazaar leaders were facing bankruptcy, and there was a pervasive perception, both inside and outside Iran, that the Shah's regime was faltering. The recent revolutions in Cuba and Iraq, where corrupt pro-Western regimes had been replaced by increasingly pro-Soviet ones, added to Western anxiety. On December 14, 1959, President Eisenhower, during a six-hour visit to Teheran, warned Iran's leaders that "military strength alone will not bring about peace and justice."[5] When John F. Kennedy became president, his administration applied to Iran a version of its Alliance for Progress policy, urging reform from above buttressed by military might.[6]

Eager to show his commitment to democracy, the Shah, who wrote in his autobiography that he would never establish a one-party system since that was what the communists and Hitler had done,[7] had encouraged the formation of two parties. One, the Melliyun, or "Nationalist" party, was led by Eqbal, the other Mardom, or "People's" party, was led by Asadollah Alam and constituted what was termed the "pseudo-opposition" in chapter 1. Both Eqbal and Alam were trusted and loyal friends of the Shah. These two parties were to contest the elections to the twentieth Majles, scheduled for the summer of 1960, and which the Shah promised to be free. Coming in the wake of Eisenhower's warning and Kennedy's criticisms in the Senate, the Shah's promise of free elections was interpreted by the opposition as resulting from American pressure. This emboldened the Nationalists to start organizing again.

---

[4]Homa Katouzian, *The Political Economy of Modern Iran* (1981), p. 213.

[5]Quoted in James A. Bill, *The Eagle and the Lion: The Tragedy of American-Iranian Relations* (1988), p. 120.

[6]Ibid., pp. 132ff.

[7]His Imperial Majesty Mohammed Reza Shah Pahlavi, Shahanshah of Iran, *Mission for My Country* (1960), p. 173.

The Second National Front

On the whole the Nationalists had weathered the post-1953 regime much better than the Tudeh, which by the early 1960s was a mere shadow of its former self.[8] The Nationalists' renewed activism led to the founding of the Second National Front. The animators of the old NRM saw themselves as part of the National Front, therefore a discussion of the reasons why its leaders decided to found the LMI must deal with the internal workings of the National Front too.

Revival of the National Front

The events leading to the reconstitution of the National Front in 1960 are a matter of disagreement. According to an LMI source, the initiative came from NRM leaders who had been freed from prison. Having concluded that the Shah wanted to defuse mounting tensions in Iranian society by opening up the political system, the NRM leaders decided to take the initiative in reconstituting the National Front. Small teams of NRM activists contacted leading Nationalist figures. When it transpired that the majority of those approached favored a new beginning, the Executive Committee of the NRM decided to invite all those whose response had been positive to come together to deliberate on an action plan. The invitation went out in the name of Ay. H. S. Reza Firuzabadi, and was convened at the house of his son.

Before this invitation went out, however, Saleh seized the initiative, and invited many leading collaborators of Mosaddeq to his house for a meeting. He did not include any of the former NRM figures. Not content with this snub, Saleh then published, with a few changes, a draft-declaration on the future of the National Movement (prepared by the NRM and submitted to him for his comments) as his own declaration. Upon the intervention of common friends, however, Bazargan and Taleqani were invited to join the Central Group that met regularly at the house of Saleh. This group eventually constituted itself as the High Council of the National Front.[9]

Gholamhosein Sadiqi tells a different story. According to him, leading collaborators of Mosaddeq, including Saleh, Sadiqi himself, Mo'azzami,

[8]The reasons for this decline were many and not only due to government repression. See Ervand Abrahamian, *Iran between Two Revolutions* (1982), pp. 451–57.

[9]One LMI source indicates that Saleh had at first been unenthusiastic about the NRM's plans, but changed his mind after a meeting with the U.S. ambassador. See *Chegunegi-ye tashkil-e jebhe-ye melli-ye dovvom va naqsh-e nehzat-e moqavemat-e melli-ye Iran* (How the Second National Front was founded and the role of the National Resistance Movement) (1977), p. 11. The veracity of this could not be ascertained independently, and Saleh died in 1981 and cannot give his side of the story.

and Kazemi had begun meeting regularly in the autumn of 1956 (Azar 1335). Later they were joined by a few others, including Bazargan, Haqshenas, and Ali-Akbar Akhavi. In mid-June 1960, Dariush Foruhar went to see Sadiqi and proposed the revival of the NF. Sadiqi made his participation in the enterprise contingent on Saleh's agreement, which Foruhar obtained on a visit to Kashan.

Sadiqi then convened a meeting of all those who had been participating in the meetings of the late 1950s plus a few others, and on July 13 (Tir 22) all eighteen of them met in Sadiqi's house and revived the National Front. One week later, on July 20, the same group was joined by Saleh, who had come back from Kashan, and a few others, and the reconstitution of the National Front, NF (II), was officially announced.[10]

Meanwhile, preparations went ahead for the elections. The Nationalists named a five-member committee, of which Bazargan was a member, to coordinate the National Front's participation in the elections. The committee campaigned for free elections, but Teheran's two major newspapers, *Keyhan* and *Ettela'at*, refused to print any of its declarations. Exasperated, the Nationalists mandated a delegation of five members, which included Bakhtiar, Bazargan, Kazemi, Keshavarz Sadr, and Sadiqi, to meet with the minister of the interior, R. Atabaki, to ask for assurances that the NF (II) would be allowed to participate in the elections. The leadership of the National Front had wanted this meeting to be discreet, but NRM militants nevertheless mounted a small demonstration outside the ministry while the NF delegation was inside, causing the leadership to take umbrage. Atabaki had been very courteous and promised a reply to the NF's request, but an answer never came. Worse, Prime Minister Eqbal said in one of his speeches that the elections would indeed be free, but not for Mosaddeqists.

According to the LMI source, the NRM activists convened a public meeting for July 20 (Tir 29, 1339), even though the NF leadership would have preferred a smaller, more discreet gathering. The meeting took place at the house of the younger Firuzabadi.[11] The next evening another meeting was held at the same place, and Hasan Nazih read a declaration officially announcing the reconstitution of the National Front. All sources agree that on the eighth anniversary of the uprising that restored Mosaddeq to the premiership, amid the cheers and outpourings of joy of everybody present, the Second National Front was born. The rebirth of the National Front thus coincided with the elections to the twentieth Majles.

[10]Personal communication, December 1987.
[11]*Chegunegi*, pp. 19–20.

The Summer Elections of 1960

After the unsuccessful demarche at the Ministry of the Interior, the National Front decided that it could only boycott the elections. After many postponements, balloting finally began in the provinces on July 26, and by August 12, when the last results came in, the prime minister's Melliyun party had obtained 104 seats, and the "opposition" Mardom party won about 25. But two provincial towns had not voted: Kashan, where the IP's leader Allahyar Saleh was running, and Kerman, where Mozaffar Baqa'i was a candidate. Certain elements within the government wanted to co-opt the Nationalists, and the prospect of a parliamentary mandate from Kashan was perhaps meant as an incentive for Saleh to join the system. Baqa'i, for his part, contributed with his characteristically vitriolic style to a general heightening of the temperature of the campaign, ultimately forcing even the leader of the pseudo-opposition, Alam, to denounce the irregularities of the elections.

In Teheran a group of independent candidates under the leadership of Amini were also contesting the elections. As they were untainted by any recent association with Mosaddeq, the government allowed them greater leeway, and thus their campaign quickly gathered momentum, so much so that it seemed as if Amini and his followers were becoming a more dynamic force in Iranian politics than the NF. To be sure, Amini did not have the popular backing that the Nationalists could count on, but on the other hand he had a well-defined political program of reforms, which the Nationalists lacked. Thus in Teheran the elections quickly turned into a duel between Eqbal and Amini, who accused the prime minister of betraying the Shah's wishes by allowing so many flagrant irregularities.

The Shah had invited the foreign press to cover his free elections. When it became clear that nobody inside or outside Iran believed this emerging *chambre introuvable* to be representative of the Iranian people, the balloting in Teheran was halted and the Shah advised all already elected members of parliament to resign, so as to pave the way for fresh elections. Eqbal himself resigned as prime minister on August 27, 1960 (Shahrivar 5, 1339), and was replaced by Ja'far Sharif-Emami, a Swedish-trained engineer and fellow member of Bazargan in the Engineers Association.

Internal Conflict in the Second National Front

One day after the July 21 meeting that saw the resurrection of the NF, another one was held at the same place, but it was broken up by SAVAK.

The meetings then moved to the house of Abbas Sheibani, a young NRM activist. After these were in turn stopped, they moved to the house of H. Abolhasan Lebaschi, a Bazaar leader. These meetings were arranged and organized by NF activists who had been members of the NRM. The latter, now that the National Front existed, had no official existence of its own, but former NRM activists formed a well-organized network within the National Front and operated as a current within it, a current calling itself *nehzat*, or "movement." The moderate leadership of the National Front resented their initiatives and with few exceptions did not attend the meetings.

After the annulment of the summer elections and the opening up of the political system that ensued, factions hardened inside the National Front, with two clearly distinguishable wings confronting each other on several issues. Among the people on one side were those who would in 1961 found the Liberation Movement of Iran. The issues that arose in 1960 are relevant to an understanding of the emergence of the LMI. They remained unresolved, contributing to the ultimate failure of the Second National Front. But before considering these issues, let us turn to the composition of the National Front's High Council. It consisted of a number of former collaborators of Mosaddeq without a party affiliation, such as Baqer Kazemi, Gholamhosein Sadiqi, Nosratollah Amini, and Keshavarz Sadr; members of the Iran Party, such as Allahyar Saleh, Shapur Bakhtiar, Karim Sanjabi, and Baqer Kazemi, who acted as chairman; H. Mahmud Manian and H. Hasan Qasemieh representing the Bazaar; four leaders of the former NRM, namely Nazih, Bazargan, Y. Sahabi, and Taleqani; Dariush Foruhar of the PIN and Hosein Razi of the PIP; plus Khonji and Hejazi, the dissident socialists. Khalil Maleki's membership in the High Council and that of his party in the National Front were met with resistance, especially from Shapur Bakhtiar.[12] Most other members were not very prominent and owed their membership in the NF's ruling body to their friendship with one or another of members just listed. The total membership of the body reached thirty-six at its peak. Within the High Council the rule of unanimity prevailed, which made the simplest decisions, such as the wording of a declaration, difficult to reach.[13] Moreover, representatives of political parties were vastly outnumbered by "independent personalities." This had a certain bearing on the issues that divided the National Front.

The first bone of contention was the National Front's very structure.

[12]Bakhtiar confirmed this, but preferred not to give the reason for it. Personal interview, Suresnes, August 19, 1983.

[13]Homa Katouzian's introduction to Khalil Maleki, *Khaterat-e siasi* (Political memoirs) (1979), p. 135.

The Iran Party, the "independent personalities," and Khonji wanted a unified party. In the autumn of 1960 Khonji circulated a paper in which he demanded the self-dissolution of all parties in the NF. To give an example, he announced the dissolution of his own "Socialist party," which he had apparently created for the sole purpose of dissolving it to prove his commitment to a unitary structure. Khonji's plans were opposed by the PIN; some of the PIP; the socialists led by Maleki, who hoped to be admitted into the NF; and, after May 1961, the LMI.

The second issue concerned the strategy of the NF. The radical wing proposed mass mobilization to block any retreat of the Shah, while the elder statesmen preferred behind-the-scenes maneuvering and discreet talks with the Shah, hoping that American pressure would induce him to turn to them.

The third issue was linked to the second and had to do with the Shah himself. The radicals wished to single him out as the root of Iran's troubles and include him and his role in all discussions, whereas the leadership of the NF addressed their attacks to various government bodies.

Organizationally the radical wing of the NF (II) consisted of the former NRM activists, the PIN,[14] and the students, who formed the Student Organization of the National Front when the academic year 1960–61 (1339–40) began in the autumn of 1960 and students returned to campuses and high schools. The majority of student leaders were secular-minded; they admired Bazargan and the NRM/LMI for their courage and dynamism, but most had no taste for their religious tendencies. The Student Organization itself, however, was pluralistic. The radicals of the NF also enjoyed the sympathy of the majority of the lower-level activists. It should be pointed out, however, that as the conflict inside the NF smoldered under the surface, both sides took care not to let the public know about it.

After the National Front's new incarnation had been made public and the houses of individual members had become inadequate to contain the ever-increasing numbers of sympathizers who attended meetings, the radical current within the NF decided to hold its first public but unofficial meeting at a corner of Jalalieh Field, an open tract of land in Teheran's northwest mainly used for horse racing and polo. This gathering, held on August 17, 1960 (Mordad 26, 1339), was the first public gathering of Nationalists after the 1953 coup. The NF's leadership had been skeptical about its opportuneness, and to assuage

---

[14]In 1961 the Party of the Iranian Nation held a congress that eliminated the term *Pan-Iranism* from the party program and also did away with the fascistoid trappings of the organization. Yet a certain element of style inherited from pre–World War II fascism would always remain.

their feelings the meeting was officially held by the "Student Supporters of the National Front," consisting in the main of NRM supporters
and followers of Dariush Foruhar's PIN. None of the Nationalist
leaders attended.

The major organizer of the meeting was Abbas Sheibani, and roughly 3,000 people came. Three speeches were given, a poem was read,
and the meeting ended with a declaration demanding the annulment
of the summer elections.

The relative success of this meeting emboldened its organizers but
irritated the NF leadership, who sensed that the initiative was slipping
away from them. The students wanted to organize another, bigger
meeting on Baharestan Square, in front of the Majles. Leaflets distributed all over Teheran announced the meeting for September 1 (Shahrivar
10). The NF leadership again opposed the meeting, and the government declared that it would not tolerate it. The organizers backed
down and instead announced a meeting for September 4 (Shahrivar
13), again at Jalalieh Field. Security forces sealed off the area and thus
the proposed meeting degenerated into antigovernment demonstrations that lasted the whole day. A few weeks later another meeting was
convened at the Hedayat Mosque, but on that evening Taleqani was
prevented from entering his mosque by government forces. New
demonstrations were the result. These demonstrations, the biggest in
Iran since the coup, received widespread coverage outside the country.
One of the consequences was the beginning of Nationalist activities
abroad.

After the summer elections were canceled and Sharif-Emami became
prime minister, Teheran calmed down somewhat. The NF was still very
cautious in its approach. On the one hand it had always asked for "free
elections," since that was all the diverse groupings within it could
agree on, and on the other hand it was incapable of pulling itself
together. It could not even come up with a nationwide list of candidates. In November John F. Kennedy was elected president of the
United States, and that event raised hopes in Iran that his administration would exert enough pressure on the Shah to lead Nationalists to
power.

All this time the radical wing's impatience with the leadership grew.
Ultimately, the former NRM activists were led to write a letter to the
High Council. The letter, dated November 15, 1960 (Aban 24, 1339),
was accompanied by a lengthy paper analyzing the international situa-
tion and its bearing on the domestic policies of Iran, written by Rahim
Ata'i.[15] The two texts are fundamental to an understanding of the

[15]Both are reprinted in *Chegunegi,* pp. 39–69.

reasons that led the former NRM members to constitute themselves as a party a few months later.

The letter claimed that the leadership of the NF was weak, had an insufficient understanding of political matters, and was out of touch with reality and the wishes of the people. To make up for these deficiencies the former NRM members had tried to organize mass meetings and to bring about changes in the leadership structure of the NF, but on that last point nothing had been achieved. So far the former NRM leaders had refused to act independently of personalities who, because of their past association with Mosaddeq, had a good reputation among the population. But since the last successful meeting at Jalalieh Field two months had passed and still the High Council had shown no initiative. Apologizing for its frankness, the NRM outlined a plan of action.

The paper lamented that "the Salehs, Kazemis, Sanjabis, and Sadiqis" became active only when foreign newspapers began to criticize the Iranian regime, when the Shah promised free elections, and after the likes of Baqa'i and Makki had come out of their holes too. Neither the Nationalists nor the Shah had responded adequately to the pressures from abroad. The Shah did not realize that foreign pressure to liberalize his regime was meant precisely to *save* his throne; thus, by suppressing the NF he was acting against his best interests. The Nationalists, for their part, did not realize how serious foreign interests were about the liberalization and therefore did not take full advantage of it. A stalemate had ensued.

The paper then analyzed the world situation and concluded that everywhere in the underdeveloped world people were seeking revenge against those responsible for their plight. Communism was waiting precisely for that, and its danger had decreased only in those countries (Egypt, Iraq, Syria) where revolutionary governments had been able to satisfy the people's thirst for justice. If the leaders of the NF could not provide the necessary leadership for a similar development to take place in Iran, they should step aside and save Iran from either falling victim to communism, to which people would turn if the Nationalists failed, or remaining under the rule of colonialism.

The paper claimed that alone in the National Movement the *nehzat* or "movement" had a concrete program. Its goals were threefold: to preserve Iran's interests, to eliminate the danger of an upset in East-West relations and prevent Iran from taking up communism, and to make sure that Iran played its part in world politics and contributed to world peace. The NF leadership was asked not to impair these efforts and to allow them to be carried out in good understanding with the West, to put aside their overcautiousness and doubts, and forcefully to enter the forefront of the political stage. The paper further argued that Nationalists lacked the capacity to carry out a military coup, but that if any sign of unrest should emerge in the army, and if it were led by honorable men, Nationalists should seek to strengthen it. The authors were in favor of lawful and open political struggle, but that excluded any flirtation with the regime. The truth should be said aloud: when the Shah called Nationalists traitors, their answer should be that the traitor was he who had taken the rights of the people away from them, had deprived them of the right to choose their deputies and their government, and had wasted the national income in ways dictated by foreign interests.

The paper then proposed a minimal action program, drawn up "with due regard for the leadership's state of mind and capacities." The National Front should

1. Get a permanent locale and put up a sign.
2. Protest against the delay of the elections in an open letter, with meetings and sit-ins.
3. Ask for a permit to print a newspaper, and to proceed to publish it.
4. Recommence electoral meetings at the homes of prominent members.
5. Draw up a list of 200 parliamentary candidates and an electoral program.
6. Hold press conferences.
7. Hold electoral meetings.
8. Arrange for all leaders to travel to the provinces and present the candidates.
9. Take good care of and provide a livelihood for the victims of repression.
10. Establish contacts with the representatives of foreign powers to remove their doubts and provide them with the National Movement's program.
11. Encourage structured groups to take a bigger part in [the National Front's] executive affairs.
12. Oblige every member of the High Council to accept the responsibility of directing one student, worker, or local group, so as to get acquainted with [the activist base].

The paper ended by noting that all twelve articles were within the realm of the law. If the government were to use force against its implementation, strikes, demonstrations, and meetings should be organized in response. If these were stopped by the regime, bolder methods would have to be used.

In these two texts one is struck by the total absence of any reference to religion. This is one more proof that religious motivations did not play a major role for all founders of the LMI. The two texts also reflect the former NRM activists' impatience with the disproportionate influence of the "independent personalities" within the NF.

The letter did not please the NF leadership at all, and elicited a sharp reply from Sanjabi. On at least one point, however, the radicals gained, for the National Front moved into a house at 143 Fakhrabad Avenue, although most meetings there were broken up by *chaqukesh* elements.[16]

With Bazargan and his friends still members of the High Council, but the rank and file of the old NRM and the students ever more thirsty for action, the campaign began again for the second elections to the twentieth Majles, elections known as the winter elections of 1961.

The Winter Elections of 1961

The election campaign started toward the end of 1960. Conditions were hardly better than in the previous round. After the annulment of the summer elections, Amini and Baqa'i had become very active, both developing more dynamism than the NF could muster. This was due partly to the asthenic nature of the Nationalist leadership, and partly to the fact that Amini and Baqa'i were less objectionable to the regime, having both distanced themselves from Mosaddeq. The Nationalists boycotted the elections, mainly because they could not agree on a list of candidates, either for Teheran or the rest of the nation.

On January 30 (Bahman 10, 1340), 1961, the headquarters of the National Front was closed down by the police. At that point the NF leadership, exasperated, decided to attract attention with a sit-in in the Senate building. The delegation, including, among others, Kazemi, Keshavarz Sadr, Hasibi, Sadiqi, and Bazargan, was received with courtesy by two elder statesmen of the regime, Hasan Taqizadeh and Sardar Fakher Hekmat. The Nationalists were treated well, but the government forbade them to leave, and thus while the election campaign raged in Teheran, a good part of the Nationalist leadership was imprisoned in the Senate, whose reading room had been converted into a dormitory. They were not allowed to leave until the Teheran elections were over.[17]

During this time the students of the National Front also intensified their activities, culminating in serious rioting when Eqbal visited Teheran University on February 23 (Esfand 4): his car was set on fire and completely destroyed, and he himself was threatened. The burning of Eqbal's car had a tremendous impact on the populace and was seen as a major victory by the opposition. The government responded by closing the university until after the New Year recess (April 3,

---

[16]Bazargan, *Modafe'at*, p. 198.
[17]A full and instructive account of this episode is given in Bazargan, *Modafe'at*, pp. 198–201.

1961/Farvardin 14, 1340).[18] Meanwhile, on February 11 the Bazaar closed in response to a call for a general strike issued by the National Front.

With the National Front paralyzed, Amini seemed to benefit more and more from the disturbances. Iran's economic situation was worsening, and the new Kennedy administration made further U.S. aid contingent on the enactment of bold reforms. With the idea of reforms in the air, Amini had the advantage of a clear program, while the National Front's only program was "free elections" and the establishment of "the rule of law," points that were beginning to lose their mobilizing power.

When the election results were announced, the Melliyun party had obtained about 45 percent, and the Mardom party 35 percent of Majles seats, with the rest going to independents. In Teheran, pro-Amini independents had gained six out of fifteen seats, but Amini himself had not run. Nationalist candidates running individually, like Borumand in Isfahan, had been forcibly prevented from campaigning, with one exception: in Kashan, Saleh ran unopposed and was elected. After the Shah opened the new parliament on February 21, Saleh, knowing that his presence in the chamber could easily be construed as an act of complicity with the regime, gave a strong and courageous speech in which he denounced the irregularities of the elections. Student demonstrations continued, and the National Front made an ill-prepared and therefore unsuccessful attempt to close the Bazaar in a one-day general strike. To defuse the rising tide of dissatisfaction the Shah decided to depose all major security chiefs, including SAVAK's ambitious Teimur Bakhtiar, and make scapegoats out of them.[19]

The new parliament had a majority of conservative members of the old establishment, often big landowners, who were not likely to assent to any reform program the government might present under American pressure. The central issue became agrarian reform, and its most prominent proponent was Hasan Arsanjani, Amini's close associate. On March 29, 1961 (Farvardin 9, 1340), Ay. Borujerdi, the undisputed leader of Iran's Shi'ites who had opposed legislation for agrarian reform (discussed later), died and thus a major obstacle to the enactment of reforms was removed. The Shah had the alternative of either turning to the National Front or to Amini to carry out the reforms. He had a long talk with Allahyar Saleh, whose brother Jahanshah was loyal to the regime, but because of Saleh's intransigence on key points

---

[18]The chronological account can be found in *Keesing's Contemporary Archives* (London) (hereafter cited as *Keesing's*). April 1–8, 1961, p. 18012.

[19]Cottam, *Nationalism*, p. 302.

nothing came of the conference. Besides, the position of the National-ists on agrarian reform was not at all clear, as we will see.

On May 2 (Ordibehesht 12) the teachers of Teheran went on strike to demand higher salaries. During a demonstration outside the Majles the police opened fire on the strikers and killed one teacher. Embarrassed, Sharif-Emami resigned on May 4. On May 6 Prime Minister Amini presented his cabinet. The same month of May 1961 saw the birth of the LMI.

Political Action under the Sign of the Qoran

The radical former NRM elements within the NF felt that the struc-ture of the NF and its lack of dynamism impeded any meaningful action; they decided to form a party, which would be the continuation of the old NRM. According to Hasan Nazih[20] the object was at first to form an action group to demand free elections, which would have been called Nehzat-e azadi-ye entekhabat, Movement for Free Elections, but since that would have become a misnomer after elections, agreement was reached on Nehzat-e azadi-ye Iran, Movement for the Freedom of Iran.[21] But for Bazargan, Sahabi, and Taleqani, the aim was to form a party with an Islamic coloration. As Bazargan saw it,

> The National Front was, as its name indicated, a Front. That is a union of social philosophies and prominent personalities which had a common goal, namely the independence of the country and the freedom of the people. But having a common goal is not tantamount to having common motivations. One cannot expect that. Some may be motivated by national-ism, others by humanitarian feelings, race consciousness, or socialism. . . .
>
> However, for us, for many of our friends, and perhaps for a majority of the Iranian population, there could be no motivation other than the principles and religious tenets of Islam.
>
> I am not saying the others were not Muslims or that they were opposed to Islam. Only, for them Islam did not constitute a social and political ideology. But for us it was the basic motivation for our social and political activism.

Bazargan recalls that near the end of the summer of 1960, he

> went to Borqan . . . with Dr. Sahabi. In that verdant valley we talked about founding a party, something our friends, the young, and even our con-science were urging us to do. Three things were clear to us:

[20]Personal interview, Paris, July 1982.
[21]See the Introduction for a discussion of the party's name in English.

1. Under present conditions it was incumbent upon us to be politically active and to found a party.
2. The ideology and program of such a party would have to be based on Islam.
3. We had neither the talent, nor the time, nor the forcefulness to do it.

Seven or eight months went by in doubt and delay. Finally, at the end of 1339 [March 1961] our doubts ceased and we decided to found the Liberation Movement of Iran.[22]

Bazargan and Sahabi invited Taleqani to join them. In early May he performed a Qoranic bibliomancy and the result[23] encouraged him to answer Bazargan's call.[24] Joining a political party was a rather novel step for a mulla; Ay. Zanjani, for instance, did not join. At his trial in 1963 Taleqani explained his participation. To understand the reasoning it should be noted that *hezb* is the common Persian word for "political party." The same word *hizb* (in Arabic) is used in the Qoran and it usually is translated as "sect" or "party." After pointing out that groupings based on common beliefs are a more advanced form of social organization than those based on national, racial, linguistic, and geographic distinctions, Taleqani continued: "The Qoran is the first book and Islam the first system of beliefs that ignored racial, ethnic, geographic, and linguistic bonds and instead organized their primary grouping on the basis of belief. The word *hezb* was brought up and in the Qoran there is a sura called *Ahzab* [confederates]. The Prophet organized committed and believing people from Mecca and Yathrib . . . and the Qoran calls these people '*hezbollah*' [Party of God], while every adversary *hezb* that arose from reaction, ignorance, . . . was called '*hezb osh-sheitan*' [Party of Satan]."[25] Taleqani thus adroitly took advantage of one word's two meanings to legitimize his party by presenting it as an avatar of the original group of Muslim believers gathered around the

[22]Bazargan, *Modafe'at*, pp. 207–8.

[23]The Qoran opened on Sura al-Nisa'. Here is an excerpt relevant to Taleqani's decision: "Such believers as sit at home—unless they have an injury—are not the equals of those who struggle in the path of God with their possessions and their selves. God has preferred in rank those who struggle with their possessions and their selves over the ones who sit at home; yet to each God has promised the reward most fair; and God has preferred those who struggle over the ones who sit at home for the bounty of a mighty wage, in ranks standing before Him, forgiveness and mercy, surely God is All-forgiving, All-compassionate" (4:95).

[24]"Jarayan-e ta'sis-e nehzat-e azadi-ye Iran" (How the LMI was founded) in *Safehati az tarikh-e mo'aser-e Iran: Asnad-e nehzat-e azadi-ye Iran* (Some pages from contemporary Iranian history: The documents of the Liberation Movement of Iran), vol. 1 (1982), p. 48.

[25]Teleqani's full text can be found in B. Afrasiabi and S. Dehqan, *Taleqani* (1981), pp. 187–93.

Prophet. His use of the word *hezbollah* caught on, and after the revolution many a meeting of the LMI was broken up by ruffians calling themselves *hezbollahi*, a prime case of "unanticipated consequences."

These three versions of the LMI's founding show that from the very outset the new party's leadership and membership were not homogeneous, as key members were driven by different, although by no means mutually exclusive, motivations. What united them, then, was a radical stance vis-à-vis the Shah and, as we saw in chapter 2, a common background in the Bazaar.

The timing of the founding of the new party must be seen against developments in the religious sphere, for in May 1961 a large congress in Teheran brought together the Muslim Student Associations as well as Islamic associations of engineers, physicians, and teachers, Mohammad-Taqi Shariati's Mashad-based Center for the Propagation of Islamic Truth, and a few other groups (thirteen total). Ays. Shariatmadari and Milani sent delegations as well, and there were signs that the modernists and the *howzeh* might move toward greater cooperation.[26]

The LMI, however, which still considered itself part of the National Movement, would soon apply for membership in the National Front, and in a letter dated Ordibehesht 21, 1340 (May 11, 1961), Bazargan, in the name of the founding members of the new party, informed Mosaddeq of their initiative. The letter speaks of the founders as "believing" *(mo'men)* and invokes the help of God,[27] but is silent on the new party's ideology. In his reply of May 15 (Ordibehesht 25) the old man of Ahmadabad gave his blessing.

The LMI and Its Activities

The beginning of the LMI's short existence as a political party coincided with Ali Amini's tenure as prime minister.

Amini's Premiership

Ali Amini was a self-respecting politician who opposed dictatorship and corruption, and who was nonetheless pro-Western. A relative of Mosaddeq's, he had been minister of economic affairs in one of Mosaddeq's cabinets without being associated with the National Movement. He had later made many enemies in the Nationalist camp by putting his signature under the 1954 oil agreement.

[26]Mehdi Bazargan, *Enqelab-e eslami dar do harekat* (The Islamic revolution in two movements) (1984), pp. 18–21.
[27]"Jarayan," p. 4.

In a radio broadcast on May 8 Amini warned that Iran faced "economic poverty" because "vast resources [had] been squandered and financial laws ignored," and added that Iran's "financial and economic systems" were "at their last breath because incompetent and dishonest men in responsible positions [had] misused public funds and enriched themselves at the expense of the Treasury."[28]

As prime minister, Amini had to navigate a hazardous course between the Shah, who mistrusted him, the National Front, which was jealous of him, and the conservatives who dreaded his plans for land reform. He tried to appease the Nationalists by easing restrictions on their activities, and encouraged press freedom. Faced with a hostile parliament, he obtained the dissolution of both houses from the Shah on May 9, arguing that Iran could only have honest elections once the electoral laws had been rewritten.

His cabinet included some notable personalities. Mohammad Derakhshesh was named minister of education and ended the teachers' strike to the satisfaction of the strikers. Arsanjani was named minister of agriculture, but Amini decided to postpone action on agrarian reform until he had consolidated his position. The new prime minister moved against corruption by removing many generals from their positions as heads of state agencies. In so doing, he made many enemies. He then proceeded to stabilize Iran's balance of payments by restricting foreign travel and stopping the sale of foreign currency to importers of alcoholic beverages, cosmetics, electrical appliances, and other "luxury items."[29]

In the winter of 1961 the Amini government issued the first land reform decrees. But Amini's apparent successes did not earn him the gratitude of his monarch, as the very presence of an independent prime minister was perceived as a threat by the Shah. When in July 1962 (Tir 1341) a difference of opinion surfaced between the Shah and his prime minister over the military's budgetary allocation, Amini resigned and was replaced by Amir Asadollah Alam, a landed aristocrat.

The Founding of the LMI

The founders of the LMI numbered twelve: Bazargan, Taleqani, Yadollah Sahabi, Hasan Nazih, Mansur Ata'i, Rahim Ata'i, Abbas Radnia, Abbas Sami'i, Abbas Sheibani, Ezzatollah Sahabi, Ahmad Alibaba'i, and (probably) Ahmad Sadr Hajj-Seyyed-Javadi. All except the last two men have been discussed so far. Ahmad Alibaba'i, born in

---

[28]Quoted in *Keesing's*, May 27–June 3, 1961, p. 18117.
[29]For details see ibid., pp. 18117 and 18882.

1925 in Teheran, is a Bazaar merchant with a keen interest in religious affairs. Ahmad Sadr Hajj-Seyyed-Javadi, a lawyer, comes from a prominent Qazvin family long active in Nationalist politics. The highest echelon of the new party was its Executive Committee, which consisted of Bazargan, Taleqani, Y. Sahabi, and Rahim Ata'i.

Like that of the NF (II), the inaugural meeting of the LMI was held at the house of Sadeq Firuzabadi. It took place on May 17, 1961 (Ordibehesht 27, 1340), organized (and briefly addressed) by a young LMI member who was to reach a certain prominence during the Iranian revolution, Abbas Amir-Entezam.

Bazargan gave the first speech. He began by justifying the founding of yet another party. Iranians had become mistrustful of political parties for two reasons. First, the performance of parties had been deeply disappointing, and they had hitherto served mainly as vehicles for the personal ambition of individual politicians, and second, Iranians were too individualistic to cooperate. Still, this general disenchantment with political parties did not diminish the objective need for them, for if Iranians wanted to live and breathe freely they had to overcome their internal and external oppressors, and to achieve that, they had to organize. The concessions wrought by the NF from the government in recent months showed that if people organized they could contribute to change.

Bazargan went on to say that to found a party was not easy. The political arena was one of the toughest fields of action, and finding solutions and formulating alternative policies for pressing economic, cultural, administrative, and political problems was a mighty task. It also meant that one had to leave one's other occupations and be ready to go to prison periodically. Given all these obstacles and popular disenchantment with parties, one had a tendency to give up and mind one's own business. But one's conscience would not rest. The task was therefore arduous, but they planned to overcome the difficulties by trusting in God.

Bazargan added that he and his friends were not suggesting that the existing parties were bad. The other Nationalist parties were honorable and their leaders good people. But in their programs, methods, and record the majority of the population had not found a reflection of its beliefs and hopes, and some might find in the principles of the LMI a better answer to their convictions and yearnings. Therefore, the LMI was not setting up shop in opposition to the National Front but rather wished to be a constitutive member of it. If its membership was accepted, it would cooperate sincerely. If not, the LMI would manifest no hostility or grudge.

Finally, Bazargan summed up the four basic principles of the party.

Its members were Muslim, Iranian, adhered to the Constitution, and were Mosaddeqist:

1. We are Muslims, but not in the sense of considering prayers and fasting our only duties. Rather, our entry into politics and social activism was prompted by our national duty and religious obligations. We do not consider religion and politics separate, and regard serving the people . . . an act of worship. We recognize freedom as a primary divine gift and its achievement and keeping are for us an Islamic tradition and a hallmark of Shi'ism. We are Muslims in the sense that we believed in the principles of justice, equality, sincerity, and other social and humane duties before they were proclaimed by the French revolution and the Charter of the United Nations.

2. We are Iranians but do not claim that Iranians are superior to other peoples. Our love for Iran and our nationalism imply no racial fanaticism, and are on the contrary based on an acceptance of our own shortcomings and honoring of others' virtues and rights. We insist on our country's standing and independence but are not opposed to contacts with other nations, [as we live] in an [increasingly interdependent] world.

3. We respect the Iranian Constitution as an integral whole, and will not accept that its basic principles, namely the freedom of thought, press, and reunions, the independence of judges, the separation of powers, and finally honest elections be forgotten and sacrificed, whereas minor details and misinterpreted legal formalities occupy the major role, resulting in the abrogation of national sovereignty and the rule of law.

4. We are Mosaddeqists and regard Mosaddeq as one of the great servants of Iran and the East, but not such as he has been accused of out of stupidity and hindthought, where his school is presented as synonymous with lawlessness, the strengthening of communism, xenophobia, and the separation of Iran from the rest of the world. We honor Mosaddeq as the only head of government in Iran's history who was truly chosen and loved by the majority of the people, who acted in a direction desired by the people, enabling him to establish bonds between the rulers and the ruled and explain the true meaning of government and thus achieve the greatest success in Iran's recent history, namely the victory over colonialism.[30]

After Bazargan, Hasan Nazih gave a speech. In it he analyzed the current situation, noting that all of the LMI founders' predictions and warnings had come true and were now even admitted by the prime minister. He went on to quote regime members' rosy predictions and later admissions of defeat. The main reason for these repeated failures had been foreseen by Mosaddeq at his trial when he had said: "Even if billions of pounds and dollars are channelled to a ruling group that is not chosen by the people, not only will no ill be remedied, but poverty,

[30]"Jarayan," pp. 17–18.

debts, and the economic crisis will increase day by day." Nazih concluded that the best guarantee for the maintenance of the regime was an integral application of the Constitution, so that the people would choose their own government, as was the case in other monarchies, for example Sweden, England, Denmark, and Belgium.[31]

The seven members of the founding council (Bazargan, Taleqani, Y. Sahabi, Nazih, Mansur Ata'i, Rahim Ata'i, and Abbas Sami'i) then issued a formal declaration announcing the establishment of the LMI. Taleqani and Ay. Reza Zanjani issued statements of their own, although the latter did not join formally. The LMI also published its program that day; it is reproduced in Appendix A. Politically, the program was in line with the Nationalist demands for honest and constitutional government. In the realm of economics, the program reiterated the old Nationalist demand that oil revenues not be used to cover current expenditures, but rather to finance development projects. Significantly it did *not* call for agrarian reform. In view of the overall failure of the Shah's land reform, it would be tempting to attribute this to foresightedness. But the failure of the land reform was not necessarily predictable in 1961, and it is more probable that the LMI's reluctance to commit itself to sweeping changes in property relations reflected the fact that the conformity of such changes to Islamic laws was an unsettled question then. (A few months later, in October, Taleqani would attempt to clarify this thorny issue, as we shall see.) Also, the party was above all urban and Bazaar-based, which helps explain why agrarian questions were peripheral to its concerns. It should also be added that Mosaddeq himself had not advocated radical agrarian reform; instead during his tenure as prime minister a program was elaborated whereby landowners would have been required to pay 20 percent of their profits back to the village, half for the peasants and half for community improvements.[32] In the program of the LMI this became a call for the establishment of "just relations between peasants and landowners."

The main thrust of the party program was the desire to create an atmosphere of trust and predictability in society. Words such as "genuine," "principle," "correct," and "principled" abound and reflect the view that so long as the government and the ruling group did not enjoy the public's confidence, all changes, reforms, and programs would only be cosmetic and have no lasting effect. There was also the idea that reform proposals coming from an illegitimate government could not be sincerely meant. All of this bespeaks the LMI's frustration over the lack of a legal-rational order in Iran.

[31]Ibid., pp. 11–24.
[32]See Cottam, *Nationalism*, pp. 271–72.

From the outset the LMI was somewhat handicapped by its internal heterogeneity. To be sure, all founders were Nationalists and believing Muslims. But the Islamic orientation was more pronounced in Bazargan, Taleqani, and Sahabi, while others, especially Ata'i, Radnia, and Sami'i, had vaguely socialist tendencies. The rank and file consisted mostly of members of the Muslin Student Associations who generally came from lower middle-class backgrounds, were often provincial, and were thus less sophisticated and more narrow-minded than many key figures in the party leadership, people who spoke foreign languages, were financially well-off, and had traveled abroad. Some people joined the new party because of their past association with the NRM and were thus attracted more by the LMI's radical stance vis-à-vis the Shah than by its religious bent. A certain amount of tension thus existed from the outset.[33]

The LMI's Activities as a Party

The Liberation Movement of Iran operated openly as a party within the political system for nineteen months. In May 1961 it was founded, in January 1963 most of its leaders went to prison. During these nineteen months no elections took place which would allow us to gauge its popularity, the party held no congress that would permit us to investigate its internal workings, and the two governments in this period did not include the LMI in their discussions with the opposition. Precious little can be said about the LMI as a party.

At the outset the party was allowed to open a club on 141 Kakh Street, in what was then an upper middle-class neighborhood of Teheran. The house was owned by Bazargan. On the day the club was inaugurated it was packed with people, which the LMI interpreted as a sign of the public's impatience with the National Front. On May 22, 1961 (Khordad 1, 134), Bazargan, in the name of the party founders, sent a short letter to Baqer Kazemi, the chairman of the National Front's High Council, requesting NF membership for the LMI. The High Council never responded officially, but in spite of all the differences that would arise between the LMI and the NF's leadership it was always understood that the LMI's leaders were members of the NF, unlike Khalil Maleki.

The LMI also proceeded to put out regular publications. The party did not have an organ, but published a number of "internal publications," digests, and so on, carrying news, comments, and translations

---

[33]Ezzatollah Sahabi's interview in Naser Hariri, *Mosahebeh ba tarikhsazan-e Iran* (Interviews with makers of Iranian history) (1979), pp. 179–82.

from foreign newspapers.[34] In addition, the party produced declarations at important junctures which were widely distributed in Teheran.

In the few months that it existed regular meetings were held which would be addressed by party leaders. On several occasions members of the Student Organization of the NF would visit and exchange views with LMI members. After the closing of the club the meetings of the Monthly Talks Society (discussed later) and of the various Islamic associations (of students, engineers, physicians, and so on) provided opportunities for leaders and sympathizers to come together.

During this period of more or less open activity the LMI also issued a number of more lengthy declarations in which it analyzed the current situation. One was an "Open letter to His Majesty Mohammad Reza Shah Pahlavi," published in July 1962. In it the LMI introduced itself and its program to the Shah and painted a dire picture of the country's current situation. It contrasted Prime Minister Amini's gloomy analyses of Iran's woes with the Shah's own optimistic views, and compared the Shah's practice with what he had written in his book *Mission for My Country*. Basing itself on a remark the Shah had made at the American Press Club during his visit to the United States in March to the effect that he welcomed constructive criticism, the LMI exhorted the monarch to reign and not to rule.[35]

The LMI's emphasis on religion was a major controversy between the LMI and the NF. To be sure, no NF leader could politically afford openly to attack the LMI for its religious orientation: Iran was an Islamic country. While some members of the NF leadership were more or less believing Muslims who did not want to mix religion with politics (such as Saleh and Sanjabi), others (such as Sadiqi and Bakhtiar) were quite openly freethinkers. We have no records of debates between the two sides on the proper role of religion in politics, but informal talks with political leaders of that time indicate that very often discussions on the High Council of the NF concerned just that. At the same time, leaders of both the National Front and the LMI always took pains to assure the public that the founding of the LMI did not represent a split in the National Movement.[36]

During its brief existence the LMI also tried to demonstrate what properly motivated and honest people could accomplish if they organized. The most visible outcome of this effort was an entire village that the LMI financed and built (recall that many party leaders were engineers and/or in the construction business) for victims of a strong

[34]They are collected in *Safehati az tarikh-e mo'aser-e Iran: Asnad-e Nehzat-e Azadi-ye Iran,* vol. 2 (1983).
[35]*Safehat,* 1, pp. 133–56.
[36]See for instance *Safehat,* 2, p. 57.

earthquake that shook the region of Qazvin in 1962.[37] The effectiveness of that relief effort was contrasted with the government's allegedly inefficient and corrupt handling of the international aid it received for the same purpose.

The LMI's political aims were more or less shared by the National Front. There was, however, one more issue which the LMI placed on the agenda of Iranian politics, a move that would have a lasting effect on the political outlook of Iranians: Iran's relations with Israel.

The LMI's religious orientation obviated the anti-Arab feeling that some Iranians harbored, even inside the National Movement, which allowed them to contemplate normal relations with Israel. Israel was depicted in LMI party publications as a surrogate for Western imperialism in the Middle East, and the Shah's government was repeatedly chided for maintaining relations with Israel. The impetus for the LMI's vehemently anti-Israeli policy originated from Taleqani's two trips to what was then East Jerusalem, to attend Islamic congresses sponsored by the Jordanian government (1959 and 1961). In 1959 he also headed a clerical delegation to Cairo bearing a message from Ay. Borujerdi to Sheikh Shaltut, the rector of the Al-Azhar University and Grand Mufti of Egypt. Sheikh Shaltut officially recognized Shi'ism as a legitimate branch of Islam, alongside the four traditional Sunni schools, a move that greatly facilitated later manifestations of Muslim unity. Taleqani left Egypt impressed by the Egyptian revolution,[38] and that probably laid the ground for the LMI's sympathy for the Egyptian dictator.

The main focus of the LMI's attacks was Israeli involvement in agricultural development in the area of Qazvin. Both the Iranian and the Israel governments tried to keep these contacts secret,[39] and it is perhaps only because of their efforts on behalf of the earthquake victims that the leaders of the LMI became aware of the increasing Israeli presence in Iran. This antipathy toward the Jewish state had at times clearly anti-Semitic overtones.[40] That the LMI objected mainly to the presence of Israeli experts in Iran shows that the party was not aware of (or dared not bring up) a far more sinister link between the two countries, namely the close cooperation between the Israeli secret service, MOSSAD, and SAVAK.[41]

A corollary of the hostility to Israel was strongly expressed sympathy

[37]*Safehat*, 1, p. 94.

[38]Afrasiabi and Dehqan, *Taleqani*, pp. 169–76.

[39]Robert B. Reppa, *Israel and Iran: Bilateral Relationship and Effect on the Indian Ocean Basin* (1974), pp. 98–99.

[40]In the internal publication of the LMI we find only one joke, and that is anti-Semitic (as opposed to anti-Zionist). See *Safehat*, 2, p. 121.

[41]On SAVAK's cooperation with MOSSAD and other Western intelligence agencies see Harald Irnberger, *SAVAK oder der Folterfreund des Westens* (1977).

for Arab causes. The LMI celebrated Algerian independence and the union of Egypt and Syria in the United Arab Republic. Since Nasser was becoming increasingly hostile to the Shah, this LMI policy was a direct challenge to the Shah's foreign policy.

While the LMI functioned openly as a political party, it was both an ally and a rival of the National Front. The religiously colored discourse that the LMI increasingly adopted could not be matched in terms of effectiveness by anything the other factions of the National Movement had to offer: the vague Fabianism of the IP, the exalted nationalism of the PIN, the Islamic socialism of the PIP, or the socialism of Khalil Meleki. In the end even veteran leaders of the NF had to admit that the LMI was the more popular of the National Movement's two wings.[42]

The LMI failed to reap the benefits of its popularity, however. The Shah, of course, was unwilling to grant a genuine democratization, but perhaps the LMI itself could have done more to advance its cause. Altogether too much time was spent in internal debate between the two constitutive elements within the party (NRM and MSA people) and in quarreling with the NF. There were no membership drives and the LMI always remained only a potential cadre party. Organization in the provinces was minimal. Thus, when the top LMI leadership was arrested in January 1963, for all intents and purposes the party was at its end.

The LMI, the Nationalists, and Amini

In its reaction to Prime Minister Amini the National Front divided along the same lines as on the other issues. The radical wing clearly perceived and wanted to take advantage of the difference between Amini and the Shah. The plan was to weaken the Shah by strengthening Amini. The students of the NF had actively supported the teachers' strike. To the more religious elements in the radical wing, basically the LMI, Amini's tact and consideration for religious sensibilities were added incentives to give him a chance, at least for the time being.

The moderate wing, by contrast, resented Amini. They had never criticized the Shah personally, arguing that the Shah must reign and not rule, and now they transferred their opposition to Eqbal and Sharif-Emami to Amini. Their political program consisted in the demand for free elections, which the prime minister *could* not grant: the old conservative establishment was still so deeply entrenched in the

---

[42]Allahyar Saleh, as quoted in the secret U.S. documents published by the "Students following the Imam's Line," reprinted in *Iran Times* (Washington, D.C.), January 13, 1984, p. 15.

rural districts of the country that elections free of government interference would have resulted in a chamber dominated by landlords who would have toppled Amini. On the question of land reform the National Front was also most cautious, for many reasons. The National Front did include a number of major landlords on its High Council, and it appears that the National Front did not want to antagonize high members of the clergy, among whom many opposed agrarian reform.

Prime Minister Amini had hoped to reach a truce with the Nationalists, and as a goodwill gesture allowed them to hold a mass meeting at Jalalieh Field. This meeting, the first and last mass meeting of the Second National Front, was held on May 18, 1961 (Ordibehesht 28, 1340) and about 80,000 people came, demonstrating to the world the vitality of Mosaddeqism. The speakers, however, attacked Amini mercilessly and Sanjabi declared that the people of Iran did not want a prime minister imposed by America.

The next step in the confrontation between the moderate wing of the NF and Amini came on July 21 (Tir 30), when the Nationalists wanted to commemorate the anniversary of the 1952 events that had led to Mosaddeq's return to power. As prime minister Amini *could* not countenance this public humiliation of his sovereign, but he let it be known that any other day would be all right. The NF was adamant, and went ahead with its preparations for a show of force. The result was that the meeting did not receive official authorization and degenerated into riots. Many Nationalist leaders were arrested, and the clubs of both the NF and the LMI were closed down. Not to be outdone by the Nationalists, the Shah organized his own celebrations of the day he was brought back to power (August 19/Mordad 28) at Dowshan Tappeh. In his speech he reminded his opponents of the disorder they were creating and sent a warning both to the Nationalists and to Amini.

On November 15, 1961 (Aban 24, 1340) the Shah issued a proclamation addressed to Prime Minister Amini in which he spelled out details of the reform program he wished the government to enact. The reactions from the National Front and from the LMI differed only slightly. Both emphasized that the regime's pretexts for not holding elections were invalid and that elections were a cornerstone of Iran's Constitution. But whereas the NF's reasoning was mainly legal and included Amini in its reproach,[43] the LMI ignored the prime minister completely and instead prefaced its declaration with statements by the Shah in which he had said the opposite of what he was now proposing

[43]The Shah's proclamation and the National Front's response are available in English. See *Middle East Journal* 16 (Winter 1962), 86–92.

to do. This use of irony is typical for the LMI (also in later periods): essentially they were calling the Shah a liar.

On January 21, 1962 (Bahman 1, 1340), a National Front demonstration by Teheran University students led to an attack by paratroopers under the command of Major Manuchehr Khosrowdad on the university, where they beat students, broke windows and doors, and destroyed much expensive laboratory equipment. Most leading members of the Student Organization and some NF leaders, who had had no hand in the affair, were arrested. On January 24 (Bahman 4) the National Front leadership called for a general strike, which was so ill-prepared that it failed badly.

After that fiasco the National Front was exposed as ineffective, and its most active members, the student leaders, were in prison. Amini, for his part, let it be known that he had had nothing to do with the severe repression and refused to be identified with it. He declared that the disorders had been provoked by opponents of agrarian reform and by Tudeh agitators.[44] Amini also formed a commission of inquiry, consisting of two Justice Ministry officials and one army representative to look into the matter. The commission absolved the National Front of any guilt (as a result of which its leaders were freed), and instead concluded that the demonstration had been provoked by opponents of agrarian reform, such as Ja'far Behbahani (who had broken with the regime in 1959), Asadollah Rashidian, and Fathollah Forud.[45]

Soon after the attack on the university a publication of the LMI claimed that in Europe Teimur Bakhtiar had announced the cabinet he would have formed after a successful coup. The list, as reproduced by the LMI, contained two NF leaders: Shapur Bakhtiar (Teimur Bakhtiar's first cousin) as minister of labor, and Khonji as minister for the land reform. This hint at collusion with the former head of SAVAK amounted to a grave accusation and certainly did not improve relations between the NF and the LMI.[46]

On July 17, Asadollah Alam took over from Amini as prime minister. The conservatives hoped that the appointment of a landed aristocrat

---

[44]In early November 1961, ninety members of the outlawed Tudeh had been arrested, and one of the arrested had confessed that he and others had received orders to join the National Front. *Keesing's*, July 21–28, 1962, p. 18882.

[45]Personal communication from Gholamreza Sadiqi, December 1987. It should also be pointed out that leftists in the National Front have always claimed that the opponents of land reform had collaborated with conservative elements inside the National Front.

[46]*Safehat*, 2, pp. 267–68. The original news item had been published in London by the National Front paper *Bakhtar-e emruz*, which, according to Cosroe Chaqueri (personal communication, January 1989), was heavily infiltrated by Tudeh members at the time. Shapur Bakhtiar has consistently denied any collusion with his cousin.

would herald an end to their travails, but the land reform could not be rolled back since it had the full support of the United States. Alam vowed to continue Amini's reforms.

The new prime minister initiated high-level talks with Allahyar Saleh and Mehdi Azar, two top leaders of the NF, and intimated that he might take a few Nationalists into his cabinet. Again the gap between the Mosaddeqists and the Shah's government was too wide to bridge, but at least the negotiations kept the NF in check for a while.[47]

In the fall of 1962 (Aban 1341) the government extended the suffrage to women and declared its intention to establish provincial assemblies, without stipulating that their members would have to be Muslims. The LMI's response was to call this irrelevant, since men, who had enjoyed the suffrage, did not have any political rights either. Members of the clergy immediately opposed the two measures, putting the LMI in a difficult position: on the one hand the party had always urged more clerical support for the opposition, but on the other hand the terms of the clerical opposition differed from the LMI's. The LMI praised the ulema for opposing the regime, but sought to "clarify" their position. The party argued, somewhat disingenuously, that the ulema's statement that "women's involvement in social affairs is forbidden and must be prevented" should not be interpreted as discrimination against women.[48] It declared that the clergy's struggle was directed against lawlessness and against the Baha'is, who as agents of Israel were penetrating all levels of government, and that the clergy fought for free elections to a parliament, in which women's rights would be well looked after.[49]

The long-simmering tension between the LMI and the NF continued, finally culminating in an angry exchange over a photograph. Both sides in the internal conflict of the National Movement claimed to represent Mosaddeq's thought. In late October 1962, Mosaddeq, in response to an LMI request, sent them a photograph bearing an inscription: "To those who, when the public good is at stake, sacrifice their personal interests; to those who in political matters have not compromised and who sacrifice everything for Iran's freedom and independence, this unworthy picture is presented." Members of the LMI youth organization affixed the name of the party to the top of the photograph, reproduced it in large numbers, and distributed the copies widely in Teheran, claiming that with it Mosaddeq had designated the LMI as the true continuator of his way. The real significance of Mosaddeq's words

---

[47] Homa Katouzian's introduction to Maleki, *Khaterat*, pp. 159–60.
[48] *Safehat*, 1, pp. 171–73, 175, and 178.
[49] Ibid., pp. 196–202.

was that he was in effect warning the leaders of the National Front not to enter any shady deals with Alam.

To this day National Front people resent the LMI's claim to exclusiveness. They argue that Mosaddeq used to dedicate his photographs to people by name, and had he wished to do so there is no reason to believe that he would not have specifically dedicated it to the LMI. Indeed, to conclude from the inscription alone that Mosaddeq regarded LMI adherents as his true followers is not realistic. The incident of the photograph strikes one as trivial today, but it created bad blood between the NF and the LMI and kept coming up in the two organizations' publications for a long time.

In exchange for the NF leadership's lack of zeal the government allowed preparations to go ahead for the first congress of the National Front. In these preparations the cards were heavily stacked against radicals. Different groups were to elect delegates according to the following key:

Students	35
Bazaar	10
Workers	10
Neighborhood Councils	10
Teachers	8
Guilds	7
Government employees	5
Private sector employees	5
Administrations	7
Suburbs	9
Clergy	2
Women's Organization	2
Athletes	2
Students abroad	7

That meant that more than 100 participants were to be sent by the various organizations affiliated with the National Front, while about 60 were there as individuals, a number that included party leaders. Some organizations, such as that of the private sector employees, existed only on paper and sent no delegates. According to one source, the Neighborhood Councils did not send any delegates either as the elections that would have designated them were sabotaged by the NF because the councils were thought to be dominated by the PIN.[50] The inclusion of athletes, perhaps curious to the Western reader, is explained

---

[50]Sadeq Qotbzadeh in a speech given in 1964 to the NF's Munich branch, the text of which is in my possession.

by the important place traditional athletics occupy in Iranian society.[51] Most participants came from Teheran, as the NF had developed little activity outside the capital, except for individual leaders' efforts in their hometowns (for example, Saleh in Kashan). Of the 35 student members, 29 seats were for students from Teheran, the rest for their provincial comrades. The 7 seats initially reserved for students abroad were not filled after student leaders in Europe and the United States expressed doubts about being able to leave Iran again after the congress.

The LMI at the Congress of the National Front

Four leaders of the LMI had been invited to participate: Bazargan, Taleqani, Nazih, and Sahabi. But like other party leaders they were there in their own right, not qua LMI representatives. The ranks of the LMI were strengthened by a number of student delegates who were LMI members, such as Abbas Sheibani and Mohammad Moqaddam. The congress elected Mosaddeq honorary president of the National Front, and then elected a new High Council of thirty-five members. These were elected by the congress at large in a secret vote, as a result of which the student member of the council, Abbas Naraqi, was not the choice of the thirty-five member student delegation to the congress.[52]

The congress of the National Front was dominated by the old debate: should it be a unitary organization, or should it encompass a variety of parties and personalities? The membership of the LMI in the National Front was another aspect of this problem. Both issues were hotly debated, and three factions developed.[53] The unitarist faction, whose most prominent leaders were Sanjabi and Saleh, essentially wanted to transform the National Front into a unified party.

The unitarists were opposed by a faction that came to be known as the Congress Minority: this was essentially what we have called the radical wing. It included party leaders, such as the four LMI leaders, but also Dariush Foruhar of the PIN and Hosein Razi, general secretary of the PIP (Nakhshab was still in New York). Numerical strength was provided by the very important Student Organization of the National Front, whose thirty-five delegates were overwhelmingly favorable to the minority. Some leaders would later rise to political prominence, such as Abolhasan Banisadr, Hasan Habibi, and Bizhan Jazani. Between these two factions were the other participants, undecided dele-

---

[51]See A. Reza Arasteh, *Man and Society in Iran* (1964), pp. 29–33.

[52]*Mokatebat-e Mosaddeq: Talash bara-ye tashkil-e jebhe-ye melli-ye sevvom* (The correspondence of Mosaddeq: The efforts to organize the Third National Front) (1975), p. 71.

[53]The following account of the National Front's congress was given to me by Hedayatollah Matin-Daftari during interviews in Paris, in July and August 1983.

gates whom the two factions tried to sway their way. The most prominent member here was Sadiqi, Mossadeq's last minister of the interior, who made some feeble efforts to reconcile the two sides.

At the end of the second day of the congress, the LMI's Central Committee met privately to decide whether to continue their participation in the congress or to walk out, given that so many historic leaders of the NF were opposed to its existence as a party inside the National Front. Rahim Ata'i, Ezzatollah Sahabi, Hasan Arabzadeh, Mohammad Moqaddam, and Abbas Sheibani voted against staying inside the NF. They were outvoted, however, and with a majority of two it was decided that the LMI should continue its struggle *inside* the National Front.[54]

On the third day of the congress, the Congress Minority was making headway in its campaign to win over the undecided delegates, when the debates degenerated and Bazargan left the congress in a huff, followed by some other LMI delegates. The Student Organization attempted to avoid an open break, and following Bazargan and the other LMI leaders out of the hall, tried to bring about a reconciliation—to no avail. The Congress Minority had now lost the crucial votes of LMI leaders and sympathizers. The congress then voted to accept a motion that if the LMI purged itself of some of its more unruly members, the High Council would again consider the party's membership in the NF. The question of the LMI's participation in the National Front therefore was never resolved.[55]

The end of the congress coincided with preparations for the Shah's referendum on his so-called White Revolution. But first we need to turn our attention to religious developments. The period 1959–63 witnessed the first attempts by Islamic modernists to create a coherent body of political positions and to present their views to a wider audience: people associated with the NRM and later the LMI played a prominent part in this.

The Religious Reform Movement of the Early 1960s

The hitherto harmonious relations between the Pahlavi state and the ulema began deteriorating in 1959. The rift became apparent in May 1960, when Ay. Borujerdi, who was at the peak of his prestige as sole *marja'* of Iranian Shi'ites, denounced the agrarian reform bill of 1959 (presented to parliament in early 1960) as contrary to both Islam and

[54]This episode was related to me by Ahmad Alibaba'i, who was present. Interview, Cologne, August 23, 1983.
[55]Gholamhosein Sadiqi, personal communication, December 1987.

the Constitution. He did not attack the Shah personally, but instead blamed his advisers. Given the general state of corruption and economic crisis that pervaded the country, the sentiment was appearing among the religious classes that tyranny and despotism were reaching intolerable levels. At long last Borujerdi had left his lofty indifference to politics, but not all religious people could agree with his motives. While it is true that the clergy as a whole stood to lose from agrarian reform, which impelled many of them to adopt conservative positions, other sectors, including many modernists, were alive to the need for agrarian reform, but mistrusted the Shah's motives and sincerity in championing the cause. A purely negative attitude toward the Shah's proposed reform program therefore would not do. This led to a monthly lecture series in which socioeconomic problems of Iran were discussed in the light of Islam.

The Monthly Talks Society

As already mentioned, Taleqani's Hedayat Mosque was a center of political opposition against the Shah. Prominent Nationalist politicians would attend the lectures given under its aegis.

During the time of the summer elections of 1960 SAVAK closed down the lecture series. As a result, the organizers of these talks decided to move them to the house of Ahmad Alibaba'i, in the Bagh-e Shah section of Teheran. The first occasion was provided by the mourning period in the last third of the lunar month of Safar,[56] a period of extensive *rowzehkhani*. But instead of the usual format, in which the audience sits on the floor and hardly listens to the ritualized outpourings of grief offered by professional *rowzehkhans*, the organizers of these meetings decided to change the setting. For the first time a tribune replaced the traditional pulpit, and chairs were set up in the garden, to convey the impression of a lecture rather than a traditional *rowzehkhani*. The aim was to get people to *listen*. As one organizer put it: "We started from the premise that the speaker was for the audience, not the audience for the speaker," an allusion to the well-known and often derided narcisistic tendencies of many *rowzehkhans*. Taleqani and S. Morteza Motahhari took turns addressing the audience. For the first time tape-recorders were used to record the talks, which were then transcribed and published.[57] The first evening about 200 people came;

---

[56]This ten-day mourning period begins forty days after Ashura, and also includes the anniversaries of the deaths of the Prophet, and the Second and the Eighth Imams.

[57]Ahmad Alibaba'i, personal interview, Cologne, August 1982. The talks were published as *Goftar-e mah dar namayandan-e rah-e rast-e din* (Monthly talks for revealing the straight path of religion) (n.d.).

more showed up the next evening, and on both occasions many Nationalist statesmen put in an appearance. On the third night police broke up proceedings at midnight and arrested Alibaba'i, who spent a night in jail. At the time the meetings were considered a solid popular success, which shows the modesty of the religious modernists' ambitions and expectations. At the end of the ten-day mourning period, the innovative format of the talks was deemed such a success that it was decided to organize one talk a month. For this purpose a "Society of Monthly Talks for the Propagation of the True Path of Religion" (Anjoman-e goftar-e mah dar namayandan-e rah-e rast-e din) was formed. The main movers for the Monthly Talks Society were Alibaba'i and H. Ja'far Khazzazi, a prominent and trusted Bazaar leader, whose spacious house could accommodate up to 1,000 listeners. Speakers were assigned topics and had one month to prepare their lectures; and the foreknowledge that these talks would be taped and printed was a strong incentive for them to do their homework. At each session the previous session's talk would go on sale for 5 rials (7 cents).

The talks dealt with the interfaces of religion and socioeconomic matters and therefore had a decidedly this-worldly emphasis. This new emphasis was seen (and is often seen even now) as a mark of the movement's "reformism." In fact, since such an important ingredient of the series' "modernity" lay in its novel form rather than any new content, it is not surprising that we find among its participants people who would later become prominent in the fundamentalist movement. A total of thirty-one talks were given. The most prominent speaker was S. Morteza (later Ay.) Motahhari, who gave a total of seven talks, including the first two. Taleqani gave two lectures. The first, given on October 27, 1961 (Aban 5, 1340), formed the basis of his later book *Islam and Ownership*. In it he attempted to transcend the alternative between the traditional ulema's preference for the economic status quo and the Shah's agrarian reforms.

It would be impossible to summarize here the contents of all the articles contained in the three published volumes. The object of all speakers was to shake up the religious community, to put an end to the lethargy that had characterized it, and to attempt to make Islam relevant to social, economic, and political problems of the day. Interwoven through all of them was the idea of work, deed, action, as opposed to listening, talking, and thinking. Religious circles must listen to the young and attempt to speak to their problems. Islam as an internalized outlook on the world should be rejected in favor of the conception of Islam as a total way of life, with answers to all problems as might occur. These answers were to be found in the Qoran itself and not necessarily in *feqh*, jurisprudence, which had become the primary branch of the religious sciences. Of paramount importance was the Islamic injunction of "enjoining what is good and preventing what is evil," which was interpreted in an all-encompassing way. The social dimension of all ethical commands was emphasized over the private side; Ay. Motahhari, for instance, took the widespread irregularities in the two elections to the twentieth Majles as an example to demonstrate the disappearance of piety among the authorities.

Although the talks avoided any direct attacks on the Shah, Bazargan and Yadollah Sahabi avoided participating as speakers, so as not to make the society suspect in the eyes of the regime. The lectures continued for two more months, until they were banned by the government in March 1963. The proceedings were published in book form in 1964 and regularly reprinted thereafter.

The Discussions of Marja'iyat

The death of Ay. Borujerdi in March 1961 (Farvardin 1340) evoked considerable uncertainty among believers. Iranian Shi'ites had become used to the idea of *one* supreme *marja'*, who was clearly more learned (*a'lam*) than all other *mujtahid*s. At the passing of Ay. Borujerdi a number of major ayatollahs were plausible successors, but none had enough of a personal following to be clearly recognized as *a'lam* by the entire community. At the same time the Shah attempted to influence the course of events by clearly indicating his preference for Ay. Muhsin Hakim, who, from the Shah's point of view, had the advantage of being an Arab resident in Iraq, which lessened the likelihood of his involvement in Iranian politics.

When, a few months after his death, still no successor had emerged to Ay. Borujerdi, members of the Islamic associations began taking an active interest in the question. A few discussion meetings were held, and finally it was decided to organize a symposium in Teheran and invite certain progressive mullas to give papers dealing with various aspects of the "succession problem." Practical difficulties prevented the symposium from taking place, but the papers were collected and published in December 1962 (Azar 1341).[58] The volume includes ten essays, and among the authors we find many who also participated in the Monthly Talks Society. Ay. Motahhari contributed three pieces, and Taleqani wrote an essay advocating the decentralization of *marja'iyat*. Bazargan, the only lay member of the group, wrote an essay titled "People's Expectations of the *Maraje'*."

[58]*Bahsi darbareh-ye marja'iyat va rowhaniyat* (A discussion on *marja'iyat* and the clergy) (1962).

In the collection's introduction the institution of *taqlid* was specifically upheld: "The Qoran does not forbid imitation, it forbids blind imitation." It argued that the contemporary world is characterized by growing specialization, therefore the institution of *taqlid* is in no way opposed to the spirit of the times. People tend to follow preestablished and well thought-out plans, but in our day and age planners and decision makers are well-intentioned experts in such fields as politics, commerce, medicine, the science and technology, whom the people freely chose as members of parliament, ministers, directors, physicians, savants, and so on. The position of the *marja'* was elective even before democracy was developed in the West, therefore the imitator must do thorough research before he chooses a *marja*.'[59] The question of who becomes *marja'* is a serious national question, for non-Muslims, too, given the enormous weight that he has in the life of the Iranian nation.

Far from wishing to do away with the institution of *taqlid*, the writers upheld it and merely wanted to make it responsive. They argued that the openness of the gates of *ijtihad*, a matter of pride for Shi'ites, was meaningless if it remained a theoretical possibility only and if the *mujtahid*s did not actually make use of their authority to interpret religious principles to find answers for pressing problems of the day. This point was made with particular vehemence by Bazargan, who claimed to write as someone occupying a position between the laymen and the ulema, and who, because of his experience as a teacher, was well attuned to the needs and expectations of the young.

For our purposes it is worthwhile to try to gauge the significance of the collection for the development of modernist Shi'ism's political activities. It is of great import that the most learned of all the participants, Allameh Tabataba'i, expressly rejected the idea of a congruence between Islam and democracy, and instead candidly discussed their fundamental differences. Bazargan himself in his piece reproached the clergy for not having been politically active enough. This has to be seen in light of Ay. Borujerdi's courteous and at times cordial relations with the Shah. Bazargan and his friends wanted the clergy to lend their authority to the creation of an Islamic force in politics.

It is difficult to assess the ramifications of the religious "reform" movement of the 1960s. As far as the content of the talks and articles is concerned, one must admit that although many questions were posed, few answers were given. That could not have been otherwise: it has always been up to the clergy to make pronouncements on articles of faith, and of the personalities involved in the movement none was a major *mujtahid*. All the "reformers" could hope to do was to suggest

[59]Ibid., p. 3.

directions of research, to provide some basic ideas, and thus prod the higher ranks of the ulema to become more sensitive to the urgent questions of the day.

The movement's impact on the population was quite small. The language used in the talks and articles was often scholarly and abstract, and therefore could not compete with the simple words of preachers or the emotional and yet easily understood sermons of Khomeini. As mentioned earlier, attendance at the meetings of the Monthly Talks Society was about 200, whereas when Khomeini spoke in Qum thousands would come and listen.

To expand their audience, the organizers contacted the Ministry of Education and the Department of Religious Endowments and asked for financial help to distribute the texts in high schools. The government had always looked askance at these stirrings, however, and preferred the quiescent and scholarly mullas oblivious to the world around them to these self-styled "religious intellectuals." The state thus lost a chance to ally itself with religious modernists, and thus include religion in the process of modernization. The efforts of the reformers were in the short run frustrated, although they had great impact on the young, who were introduced for the first time to a whole new style of thinking about religion and to a novel type of religious discourse. The ideas first formulated in the monthly talks and articles would later be developed in the Hoseiniyeh Ershad Institute. By then, however, far more momentous developments were taking place among the clergy, who, under the impact of the Shah's policies and societal developments, were becoming politicized.[60]

In this context, a reexamination of cultural values among nonreligious Iranians began, a movement that arose with Jalal Al-e Ahmad's indictment of the Iranian elite's beholdenness to Western values. His book *Gharbzadegi* contributed to a new intellectual climate in Iran in which Western models (liberal or Marxist) were no longer seen as providing answers.[61] Secular intellectuals became increasingly curious about their own indigenous cultural traditions.

---

[60]For a more detailed summary of the ideas put forth in the reform movement of the early 1960s, see Shahrough Akhavi, *Religion and Politics* (1980), pp. 117–29; and A. K. S. Lambton, "A Reconsideration of the Position of the *Marja' Al-Taqlid* and the Religious Institution," *Studia Islamica* 20 (1964), 115–35.

[61]Jalal Al-e Ahmad, *Gharbzadegi* (Weststruckness), trans. John Green and Ahmad Alizadeh (1982).

The End of Traditional Politics

After Alam became prime minister, the Shah fully assumed the governance of the country and claimed for himself the reforms begun by Amini. He issued a program of six points,[62] which the people of Iran were invited to approve in a plebiscite scheduled for January 26, 1963 (Bahman 6, 1341). To nobody's surprise on this occasion only 4,115 people out of more than 5 million voted against what would later be called the Shah's White Revolution, a mandate that the Iranian press compared favorably to the 77.3 percent approval rate de Gaulle had received in 1962.[63]

The LMI reacted to the plebiscite by publishing a long declaration in which it contended that the Shah's so-called revolution was not genuine because the people were not involved with it. Land reform, the text went on, would only increase Iran's dependency on foreign experts, especially Israelis.[64] The National Front responded to the Shah's move by contending that the use of the plebiscite procedure was unconstitutional since Iran had been without a parliament since May 1961, and denounced the "arbitrary and despotic regime and the Shah's interference in the affairs of State."[65] A protest demonstration called by the NF for January 25 was banned by the government, and on that day most of the leadership of both the NF and the LMI was arrested. The total number arrested would eventually reach about 400. Earlier, religious leaders had also opposed the plebiscite and called for a strike. The NF had supported that action and on January 22 the Bazaar of Teheran closed for three days and there were demonstrations. The arrest of the Nationalist leadership did not immediately end political activity of the old type, however, and this took some time to fizzle out. The LMI, too, attempted to continue functioning.

The LMI after the Arrest of Its Leaders

After the arrest of Taleqani, Sahabi, and Bazargan, lower-ranking members of the LMI tried to keep the party going. Rahim Ata'i was already quite ill and had had to abstain from party activism for quite some time. Other leaders had been traveling when the arrests came and thus escaped prison for the time being. In February, Ezzatollah

---

[62]Later more points were added, until eventually the White Revolution comprised twenty-one points.

[63]Marvin Zonis, *Political Elite* (1971), p. 76.

[64]*Safehat*, 1, pp. 203–21.

[65]*Keesing's*, March 9–16, 1963, p. 19293.

Sahabi established contacts with these elements and took charge of what remained of the party organization.[66]

The party's outlook now became markedly more Islamic. In late winter 1963 (Esfand 1341) it published a major ideological statement, "Political Struggles and Religious Struggles."[67] So far the LMI had presented itself as a party that was Muslim, Iranian, constitutionalist, and Mosaddeqist. Without breaking with this definition, the party now presented a rationale for harnessing the people's religious aspirations for political action. This was the result of, on the one hand, the Nationalists' failure to reach their most minimal goals, and on the other the ulema's abandonment of their lofty indifference to politics. The 1963 text's argument is outlined in the following paragraphs.

First, the statement defines "struggle" as "the confrontation of a person, or organization, or a people with the existing state of affairs in order to change it and transform it to the desired state." It then alludes to the axiom that all progress is the fruit of struggle thusly defined, and that the opposite of struggle, immobilism, is a form of corruption. The agents of this change have to be the people themselves, for the Qoran says "God changes not what is in a people, until they change it themselves" (13:12). The text pointedly notes that the verse makes no reference to foreign elements.

The text continues that while struggles in the West had been mostly political, all major religions had sprung up in the East. This legacy meant that Eastern peoples responded more readily to spiritual appeals than to appeals based on nationalism and the promise of material benefits. Nationalist political activity had come to a standstill; what was left of the LMI now sought a rapprochement with the newly politically active ulema.

With great difficulty, the remaining LMI cadres put out some issues of the party's fortnightly "internal publication," and in them attacked the government harshly. Earlier on, the LMI had in its declarations respectfully counseled the Shah to change his ways. Now all pretense was dropped and the Shah himself became the target of opprobrium.

Israel was held responsible for many of the ills that were afflicting Iran, and anti-Semitism grew. Some leaders of the party may have been embarrassed by this, for in the ninth issue the publication inserted a disclaimer that distinguished between Zionism and Judaism and denied any animosity toward the latter.[68] The disclaimer suggests that the rank and file of the LMI, especially the more committed elements (who

[66] *Modafe'at-e mohandes Ezzatollah Sahabi dar dadgah-e gheir-e saleh-e tajdid-e nazar-e nezami* (The defenses of Engineer Ezzatollah Sahabi in the illegitimate Court of Appeals) (1976), p. 13.

[67] "Mobarezat-e siasi va mobarezat-e mazhabi," in *Safehat*, 1, pp. 229–59.

[68] *Safehat*, 2, pp. 197–98.

were taking the considerable risk of publishing the newsletter), were in general less sophisticated and enlightened than the party leadership. No wonder, then, that soon many began to look toward Qum for guidance.

These lower-ranking members, many of whom came from traditional lower-middle class families, also established closer relations with clerical circles. All major *maraje'* were approached and asked to issue declarations in favor of the imprisoned leadership of the LMI. Ays. Milani and Shariatmadari responded favorably, but Khomeini hesitated, and only after much prodding did he issue a declaration, *without,* however, mentioning Bazargan's, Sahabi's, and Taleqani's party affiliation or their Nationalist persuasion. In March, when government troops attacked the Feiziyeh *madrasah* in Qum, the LMI issued another statement. But on the whole, SAVAK made any sort of activity ever more difficult.

Taleqani alone was released from prison on May 25, 1963 (Khordad 4, 1342; Muharram 1, 1383 A.H.L.). He wanted to resume political preaching at his Hedayat Mosque but was prevented from doing so when the government closed it. SAVAK then laid an elaborate trap. An agent gained access to the Taleqani household and stole drafts of declarations, which were then printed and distributed. The resulting pamphlets subsequently were used against Taleqani after his rearrest. At his trial he admitted having written them, but denied having had anything to do with their publication and distribution. It seems safe to say that they represent Taleqani's thinking at the time. One draft was addressed to the military and exhorted soldiers not to follow orders.

One is struck by the extreme paranoia of these tracts. They attacked the Shah's repression, as was normal and understandable. But in last analysis all evils were blamed on Jews, Baha'is, Israelis, Freemasons— all international spies who had colonized the Iranian government and administration and turned women into prostitutes, who were exploiting Iranian peasants and spreading corruption through their domination of the media, and who had given orders to the security forces to kill the ulema en masse.[69] One month after his release Taleqani was again arrested, together with Ezzatollah Sahabi, Rahim Ata'i, Abbas Radnia, and some other lower-ranking activists of the LMI. Now even the

---

[69]These declarations were contemporary with the riots of June 1963, in which many people were killed. They may only reflect Taleqani's momentary rage and his frustration over his powerlessness. But then, they may also reflect his true beliefs, now coming to the fore and unrestrained by political considerations. According to Homa Katouzian (personal communication, February 1988), this type of thinking, blaming international conspiracies for all ills in Iran, was prevalent at that time in Iran, both among secular and among religious Nationalists. For details on Taleqani's declarations and the SAVAK plot see Afrasiabi and Dehqan, *Taleqani,* pp. 198–218.

occasional publications ceased appearing and the LMI went into hibernation.

In the months after the plebiscite, rumors circulated that the imprisoned leaders of the NF(II) were negotiating with the regime about some form of cooperation. Some were freed from prison. But the June 1963 riots put an end to all these contacts, real or imagined.

The Rise of the Clerical Opposition and the Riots of June 1963

The riots of June 1963 had a dynamic totally independent of that of the National Movement. Khomeini was the leader, and his prominence in Iran's political scene dates from that year. The later fate of the LMI would be conditioned by the displacement of the moderate Islamic forces by the radical elements led by Khomeini.

To understand the causes behind the riots we need to go back a few years. Khomeini was a minor contender for the succession to Ay. Borujerdi at the latter's death in March 1961. Around that time he began making fiery speeches against such government reform programs as the enfranchisement of women and the Local Government Election Bill (which had done away with the requirement that candidates and voters be Muslims), speeches which got him arrested for the first time in 1962. Just before the January 1963 plebiscite on the White Revolution, he was again arrested for allegedly opposing agrarian reform. On March 22 (Farvardin 2) a minor incident led to an attack by security forces on the shrine in Qum, which resulted in much destruction and in which many students were wounded. Khomeini's house in Qum now became the headquarters of clerical opposition to the Shah. Due to his unquestionable courage and outspokenness, he assumed a major political role and became the leader of the most militant sector of the ulema. His popularity among the faithful also grew and he became a major *marja'*.

On Ashura day (June 3, Khordad 13, Muharram 10) of 1963, the traditional processions in Teheran were politicized as people carried portraits of Khomeini with them and chanted their support for him. The organizers tried to prevent anti-Shah slogans, but when the processions reached the Marble Palace they occurred nevertheless.

On that same day the clergy had planned large-scale speeches in the various schools and mosques of Qum. The government sent its agents and threatened to attack the city if they did. Many clerical leaders backed down, but Khomeini delivered a sermon in the Feiziyeh *madrasah* in which he defended the ulema against the Shah's attacks and once again, but in blunt language, warned the Shah to behave.[70] As a result

[70]An English translation of that powerful and moving sermon is available in R. Khomeini,

he was arrested in the wee hours of June 4 (Khordad 14, Muharram 11) and brought to Teheran.

Within a few hours crowds of protesters began to form in front of the Teheran Bazaar and by mid-morning troops opened fire. The rioting then spread to Mashad, Qum, Isfahan, and Shiraz, reached its climax on June 5 (Khordad 15, Muharram 12), but was finally put down with a heavy loss of life. The riots were the heaviest Iran had known in recent memory and amounted to a veritable uprising.

Khomeini was released on August 3, but detained again in October, after he had urged his followers to boycott the long postponed elections to the twenty-first Majles. This time he was jailed until May 1964. In October 1964 the parliament passed in close succession two bills, one to grant American military personnel diplomatic immunity, the other to accept a loan of $200 million from the United States for the purchase of military equipment. When Khomeini issued a sharp attack on the bills, the government decided to exile him, first to Turkey, then to Najaf, in Iraq, where he would remain until 1978.

The events of June 1963 are the starting point of the religious movement that ultimately led to the revolution of 1978–79. The secular National Front could not hide its distaste for the new type of politico-religious activism. Allahyar Saleh in 1964 told U.S. embassy officials that under no circumstances would the National Front support the religious movement, since the latter's aims were the opposite of what the National Front stood for.[71] Saleh's lucidity was not matched by the LMI, for on the second day of the rioting the party issued a statement in support of the movement, and party activists participated in the demonstrations. They tried to introduce Mosaddeqist slogans, apparently without major success: far deeper emotions and longings had been awakened and set free.[72] The themes, catchwords, and methods used by the militant clergy in 1963 would fifteen years later be used again, but this time with the backing of far better-organized support networks.

The End of the NF(II) and the Third National Front

In late summer 1963 the regime started preparations for the elections to the twenty-first Majles, with the customary assurances that they

---

Islam and Revolution: Writings and Declarations of Imam Khomeini, trans. and ann. Hamid Algar (1981).

[71]From the secret documents published by the "Students following the Imam's Line," reprinted in *Iran Times,* January 13, 1984, p. 15.

[72]Factual information for this account of the beginning of clerical opposition to the Shah is based on S. Jalaleddin Madani, *Tarikh-e siasi-ye mo'aser-e Iran, II* (The political history of contemporary Iran, vol. 2) (1983/1361), pp. 10–62, and Zonis, *Political Elite,* pp. 44–47.

would be free. The Student Organization of the National Front (the NF's leadership was still in prison) decided to hold a public meeting in support of free elections on September 6, 1963 (Shahrivar 15, 1342), on Baharestan Square, in front of the Majles.[73] They communicated their decision to the police and asked for an official authorization, so as to comply with the law. The police evaded giving an answer, upon which the students informed the authorities that the meeting would be held, and that they considered the authorities responsible for security arrangements. Preparations now went ahead, and the Bazaar, the clergy of Teheran, and Ay. Milani of Mashad issued supporting statements as well.

At this point the regime countered with a masterstroke: while all LMI prisoners were kept in jail, the NF leaders were released the day before the demonstration was scheduled (Saleh, who was in the hospital, was told he could consider himself free). They were told that it was up to them to stop the demonstration, if they wanted to avoid a bloodbath. Sanjabi wrote a letter to Saleh, and Saleh, in a letter addressed to the students and dated "Thursday afternoon, Shahrivar 14," ordered the meeting canceled, arguing that the Military Command had not authorized the meeting and that it was NF policy to abide by the law.

It was too late to call the meeting off, and on the next morning masses of people converged upon Baharestan Square, all accesses to which had been sealed off by the police during the night. Scuffles ensued, and people demonstrated in the surrounding streets until the evening. Roughly 100 demonstrators were arrested.

By keeping the leaders of the LMI in prison and releasing the NF leaders, the regime achieved four goals: first, the students, the most active element in the National Front, were disavowed by the leadership and thereby lost face and credibility; second, the gap between the NF leadership and the activists widened; third, the gap between the religious and secular wings of the National Movement was exacerbated; and fourth, the government did not have to go on record as prohibiting a meeting in favor of free elections.

When the High Council of the NF met after this incident, Saleh argued that times were not propitious for active political opposition to the Shah: "With all that has taken place, such as the events of Khordad 15 [the June riots], the prisons are filled and there is no sense in giving martyrs. I think there is nothing to be gained from getting many people killed. On the contrary, the loss would mean that we will have fewer people to count on when conditions are right again. . . . In my

[73]The following account is based on documents collected in *Mokatebat*.

opinion the NF has to spend this period with patience and calm."[74] In the fall of 1963 what remained of the High Council met a number of times and adopted Saleh's thesis, which became known as *siasat-e sabr va entezar,* "policy of patience and waiting." Saleh was asked to be plenipotentiary chairman of a new executive committee, but with one exception nobody volunteered to serve on such a committee. Saleh himself was quite ill and unwilling to take on the responsibilities. The National Front's activities thus fizzled out little by little; the last issue of its newsletter came out in March 1964.[75]

After the leadership of the NF in effect sabotaged the demonstrations of September 6, the students, exasperated by the leadership's cunctative tactics, decided to secede. Their organ, *Payam-e daneshju,* was published again in October 1963, and from then on the students refused to have anything to do with the leaders of the National Front. They did decide, however, to maintain contact with other activist sectors of the National Movement, and Hedayatollah Matin-Daftari, who as Mosaddeq's grandson had access to him, was designated as the students' representative to other groups.

A letter written by Mosaddeq in late March 1964 to the leaders of the National Front in Europe, in which he complained that first the leaders of the NF had insisted on having his advice, only to disregard it afterward, was widely reproduced and distributed in Teheran by the students. This impelled the leadership of the NF to write a letter to Mosaddeq, defending its record. A three-way correspondence followed between Mosaddeq, the NF High Council and the students, in which each faction of the NF (the LMI leadership was in prison) made charges against the others and defended itself against accusations. Charges and countercharges concerned points of principle and personal conduct. It is clear from Mosaddeq's letters that he favored the point of view of the students. The issues cannot be dilated upon here: the debate was a continuation of earlier disagreements and was by now academic anyway, since neither side could realistically expect to develop much political activity. The upshot was that the NF leadership, feeling disavowed by Mosaddeq and arguing that it could not function without the full confidence of the leader of the National Movement, resigned as a group in late spring 1964. Mosaddeq accepted the resignation and in a private letter, dated September 26, 1964 (Mehr 4, 1343), to Ali Shayegan, who was in the United States, he is on record for having declared the National Front dissolved.[76]

Parallel to the break between the students and the leadership,

[74]Ibid., p. 129.
[75]Ibid., pp. 57 and 126–34.
[76]The originals of all the mentioned letters are reproduced in *Mokatebat.*

preparations went ahead for the formation of a new National Front, to be composed of political parties, as wished by Mosaddeq himself. This grouping became known as the Third National Front, and encompassed the LMI, represented by Ata'i and Sami'i, the PIN, the PIP, Maleki's socialists, and the Student Organization of the NF. Shapur Bakhtiar also participated as representative of the Iran Party. The NF(III) issued a few statements in the spring and summer of 1964 and formally announced its existence in July 1965, but essentially nothing came of it: the dictatorship of the Shah would no longer tolerate any opposition.

The Trials

The Special Tribunal no. 1 of the Military Court of Justice began the public trial of the eight arrested leaders of the LMI and their nonmember co-defendant on October 22, 1963. The court appointed a number of retired army officers, some of them NF sympathizers, as defense lawyers.

The prisoners were accused of plotting against the constitutional monarchy in Iran. Since party statutes had clearly defined the party as operating within the Constitution, evidence for the accusation was taken mainly from tracts and pamphlets distributed by lower-ranking LMI activists after the arrest of the leaders, for which Bazargan and Taleqani refused to accept responsibility. Throughout most of the proceedings Taleqani remained silent, refusing to recognize the court's jurisdiction. Bazargan and Ezzatollah Sahabi, however, defended themselves and at times engaged the prosecutors in oral debates. Profiting from the public nature of the trial, members of the Student Organization of the NF recorded the proceedings, smuggled them out of the court, transcribed them, and distributed mimeographed copies in Teheran. They also tried to hold public meetings in support of the LMI prisoners, while the National Front ignored the trial completely and did not even bother to issue a statement in support of the LMI, an omission of which they would henceforth always be reminded.

The cases were then taken to a court of appeals. Here Bazargan defended himself eloquently, and his defense, not all of it delivered orally in court, was eventually published. He concluded by issuing the warning that theirs would be the last trial in which a political group was persecuted for upholding the Constitution.

The court of appeals modified the sentences only slightly. Bazargan and Taleqani were each condemned to ten years,[77] while Yadollah

[77]As chairman of the Engineers Association, Abbas Sharif-Emami tried to persuade the

Sahabi, Abbas Sheibani, Ahmad Alibaba'i, Ezzatollah Sahabi, Abolfazl Hakimi, Mehdi Ja'fari, Abbas Radnia, Parviz Edalatmanesh, and Mostafa Mofidi received sentences ranging from two to six years. Ata'i had been freed on account of his precarious health. After 1964 the top leadership of the LMI was in prison, with the exception of Nazih, Ata'i, and Sami'i. Ata'i was too ill to be politically active, Nazih stayed quiet, but Sami'i was arrested when the regime began rounding up the leaders of the constituent groups of the NF(III). Dariush Foruhar of the PIN was arrested in September 1964 and jailed. The NF Student Organization leadership's turn came in May 1965, and finally, Maleki and three other socialist leaders were arrested and jailed in August 1965.

In that same year, 1965, the regime also arrested and tried four of the LMI's defense lawyers, General Ali-Asghar Mas'udi and Colonels Azizollah Amir-Rahimi, Ali-Akbar Ghaffari, and Esma'il Elmiyeh, for essentially having done the job they had been assigned by that same regime. The travesty of justice was complete.[78]

The Shah offered Iran a liberalization in the period 1960–63. The Nationalist opposition, however, would accept nothing short of a democratization. There is no reason to believe that by granting a full democratization the Shah would have lost his throne. Few people in the early 1960s contested the institution of the monarchy, and in the country at large the traditional legitimacy of the monarchy was still strong, as could be witnessed when the birth of the Crown Prince in 1961 produced genuine joy in the population. Yet the Shah chose to govern autocratically rather than to reign constitutionally, with the result that in due course the very institution of the monarchy became increasingly delegitimized.

There is no evidence that the Kennedy administration actually pressed the Shah to democratize Iranian politics. The basic fact that his regime, because it had been imposed on Iran by the CIA, was considered illegitimate by key sectors of Iranian society, was either unknown or considered irrelevant in Washington. We now know that throughout 1960–63 American embassy officials were in contact with members of

---

Shah to pardon Bazargan, his predecessor in the association. The Shah insisted that Bazargan come and ask for forgiveness, which Bazargan refused to do. Secret U.S. embassy document, reproduced in the *Iran Times*, April 1, 1983, p. 15.

[78]Excerpts from the proceedings are available in Paul Vieille and Abol-Hassan Banisadr, eds., *Pétrole et Violence* (1974), pp. 185–277.

the Nationalist opposition (not, however, with the LMI, whose importance they probably underestimated). The comments of the U.S. diplomats are revealing. Nationalists who defended the work of Mosaddeq,
explained the aims of the National Movement, and gave their reasons
for their opposition against the Shah were invariably described as
"dreamers," "ideologues," and the like. One sees no trace of any
empathy for the aspirations of Third World elites. As the U.S. government saw it, the reasons for the instability in Iran were socioeconomic.
To use a more analytical language, the crisis in Iran was interpreted as
a crisis of distribution, rather than as a crisis of legitimacy. When the
Shah promised to carry out wide-ranging reforms (the White Revolution) and began implementing them, U.S. pressure ceased. He even
entered political science as a "modernizing monarch" whose tragedy
was that to develop his country he had to be autocratic so as to
neutralize conservative opposition, and thereby aroused the hostility of
those strata who stood to gain most from these reforms.[79]

The year 1963 represents a watershed in recent Iranian history. Until
the early 1960s the Shah had enjoyed the support of certain sectors in
Iranian society, but with his assault on religion and the landowners he
deprived himself of that support, while at the same time forces of
progress were antagonized by the regime's increasingly dictatorial
methods and corruption. Symptomatic of this qualitative change is the
fate of a famous *chaqukesh*, Tayyeb Hajj-Reza'i. He had been one of the
leading figures of the August 1953 riots that toppled Mosaddeq. Yet in
June 1963 he rioted for Khomeini and was killed. On a more elite level,
one can mention the experiences of Sardar Fakher Hekmat, Abdollah
Entezam, General Yazdanpanah, and Hosein Ala', all elder statesmen
of Pahlavi Iran. After the June riots they went to see the Shah and
beseeched him to be less harsh in the repression of the opposition. The
Shah dismissed the four angrily and demoted them.[80] Also, until 1963
most ministers had been seasoned politicians with some claim to
statesmanship; after 1963 cabinet ministers tended to be dull technocrats
or cronies of the Shah: the regime would become increasingly sultanistic
and thus make it almost impossible for any independent personality to
have a role in it.

More important, perhaps, a quantum jump had occurred in the level
of oppression. Let us remember that in May 1961 the death of *one*
teacher had brought down a government. Two years later hundreds,
and many believed thousands, were killed and the regime did not

[79]See Samuel P. Huntington, *Political Order in Changing Societies* (1968), pp. 148–91.
[80]See Zonis, *Political Elite*, pp. 62–66, for an account of this incident.

budge. A corollary of this intensification of repression was the treatment of the press. After 1963 about seventy publications which had generally supported the Shah's regime but were not directly controlled by the government were closed down. The severity of the repression abolished political life in Iran.

The explosion of the clerical opposition movement on the political scene of Iran meant that Nationalists lost the capacity to mobilize the masses at critical junctures. As Saleh's reaction to the 1963 riots shows, human lives meant far more to the NF leadership than to the militant clergy led by Khomeini, for whom martyrdom was an essentially positive phenomenon. The many deaths caused by the religiously inspired riots of June 1963 posed a challenge to the Nationalist cause, for compared to the religious opposition they had very few martyrs to show: Hosein Fatemi, Mosaddeq's foreign minister, one or two of the three students killed on December 7, 1953 (Azar 16, 1332), the teacher slain in May 1961, and a few more students killed here and there.

After June 1963 the secular, liberal opposition to the Shah embodied by the National Front, fell silent inside Iran. New methods of opposition had to be found, and these are studied in our next chapter.

CHAPTER 5

_____

Crossing the Desert:

1963–1977

After the LMI's top leadership went to prison in 1963, lower-level activists tried to keep the movement going. But as the Shah's personal dictatorship became increasingly repressive in the years after his White Revolution, these activities soon petered out. Of those LMI members or sympathizers who did not go to prison, some gave up political activity altogether, preferring to wait for better times. Those who did not wish to give up, chose one of three ways of action. One group carried on political action from abroad. Another group came to the conclusion that the people's political and religious awareness had to be raised before any opposition to the Shah could have a chance of success. The Hoseiniyeh Ershad movement, discussed later in this chapter, is the embodiment of this political option. Still others, mostly younger people, gave up the idea of political activism, which had become impossible anyway, and resorted to armed struggle. They founded the Mojahedin guerrilla group. As we shall see, the three courses of action sometimes overlapped and there was considerable interaction among them. All these efforts notwithstanding, the period 1963–77 witnessed a rise of Islamic fundamentalism rather than modernism. But before we turn our attention to these movements, we should introduce the main figures of the LMI's second generation.

The LMI's Second Generation

The leaders of the second generation of the LMI were people who got their first taste of politics and religious activity during the relatively free period from 1941 TO 1953, and whose youth coincided with the Shah's dictatorship, a regime seen by Nationalists as foreign-imposed. The main figures were Ali Shariati, the most influential intellectual in recent Iranian history, Ebrahim Yazdi, Mostafa Chamran, Abbas Amir-Entezam, and, to some extent, Sadeq Qotbzadeh.

Ali Shariati

A wide range of political groupings in contemporary Iran vie for association with Shariati's name. Some may object to his inclusion in a study of the LMI. The fact is that during the LMI's first period of open activity Shariati was in Paris, and that, before his death, he did take part in the preliminary discussions concerning a possible revival of the LMI, held in early 1977.

Whatever one may think of the substantive value of his intellectual production, it is undeniable that, next to Khomeini, Shariati is the most influential figure in the Islamic movement that led to the revolution of 1979. His restless life, fiery oratory, iconoclastic style, and early death at the age of forty-four have made him a quintessentially romantic hero. It is not surprising that a cult has developed around his name, and his life and action have been the object of an extensive hagiography.[1]

Ali Shariati was born on November 23, 1933 (Azar 2, 1312), in Mashad into a religious and Mosaddeqist family. The greatest influence during his early years was his father, Mohammad-Taqi Shariati, whose 2,000-volume library and Center for the Propagation of Islamic Truth provided intellectual stimulation. In high school he was not content to follow only the normal curriculum, and studied Arabic and the religious sciences with his father. He also learned some French before he entered the university. While still in high school, he entered Mashad's Teacher Training College. He taught elementary school in several villages outside Mashad, and at the same time studied for his high school diploma and then for his degree from the Teacher Training College. In 1956 a Faculty of Letters was founded in Mashad. Shariati, by now a teacher, enrolled for a degree in modern languages. For the next few years he would teach in local schools, lecture at his father's institute, and pursue his studies at Mashad University. In 1958 he received his *licence* (B.A.). Shariati was also active in Nationalist politics and he was the youngest of the NRM activists arrested in 1957.

In these years Shariati published his first books and translations. His first translation, Alexis Carrel's *Prayer*, came out in 1948. Two more

---

[1]See for instance the publisher's preface and the translator's introduction to Ali Shariati, *Man and Islam* (1981), pp. vii–xxi.

works were published in the 1950s. The first was *Maktab-e vaseteh* (The median school), on the philosophy of history. In this book, published in 1955 (Tir 1334), he argued that Islam was a "median school" between communism and capitalism, which combined the advantages of all other schools of thought but had none of their defects. In 1958 (1337) Shariati published in Mashad a book entitled *Abu Zarr: Khoda parast-e sosialist* (Abu Dharr: The God-fearing socialist). This book, whose title in the Persian translation may reflect Shariati's membership in Nakhshab's movement (discussed in chapter 3) was loosely based on the work of the radical Egyptian novelist Abdulhamid Jawdat as-Sahar. It traced the life of one of the Prophet's first followers, Abu Dharr, who had upheld egalitarian values after Muhammad's death, supported the Imam Ali, and, as a result, had been exiled to the desert by the third caliph. For Shariati, as for left-leaning Muslims in other countries,[2] Abu Dharr was the first Muslim socialist. In 1959, Shariati was finally granted the scholarship that had been his due since he had graduated at the top of his class two years earlier; it had been refused on account of his political activities. With it, he went to Paris for graduate studies. Before his trip, he had visited Bazargan in the company of his father, and Bazargan had counseled him to study sociology.[3]

The France that Shariati found in 1960 was rather different from the Third Republic Bazargan had known. The Algerian crisis was at its height, more and more colonies were becoming independent, and Paris was teeming with Third World intellectuals struggling with identity crises. The West was an uncontested model no more. Shariati soon made the acquaintance of a large number of Algerians and became an active supporter of Algerian independence. He contributed articles to *El-Moudjahid*, the organ of the FLN (National Liberation Front), and was on occasion beaten up by French police.

The growing corpus of secondary literature on Shariati has emphasized his contacts with left-leaning intellectuals during this period. The sociologist Georges Gurvitch, Jean-Paul Sartre, and Frantz Fanon are often mentioned. While Shariati was certainly influenced by these men, his actual personal contacts with them have been vastly exaggerated. With Fanon he corresponded for a short time, and Sartre he met once in a café. He did attend Gurvitch's lectures at the Sorbonne, and he also frequented the company of Jesuits. A widely held belief has it that he took a Ph.D. in sociology. His most enthusiastic admirers even claim that in the four years he spent in Paris, he received doctorates in

---

[2] Manfred Halpern, *The Politics of Social Change in the Middle East and North Africa* (1963), p. 158n.

[3] Abdolali Bazargan, ed., *Masa'el va moshkelat-e nakhostin sal-e enqelab* (The problems and difficulties of the first year of the revolution) (1983), p. 312.

both sociology and the history of religions.[4] The truth is, however, that he only studied for a *doctorat d'université* (at the time the lowest doctoral degree in France; it presupposed neither course work nor exams, was reserved for foreigners, and ceased being recognized as a doctorate in Iran sometime in the early 1970s) in "Letters" at the Sorbonne. His dissertation, written under the direction of the eminent Iranologist Gilbert Lazard and presented in 1963, consisted of an edition and translation of a medieval book, *Faza'el ol-Balkh*.[5] This book contains references to the moral degeneration and political corruption, and the resulting rise of superstition, in the city of Balkh before its sack by the Mongols.[6]

In Paris Shariati became the main founder of the external branch of the LMI, as will be related later. He returned to Iran in 1964, and was immediately arrested and jailed for six months. Upon his release, he was made an elementary school teacher outside Mashad, which he resented, given his qualifications. After a few months, however, he received a teaching appointment at Mashad University, his alma mater. But soon the style and content of his lectures incurred the displeasure of the authorities, and he was suspended from academia. After a while he went to Teheran, and began his cooperation with the Hoseiniyeh Ershad Institute.[7]

Ebrahim Yazdi

Ebrahim Yazdi was born in about 1931 (1310) to a traditional middle-class family in Qazvin. When he was six, his family moved to Teheran, where his father would operate a large grocery store. He received his secondary education at the Dar ol-Fonun, where he started his activism by founding the Ami Kabir Islamic Association, named after the great nineteenth-century reformer who had founded the school and who was eventually killed by the then Shah because of his reformist zeal. In high school he was consistently the best student in his class. After graduating, he entered Teheran University's Faculty of Pharmaceutics, where he became a leading member of the Muslim Student Association, to whose various publications he regularly contributed. Early on

---

[4]Introduction to Shariati, *Man and Islam*, p. x.

[5]Ministère de l'éducation nationale—Direction des bibliothèques de France, *Catalogue des thèses de doctorat soutenues devant les universités françaises—Année 1963* (1964), p. 381.

[6]Editor's Introduction, Abdolhayy Habibi, ed., *Faza'el ol-Balkh* (1971).

[7]Biographical data for Shariati are taken from *Payam-e Mujahid*, no. 49, Tir-Mordad 1356 (July 1977); Introduction to *On the Sociology of Islam*, by Ali Shariati, trans. Hamid Algar (1979); and Shahrough Akhavi, *Religion and Politics in Contemporary Iran* (1980), pp. 144–45; and personal testimonies from Iranian residents in Paris who knew him well (including a former roommate) and who wish to remain anonymous.

he had some contacts with the Devotees of Islam and collaborated with them, but after their break with the National Movement he sided with the latter. During the July 1952 (Tir 1331) events, he organized student support for Mosaddeq.

After the 1953 coup he joined the NRM, his activities centering on the NRM's University Committee and the movement's publications. During these years he also worked for a trading company in Teheran. It was his employer who finally managed to get him a passport (for his anti-Shah activities he had been barred from leaving the country). He left Iran in about 1960 (1339). Yazdi eventually settled in the United States, and pursued his studies in pharmacology, specializing in oncology. He did postdoctoral work at the Massachusetts Institute of Technology, then worked in the Veterans Administration Hospital affiliated with Baylor Medical College in Houston, Texas, where he also received an appointment as assistant professor. He was the main driving force behind the LMI's American branch and the burgeoning network of Muslim Student Associations in the United States.

Ebrahim Yazdi is the most controversial leading figure of the LMI, among whom he was closest to Khomeini. As Shariati has become a cult figure in Iran, Yazdi has been the target of slander campaigns, which centered on the rumor that during his long stay in the United States he had acquired American citizenship.[8]

Mostafa Chamran

Mostafa Chamran was born in 1933 (1311), into a devout family in south Teheran. His father had to work hard to give all his children an education. Young Mostafa attended first the Dar ol-Fonun and then Alborz High School. At the age of fifteen he began frequenting Muslim Student Associations and Taleqani's Hedayat Mosque.

In 1953 (1332) he entered Teheran University to study electrical engineering. He also became an active member of the NRM and was responsible for the distribution of the movement's paper on the campus of Teheran University. In 1959 Chamran graduated at the top of his class. After that, he spent one year teaching at his alma mater and in 1959, taking advantage of the state scholarships offered to top students, left for the United States to pursue graduate studies. First he took an M.S. at Texas A & M, then went to the University of California at Berkeley, where he completed a Ph.D. in only three years. In

---

[8]To counter these rumors, Yazdi asked Khomeini for a formal denial. It may or may not be significant that Khomeini confirmed in his letter that Yazdi was "of Iranian origin and a Muslim."

California he founded Muslim Student Associations. Upon graduation Chamran moved to the East Coast to work at Bell Laboratories in New Jersey. His job did not satisfy him, however, and in 1964 he embarked on a trip to the Middle East, never again to resume his scientific career.

In a political movement characterized by its attempts to bring out the rational elements in Islam, Chamran stands out for his mystical tendencies. He was an *aref*, loved the mystical poetry of Rumi, and was a practitioner of traditional Iranian athletics, a passion which earned him the acquaintance of Gholamreza Takhti, Iran's legendary wrestling champion and member of the National Front's High Council who was allegedly killed by SAVAK in 1967. His penchant for military organization and his activities in Lebanon with the Shi'ite Amal movement, which he helped establish, should be seen in this light. After the revolution he returned to Iran and helped reorganize the country's armed forces. Chamran, who was the LMI's foremost military expert, was killed in the Iran-Iraq war on June 21, 1981 (Khordad 31, 1360), under dubious circumstances.[9]

Abbas Amir-Entezam

Abbas Amir-Entezam was born in about 1933 (1312) into a wealthy carpet-manufacturing family. He studied at Teheran University, taking his *licence* (B.S.) in engineering in 1955. As a student he was active in the NRM, and later became a founding member of the LMI. Upon graduation he worked as a consulting engineer in Teheran, until he went to Paris for eleven months in 1963. From 1964 to 1966 he studied at the University of California at Berkeley, where he received a master's degree in engineering. Here he became active in the Muslim Student Association founded by Chamran and also in the Confederation of Iranian Students, the umbrella organization of anti-Shah students abroad. He worked in the United States from 1966 to March 1969, at which point he returned to Teheran as a consulting engineer. In 1971 he set up his own firm, which soon flourished. After his return to Iran, he maintained contacts with Yazdi, and in 1977 became one of the chief interlocutors of the U.S. embassy in Teheran.

Abbas Amir-Entezam is the most secular among prominent LMI figures. He is also the only one who is currently in prison.[10]

---

[9]Biographical information on Chamran is adapted from *Zendeginameh-ye sardar-e rashid-e eslam shahid doktor Mostafa Chamran* (Biography of . . . Dr. Chamran) (1982).

[10]Biographical information on Amir-Entezam has been obtained from Daneshjuyan-e mosalman-e peirow-e khatt-e emam, *Asnad-e laneh-ye jasusi* (Documents of the spies' nest), vol. 10 (n.d.).

Sadeq Qotbzadeh

Sadeq Qotbzadeh (d. 1982) was born in about 1936 (1315) in Isfahan into a wealthy Bazaar family. He attended the Dar ol-Fonun in Teheran, where he became politically active. First a supporter of Ay. Kashani in the early 1950s, he remained loyal to the National Movement after 1953 and was both a high school delegate in the NRM's ruling council and an active member of the MSA.

In 1958 he left Iran for the United States, where he became active in Iranian student politics. Beginning in 1954 the Iranian Students Association had been receiving $10,000 per year from a group called the American Friends of the Middle East, the funds coming from the CIA, according to Qotbzadeh. In 1959 payments were stopped. The Iranian embassy in Washington, under the new and dynamic ambassador Ardeshir Zahedi, a former son-in-law of the Shah, offered to fill the gap. The Iranian Students Association held its next meeting in Ypsilanti, Michigan, in September 1960. At this congress Qotbzadeh attacked the Shah and his system in most virulent terms and was elected to the central council of the association. Zahedi had to retreat, and Qotbzadeh was thus instrumental in freeing the Iranian Students Association from government control. At that congress the association also affiliated with the Confederation of Iranian Students. A strong anti-Shah speech delivered in January 1961 (1339) in a Washington hotel, during which he slapped the Iranian ambassador in the face, brought him notoriety as the most famous Iranian student organizer abroad. Always active in student politics, Qotbzadeh never finished any degree requirements.

During these years he was a member of the National Front's Council in the United States. At the end of 1962 (1341) he left the United States, and in 1964 arrived in the Middle East, where at one point he acquired Syrian citizenship. He then began to organize MSAs outside Iran, and these associations would become the central focus of his attention after 1969 (1348). In 1966 (1345) he left the Iranian Students Associations after National Front sympathizers united with leftists to attack him personally.[11]

From the mid-1960s onward Qotbzadeh was constantly on the move, dividing his time between the United States, Canada, and Europe (where he occasionally spoke to church groups), and the Middle East. He was the main intermediary between the MSAs and various radical Arab states. Once or twice a year he would meet Khomeini in Najaf, and in due course became quite close to him, despite his rather

---

[11]Details of Qotbzadeh's activities among Iranian students are taken from a personal letter, dated October 2, 1967, and written in Washington, D.C., to Schapur Ansari, of Bad Homburg, West Germany, who kindly made it available to me.

latitudinarian private life. In 1970 he became directly involved with the LMI(a). In 1976 (1355), in Paris, SAVAK hired a small-time criminal to kill Qotbzadeh, but the putative gunman preferred to give himself up to French police, and a minor scandal ensued.[12] Qotbzadeh's links to the LMI core in Teheran were rather loose, and in 1978 he attempted to found a break-away LMI in Paris, claiming that he had Taleqani's support. In September 1982 he became the first prominent revolutionary figure to be executed by the Islamic Republic.[13]

As these biographical sketches show, the leading figures of the LMI's external wing were all good students in high school, which for many was the Dar ol-Fonun.[14] It may or may not be a coincidence that those who were most deeply committed to Islam had gone abroad on state scholarships, which they had had some trouble obtaining. If one tries to understand ideological commitment as a result of strain,[15] one might argue that the LMI's second generation experienced more strain and conflict in their youth than, for example, Bazargan or Y. Sahabi. They are thus an intermediary generation between the liberal founders of modernism, and the proponents of totalitarian fundamentalism who dominate today's Islamic Republic.[16]

LMI Activities outside Iran

Little has been said so far about Nationalist activities outside Iran. Such activities did not begin with the crackdown of 1963; we need to go back to 1960 to chronicle the oppositional role of Iranian Nationalists abroad. But first, a glance at the history of oppositional activities outside Iran in general will be useful.

The Opposition in Exile before 1960

From the end of the nineteenth century, many Iranian intellectuals, faced with the impossibility of being politically and journalistically active in their own country, took advantage of the freedom of speech in Europe (and to a lesser extent India) to agitate for their ideas where the

---

[12]For details, see J.-C. Guillepaud, "Les Tribulations d'un 'tueur' de la Savak," *Le Monde*, April 8, 1977, p. 2.

[13]Biographical information on Qotbzadeh is from *Bamdad* (Teheran), January 16, 1980 (Dey 26, 1358), p. 12.

[14]See chapter 2 for the significance of this.

[15]See Clifford Geertz, "Ideology as a Cultural System," in *Interpretation of Cultures* (1973), pp. 203–4.

[16]On the generational aspect of modernism and fundamentalism see Michael M. J. Fischer, "Islam and the Revolt of the Petit [sic] Bourgeoisie," *Daedalus* 111 (1982).

arm of the state could not reach them. In the nineteenth century this was the path taken by two of the great reformers Iran has produced, Mirza Malkam Khan, and S. Jamaleddin Asadabadi, "al-Afghani." After the end of the First World War and the beginning of Reza Khan's rule in Iran, many Iranian students went to Europe, some sponsored by the state, others relying on private means. By far the most popular destinations of these Iranians were France and the French-speaking areas and universities of Belgium and Switzerland, followed by England and Germany.

Germany, however, became the main center of anti-Pahlavi political action in the interwar period. Reza Shah sent more students to Germany than to any other country, and the Weimar Republic, in keeping with its liberal political culture and constitution, had very progressive laws on political asylum. This made it easier for Iranian dissidents to live and be active in Germany than in France. The other reason for Germany's prominence is more elusive. It seems that Iranians in France were housed in boarding schools, whereas in Germany the Iranian students lived by themselves. Moreover, the Iranian counselor for students abroad, Esma'il Mer'at, had his residence in Paris. This meant that Iranians in France were under constant surveillance, a circumstance that helps explain the higher degree of student activity in Germany, as opposed to France. These favorable conditions ended in 1932, when Chancellor H. Brüning was persuaded to sacrifice Germany's hospitality toward political dissidents to the country's economic interests: Reza Shah had threatened to place his import orders elsewhere.[17] This early foreign-based Iranian opposition was overwhelmingly leftist. Of those members of the "group of 53" who had received a higher education in Europe, five, including the central figure Taqi Arani, had studied in Berlin, and only one each in Paris, Grenoble, and Moscow.[18]

After 1945, many Iranian students went abroad again. There have always been fewer places available in Iranian universities than there are applicants (the ratio of available places to applicants has hovered around one to ten). The reason for this discrepancy lies primarily in the highly academic curriculum of Iranian high schools, which, at least until the mid-1970s, did not prepare students for anything but a university education.[19] Therefore, getting a university education abroad was a normal, not an extravagant option. Given the high status of education in Iran,[20] it was not uncommon for entire families to tighten

---

[17]Ahmad Mahrad: "Lag Berlin in Persien? Iranische Oppositionelle in der Weimarer Republik," in Kurt Greussing, ed., *Revolution in Iran and Afghanistan* (1980), pp. 77–122.

[18]Ervand Abrahamian, *Iran between Two Revolutions* (1982), pp. 156–61.

[19]A. Reza Arasteh, *Education and Social Awakening in Iran, 1850–1968* (1969), pp. 94–96.

[20]See Marvin Zonis, *The Political Elite of Iran* (1971), pp. 163–64.

their belts to allow one son to study in the West. In 1960 there were 15,000 Iranian students abroad, and by 1966 this number had risen to 30,000. Of these, only about one-tenth were state-financed.[21]

In 1949 Iranians started flocking to German universities again. They were lured by the relatively low cost of living in postwar Germany and attractive offers from German universities eager to end the international isolation of the Hitler years, to which one can add a widespread Germanophilia among Iranians.[22] By the end of the 1960s Germany had the highest Iranian student population, closely followed by the United States.[23] It was natural, therefore, that Germany became one of the centers of antiregime activity by Iranian students, especially until the mid-1960s.

France had always been a popular country with Iranian students too, but not England, which was considered too expensive. An American education was unaffordable for most Iranians in the years immediately after the war, but beginning in the early 1960s, more and more Iranians found the resources to study in the United States, which soon became the country with the most Iranian students. All these students constituted a fertile base, sometimes the only one, for the Iranian opposition against the Shah. Serious organizational efforts began in 1960, as oppositional activities burgeoned inside Iran.

Nationalist Opposition Abroad after 1960

Students were among the first to organize. In Europe, the Confederation of Iranian Students attracted for a while both Nationalist and Tudeh students. In the United States, Shahin Fatemi (a nephew of Mosaddeq's slain foreign minister) was active. So was Nakhshab, who in September 1960 led a modest anti-Shah demonstration of seventeen students outside the United Nations in New York. News of this act was received enthusiastically in Teheran, and although small, it also served to galvanize the anti-Shah opposition in America. A few weeks later at the congress of the Iranian Students Association, Nationalist elements around Nakhshab and Qotbzadeh managed to wrest control of the association from pro-regime elements.

Meanwhile, efforts were made to create organizations of the National Front in the United States and in Europe. In the United States the presence of Ali Shayegan (d. 1980), one of Mosaddeq's closest collaborators, facilitated the formation of a National Front organization. Its

---

[21]Arasteh, *Education*, p. 41.
[22]Issa Chehabi, "Kulturelle Beziehungen zwischen Deutschland und Iran," *Die Horen* 26 (123) (Autumn 1981), 163–64.
[23]Arasteh, *Education*, p. 42.

establishment was announced on February 2, 1962, and it held its first congress in New York City in 1963. At that congress a split occurred, as a result of which the National Front in the United States did not hold its next congress until April 1966, again in New York City. Two more congresses were held in 1967 and 1968.

In Europe a preliminary meeting had been held in Stuttgart, Germany, in 1961. Khosrow Khan Qashqai, in Europe since the 1950s, began publishing a newspaper, *Bakhtar-e emruz* (Today's Evening—this was the name of Hosein Fatemi's old paper), which started appearing on April 4, 1961. Most of his collaborators, however, were Tudeh sympathizers.[24] In May 1962 the establishment of the National Front's European organization was announced. At its first regular congress in August 1962 in Wiesbaden, Germany, the newspaper's name was changed to *Iran-e azad* (Free Iran); Ali Shariati became one of its chief editors and the first issue appeared in November 1962.

Ali Shariati had been active among Nationalist circles in Europe from the very moment of his arrival in Paris. After working with an ephemeral group, Javanan-e nehzat-e melli-ye Iran—Orupa (Youth of the Iranian National Movement—Europe), he became involved in the attempts to create a National Front organization abroad. In early 1962 he traveled to Iran to see his ailing mother. There, he renewed his contacts with his old friends from the NRM times, who had now created their own party, the LMI. After his mother's death he returned to Paris. Influenced by the recent examples of Cuba and Algeria, he came to the conclusion that violent struggle had to be prepared against the Shah. In February he circulated a letter to other LMI sympathizers in Europe in which he proposed the creation of a "special unit" inside the National Front, which would not have any open links with the NF so as not to jeopardize the parent organization's activities in Iran, but which would be charged with preparing the revolution. He added that if the NF agreed with this proposal, so much the better. If it did not, LMI sympathizers in the NF would have to go it alone.

With the National Front established, Shariati decided to pursue the matter. In a letter dated September 24, 1962, which he again circulated among LMI sympathizers, he proposed for the first time the establishment of an external branch of the LMI. He argued that until that point the constitution of a National Front organization in Europe had top priority: now that this task had been accomplished, one had to go further. The heritage of the NRM had to be safeguarded from the vagaries of everyday politics. The LMI should be established under the umbrella of the National Front, which was by definition a heterogene-

[24]Cosroe Chaqueri, personal communication, March 1989.

ous coalition formed for a limited purpose. It lacked an ideological underpinning. The spiritual void in the National Front was terrifying, for people who entered a political movement at a moment of excitement would stay only if they were offered spiritual nourishment. Otherwise, once the initial exuberance had passed, they would either become disenchanted or leave politics after the excitement was over. Thousands of Iranian students were going back to Iran every year, but they were going back empty-handed. The world faced pressing questions: socialism, the role of religion, the reform of property laws in Islamic countries, national liberation movements. These were all substantive issues that transcended the establishment of the rule of law (a reference to the main programmatic point of the National Front). If they (that is, Shariati and his friends) did not try to find solutions, others would. The LMI sympathizers loyally had helped to build the National Front. Now that that had been done, they could start building up an external organization of the LMI. This organization would have to be totally secret. At the same time its members should continue their sincere and loyal participation in the NF.

In a letter to the National Front's Executive Committee dated January 16, 1963, a few days before the arrest in Iran of the National Front's and the LMI's top leadership, Shariati proposed his other plan; namely, the establishment of a secret unit within the NF to prepare the revolution in Iran.[25]

But inside the National Front tensions had appeared, tensions that had partly personal and partly ideological causes. Shariati became disenchanted with his work at *Iran-e azad*, feeling that he was surrounded by "capricious, untrustworthy, egocentric" people who made life difficult for him. He resigned. Shariati did not participate in the second congress of the National Front, held in 1963 across the river from Wiesbaden in Mayence, and in 1964 he returned to Iran, ending his involvement in the LMI's external wing.[26] We will find him again, when we discuss the Hoseiniyeh Ershad movement.

Before we turn our attention to the LMI(a) proper, a few words are in order about other National Front activities outside Iran. The organization held several congresses, but they were plagued by splits. In the United States activities dwindled in the late 1960s, in Europe they went on until the mid-1970s. In 1970 leftist Nationalists established a new Middle Eastern branch of the NF in Beirut, where they published their

[25]Secular Nationalists also thought of organizing their own "secret unit." They held discussions with Egyptian authorities, but these talks came to naught and were broken off in 1962. Cosroe Chaqueri, personal communication, March 1989.

[26]Information on Shariati's involvement in the National Front is taken from *Payam-e Mujahid*, no. 49, Tir-Mordad 1356 (July 1977).

own organ, again called *Bakhtar-e emruz*. This journal gave broad coverage to the anti-Shah activities of the Fada'iyan (discussed later).

The LMI (Abroad)

The first meetings of the LMI(a) were informal. Shariati was chosen to head its secretariat, but the group did not publicize its activities. After the Third National Front, of which the LMI was a member, was constituted in 1964, the LMI(a) would upon occasion issue statements in its own name.[27]

In the spring of 1963, LMI sympathizers abroad, mainly Shariati, Yazdi, and Chamran, decided that armed struggle was the only way to get rid of the Shah regime. But revolutions required technical know-how, which Iranians lacked. Leftists could acquire this know-how in communist countries, and indeed some former Tudeh members did venture to China, and others established contacts with Cuba and Albania. Muslims, on the other hand, had fewer choices: Algeria and Egypt seemed the only options.

Using Shariati's old contacts with the FLN newspaper *El-Moudjahid*, a Paris-based LMI member was dispatched to Algiers to try to get FLN help in teaching young Iranian volunteers the use of weapons, techniques of underground organization, and so on. Although the Algerians seemed accommodating, concrete arrangements were made with Egypt. The first LMI(a) delegation, consisting of Yazdi, Chamran, and Qotbzadeh, went to Cairo in December 1963 (Dey 1342). Shariati, having opposed the choice of Egypt, did not go along. Nasser's representatives promised help and the two sides agreed that the LMI(a) would set up its organizational structure there. In July 1964 (Tir 1343) Chamran, Qotbzadeh, and Yazdi established the Sazeman-e makhsus-e ettehad va amal (acronym: SAMA'), Special Organization for Unity and Action, in Egypt. SAMA' maintained links with the imprisoned LMI leadership in Iran and informed them of its plans. These included training young Iranians for guerrilla warfare against the Shah. Chamran was chosen to head the training program. In Teheran a group of three LMI figures, including Rahim Ata'i, was formed to supervise contacts with the exiles and to select and send recruits to Egypt.

From early 1962 on, Chamran and Yazdi had started collecting material on guerrilla warfare from around the world, much of it communist-inspired. After 1964 they used translations of these materials in the training program, and also smuggled them into Iran, where

---

[27]Information on the early activities of the LMI(a) is from *Zendeginameh*, pp. 18–35.

they were made available to those young LMI members, such as M. Hanifnezhad, who were preparing to organize the Mojahedin.

In mid-1966 clouds of discord began to overshadow the harmonious relations between the Egyptian government and the LMI(a). Nasser wanted SAMA' to start anti-Shah broadcasts over Radio Cairo. The LMI(a), however, preferred to go on preparing quietly for the armed uprising against the Shah. Another source of friction was the United Arab Republic's increasingly nationalistic policy vis-à-vis Iran. Having always loyally supported Arab causes (Suez, Algeria, Palestine), LMI members were disappointed and annoyed that Nasser's Arab national-ism had turned anti-Iranian. They complained to both the Egyptian government and to the Arab League about the toponymical changes introduced by Arab governments (Arabian Gulf for Persian Gulf, Arabistan for Khuzistan), pointing out that a rift between Arabs and Iranians would only benefit the common enemy. They were politely listened to, but they did not achieve much. Nasser, for his part, was disappointed with them, for he wanted anti-Shah action, which SAMA' had failed to produce. As a result, in 1966 SAMA' left Egypt, and in effect disbanded.

At the close of the Egyptian episode, LMI(a) leaders gathered and concluded that the Shah regime was now so consolidated that armed struggle was futile. They decided to concentrate on the religious education of Iranian students abroad. Young Iranians were seeking foreign educations in ever-increasing numbers, and many now came from traditional, less Westernized, middle-class backgrounds and were thus amenable to organization along religious lines. New MSAs were to be created and the existing ones expanded. In Germany this was done by Sadeq Tabataba'i,[28] in France by Sadeq Qotbzadeh and Hasan Habibi,[29] in the United States by Yazdi and also Nakhshab, who ceased political activity in the mid-1960s and concentrated on Islamic mission-ary work, also among Americans.

By 1977 the MSAs in the United States had about 600 activist members, but many more Iranian students sympathized with the network, at least to some degree. The majority of MSA members sympathized politically with the LMI(a). In California, however, the MSAs developed a life of their own, and Paris-based NF organizer Abolhasan Banisadr had a number of supporters in California.

The decision to concentrate on religious organizations meant the end

[28]Tabataba'i had studied at the Technische Hochschule in Aix-la-Chapelle (Aachen), Germany, and then settled in that country as a businessman. He married into the Khomeini family, and went to Iran after the revolution.
[29]Habibi studied in Aix-en-Provence, and was close to both Shariati and Banisadr. Although religiously oriented, he never joined the LMI.

of cooperation with nonreligious groups, such as the National Front
(which had become inactive anyway), and the Confederation of Iranian
Students, which was by now under firm leftist control. This exacerbated the estrangement between the secular and the religious sectors of
the National Movement. In light of later, postrevolutionary developments, the situation that obtained in Paris is of great significance.
There, one of the most active National Front organizers was Abolhasan
Banisadr, who had gone to Europe in late 1963. Although himself very
religious, Banisadr stood for a united National Front; he consistently
tried to win the cooperation of Europe-based sympathizers of the LMI
and of the Maleki socialists. He collaborated both with secularists,
such as Ahmad Salamatian, and with more religiously oriented people,
such as Hasan Habibi. To these National Front activists it appeared that
the LMI(a) had given up the fight against the Shah.[30] Qotbzadeh
maintained some degree of cooperation with Banisadr, but also operated independently. One minor incident can, with the benefit of hindsight, be interpreted as indicative of the LMI(a)'s growing closeness
with Khomeini, a development that paralleled the LMI(a)'s estrangement from the National Front. In the mid- and late 1960s Nationalists
in Paris were preparing and publishing the collected papers, speeches,
and letters of Mosaddeq. The volumes were being published by
"Mosaddeq Publications." After a few volumes came out, Qotbzadeh,
without consulting anyone, changed the publisher's name to "Modarres
Publications." Secular Nationalists saw this as a gesture toward Khomeini.

From the LMI's point of view, the relative consolidation of the Shah's
regime in the years 1963–66 meant that change would take time;
therefore it was necessary to concentrate on the ideological preparation
of Iranian students abroad, to "raise their consciousness," one might
say.

In Houston, Yazdi also established a publishing house to distribute
modernist Islamic books sent from Iran. After 1974, such books could
no longer be printed in Iran, and Yazdi therefore proceeded to found
the Book Distribution Center, which has reprinted and translated
religious texts ever since. In 1977 the center issued the first translation
of a book by Shariati. It also sends books and pamphlets to other
Muslim countries and maintains ties with black Muslim groups in the
States. The center caters exclusively to religious tastes: the whole
spectrum of Muslim writing is covered, from fundamentalists, such as
Mawlana Mawdudi, to Shariati and Bazargan, and Taleqani. With one
or two exceptions, the organization's catalog offers no works by secular
Nationalist writers on nonreligious subjects. The funds for all these

[30]Abolhasan Banisadr, personal interview, Auvers-sur-Oise, July 1982.

activities were provided by wealthy bazaaris, who, under the Shah's liberal foreign exchange rules, were free to transfer the necessary sums abroad.

In about 1970–71, with the beginning of Mojahedin operations in Iran imminent, the LMI(a) came to the conclusion that the groundwork for the revolutionary uprising had been laid. The revolution now entered its active phase. The LMI(a) began to operate openly as a political group. With the help of such sympathetic academics as Richard Falk of Princeton University, and Richard Cottam of the University of Pittsburgh, contacts were made with various human rights groups (such as Amnesty International and the Unitarian Universalist Service Committee), and the abuses of the Shah regime were thus given wide publicity.

Relations were reestablished with the Mojahedin, and the LMI(a) at long last gave up its own military ambitions. In Houston, Yazdi began publishing a monthly organ of the LMI(a), which he called *Payam-e Mujahid* (The Warrior's Message). It publicized oppositional activities in Iran, covering the left, the Mojahedin, and fundamentalists. The Shah's regime and its excesses were denounced, Muslims around the world were supported, and every May a leading article commemorated the founding of the LMI in Iran and provided a rare but regular reminder that the LMI(a) traced its lineage to the National Movement. Mosaddeq himself was mentioned, even commemorated, but the National Movement was more often than not presented as a forerunner of the Islamic revival. This view is congruent with the self-image of the LMI as a religious *and* Nationalist group, but it misrepresents the relationship between the National Movement and the Islamic Movement, which are quite independent of one another. By the mid-1970s, *Payam-e Mujahid* had reached a circulation of up to 6,000. Reprints were sometimes made in Europe.

Meanwhile, in 1970, Chamran moved to Lebanon. Given that country's open society, it was a convenient base for the LMI(a) Middle Eastern operations, such as there were, and a good place to maintain contact with the Mojahedin. Chamran also established close relations with an old acquaintance, Imam Musa al-Sadr, the leader of Lebanon's Shi'ites since the late 1950s and an Iranian by birth, who was beginning to make that community's voice heard in Lebanese politics. Chamran took a leading part in the formation of the Shi'ite Harakat al-mahrumin (Movement of the Deprived), and his martial proclivities found a new outlet in the militia organization of the Shi'ites, the Amal. He accompanied Imam Musa al-Sadr on all his foreign trips, but not on his last, to Libya, where he disappeared in August 1978.

In Lebanon Chamran settled in the outskirts of Tyre where he became the director of the Burj-al-Shimali Technical Institute, destined to provide education for indigent Shi'ites.[31] In addition to vocational training, pupils were also given "ideological training," for which purpose many of Shariati's works were translated into Arabic. It so happened that the school was in the immediate vicinity of a large Palestinian refugee camp. Some LMI(a) members had already met Palestinian guerrillas in Egypt, when the nascent al-Fatah was starting its military training program there. In 1970, after al-Fatah had expanded its operations in the wake of the 1967 Arab-Israeli war, relations became closer. The Mojahedin were sending some of their members to Palestine Liberation Organization (PLO) camps for training, and Chamran was in contact with them. Soon, however, the LMI(a)'s relations with the Mojahedin deteriorated somewhat, because of the Mojahedin's publication of a book called *Shenakht* (Cognition), with whose leftist content the LMI(a) could not agree. It refused to reprint it. After the rift between Amal and the PLO, the LMI(a)'s relations also deteriorated with the PLO, who found new friends in Iran.

In 1978 Yazdi left for Iraq to be closer to Khomeini. The last proclamation of the LMI(a), in the last issue of *Payam-e Mujahid*, December 1978 (Azar 1357), condemned the LMI's not-quite-revolutionary-enough stance vis-à-vis the Shah. While maintaining perfect courtesy toward Bazargan, the proclamation stated that the LMI(a) was firmly following the policies of Khomeini. By this time, *Payam-e Mujahid* had relegated the traditional Iranian solar calendar to second place behind the lunar calendar favored by the clergy and usually only used for ritual purposes.

The Hoseiniyeh Ershad Institute

In Iran, a *Hoseiniyeh* refers to a place where the sufferings and martyrdom of Imam Husein, the Third Shi'ite Imam, are related, usually during the lunar month of Muharram. Traditionally these ceremonies have a purely emotional and cathartic purpose. The word *Ershad* can be translated as "guidance." The addition of *Ershad* in the name of the Hoseiniyeh Ershad Institute meant that the purpose of this particular *Hoseiniyeh* was not the lachrymose emotional gratification obtained at a traditional *Hoseiniyeh*. Rather, it was to be a place where Iranians were to be guided toward fundamental change in the affairs of society. The choice of a *Hoseiniyeh* as a center of religious modernism also reflected the fact that traditionally *Hoseiniyeh*s were not directly controlled by the ulema.

[31]Augustus Richard Norton, *Amal and the Shi'a: Struggle for the Soul of Lebanon* (1988), p. 57.

The Founding of the Institute

The institution was founded in 1964 (1343). S. Ali Shahcheraqi, a progressive *moballegh*, was its first director.[32] The original driving force was Ay. S. Morteza Motahhari (d. 1979), a cleric who was close to Bazargan and Taleqani without being a member of the LMI, and who is said to have been one of Khomeini's favorite pupils. Administrative tasks and public relations were carried out by Naser Minachi, a lawyer from Teheran, and Mohammad Homayun (d. 1978), a prominent Bazaar merchant and wealthy philanthropist who had been a keen supporter of the Monthly Talks Society. Homayun bought the 4,000 square meters of land in Teheran's northern suburb of Qolhak on which the buildings were to be erected. While he remained the main financial benefactor of the institute, other merchants also made commitments to pay 5,000 rials ($70) per month to help meet expenses.

In 1967 (1346) the Hoseiniyeh Ershad moved to its new premises. Its location was both practical and symbolic. The clergy's domination in the southern, more traditional parts of the city was such that it would have been very difficult for an innovative religious center to function there. Eschewing Teheran's traditional and more religious south for the city's secular north would also bring Islam to the educated, secularized bourgeoisie, society's modern segment, which lives in Shemiran, the northern suburbs of Teheran.[33] For the same reason, perhaps, no expense was spared to make the building physically attractive: a blue tiled dome, in the manner of the grand mosques of Isfahan, topped a building whose façade was of marble. The only constraint the founders imposed on themselves was that all materials were to be produced in Iran. The institute boasted a library, a mosque, a lecture hall, and, for the first time in Iran, closed-circuit television to ensure that speakers could be seen from all parts of the complex and that women would be encouraged to attend the meetings. In the same year the institution

---

[32]Unless otherwise indicated, all information on the Hoseiniyeh Ershad is based on an interview with Naser Minachi commemorating the eighth anniversary of the closing of the Hoseiniyeh Ershad, in *Mizan* (Teheran), November 5, 1980 (Aban 14, 1359); Ahmad Alibaba'i, "Hoseiniyeh ershad ra motejaddedin az moteqaddemin! bastand," in *Keyhan* (Teheran), November 15, 1980 (Aban 24, 1359); Ahmad Alibaba'i, "Shariati goft: Raftam haram-e Emam Reza dard-e del va da'va ba hazrat," in ibid., June 19, 1980 (Khordad 29, 1359), and interviews with Ahmad Alibaba'i in Cologne, August 23 and 24, 1982.

[33]As discussed in chapter 1, in Teheran the socioeconomic diversity of the population is clearly reflected in the city's geographical layout. For a study of the urban geography of Teheran, see Martin Seger, *Teheran: Eine stadtgeographische Studie* (1978), esp. pp. 56–124. See in particular fig. 44 (p. 103), which shows the location of religious edifices in the city. Within Shemiran, Qolhak has always been a somewhat less "Godless" section than other parts. The reason is that unlike most of the other neighborhoods, Qolhak developed around an old village core and therefore kept a more diverse population.

was officially registered as the Hoseiniyeh Ershad Research and Educational Institute (Mo'aseseh-ye Tahqiqati va Ta'limati-ye Hoseiniyeh-ye Ershad).

Bazargan, Taleqani, and Yadollah Sahabi, who were freed from prison in 1966, were not consulted by the institute or invited to give talks, as their previous political visibility would have attracted the attention of SAVAK.[34] Ay. Motahhari, on the other hand, until the early 1970s maintained courteous relations with the regime. Speakers at the Hoseiniyeh Ershad included lay figures like Kazem Sami and Habibollah Peiman, both of whom had been active in Nakhshab's movements and then founded the Liberation Movement of the People of Iran (discussed later in this chapter), but also some intellectual ulema such as Mohammad Beheshti, Ho. Hashemi Rafsanjani, Ho. S. Javad Bahonar, and Ho. Sadreddin Sadr Balaghi, a Mosaddeqist cleric with links to Ay. Shariatmadari. The Shah's regime did not impede these activities, hoping that they would weaken the appeal of the traditional clergy and the leftists.

Some organizational and research work had started on a modest level in 1964 (1343), but large-scale activities were inaugurated in 1967. In April 1970 (Ordibehesht 1349) the Hoseiniyeh Ershad organized a conference to commemorate Muhammad Iqbal, the Indian Muslim modernist philosopher and poet. Shariati gave a talk on that occasion, and in his preface to the proceedings he wrote that Iqbal "thought like Bergson, loved like [Rumi], wrote poetry for his faith like Naser Khosrow, fought imperialism like Seyyed Jamal [al-Afghani], endeavored to rid civilization of the evils of the lust for power like Tagore, tried to breathe love and spirituality into the life of contemporary man like Carrel, and wanted to reform his religion like Luther and Calvin." The relevance of these comparisons to Iqbal might not meet with universal agreement; they do, however, tell us something about Shariati's view of himself, as he acknowledges Iqbal as a role model.[35]

Shariati Takes Over

Until 1969 (1348) the main figure, and most popular speaker, of the institute was Ay. Motahhari. In that year Ali Shariati, who had been invited to come to Teheran by none other than Motahhari (to whom he was related) himself, began to become quite visible in the institute's activities. Soon his popularity eclipsed that of Motahhari: it is said that while Shariati's lectures attracted huge crowds, fewer and fewer people

---

[34]Mehdi Bazargan, personal written communication, June 1988.
[35]Ali Shariati, *Ma va Eqbal* (We and Iqbal) (1978), p. 9.

went to Motahhari's. Until the closing of the Hoseiniyeh Ershad in 1972 Shariati remained its new driving force.

Shariati's thought was discussed in chapter 2. His innovations, both in style and in substance, his anticlericalism and consistent attacks on the clergy, displeased large sectors of the ulema. They were presented by Shariati as the contemporary representatives of Safavi Shi'ism, which was characterized by its connivance with the despotic regime of the Shah.

Motahhari was something of a maverick himself and had on occasion been rebuked by the conservative clergy, who found fault with his supposedly unorthodox views on, to give but two examples, the Islamic veil (as expressed in his book *Hejab*), or with his opinions concerning the problem of *marja'iyat*. But his credentials as a cleric were impeccable. In the face of these attacks, Motahhari moved toward more and more orthodox positions. In contrast to Motahhari, Shariati had, in formal terms, only a Western education. Soon frictions arose between him and Motahhari, who was goaded by some ulema far more conservative than himself. Given Motahhari's relative loss of popularity, jealousy may have been a factor in this friction.[36] Hosein Dabbagh, who claims to have had direct contact with Motahhari, relates that Motahhari "questioned all the basic concepts that Shariati put forward . . . [and] thought that Shariati was an instrumentalist, in the sense that he used religion as an instrument for his political and social objectives."[37] Akhavi relates that Motahhari confided to him in 1975 how he thought that Shariati had jeopardized the institution by giving an overtly political coloration to the Hoseiniyeh Ershad's activities.[38] Be it as it may, after Shariati's success became apparent, Motahhari and some other ulema, such as Beheshti and Ho. Hashemi Rafsanjani (but not Ho. Sadreddin Sadr Balaghi) left the institute.

At no point did Motahhari object openly to the content of Shariati's writings. Rather, he preferred to direct his attacks against Naser Minachi, whose management he ostensibly questioned. Minachi was obliquely accused of being authoritarian, even corrupt. The Bazaar and other conservative circles did not like what Shariati had to say, but given Shariati's popularity, Minachi became the scapegoat.[39]

Motahhari's departure meant that the institute was now besieged from two sides. Within the clergy unease grew because of the heterodox innovations in Shariati's teaching. In conservative circles the Hoseiniyeh Ershad was soon called *Kaferestan*, place of the infidels, and

[36]Hamid Algar, *The Roots of the Islamic Revolution* (1983), p. 88.
[37]Quoted in ibid., p. 90.
[38]Akhavi, *Religion and Politics*, p. 144.
[39]Ahmad Alibaba'i, personal interview, Cologne, August 23, 1983.

Yazidiyeh, the opposite of *Hoseiniyeh,* since Husein was killed during the rule of the caliph Yazid. Shariati was accused of being a Wahhabi, a Sunni, a communist, a savak collaborator, and of being against the principle of *velayat-e faqih,* the cornerstone of Khomeini's ideology which was beginning to be known in those years (Khomeini's book appeared in 1971). Doubts were voiced about whether Shariati performed all his daily prayers. His wife was denounced for not wearing the complete Islamic veil. The Bazaar, which, it is not unfair to assume, had little use for Abu Dharrian socialism, also openly turned against him.

In a letter to Homayun and Minachi dated November 25, 1972 (Azar 4, 1351), a few days after the institute's closure, Shariati summarized what the Hoseiniyeh Ershad had meant to him:

> My revered father: Homayun; my brother, my hope: Minachi.... Even if they raze this building, the empty land, its address, will have their own place in the history of ideas, the Islamic movement, and the awakening of the people. Thus, you were first the builders of a building and have now become the founders of a movement. For me the Hoseiniyeh is not [merely] a place where I lectured and taught. [It] has infused my blood, thought, personality, my faith. The Hoseiniyeh Ershad will become the foundation of a Party, one whose ideology will be Alavi Shi'ism.... The Hoseiniyeh has now become the honor and love of our religion. [I want you to know] that from now on until my death or murder, like Bilal who under torture would repeat one word: ahad! ahad! ahad! [one God] with every torture I will only utter one name: Ershad! Ershad! Ershad![40]

Ali Shariati had meant the Hoseiniyeh Ershad to become a major institution of learning, research, and teaching. By training Muslims in modern methodologies, he wanted to break the traditional clergy's domination in the *howzeh*s. His project called for four units: research, teaching, the propagation of Shi'ism, and logistics (publishing and translation).[41] Shariati's project, with its methodological innovations (he planned an idiomatic translation of the Qoran) and opening to the West, was both ambitious and a major break with the past. Its implementation would have made the traditional clergy's learning unattractive to the youth. Although the ulema had attempted a minor reform of the curricula of the Qum *howzeh,* they could not go as far as Shariati had

---

[40]Quoted in Naser Minachi, "Hoseiniyeh ershad yek sakhteman nist, yek jarayan ast," in *Ettela'at* (Teheran), December 21, 1980 (Azar 30, 1359).

[41]"What Is To Be Done: A Practical Plan for the Husayniah Irshad," in Ali Shari'ati, *What Is To Be Done: The Enlightened Thinkers and an Islamic Renaissance,* ed. and ann. Farhang Rajaee (1986), pp. 103–60.

proposed.[42] His questioning of the age-old ways of organized Shi'ism's educational establishments contributed to the clergy's dislike for him.

The End of the Hoseiniyeh Ershad and Shariati's Last Years

The government, which earlier on had been too busy fighting the Mojahedin to pay much attention to the Hoseiniyeh Ershad, became increasingly alarmed. Initially the Shah regime had tolerated the founding of the Hoseiniyeh Ershad because it was thought that the religious modernism the institute stood for would weaken the clergy. Later, by letting Shariati continue, the government also hoped that his activities would sow discord in religious circles. For this purpose, the regime consistently admonished him to understate sociology and concentrate on *aqa'ed* (Shi'ite beliefs).[43]

The withdrawal of the clerics meant that the price of repressing the Hoseiniyeh Ershad was considerably lowered. Several attempts were made, by relatively progressive Bazaar merchants both in Teheran and in Mashad, to reconcile Motahhari and bring him back to the institute; but to no avail. In the autumn of 1972 (1351), during the month of Ramadan, Ahmad Alibaba'i, apparently with some help from Beheshti, argued that if ever some SAVAK-instigated mob came to attack the institute, the damage would also affect those members of the clergy's progressive wing (that is, Motahhari himself) who had at one point collaborated with it. Alibaba'i attempted to talk Motahhari into giving at least a few talks at the institute, so as to signify to the government and to public opinion that the Hoseiniyeh Ershad still had some support from the clergy. Motahhari refused.[44]

It is alleged that the Shah himself ordered the institute's closure and the punishment of those who ran it. On October 24 and 25, 1972 (Aban 2 and 3, 1351), Shariati gave two parts of a long lecture entitled "Shi'eh yek hezb-e tamam" (Shi'ah: A total party), in which his conceptions of Shi'ite Islam as a political force were spelled out in detail by comparing and contrasting it with other political and social movements. In November 1972 (Aban 1351) the Hoseiniyeh Ershad hosted performances of the modern play *Sarbedaran*, based on a fourteenth-century Shi'ite social movement that attained power for a few decades in Khorasan.[45] At the

---

[42]On the ulema's efforts in this direction, see Michael M. J. Fischer, *Iran: From Religious Dispute to Revolution* (1980), pp. 78–86.

[43]Akhavi, *Religion and Politics*, p. 147.

[44]Ahmad Alibaba'i, personal interview, Cologne, August 23, 1983.

[45]The left-modernist view of the Sarbedaran movement is directly influenced by I. P. Petrushevsky's Marxist interpretations of Iranian history, widely available in Persian in the 1970s. See his *Islam in Iran* (1985), pp. 304–9.

same time Shariati gave a new lecture titled "The Philosophy of Existentialism, the Historical Philosophy of Islam." A week later the institute was closed by government order. Toward the end of its life, about 5,000 students had been enrolled in its classes, which were typically held on Friday afternoons after communal prayers at the mosque. After the closure Shariati went into hiding. To drive him into the open, the government arrested his father, whereupon, in 1973, he gave himself up.[46] In 1974 (1353) Minachi was arrested. Motahhari was also arrested, but freed after two nights in prison.

Attacks against Shariati continued. They reached such proportions that even Motahhari rose to his defense. In a letter dated October 3, 1973 (Mehr 7, 1352), in which he never mentions Shariati by name, he denounced the attacks and stated that differences of opinion were natural among Muslim scholars and the proper way to resolve them was by discussion and debate. If somebody called for unity among various groups of Muslims because they faced the same enemy, that did not mean he was a Sunni.[47]

Shariati's works continued to be reprinted for another two years. Censorship was avoided by printing the old dates on them. About 2 million volumes were circulated in this way before the revolution. The regime's attempts to implicate more people did not succeed, however, and nobody else was arrested. The publishers' correspondence with the various student groups abroad was not decoded. Shariati's many lectures, articles, and books were also reproduced and distributed outside Iran by the MSAs that were expanding in Europe and North America, as related earlier. Many of his works also found their way to Afghanistan, where Persian is the lingua franca.

After the Hoseiniyeh Ershad was closed down, some of its activities moved to the nearby Qoba Mosque, where Ho. Mofatteh was *pishnamaz*. The government decided to take over the premises of the Hoseiniyeh Ershad. In prison, Homayun was made to agree to transfer his title to the institute to the Organization of Endowments, a state agency administering religious endowments (*owqaf*).[48]

At the 1975 meeting of the Organization of Petroleum Exporting Countries (OPEC) in Algiers, where Algerian diplomacy brought about a reconciliation between Iran and Iraq, the then Algerian foreign minister, Abdelaziz Bouteflika, intervened on Shariati's behalf and

---

[46]S. Jalaleddin Madani, *Tarikh-e siasi-ye mo'aser-e Iran, II* (The political history of contemporary Iran, vol. 2) (1983/1361), p. 198n.

[47]The letter is reproduced in *Payam-e Mujahid*, March 1974 (Esfand 1352), pp. 1 and 6.

[48]*Payam-e Mujahid*, November 1972 (Aban 1351), p. 8. Earlier, the government had taken over the Hedayat Mosque in a similar way.

asked for his release. The release was ordered by the Shah after he returned to Iran. In early March 1976 Shariati was freed, followed six weeks later by Minachi.

After his release, Shariati learned that the clergy and the government had prepared a final humiliation for him. One of his work, *Ensan, eslam, va maktabha-ye maghrebzamin* (Man, Islam, and Western schools of thought) had been serialized in the daily newspaper *Keyhan* from February 15, 1976, to March 15, 1976 (Esfand 1354). The regime thus conveyed the impression that Shariati had collaborated to obtain his own release,[49] and by the same token they hoped to exacerbate the rift between the Muslim and Marxist wings of the opposition, which had flared up after the recent split in the Mojahedin organization.

Shariati was not allowed to resume his teaching. For a while he went to his native Mazinan. He held a few more secret meetings, in which he discussed writings on which he had worked in prison. In the face of harassment by SAVAK, however, he decided to leave Iran and went to England. He hoped to get a teaching appointment in Algeria.

Ali Shariati died on June 19, 1977 (Khordad 29, 1356), in Southampton of a heart attack, after his wife had been prevented in the last moment by SAVAK from joining him in England. The coroner's report did not mention any unnatural causes for his death, but his followers claim that he was assassinated by SAVAK. This claim may be a result of the usual mythopoeic tendencies inherent in all revolutions, but it is not implausible that the reportedly harsh treatment he endured in prison weakened his constitution.

When news of his death reached Teheran, preparations were made to receive his remains. The government had instructed the Iranian embassy in London to cooperate fully. Many supporters of Shariati hoped to turn the arrival of his body into an antiregime demonstration, which was conceivable since in the summer of 1977 the first effects of the Shah's new liberalization program were making themselves felt. Twenty-four hours after his death, a meeting was held in England, which the following men attended: Sadeq Qotbzadeh and Abolhasan Banisadr from Paris, Ebrahim Yazdi from America, Sadeq Tabataba'i from Germany, and Naser Minachi, who happened to be in England at the time. It was decided that the Iranian government would attempt to use the return of Shariati's body to discredit him by giving him full honors. To prevent that, arrangements were made, mainly through Yazdi, for his body to be flown to Damascus. He was buried at the

[49]Hamid Algar, Introduction to Ali Shariati, *Marxism and Other Western Fallacies*, trans. R. Campbell (1980), p. 13.

Zeinabiyeh, the tomb of Imam Husein's sister, a major Shi'ite shrine. Imam Musa al-Sadr officiated at his burial.[50]

After Shariati's death both the clergy and the government tried to associate themselves with his name. In Shiraz two major ayatollahs held memorial services for him. The LMI dispatched Sadeq Qotbzadeh to Najaf, Iraq, to get Khomeini to send a message of condolence to Shariati's father, but this Khomeini refused to do. In response to telegrams of condolence sent to him, Khomeini only issued a statement in which he exhorted Iranian youth to lead the people out of the wilderness of autocracy, corruption, and foreign domination. On the government side, a laudatory article appeared in *Keyhan* on June 23, 1977 (Tir 2, 1356). Mashad University announced that it too would hold a memorial service.[51]

The Shah regime did not dare reopen the Hoseiniyeh Ershad; after the revolution it was reopened and sponsored a few lectures and discussions on matters of topical interest. The founders would have liked to start again where they had left off and implement the ambitious program Shariati had outlined, but many of them now had official responsibilities in the Provisional Government and thus lacked the time to dedicate themselves to the Hoseiniyeh Ershad. With the fall of the Provisional Government in November 1979 their position became too insecure to resume widespread activities at the institute.

The Mojahedin

After the leaderships of all Nationalist parties either went to prison or opted to cease overt political activity after 1963, many younger members and sympathizers of these parties came to the conclusion that political struggle, whether open or clandestine, was ineffective in bringing about the end of the Pahlavi dictatorship.

The Guerrilla Option

The success of the recent revolutions in Algeria and Cuba, the flaring up of the war in Vietnam, and the violent repression by the Shah regime of the June 1963 demonstrations led some to opt for violent struggle.

Bizhan Jazani, who had been a leader of the National Front Student Organization, formed a group that would ultimately merge with others and become the Fada'iyan organization, a communist guerrilla

---

[50]"H.B.," "*Mardi keh zendegiyash hameh hadaf bud . . . ,*" in *Iranshahr* (Washington, D.C.), June 15, 1979 (Khordad 25, 1358), pp. 10–13.

[51]Akhavi, *Religion and Politics*, p. 234n.

movement.[52] Fundamentalist Muslims founded the Party of Islamic Nations (Hezb-e melal-e eslami), which was discovered in the autumn of 1964 and its members were arrested. The Party of the Iranian People (PIP), at its first (and last) congress in 1962 (1341), had rejected some young members' proposal to espouse violent struggle if need be. In 1964, therefore, some young party members, led by Kazem Sami and Habibollah Peiman, seceded and founded JAMA, the Persian acronym for Liberation Movement of the People of Iran. Groups were formed in Teheran, Mashad, and the north, but the nascent network was soon neutralized by the regime and the leaders arrested.[53] The PIP withered away, never again to reappear on the political scene. The younger elements of the LMI, the most vigorous opposition movement to the Shah in the previous three years, were not immune to such stirrings: in 1965 young elements of the now inactive LMI founded the Sazeman-e mojahedin-e khalq-e Iran, known in English as the People's Mojahedin Organization of Iran, or PMOI.

The LMI and the Mojahedin

The six founders of the Mojahedin movement were Mohammad Hanifnezhad, Sa'id Mohsen, Mohammad Asgarizadeh, Rasul Meshkinfam, Ali-Asghar Badi'zadegan, and Ahmad Reza'i. Hanifnezhad, the oldest, was born in 1938 into a clerical family in Tabriz. After high school he went to Teheran to study agronomy, and at Teheran University's Faculty of Agriculture he founded an MSA. He then joined the LMI, and as a result of the 1963 riots spent some time in prison, where he met Taleqani and Bazargan. He was influenced by both of them: it is said that he read Bazargan's *Rah-e teyy shodeh* over and over. After his early release, Hanifnezhad completed his degree and spent one year of military service in Isfahan, devoting much of his time to a study of other countries' revolutionary experiences.

Sa'id Mohsen was born into a clerical family in Zanjan. He entered the Teheran University's Faculty of Engineering with a state scholarship, and became an MSA activist. He also joined the LMI and served in its

[52]On the history of the guerrilla groups in Iran see Ervand Abrahamian, "The Guerrilla Movement in Iran, 1963–1977," in *MERIP Reports* (March–April 1980), 3–15; and Fred Halliday, *Iran: Dictatorship and Development* (1979), pp. 235–48. The Fada'iyan recruited primarily from among Tudeh members and secular National Front elements, but such prominent Fada'is as Mas'ud Ahmadzadeh and Amir-Parviz Puyan, both from Mashad, had started their political activities in the LMI. The former had even founded an MSA in his hometown.

[53]This short history of JAMA is taken from an election pamphlet of JAMA, published in Teheran in 1980. Just as the PIP had foreshadowed the LMI, JAMA foreshadowed the Mojahedin.

Student Organization. After the party leadership's arrest in January 1963, he was one of the lower-ranking members who tried to keep the LMI going. Like Hanifnezhad he went to prison after the 1963 riots, and thence, upon finishing his degree, to do his military service. Asgarizadeh came from a working-class background and was born in Arak. With a help of a state scholarship he studied business in Teheran. Meshkinfam, another agricultural engineer, came from a middle-class family in Shiraz. Badi'zadegan was a young professor of chemistry in Teheran who came from a middle-class family in Isfahan. Reza'i, finally, came from a Bazaar family in Teheran and was to become the group's chief ideologue. He had joined the LMI while still in high school, and had then met Hanifnezhad while doing his military service.[54]

Some members went to Jordan to receive guerrilla training from the PLO, while others, in particular Hanifnezhad and Reza'i, stayed behind to work on ideology. They followed the path of the LMI in reinterpreting Islam but came to more radical conclusions. These resemble those of Ali Shariati, but it has to be borne in mind that the main corpus of Mojahedin ideology had already been elaborated by the time Shariati's most prolific period at the Hoseiniyeh Ershad began.

The PMOI started military operations in 1971, in an attempt to disrupt the celebrations of the 2,500-year anniversary of the Iranian monarchy. In the repression that struck back as a result of these actions, the Mojahedin lost their entire original leadership, through executions or in street battles with the security forces. After this they turned more and more to the left, until, in 1975, a split occurred in the organization: a leftist faction, including Ay. Taleqani's son Mojtaba, discarded Islam altogether and became a purely Marxist-Leninist organization. Another faction kept its Islamic allegiance, although their ideology is heavily tainted by Marxism.

In discussing the Mojahedin's problematic relationship with the LMI, one should remember that throughout the period under discussion, the LMI did not function as a party and maintained no underground network inside Iran either. What matters, therefore, is the attitude individual LMI leaders took toward their party's offspring.

At first, Bazargan and his circle, in their prison isolation, were not aware of the founding of the Mojahedin. Bazargan himself, for reasons that have probably more to do with his temperament than with his assessment of political situations, always remained cool to the idea of armed struggle. This, despite his prophetic warning at the trials in 1963 that theirs would be the last group to be persecuted for their affirmation and defense of the Constitution. By the early 1970s Bazargan was a

---

[54]Biographical data on the founders of the Mojahedin are adapted from Abrahamian, *Iran,* pp. 489–90.

moderately prosperous businessman in Teheran, and while he never compromised his principles, it is not difficult to see why he should not have been too enthusiastic about the Mojahedin and their leftist leanings.

Nonetheless, until the early 1970s LMI elements did support the Mojahedin financially, and cooperation was even closer with the LMI's external organization, as we have seen. After Bazargan's and Taleqani's release from prison in 1966, it was Taleqani who had more contacts with the Mojahedin leadership, engaging them upon occasion in ideological debates. The guerrilla organization's ideology, with its leftward tilt, was clearly less distasteful to Taleqani, who had a keener appreciation of the problems posed by economic inequality than Bazargan, a man who is above all concerned with justice and freedom. Inside Iran, the other LMI personality to maintain relatively close links with the Mojahedin was Ezzatollah Sahabi. In 1971 both he and Taleqani were arrested for their links with the organization. Taleqani was exiled to inhospitable Zahedan, while the younger Sahabi went back to jail, to be released only in 1978.

Shariati's relationship with the Mojahedin is something of a mystery. On the surface their ideologies appear to have a lot in common, and yet there is no clear evidence of close cooperation between the great orator and the military activists, although it stands to reason that many a Mojahed must have attended Shariati's lectures and learned from them.

Since the LMI did not exist as a party when the Mojahedin organization was founded in 1965, this event was not perceived as a split by LMI sympathizers at the time, and the guerrilla organization was seen by many as a metempsychosic continuation of the LMI. While many former LMI leaders and sympathizers would not go so far as to risk their skins for the cause of the Mojahedin, they were also in some sense proud of it, to some extent because they had no martyrs of their own to show. Things changed after the Mojahedin's decimation in 1971. The surviving activists did not have the same attachment to the LMI that had characterized the founders, and the increasing ideological similarities with Marxist groups were surely alarming to what was left of the LMI.

In retrospect, therefore, the founding of the Mojahedin can be seen as a split. By the time the LMI revived as a political grouping, in 1977, the PMOI had developed a life of its own, with only genealogical ties to the LMI.[55]

[55]A thorough discussion of the Mojahedin is beyond the scope of this study. This is how the PMOI interpreted their split from the LMI: "In prison Badi'zadegan, Mohsen, and Hanifnezhad together analyzed the causes for the repeated failures of Nationalist movements in Iran. They came to the conclusion that these movements had failed for six reasons: They had lacked an ideology, they had not had the necessary know-how for struggle, they had been centered around personalities, they had not been professional, they had been parliamentarist, and they had been naive. The Mojahedin

From Religious Modernism to the Triumph of Fundamentalism

Fifteen years after the LMI, the political expression of Islamic modernism in Iran, was eliminated from the scene, Ay. Khomeini's mixture of traditionalism and fundamentalism triumphed in the revolution of 1978–79. What were the relations between the modernists and the fundamentalists in the intervening period?

It is understandable that Khomeini should have exercised a certain attraction on LMI leaders and sympathizers. For years Bazargan and Taleqani had been complaining about the lack of clerical enthusiasm for the anti-Shah opposition. Now, finally, one of Ay. Borujerdi's putative successors was raising the banner of revolt. Moreover, his agenda of grievances was not a priori reactionary and antidemocratic. To be sure, his opposition to women's suffrage and to the legal stipulation that voters in the elections to provincial councils had to be Muslims strikes anyone committed to universal suffrage as reactionary, but at the time the whole question was somewhat academic anyway, since it was clear that no free elections would be allowed under the Shah. At the time, Khomeini's opposition to the granting of diplomatic immunity to American military advisers, an unacceptable reminder of the much hated capitulations that had limited Iran's sovereignty until 1928, mattered more. The sympathy for Khomeini was facilitated by the fact that he was largely unknown to political leaders in Iran. Bazargan and Sahabi had met him only once, in the winter of 1962–63 (1341).

Khomeini's immediate followers were younger clerics, Mohammad Beheshti, S. Ali Khameneh'i, Ali-Akbar Hashemi Rafsanjani, and Ho. Ali Montazeri, who in the 1960s and 1970s were seen by LMI figures as intellectuals among the clergy. They had participated in the reform movement of the early 1960s (discussed earlier), they had taken part in the activities of the Hoseiniyeh Ershad until 1971, and with the notable exception of Beheshti, they went in and out of prison. Some of them (Beheshti, M. Motahhari, J. Bahonar, M. Mofatteh) were members of the Philosophy Department of Teheran University's Faculty of Theology; they combined a traditional with a modern education and enjoyed sustained intellectual contact with nonreligious intellectuals. They did not fit the image of the conservative, quietist mulla only concerned with arcane questions of *feqh* that Bazargan had excoriated in his writings.

---

endeavored to draw the appropriate lessons from these shortcomings." *Tarikhcheh, jarayan-e kudeta va khatt-e mashshy-e konuni-ye sazeman-e mojahedin-e khalq-e Iran* (A short history, the affair of the coup d'etat, and the current line of the People's Mojahedin Organization of Iran) (n.d.), pp. 1–2.

In 1971 Khomeini's book on Islamic government, based on the principle of *velayat-e faqih*, was printed, and widely circulated in Iran. Although it was very different in its content from Bazargan's vision of an Islamic ideology, the book did not compromise the unity of the Islamic Movement. In 1974–75, at the invitation of Taher Ahmadzadeh, Taleqani, Bazargan, Y. Sahabi, Mostafa Katira'i, A. Khameneh'i, Motahhari, Abbas Sheibani, and a few others constituted a secret study group to establish the main features of the Islamic ideology. They worked for a few months, until a SAVAK raid on a house in Mashad where the index cards were being kept put an end to the effort.[56]

In 1975 the unity of the Islamic movement in Iran was broken. According to Ebrahim Yazdi, the reason was the coup inside the Mojahedin, during which Marxist-Leninists took over the organization.[57] Also in 1975 Khameneh'i translated a book by the ideologue of the Egyptian Muslim Brotherhood, Sayyid Qutb. He prefaced it with a concise text comprising ten points and titled "The Characteristics of the Islamic Ideology." Point four establishes the need for a single party, and point nine posits that the population owes this party, the "party of God," *hezbollah*, full obedience.[58] Did Bazargan and his friends oppose this new trend vigorously enough? It appears that they did not take the "clerical intellectuals" seriously. Their anticlericalism prevented them from clearly assessing the fundamentalists' appeal, while at the same time the necessity of a united front against the Shah kept the modernists from engaging in polemics with the fundamentalists. By the mid-1970s religious modernists à la Bazargan had become a minority component of the rising Islamic movement in Iran. This subordinate position was due less to a decrease in the appeal of modernism than to the growth of fundamentalism.

The causes of this growth are variegated. In the 1960s and 1970s the Pahlavi regime increased its pressure on the clergy. It continued its "nationalization" of religious institutions, took over mosques, shrines, religious schools, and transferred them to the state's Organization of Endowments.[59] As the clergy's freedom of action was more and more restricted, increasing numbers of previously apolitical ulema became hostile to the Shah. This trend was reinforced by the death, in 1971, of Ay. Hakim, the major Shi'ite *marja'* of Najaf in Iraq. An Arab, he had been less involved in Iranian politics, and that had led the Shah to

---

[56]From an open letter of Bazargan to Khameneh'i of July 12, 1983 (Tir 21, 1362), reprinted in *Shesh nameh-ye sargoshadeh* (Six open letters) (1983), pp. 43–44.

[57]Ebrahim Yazdi, *Akharin talashha dar akharin ruzha* (The last efforts on the last days) (1984), pp. 12–13.

[58]Khameneh'i's text is discussed extensively in Ali Reza Irani, "Grundzüge der islamischen Ideologie im Iran," in *Politische Studien*, Sonderheft 3/1980, pp. 26–81.

[59]On these appropriations see Akhavi, *Religion and Politics*, pp. 132–43.

court him and to treat him as if he had been the sole *marja'* of the Shi'ites. Upon his death, the Shah sent telegrams of condolence to three major *maraje'*, Ay. Kho'i (Najaf), Ay. Khonsari (Teheran), and Ay. Shariatmadari (Qum). Only the latter warmly replied to the monarch's message, and thereby damaged his standing considerably. Although Ay. Shariatmadari was then, according to the traditional rules, the senior *marja'*, he lost much support among the lower-ranking clergy, who increasingly turned to Khomeini. A major moderate figure was thenceforth neutralized. Taleqani stopped speaking to Ay. Shariatmadari, but Bazargan and Sahabi maintained their contacts with him. Given the state of tension between Iran and Iraq, Khomeini was free to increase his attacks on the Shah from Najaf.

The radicalization of the clergy was also encouraged by two events that shook Mashad in 1975. In that year Ay. Milani, the head of the Mashad *howzeh* and a major *marja'* of relatively progressive outlook who had been friendly with the LMI, died. In that same year the Shah's government, represented in the city by the much-hated Gholamhosein Valian, razed the *madrasah*s and buildings surrounding the central Shrine of Imam Reza to create a park. Religious opinion was furious: many small shop-owners who had owned or rented their premises in the area were not compensated for their loss, and the annular park was seen as symbolically separating the shrine from the rest of the city. The physical destruction of the *madrasah*s and the death of Ay. Milani caused an exodus of religious students to Qum and Najaf, which were then more radical than the capital of Khorasan. Whatever moderating influence Mashad had exercised on Iran's religious life evaporated.

Parallel to this movement within the clergy, important shifts occurred in the country's demography. The Shah regime favored industrial development over agriculture. The higher number of jobs available in the urban areas led to massive migration to the cities, especially Teheran. A city that had had no slums to speak of until the late 1960s suddenly had millions of recently migrated slum-dwellers who lived under extremely precarious conditions.[60] Among these masses new forms of religious organizations sprang up, creating a fertile ground for the spread of fundamentalist ideas. Most of these organizations were founded after 1965 and were associated with the groupings of humbler occupations or of poor city quarters. Their very names, such as Religious Associations of Shoemakers, of Workers of Public Baths, of the Guild of Fruit-Juicers (on street-corners), of Tailors, of the Natives of Natanz Resident in Teheran, of the Desperates *(bicharehha)* of [Imam]

[60]Farhad Kazemi, *Poverty and Revolution in Iran* (1980). See esp. pp. 91–95.

Hosein, of the Abjects *(zalilha)* of [Imam] Musa ibn Ja'far,[61] attest to their basic difference with the associations founded by Bazargan and Taleqani. One must also not forget that while these associations were expanding, all forms of independent political activity were banned. Religion became the only outlet for oppositional leanings in the country.

At the same time, a climbing literacy rate among the masses favored the diffusion of fundamentalist ideas. Religious periodicals gained progressively wider circulation and religious books became ever more popular. In the period 1954–63 religious books had constituted about 10 percent of the total of published books, by 1975 their share had risen to 33.5 percent. In 1976 there were forty-eight publishers of religious books in Teheran, and the vast majority of the total production was fundamentalist rather than modernist.[62]

The government, meanwhile, was more preoccupied with leftists and the Mojahedin. At Iranian universities, authorities would often look the other way when members of the Muslim Student Associations, by now radicalized, terrorized other students or faculty members of whose behavior or views they did not approve.[63] In its last phase, the regime of the Shah favored religious forces over leftist forces in other ways too. Most religious political prisoners were freed in 1976 (1355), many signing statements of repentance for rebelling against the monarchy, while leftist prisoners were not let out of jail until November 1978. That move added to the momentum of the Islamic movement.

In this groundswell the likes of Bazargan and Shariati were lost. The regime had deprived them of their major forum, the Hoseiniyeh Ershad Institute. Ay. Taleqani spent most of these years in prison or in exile. The books of Bazargan and Shariati were read alongside the fundamentalist books, but they reinforced the trend toward religion rather than changing its direction. Under the circumstances, the best Bazargan and his friends could hope for was that by staying *within* the Islamic movement they might be able to guide it in a more liberal and modernist direction. The lines between the various segments of the Islamic movement were not sharply drawn. Bazargan gave occasional talks at Ay. Shariatmadari's Dar ot-Tabligh in Qum. In Qum, the seminarians read modernist writings alongside their traditional curriculum. But a shift occurred in the late 1960s: until then the most popular extracurricular texts had been books printed by the Sherkat-e Sahami-ye Enteshar, a publishing house close to the LMI that put out Bazargan's

[61]The information on these associations is taken, verbatim, from Said Amir Arjomand, "Shi'ite Islam and the Revolution in Iran," *Government and Opposition* 16 (1981), 312.
[62]Ibid., pp. 311–12.
[63]Personal communications from students and faculty studying or teaching in Iran in the mid-1970s.

writings and translations of selected foreign writers.[64] After that, the mood among the seminarians became more radical, as Marxist-inspired texts (by Petrushevsky, A. I. Oparine) and the publications of the Mojahedin (including their handbook on economics, which is a straight translation of Marx's *Critique of Political Economy*) replaced the liberal modernist fare. Ay. Golpayegani tried to stop this trend by having the dormitories raided by his disciples on occasion, but the politicization of the *howzeh* continued.[65]

Bazargan himself seemed more preoccupied with the danger from the left than with the rising tide of fundamentalism. In 1975, the split in the Mojahedin movement prompted him to write *Elmi budan-e marksism* (The scientific nature of Marxism), and in 1976 at a meeting in the Qoba Mosque he gave a talk which later became the book *Afat-e towhid* (The bane of monotheism), in which he warned against Muslims' adopting the vocabulary and thought categories of Marxists. Khomeini, on his part, lulled the modernists by always being more precise about what he stood *against*, as opposed to what he stood *for*. Thus many liberal Islamic modernists hoped that his writings on Islamic government constituted an ideal rather than an action program. Finally, the fundamentalists adopted the rhetoric of social justice and anti-imperialism popularized by Shariati, further blurring the lines between them and the modernists.

Thus, Bazargan and the old guard of the LMI looked increasingly like leaders without troops. The Bazaar, their original source of support, was dealing more and more with the clergy directly. Inside the modernist camp itself, differences could no longer be ignored. In late 1977 (Azar 13, 1356) Motahhari and Bazargan issued a joint communiqué in which they clarified their position vis-à-vis the teachings of the recently deceased Shariati. While recognizing the relevance of much of Shariati's thought, they faulted him for his insufficient knowledge of Islam.[66] This communiqué further alienated many young people, mostly students, who had long since abandoned moderates such as Bazargan for the more radical circles of the left or the Mojahedin.

The situation was different in the case of the LMI(a). Only one month after Khomeini had left Turkey for Iraq in 1964, Yazdi, Qotbzadeh, and Mohammad Tavassoli had visited him in Najaf. They thus established independent channels of communication with Khomeini, and in 1972 Yazdi became Khomeini's plenipotentiary representative in the

---

[64]Ho. Jalal Ganjeh'i, who studied in Qum in the 1960s, told me that the students at Qum read three foreign books before the 1970s: Gustave Le Bon's *La civilisation des Arabes*, Will Durant's *The Story of Civilization*, and Carrel's *Man the Unknown*. Personal interview, Nanterre, July 1985.

[65]Ibid.

[66]For the full text see chapter 2.

United States. Khomeini even authorized him to receive and spend religious taxes. As we saw in an earlier section, the LMI(a) ceased all cooperation with Nationalist groups in 1966 and concentrated on organizing religious groups. The new, purely "religious" line, is reflected in the content of *Payam-e Mujahid*. In the organ of the LMI(a) we look in vain for any articles extolling democracy, tolerance, moderation. The emphasis was on revolution, struggle, Islam. Within the Islamic movement, news items were covered generously, whether they concerned fundamentalists or the Mojahedin. Terrorist groups were eulogized alongside national liberation movements, and the IRA of Ireland and the Japanese Red Army were celebrated as revolutionaries.[67] Clearly, one cannot claim to have democratic ideals and at the same time present as heroes people who direct their armed attacks *exclusively* against those countries that have approximated the democratic ideal. The young Iranians who became members of the Muslim Student Associations in the United States were fed articles and books that had little in common with the original program of the LMI. The LMI(a) did reprint and distribute pre-1963 articles, defense statements, speeches, and books by the leading figures of the LMI, but in the annotations that were added to these it was always stated that the LMI's strict adherence to constitutional methods in the period 1960–63 had only been a tactical move, only one dimension of a tridimensional (military and ideological struggles were the other two) *guerre à outrance* against the Shah and his foreign masters. The LMI(a) thus imputed a measure of Leninesque duplicity to Bazargan that was quite incompatible with his legalistic mind-frame, not to mention his emphasis on universal standards of ethics. Muslim students breaking windows and furniture at Iranian universities were hailed as revolutionary heroes in the pages of the LMI(a)'s organ, but government troops doing the same were decried as barbarians. One notices the disappearance of a belief in universal norms, an important ingredient of a democratic frame of mind.

Unlike the generation of their grandfathers and fathers, who had gone abroad to learn something about the West, the religiously inclined young Iranians in the West tended to shut themselves off completely from their environments, concentrating on the acquisition of technical skills. Their reading, the publications of the MSAs and such newspapers as *Payam-e Mujahid*, reinforced their haughty disdain for their host countries, and no attempts were made to understand the West on its own terms. The remarkable intellectual regression that characterizes Iran's postrevolutionary political class can, at least in part, be traced

---

[67]*Payam-e Mujahid*, no. 25, December 1974 (Azar 1353), pp. 1 and 6.

back to this development. Even if we were to assume, for argument's sake,[68] that the LMI(a)'s commitment to Nationalist and liberal values was genuine, we would still have to conclude that the leaders of the LMI(a), primarily Yazdi, made the crucial mistake of assuming a Mosaddeqist "residual" in the groups they targeted with their publications, while in fact the memory of the golden age of Nationalism was dim for most Iranians studying in Europe and the United States in the 1960s and 1970s: many of them were born after 1953. No wonder, then, that upon their return to Iran many of these Iranian students turned against Bazargan and his friends and joined the camp of the fundamentalists.

It can be argued that such a policy was necessary, that to strive for revolution, one has to present things in black and white. It is true that people who are oblivious to the complexities and nuances of political and social matters make good revolutionaries. The trouble is, they are not likely to turn into pluralists the minute the revolution is over.

The LMI(a)'s policy of total subserviance to Khomeini and refusal of any cooperation with Nationalist groups contrasted with Bazargan's attitude, who always maintained relations not only with the National Front, but even with Ali Amini, and who never placed himself outside the framework of Iran's 1906 Constitution.

Summarizing the momentous shifts in Iran's dominant political culture in the years 1963–77 we can say that until the early 1960s, Nationalists commanded a majority among the *articulate* segment of Iranian public opinion. Secularism dominated the National Movement. This does not mean that all Nationalists were areligious, but one could be a believing Muslim without mixing religion and politics, that is, without being motivated in one's political action by one's religious beliefs. By 1977 things had changed: increasing numbers of Iranians had joined the ranks of the articulate, but leftists and fundamentalists had more appeal than the old Nationalists, be they secular or religious. In 1978, therefore, the Islamic movement in Iran was polarized between the fundamentalists on the one hand, and the Mojahedin on the other. Such people as Bazargan and Sahabi were somewhere in the middle. They were politicians from another era, they had great residual prestige, but no troops.

[68]Bazargan himself wrote in 1982 that the LMI(a) had contained elements more committed to the worldwide rule of Islam than to the values and traditions of the National Movement. Mehdi Bazargan, "Iran va eslam" (Iran and Islam), in *Bazyabi-ye arzeshha* (The recovery of Values), vol. 2 (1982), p. 119n.

PART III

THE LIBERATION MOVEMENT OF IRAN AND THE ISLAMIC REVOLUTION

CHAPTER 6

The Liberation Movement of Iran
and the Liberalization of 1977–1978

The years 1977–78 bear a certain resemblance to the period 1960–63. At the outset we again find a certain deterioration of Iran's economic situation, this time brought about by stagnating oil income and an economy that overheated after the boom years of the early 1970s.[1] By the mid-1970s, the Shah concluded that to ensure the continued rule of his dynasty it would be best to liberalize his regime. This liberalization coincided with the installation of a new Democratic administration in Washington, which pledged to further human rights abroad. The coincidence convinced the anti-Shah opposition that he was under pressure from President Carter, and this emboldened it. But as in the early 1960s, liberal, Nationalist, reformist, and leftist forces in Iran were not able to take effective advantage of the liberalization. Instead, under the leadership of Ay. Khomeini a revolutionary movement arose to topple the Shah.

Bazargan and his circle played an important role in these events, although by no means a determining one. The religious modernists around him had one foot in the Nationalist, liberal opposition to the Shah, the other in the religious camp under the leadership of Khomeini. Bazargan was both the chairman of the Iranian Committee for the Defense of Freedom and Human Rights and an ally of Khomeini's, hand-picked by him to serve as prime minister of the postrevolutionary Provisional Government.

---

[1]For a full picture of Iran's economic woes at the eve of the revolution, see Robert Graham, *Iran: The Illusion of Power* (1980), esp. pp. 77–127.

Carter's Human Rights Policy and Iran

American Signals

Renewed U.S. preoccupation with human rights violations by allies is usually said to have begun under the Carter administration. Yet at least insofar as Iran is concerned, the seeds of a more critical attitude toward the Shah were sown earlier. In 1975 and 1976 U.S. government officials discussed the Shah's harsh treatment of political dissidents privately with the Iranian government,[2] but Iran's strategic importance to America and the positive contribution that Iran's arms purchases made to the U.S. balance of payments, account for the fact that U.S. pressure on Iran remained relatively limited.[3]

During 1978, as opposition to the Shah mounted and the revolutionary movement expanded, the United States continued in its support for the Shah. There is no evidence that the Carterites actually pressed the Shah to democratize his country.[4] And when security forces fired on unarmed demonstrators at a sit-in in central Teheran on Black Friday (September 8, 1978/Shahrivar 17, 1357), the Shah was commended by Washington. Zbigniew Brzezinski, Carter's national security adviser, recalled,

> On September 8, violence erupted in Jaleh Square in Teheran, with troops firing on demonstrators, killing scores. [Secretary of State Cyrus] Vance and I agreed that it would be desirable for the President to call the Shah and express verbally our support for him. The conversation between the President and the Shah took place between 7:56 and 8:02 a.m. on Sunday, September 10. The President said he was calling to express his friendship for the Shah and his concern about events.[5]

Carter's statements on human rights had repercussions in Iran both on the government side and on the side of the opposition. When the

[2]See the State Department Report on Human Rights in Iran (Pursuant to the Arms Export Control Act of 1976) to the House Committee on International Relations of December 31, 1976, in Yonah Alexander and Allan Nanes, eds., *The United States and Iran: A Documentary History* (1980), p. 433.

[3]For details see James A. Bill, *The Eagle and the Lion: The Tragedy of American-Iranian Relations* (1988), pp. 226–33.

[4]This fact is borne out by the testimonies of State Department officials before the House Committee on International Relations in late 1976 and late 1977. On both occasions human rights violations in Iran were admitted, but they were put in the context of the widespread "extremist terrorism" that plagued the country; officials blithely ignored the fact that the human rights violations clearly antedated the adoption of violent tactics by parts of the opposition, as shown in chapter 5. See Y. Alexander and A. Nanes, *United States and Iran*, pp. 425–36 and 451–60.

[5]Zbigniew Brzezinski, *Power and Principle: Memoirs of the National Security Adviser 1977–1981* (1983), p. 361. Cf. also Cyrus Vance, *Hard Choices*, (1983), p. 326.

Nationalist opposition revived in Iran after a lull of fifteen years, it was under the banner of human rights. The Shah seemed more accommodating too.

The Shah's Liberalization

The Shah knew that he had been brought back to power with the help of the Eisenhower administration, and later he had enjoyed a "special relationship" with the Nixon and Ford administrations. On the other hand, the Kennedy administration had denied him arms aid and had "imposed" Ali Amini's "reform government" on him: a new Democratic administration worried the Shah.[6]

It is difficult to say to what extent the Shah's liberalization of 1977 resulted from his reading of Carter's intentions. For obvious reasons, while he was in power the Shah always claimed that he had planned a democratization of Iranian society anyway, for he could not possibly admit to being responsive to American pressure. And it is true that as early as 1975 he had allowed a delegation of the International Commission of Jurists led by Professor Georges Levasseur to conduct an in-depth study of Iran's judicial system.[7] It is also probable that his terminal illness, which he kept secret, and the failure of the Rastakhiz party to contribute to an institutionalization of his regime, induced him to open up the political system, so as to bequeath a secure throne to his son. After his fall he did admit that he had been pressured by the United States, however. At any rate, around the time that Jimmy Carter received the Democratic nomination the Shah ordered an end to torture in Iran.[8]

The Shah launched a campaign to publicize Iranian views on human rights. In the first half of 1977, Rastakhiz party leaders, members of the imperial family, and high government officials were mobilized to give speeches extolling the Shah's lofty views on democracy, human rights, and justice. Subsequently, the Iranian parliament passed laws improving the protection of human rights in the country.

Throughout late 1976 and the first half of 1977 the government released political prisoners, although the number of those freed was

[6] R. K. Ramazani, *The United States and Iran: The Pattern of Influence* (1982), p. 91.

[7] The sending of this and other delegations was at least partially due to an initiative of the LMI(a), which later translated the reports into Persian and published them.

[8] The time is inferred from a statement the Shah made to William J. Butler in May 1977, in which he said that no torture had been practiced for the last ten months. See "Testimony of William J. Butler, chairman of the Executive Committee of the International Commission of Jurists, before the Subcommittee on International Organizations of the Committee on International Relations," House of Representatives, 95th Congress, October 26, 1977.

swelled by including common criminals. It seems that the vast majority of the freed political prisoners belonged to the fundamentalist opposition.[9] Concommitantly, leftist guerrillas were killed in street battles, jailed, tried, and often executed.[10] In July, however, Ay. Taleqani was arrested and sentenced to ten years in prison. It seemed that the regime attempted to sow confusion in the ranks of the opposition by arresting some and not others, so that those not arrested would be viewed as secret collaborators with the government.

In early 1977 the Shah began a program of political liberalization. In early August Amir-Abbas Hoveida, who had been prime minister for an unprecedented twelve years, was replaced by Jamshid Amuzegar, an able and personally untainted technocrat who had hitherto been in charge of oil policy. On August 5 (Mordad 14), Constitution Day, the Shah declared: "We will have as much political freedom as the European democracies."[11] At the same time the Shah never hinted at relaxing the monopoly of the Rastakhiz party; all dissent was to be channeled through it. This was a big mistake, for until the fall of 1977, as we shall see, the initiative within the opposition belonged to intellectuals and moderates. They were thus deprived of the opportunity to form political parties, with the result that from late 1977 onward most of the mass mobilization was carried out by the clergy, who were helped by the release of fundamentalist political prisoners.

To sum up the liberalization of 1977 one could say that the Shah put an end to the worst excesses in the prisons, tolerated a few manifestations of malcontent by intellectuals, but failed to open up the political system in any way.

The Opposition and Carter's Human Rights Campaign

The anti-Shah opposition after 1953 always saw the Shah as an American puppet who could be influenced by U.S. pressure. The election of a U.S. president who pledged to work for human rights was therefore greeted with elation. For some members of the more religiously minded sectors of the opposition, Carter's strong identification with religious values was a further sign of hope. How, the argument went, could a professing Christian knowingly countenance the Shah's repression?

Iranians were aware of the Shah's apprehensions about Carter, and

---

[9]The freed fundamentalists were paraded on television, where they publicly expressed their gratitude to the Shah. One of them, Habibollah Asgar Owladi, would become a cabinet minister in the Islamic Republic.

[10]For details see *Keesing's*, April 21, 1978, p. 28940.

[11]Quoted in Ebrahim Yazdi, *Akharin talashha dar akharin ruzha* (1984), p. 14.

widely believed rumors claimed that the Shah had made hefty financial contributions to Nixon's and Ford's presidential campaigns. It was inferred that Carter had been irked by this, and according to another widespread rumor he had waited an uncommon four days before answering the Shah's congratulatory message after his election. As late as February 1980 Bazargan would write that "Carter's election made it possible for Iran to breathe again."[12]

After January 1977 the moderate middle-class opposition essentially tried to test the atmosphere, to get a feeling for how far it could go. The first initiative came from Ali-Asghar Hajj-Seyyed-Javadi, the writer and essayist. Around the Iranian New Year (March 1977) he wrote an open letter of over 200 pages to the Shah analyzing what was wrong with the country. Nothing happened to him, which emboldened the opposition.

About the same time, Hajj-Seyyed-Javadi's brother, Ahmad Sadr Hajj-Seyyed-Javadi, who was in charge of the LMI's liaison with the Muslim Student Associations abroad, issued a strongly anticommunist statement and left Iran with a considerable amount of money destined for the MSAs abroad and the Book Distribution Center in Houston. In Paris he apparently contributed nothing for Banisadr's activities, which laid the groundwork for future ill feeling between the LMI and the man who would be the first president of Iran.

After Hajj-Seyyed-Javadi's letter, the first open manifestations of opposition to the Shah were the work of intellectuals and emanated from the modern segment of society. Professional associations of lawyers, writers, university professors and physicians were created or revived; they democratically elected their leadership and sent more or less open letters to the Shah and the prime minister. Most of the prominent leaders of this movement came from the ranks of the secular component of the Nationalist, pre-1963 opposition to the Shah, although a few had had links with the Tudeh. But these associations and their letters and analyses could do little more than publicize the regime's abuses and suggest ways to improve the situation.

As far as political parties were concerned, however, the situation was less conducive to activism. The founders of the LMI had never lost touch with each other, and in 1976 they started meeting regularly at their homes to discuss a possible revival of their party. Ali Shariati took part in these meetings, but Taleqani, E. Sahabi, and A. Sheibani were still in prison.

From the outset the appropriate role of religion became a hotly

---

[12]In a letter to the editor, *Ettela'at*, Bahman 18, 1358/February 7, 1980, quoted in Ervand Abrahamian, *Iran between Two Revolutions* (1982), p. 500.

debated issue at the meetings. The debate pitted a more secular wing consisting of Sami'i, Radnia, Nazih, and Alibaba'i against the advocates of a frankly religious coloration of the party, namely Bazargan, Sahabi, Ahmad Sadr Hajj-Seyyed-Javadi, and Mohammad-Mehdi Ja'fari. Much precious time was thus lost on preliminaries and the party failed to assert an independent position on the political scene. Sami'i, Radnia, and Nazih soon dropped out of these discussions although they maintained links with the LMI, and the central core of the revived LMI became in effect quite homogeneously religious in orientation. By 1978 the LMI had a rudimentary organization, with elected executive and central committees.

Secular parties also began appearing on the scene. Rahmatollah Moqaddam Maragheh'i, member of a prominent Azerbaijani family and a lawyer previously unconnected to Mosaddeq, founded a reformist, secular party, which he called in the Latin European tradition Nehzat-e radikal (Radical Movement). Foruhar revived his Party of the Iranian Nation, the Iran party reconstituted itself with Shapur Bakhtiar as secretary general (Saleh was too old and ailing to be politically active), and one faction of what had been Khalil Maleki's Third Force became the new Society of Iranian Socialists. But none of these parties comprised more than a few old-time leaders, and they had altogether little impact on the country's political life.

Parallel to these attempts at forming political parties, efforts were made to create a wider framework for cooperation among the various Nationalist forces, which brought up the eternally divisive question of what the structure of the National Front should be.

In June 1977 Nationalist leaders decided to write an open letter to the Shah. It was drafted by Bazargan and accused the Shah's regime of "despotism in the guise of monarchy"; of creating, by its economic policies, inflation and shortages of food and housing; of squandering Iran's oil resources; of disregarding human rights; and of tolerating flattery and corruption. It called on the government "to observe the principles of the constitution and the Universal Declaration of Human Rights, forgo a one-party system, allow freedom of the press and of association, release political prisoners, permit exiles to return and establish a government based on majority representation."[13] The secular Mosaddequists wanted the letter to be signed by party leaders only, whereas Bazargan and his friends preferred a larger number of signatures, including that of Hashem Sabbaghian.[14] Sabbaghian, an

[13]Quoted from Keesing's, April 21, 1978, p. 28940.
[14]Mehdi Bazargan, Enqelab-e eslami dar do harekat (The Islamic revolution in two movements) (1984), p. 27. It appears that the secular party leaders were particularly incensed at Bazargan's insistence on including Hashem Sabbaghian among the signatories. Shapur Bakhtiar, personal interview, Suresnes, August 12, 1983.

engineer from Teheran who had left the National Front to join the LMI, was by 1977 a major figure in the circle around Bazargan. From 1963 to 1978 he had occupied a civil service post overseeing public housing projects.[15] No agreement could be reached, and finally Foruhar, Sanjabi, and Bakhtiar decided to convey the document to the Shah with their signatures only.

After this incident, five prominent Nationalist leaders, Sanjabi, Bazargan, Foruhar, Moqaddam Maragheh'i, and A.-A. Hajj-Seyyed-Javadi decided to meet regularly once a week to try to find ways to coordinate Nationalist activities. Again, no agreement could be reached. Foruhar and Sanjabi maintained that the National Front existed and consisted of the IP, the PIN, and the LMI. Bazargan and Hajj-Seyyed-Javadi, by contrast, argued that the parties existed only on paper, and that the five members of the group should issue a public invitation to other prominent figures and begin public discussions about a new National Front.[16]

The result was that the secular Mosaddeqists decided to revive the NF without the LMI. On November 22, 1977 (Azar 1, 1356), secular Nationalists met on the occasion of the religious feast of *aid-e qorban* at the garden of an NF leader at Karavansara-ye Sangi outside Teheran, with about 1,000 persons attending. The gathering was broken up by SAVAK and many were beaten up. Nobody from the LMI was present. On December 11, 1977, Dariush Foruhar announced in Teheran that the National Front had reconstituted itself under the name of Union of National Front Forces.[17] It included the Iran Party under Shapur Bakhtiar, the PIN under Dariush Foruhar, who became the NF's spokesman, and the Society of Iranian Socialists. Karim Sanjabi became the leader of the new National Front. In 1978 relations between the LMI and the NF broke down and there was very little cooperation between the two. The National Front's reluctance (at least till October) to acknowledge the religious character of the revolution may have been a factor, but one should not underestimate the lingering weight of past discords, as analyzed in chapter 4.

Given the Shah's reluctance to open up the political process to

---

[15]Biographical information on Sabbaghian is taken from a campaign pamphlet for the 1980 elections.

[16]Information on the beginnings of Nationalist political party activism in 1977 was obtained from interviews with Hasan Nazih and Ali-Asghar Hajj-Seyyed-Javadi in the summers of 1982 and 1983 in Paris.

[17]Foruhar declared that the new body would "fight the dictatorship within the framework of the law" and called for a return to constitutional monarchy and the nationalization of the major private industries, although he emphasized that the Union of National Front Forces' ideology was neither capitalist nor communist but "strictly nationalist." Quoted in *Keesing's*, April 21, 1978, p. 28940.

political parties, only unity of purpose combined with rapid and efficient organization could have enabled the Nationalists to become a political force to be reckoned with. Instead, sterile and interminable discussions about the forms of political organization and an unwillingness to carry on the type of activities one usually associates with political parties (membership drives; the creation of affiliated groups for the young, women, and intellectuals; organization in the provinces; the dissemination of position papers, and so on) frustrated the efforts. In the meantime, taking advantage of the relative relaxation of state power, the fundamentalist opposition was busy organizing.

Whatever their disagreements about the forms of political action, all Nationalist leaders did concur on the issue of human rights. Having failed to create a unified structure for the political opposition, they decided to found an association for the defense of human rights. Such an association, it was thought, would be less likely to be repressed by the government, and would also be regarded as less threatening by the United States. Members of the politically active clergy (Hashemi Rafsanjani, Beheshti, and others) with whom all sectors of the Nationalist opposition were in contact, also approved of the plan.

The Iranian Committee for the Defense of Freedom and Human Rights

The idea of an association dedicated to the defense of human rights appeared in the autumn of 1977. In due course this association became the reformist opposition's most important grouping, far more visible and active than the political parties or professional associations. After Bazargan became its chairman he would always act publicly in that capacity rather than as leader of the LMI.

Formation of the Human Rights Committee

In the fall of 1977, at the initiative of Ay. S. Abolfazl Zanjani (brother of the founder of the NRM, Ay. S. Reza Zanjani) and Fathollah Banisadr, major Nationalist figures were approached about the project. Through the usual channels—personal contacts, friendship circles—a first meeting of thirty prominent people was convened in the house of Sanjabi sometime in October. Twenty-nine of them became the "founding council" (hei'at-e mo'asses) of the Iranian Committee for the Defense of Freedom and Human Rights (ICDFHR).[18]

[18]The following information on the ICDFHR was obtained in July 1982 in Paris from interviews with Abdolkarim Lahiji, Ali-Asghar Hajj-Seyyed-Javadi, and H. Matin-Daftari.

The Founding Council included several religiously oriented figures, such as Mehdi Bazargan, Naser Minachi, Ay. S. Abolfazl Zanjani, Ahmad Sadr Hajj-Seyyed-Javadi, Yadollah Sahabi, Hashem Sabbaghian, Kazem Sami, and Habibollah Peiman. The secular members included Rahmatollah Moqaddam Maragheh'i, Rahim Abedi, founders of the Radical Movement; Karim Sanjabi, Asadollah Mobasheri, Admiral Ahmad Madani, all leading figures of the National Front; Ali-Asghar Hajj-Seyyed-Javadi and two of his political allies, Shams Al-e Ahmad and Eslam Kazemiyeh; as well as Abdolkarim Lahiji and Hasan Nazih, prominent civil rights lawyers who had defended political prisoners.

The composition of this Founding Council is instructive. Some of the individuals were largely unknown to the public, whereas others whom one might have expected to find, such as Shapur Bakhtiar or Dariush Foruhar, were missing. Most of the secular members were in fact politically close to Bazargan and the LMI. The composition of the ICDFHR's Founding Council thus mirrored that of the National Front's High Council of 1960: just as then the "independent personalities" and the Iran Party had dominated that body, offering only token representation to the religiously oriented people around Bazargan, now LMI figures and sympathizers offered only token membership to a few leading figures such as Sanjabi and Mobasheri. The most surprising absence is that of Ay. Reza Zanjani, who remained closer to the secular National Front than to the LMI.

The first conflict between the two tendencies arose over the wording of the association's charter. In an effort to build bridges to the clerical opposition, the religious wing wanted explicit references to Islam, for example, references to human rights as "Islamic human rights." They also seem to have successfully resisted some secular members' wish to include a woman in the Founding Council. On the question of the Islamic coloration of the charter a compromise was reached: human rights were to be treated in accordance with "Islamic principles" (*mavazin-e eslami*).

The members of the Founding Council then proceeded to elect a seven-man Executive Council: Bazargan, Minachi, Ahmad Sadr Hajj-Seyyed-Javadi, Nazih, Sanjabi, Ali-Asghar Hajj-Seyyed-Javadi, and Lahiji. Both Bazargan and Sanjabi were candidates for the chairmanship of the Executive Council. In the vote that followed Bazargan received six votes out of seven. The secular members of the Executive Council had voted for Bazargan, in deference to his greater part in the resistance against the Shah. A secular member, A.-A. Hajj-Seyyed-Javadi, became vice-chairman, however, and another secular figure, Lahiji, was named spokesman. On December 7, 1977, the formation of the ICDFHR was made public.

Activities of the ICDFHR

The ICDFHR began to publicize the violations of human rights in Iran and to receive guests from abroad. Among the Americans who came were Professor Richard Falk of Princeton University, Professor Richard Cottam of the University of Pittsburgh, and former attorney general Ramsey Clark. Interviews were given to the foreign press.

At the end of the year a letter, drafted by Nazih, was addressed to the secretary general of the United Nations, Kurt Waldheim. In this letter the ICDFHR said that for twenty-four years "the ruling oligarchy" had systematically violated Article 21 of the 1948 Universal Declaration of Human Rights (granting everyone "the right to take part in the government of his country, directly or through freely chosen representatives") and had prevented all effective participation of the people in parliamentary elections, that torture had not yet been abolished, and that political trials were still being held in camera by military courts. It is worth noting the essentially reformist import of the letter, which in its demands does not go beyond the Nationalist opposition's usual call for the respect of the Constitution.

The contact with Waldheim created a certain degree of immunity for the members of the ICDFHR. On January 12, 1978, the ICDFHR held its first public press conference in Teheran, with Bazargan, Sanjabi, and Ahmad Sadr Hajj-Seyyed-Javadi in attendance. Sanjabi emphasized that the committee was not a political organization and had no links with other countries but merely intended to draw the attention of world public opinion to the human rights problem in Iran. This press conference judiciously coincided with a visit by Waldheim to Teheran. Here, on January 14, 1978 (after he had paid a visit to the Shah), he confirmed that he had received an appeal from the committee signed by twenty-nine persons.[19]

Despite this relative immunity, however the members of the committee came under increasing pressure from security organizations of the state, and on April 8, 1978, bombs exploded at the homes of five founders, including Bazargan and Sanjabi.

In May the ICDFHR held extensive meetings with William J. Butler, the visiting American human rights lawyer. Shortly before that Sanjabi stopped attending ICDFHR meetings,[20] and his place on the Executive Committee was taken by Moqaddam Maragheh'i.

---

[19]*Keesing's*, April 21, 1978, p. 28940.

[20]It appears that he resented the fact that Bazargan and his allies were dominating the ICDFHR. Sanjabi himself hinted at such a motive in an interview published in *Ettela'at*, March 18, 1980 (Esfand 27, 1358), p. 8.

The offices of the ICDFHR had been set up in a house next to the Hoseiniyeh Ershad, under the cover of a legal practice for Ahmad Sadr Hajj-Seyyed-Javadi and Mobasheri, both lawyers. In the winter and spring the activities of the committee had still been quite discreet, but in the summer of 1978 it began to manifest itself more openly, and the "legal practice" became its official headquarters. Its financial needs were met by an initial commitment of the founding members to pay 100,000 rials (roughly $1,400) each.

Toward the end of the summer, mass mobilization of the populace by the clergy overtook the new dynamism exhibited by civil society, as exemplified by the ICDFHR. In August the idea came up to stage a big demonstration on International Human Rights Day, December 10. It so happened that in 1978 International Human Rights Day coincided with Tasu'a, the ninth day of Muharram. A joint demonstration was proposed to the clergy, who had made plans of their own but nevertheless accepted. As we will see, this demonstration was a resounding success. It would be naive, however, to think that millions of people paraded in Teheran for the respect of human rights. By this time the intellectual, reformist, middle-class opposition of which the ICDFHR was the main organization was merely following events.

For the sake of thematic unity, the next section jumps ahead a bit to describe what became of the ICDFHR after the fall of the Shah.

The ICDFHR in Postrevolutionary Iran

After the formation of the Provisional Government in 1979 the Executive Council of the ICDFHR decided that all those members of the Executive Council who had accepted governmental posts should resign from the ICDFHR. Their places were taken by Abedi, Reza'i, Banafti, and Tabandeh. A.-A. Hajj-Seyyed-Javadi was chosen as chairman, and Lahiji became his deputy.

The committee was now in secular hands. Its main task was now to look after the interests of the freed political prisoners of the Shah regime. Money was collected from the Organization of the Red Sun and Lion (then Iran's equivalent of the Red Cross), headed by Kazem Sami; philanthropists; Bazaar merchants; and the National Iranian Oil Company, which was then headed by Hasan Nazih.

The LMI members were now too occupied with affairs of state to take an active part in the ICDFHR's activities, but relations never broke down. The Provisional Government did not hamper the activities of the ICDFHR, but even after the demise of that government the LMI members, now free from governmental responsibility, did not resume their participation in the committee, earning the as yet silent reproach that they had tasted power and relished their part in it too much to be bothered with such associations as the ICDFHR.

After the fall of the Bazargan government, the rising tide of totalitarianism, eloquently chronicled by Ali-Asghar Hajj-Seyyed-Javadi in his articles, made it increasingly difficult for the committee to function. In November 1980 (Aban 1359) the offices of the Iranian Committee for the Defense of Freedom and Human Rights were occupied and all documents, archives, furniture, and other property were either destroyed or taken away. Ali-Asghar Hajj-Seyyed-Javadi had to leave Iran in the fall of 1981; he was followed in the spring of 1982 by Abdolkarim Lahiji.

Aborted Transition and Revolution

After the initial steps taken by members of the modern segment of society, the revolutionary movement really "took off" between November 1977 and January 1978. No longer were only lawyers, writers, and other intellectuals involved in the opposition to despotism; in early 1978 the masses entered the scene and gradually the dissident movement became a revolutionary movement.[21] After a brief summary, we will turn to Nationalist efforts to bring about a peaceful transition to a new order.

The Religious Mass Movement of 1978

It is important to note that religiously oriented Nationalists, people associated with the Hoseiniyeh Ershad Institute, the LMI, and JAMA, participated in the religious effervescence that began in 1977. They had never lost contact with the intellectual members of the clergy, Beheshti, Hashemi Rafsanjani, Khameneh'i, and the fundamentalist circle around them. In addition, Bazargan also kept in touch with more traditional clerical leaders in Qum, as represented by Ay. Shariatmadari.

During Ramadan in August 1977 intellectual clerics and lay modernists began organizing meetings at Ho. Mofatteh's Qoba Mosque in Qolhak to counter meetings that the secular, intellectual opposition was organizing at Teheran University. At the first modernist meeting the speakers included Mohammad Tavassoli, Y. Sahabi, and Bazargan; Sami and Peiman; and clerics known for their progressive views, Ho.

[21]We cannot chronicle here the important stages of the rise of the mass movement. See Abrahamian, *Iran*, pp. 504–24, and M. M. J. Fischer, *Iran: From Religious Dispute to Revolution* (1980), pp. 184–216.

Javad Hojjati Kermani, Sheikh Ali Tehrani, and Mofatteh himself. At this and similar meetings Bazargan again and again warned against too rapid mass mobilization, arguing that the people's level of understanding had to be raised first. When during these meetings the crowds would hail Khomeini's name with three salvos of benediction, Bazargan would protest, pointing out that the Prophet himself usually receives only one salvo. In the highly charged atmosphere of those months Bazargan's pleas for moderation were received with impatience, but his record and prestige as an opponent of the Shah and religious activist enabled him to remain within the movement.

After the timid liberalization of early 1977 the first opportunity for a religiopolitical mass meeting was provided by the death of Ho. Mostafa Khomeini, the ayatollah's eldest son. His memorial service was organized jointly by the clergy and the Nationalists at the Arg Mosque in the Teheran Bazaar on October 30, 1977 (Aban 8, 1356), and attracted a huge crowd. The main preacher irked the modernists by claiming in his sermon that the public's enthusiastic response was only the result of its affection for the clergy; the lay religious figures by contrast saw in that response a sign of opposition to the Shah.

Genuine mass mobilization by the clergy really began in early 1978, after Teheran's main newspaper, *Ettela'at*, on January 7 (Dey 17, 1356) published an article highly critical of the clergy. The author called them "black reactionaries" and accused them of secretly working with international communists to undo the achievements of the White Revolution. The article also seized on the fact that Khomeini's father had emigrated to Kashmir, to claim that Khomeini was a foreigner who in his youth had worked as a British spy and had written erotic Sufi poetry. The diatribe touched off angry demonstrations in Qum, in which a number of demonstrators were shot by security forces. In accordance with religious customs the deaths were commemorated forty days later, which led to new demonstrations and new casualties, resulting in a chain reaction. The demonstrations were encouraged by Khomeini, who from his exile in Najaf taped incendiary messages, which were sent to Iran and reproduced widely. Outraged by the regime's frontal attack on the religious institutions in Qum, and so as not to be left behind, Ay. Shariatmadari now also entered the picture and began demanding strict adherence to the Constitution.

In response to the demonstrations the government tried to cow the secular opposition into submission by bombing their leaders' houses. The Amuzegar government also made concessions to the Bazaar and slowed down the economy to lower inflation. It publicly apologized to Ay. Shariatmadari for an earlier attack on his home in Qum, and the Shah made a much publicized pilgrimage to Imam Reza's shrine in

Mashad. Amuzegar's strategy seemed to work for a while: for most of the summer Teheran was calm. But the government's deflationary economic policies caused widespread unemployment and after July strikes of industrial workers broke out all over Iran. In the heated atmosphere the strikes soon acquired political and religious significance.

Ramadan, the Muslim month of fasting, began on August 5 that year. Violent demonstrations took place around the country, and in Isfahan demonstrators took over the city for two days. On August 19 (Mordad 28) twenty-five years after the coup that brought the Shah to power, the Rex Cinema in Abadan burned down, killing 400 trapped men, women, and children. Government and opposition each blamed the other for the fire, but the public was more ready to believe the opposition. On August 27 the Shah replaced Jamshid Amuzegar, the technocrat, with J. Sharif-Emami, the president of the Senate. The new prime minister declared that according to the Constitution all political parties were allowed to be active.[22]

The end of Ramadan was marked with peaceful demonstrations in Teheran. Sharif-Emami had granted the necessary permission in exchange for a promise by opposition leaders to keep the demonstration calm and to refrain from any direct attack on the Shah. In Teheran about 100,000 people took part in the march. But during the next three days demonstrations intensified, in spite of government bans and opposition leaders' calls for restraint. On September 7, half a million people demonstrated in Teheran, the biggest crowd so far. The crowd began chanting radical slogans such as "Death to the Pahlavis," "Husein is our guide, Khomeini is our leader," and for the first time, "We want an Islamic republic." In response the government issued warrants for the arrest of the major opposition leaders, but Bazargan avoided arrest by seeking refuge in the house of Ay. Shariatmadari in Qum.

Martial law having been declared in Teheran on September 7, security forces fired on a crowd staging a sit-in at Zhaleh Square on September 8, Black Friday. In the working-class districts of southern Teheran the inhabitants set up barricades, and the government used helicopter gunships to dislodge them, leaving a "carnage of destruction" as the *Le Monde* correspondent called it.[23]

Black Friday spelled the end of liberalization in Iran. No opposition politician could afford to enter into any sort of coalition with the government, even if an invitation had been issued. The capital was now under the authority of General Gholam-Ali Oveisi, who had earned the sobriquet "Butcher of Teheran" for his leading role in the

[22]Yazdi, *Akharin talashha*, p. 21.
[23]Jean Gueyras's account of the events of September 8 appeared in the September 11 issue of *Le Monde*.

suppression of the June 1963 riots.[24] Jimmy Carter's telephone call to the Shah after these events enraged the Iranian opposition, which felt betrayed by the U.S. president. Strikes now appeared throughout the country, effectively paralyzing the economy. Bazaar merchants set up soup kitchens to feed striking workers and their families. In October the opposition adopted a new tactic, namely asking the population to climb on rooftops and chant *Allah akbar* (God is greatest) every night. Antiregime activism now became a quotidian affair for most of the population.

Faced with the mounting pressure, Prime Minister Sharif-Emami persuaded the Iraqi government to expel Khomeini. It was hoped that his absence from a city where he enjoyed easy contact with Iranian pilgrims and clerics might weaken his influence inside Iran. Instead Khomeini went to Paris and became the cynosure of world attention, with easy access to international mass media. In Iran demonstrations continued and after a particularly violent one on November 4 (Aban 13), Sharif-Emami was replaced with General Gholam-Reza Azhari.

On November 17 (Aban 26) the entire written press began a strike that lasted until January 8, 1979 (Dey 18). During this strike the LMI's publication *Akhbar-e jonbesh-e eslami* (News of the Islamic Movement) was the only available journal and gave regular accounts of the revolution's progress.[25]

On December 2 the holy month of Muharram began. The ICDFHR had proposed that the opposition's joint demonstration on the ninth day of Muharram, Tasu'a, start from the Ministry of Justice, but the ulema insisted that it leave from the home of Ay. Taleqani at Darvazeh Shemiran instead, to which the recently freed Taleqani consented. ICDFHR gave in and Teheran's inhabitants were invited to demonstrate in a joint declaration signed by the following: Ho. Ali-Akbar Hashemi Rafsanjani and Ay. Musavi Ardabili for the clergy, A. Eraqi and Habibollah Asgar Owladi for the Bazaar, E. Sahabi for the LMI, and A. Lahiji for the ICDFHR. As a result of this cooperation, millions of Iranian citizens of both segments of society marched together in Teheran on December 10, 1978, in one of the largest mass demonstrations in world history. The next day, on the tenth of Muharram, the demonstrations were even bigger and more clearly religious in nature. Henceforth it was only a question of time when the Shah would leave. Two months later Iran was an Islamic republic.

This has been a quick account of the outward manifestations of the revolution. The mass demonstrations and government repression thereof

[24]Oveisi was assassinated in the streets of Paris in February 1984.
[25]Bazargan, *Enqelab*, p. 48.

were beyond the control of politicians and constituted a serious constraint on their action. Let us now turn to the part played by the LMI in the events and its attempts to bring about a more orderly transition.

The LMI and the Transition to a New Order

Until the late summer of 1978 the Shah regime seemed to have the situation under control. Few people, even within the opposition in Iran, believed that the end of his rule might be near; the circumstances of his terminal illness were not known. The Shah made no attempts to defuse the situation by bringing into the government people from outside the regime: the Sharif-Emami and Azhari governments were essentially attempts to reequilibrate the regime from within. As late as July 1978 the Shah rejected any negotiations with the Nationalists on the grounds that they were "even more traitorous than the Tudeh Party."[26] More and more deputies and senators, all of whom had been "elected" under the banner of the Rastakhiz party, abandoned ship and began denouncing the government, SAVAK, and corruption in high places. The government, hoping to funnel some of the popular discontent into within-regime channels, had the state-owned radio and television network broadcast all parliamentary debates live, and the population was thus treated to unending streams of antigovernment diatribes by this parthenogenetic opposition.

With the advent of the Sharif-Emami and the Azhari governments, and their inability to bring things under control, some individuals on the margins of the regime and in the opposition began thinking about the modalities of a transition. Sharif-Emami had made some concessions to religious sensibilities (he abolished the Shah's Imperial Calendar and closed down gambling casinos), and at least some moderate elements in the opposition were willing to give him a chance. But the declaration of martial law in Teheran on September 7 put an end to these hopes.

"Bastion by Bastion"

On May 22, 1978 (Ordibehesht 1, 1357), Bazargan had told reporters of Belgian Television that so long as the Shah remained in Iran, there could be no social and political freedom in Iran.[27] The LMI participated in all demonstrations, and its members were active in the mass movement. During the summer, it seemed to Bazargan that some of Khomeini's declarations were out of touch with the concrete situation in Iran, and

[26]Quoted in *Iran Times*, July 21, 1978.

[27]*Safehati az tarikh-e mo'aser-e Iran: Asnad-e nehzat'e azadi-ye Iran* (Some pages from contemporary Iranian history: Documents of the LMI), vol. 11 (1983), p. 322.

he wanted to give Khomeini his own analysis of the situation. In August 1978 Bazargan directly contacted Khomeini in Najaf by asking a pious Bazaar merchant who planned a pilgrimage to the holy city to take a message to the ayatollah.[28] The message is a good summary of Bazargan's personal preferences in matters of political tactics:

1. The Iranian Constitution, without later amendments and changes, was the only document that could be effectively used to incriminate the Shah; moreover, under present circumstances its application was the best guarantee for the respect of Islamic laws.
2. All attacks should be directed against despotism rather than colonialism [that is, U.S. hegemony in Iran]. It was not wise to fight on two fronts, and therefore not advisable to provoke America and Europe, which would result in their hostility to the revolution and thus benefit the Shah.
3. All National and Islamic movements that had succeeded in recent Iranian history had started with their acceptance of the regime's offer of free elections. An election campaign would be an appropriate way to spread the opposition's message in the population.
4. The opposition should make use of all concessions made by the government, even if they be insincere, and all personalities who had left the regime should be welcomed to its ranks so as to encourage others to do likewise.
5. The ultimate aim was of course the overthrow of the regime. But this could best be achieved in stages: first the Shah had to leave, then his successors had to be constrained within the limits of existing laws, then one would have to work on people's minds and mentalities, and only then could the change be made to an Islamic republic.
6. Good and regular contact and counseling with the clergy was essential. For that purpose Khomeini should name a delegation in Teheran whose members could act as regular and trusted intermediaries between him and the opposition.
7. Islamic government had to be the only and ultimate aim of every Muslim. It was appropriate to mention it in the interview with *Le Monde*.[29]

[28]Unless otherwise indicated, all information concerning Bazargan's contacts and discussions with Khomeini is taken from a collection of three speeches by Bazargan published together as *Showra-ye enqelab va dowlat-e movaqqat va sima-ye dowlat-e movaqqat az veladat ta rahlat va nameh-ye sargoshadeh-ye mohandes Bazargan be emam* (The Council of the Revolution and the Provisional Government, the makeup of the Provisional Government from its birth to its death; and Engineer Bazargan's open letter to the Imam) (1983).

[29]This was an allusion to that newspaper's interview with Khomeini, the first he had ever granted a Western newspaper, which was published on May 6, 1978. An English translation was published by the *Guardian Weekly* in its May 21 issue. That version, somewhat augmented, can be found in Ali-Reza Nobari, *Iran Erupts*, (1978), pp. 9–17. Khomeini had said that his aim was the establishment of an Islamic state, that he rejected both the Shah and the monarchy, and that the 1906 constitution was only acceptable if it were amended. Bazargan's apparent approval was therefore a courteous apophasis in light of his further observations.

The content of Islamic government was not clear yet, however, and not enough acceptable work had been done on its ideological, economic, political, and bureaucratic aspects. Also, the monopolistic leadership of the clergy, which had not given good results in the past and lacked experience and technical qualifications, and the concomitant marginalization of nonreligious but well-intentioned and competent Nationalist groups was against the interests of the revolution.

On August 28 (Shahrivar 6) the LMI issued a public declaration consistent with Bazargan's message. Titled "The Way out of the Current Impasse," it identified the Shah as the root of all evil in Iran. It also declared that destruction and insecurity were growing exponentially, and although the government blamed the people for it, it alone was responsible for creating a chaotic situation from which in the end only communism would profit. If the Shah abdicated, ways could be found out of the current impasse. His successors would have learned a lesson and respect the Constitution, and the people would achieve their aims by advancing "bastion by bastion" (sangar beh sangar).[30]

In another public declaration titled "Where Are We?" issued on October 9 (Mehr 17), the LMI again proposed an orderly advance of the revolutionary forces, bastion by bastion, and warned against haste and disorderliness. Noting that Sharif-Emami had made some concessions, it concluded:

> If we commit no mistakes and no treason, don't fall victim to sentimentalism and chaos, and if we are honest, stable, intelligent, and prove that we are capable of governing ourselves and the country, despotism will evacuate its remaining positions and our independence and rights will be respected. The opportunities that have arisen should be used wisely, so that on the one hand we come closer to our main aim, and on the other hand foreign interests, which are an undeniable reality and presence, will not be forced to support and maintain the despotic order. If we advance with the tactic of "bastion by bastion," and if we are intelligent, organized, patient, and constructive, with God's help we can be hopeful about the future.[31]

Four points are obvious in these two declarations:

1. The Shah is unequivocally asked to abdicate.
2. The monarchy is implicitly accepted, and no mention is made of an Islamic republic.
3. Ay. Khomeini is not mentioned once.
4. U.S. sensibilities are taken into account.

[30]Safehat, 11, pp. 13–17.
[31]Ibid., p. 29.

The "bastion by bastion" approach reflected Bazargan's often-stated conviction that for something to succeed it had to be done methodically. It was later misquoted by radicals as a "step by step" line and Bazargan was attacked, even within his party, for being too cautious and not having enough confidence in mass action. Bazargan wanted the Islamic movement to take power gradually, to consolidate its gains after each victory. He wanted the opposition to accept the Shah's offer of free elections, as an election campaign would be the best cause for mass mobilization. Khomeini disagreed with this view, as an election campaign would in his view dissipate the popular fervor. In Bazargan's view, either the elections would be truly free, in which case the people would vote for the opposition, or they would be rigged, and the Shah's democratization would be unmasked as fraudulent before the whole world. A realist, Bazargan counted on ten to twenty opposition candidates to enter a parliament elected under the Shah.[32] He seems to have had in mind as a precedent Mosaddeq's relative victory in the election to the sixteenth Majles. Bazargan knew Sharif-Emami from their common days in the Engineers Association, and would have liked to give the prime minister time to implement a few reforms.[33] Bazargan was thus in substantive agreement with the moderate clerical leadership in Iran, which would have liked to give Sharif-Emami a chance. Shariatmadari's "broker" in the Islamic movement was Naser Minachi, treasurer of the ICDFHR and former director of the Hoseiniyeh Ershad. He and Bazargan cooperated closely, but as one U.S. embassy dispatch summed up their difference, "whereas Bazargan in the end always gives in to Khomeini, Minachi and the Shariatmadari people try to circumvent him."[34] Khomeini aborted these efforts at a rapprochement with Sharif-Emami by sending incendiary messages that called the prime minister's measures "ruses."

The events of Black Friday must have convinced both government and opposition in Iran that any solution to the crisis was impossible unless it took into account Ay. Khomeini. Ali Amini, who thought of himself as the Shah's last card, issued a statement to the effect that, if named prime minister, he would go and negotiate a truce with Khomeini, whom he had already met once in the early 1960s. The Shah did not name Amini premier, but Amini still continued his efforts to bring government and Khomeini together. He even went to Paris, but Khomeini would not see him. Bazargan was in continuous contact with Amini and it appears that he would have been willing to join an Amini

---

[32]Bazargan's interview with Hamid Algar, which appeared in the organ of the MSAs in North America, *Nasr,* February 1, 1981 (Bahman 12, 1359), p. 6.

[33]M. Bazargan, *Enqelab-e eslami,* p. 31.

[34]*Iran Times,* January 28, 1983.

government, provided Khomeini gave his blessing. Ardeshir Zahedi, the Shah's ambassador to Washington, also paid two visits to Paris in the hope of meeting Khomeini, but was also rebuffed. In October it was the turn of the leaders of the National Movement to enter into direct contact with Khomeini. Both Bazargan and Sanjabi went to pay their homage.

Neauphle-le-Château

Ebrahim Yazdi, the main political leader of the LMI(a) and Khomeini's representative in the United States, left Houston for Najaf in 1978. It was he who persuaded Khomeini to move to Paris after his expulsion from Iraq rather than to another Muslim country, such as Syria. The LMI members hoped that in France, far away from the clerical milieu of Najaf, he would be more amenable to be influenced by them in a moderate direction.

In France Khomeini and his entourage moved to the town of Neauphle-le-Château outside Paris, hitherto known only as the production site of Grand Marnier liqueur, where a longtime JAMA activist, Mehdi Asgari, put his French wife's house at his disposal.

Three men managed Khomeini's headquarters in France: Abolhasan Banisadr, who took charge of relations with the press; Sadeq Qotbzadeh, who took care of everyday matters and Khomeini's schedule; and Yazdi, who acted as Khomeini's spokesman on political matters. The latter saw to it that Khomeini and his entourage would stress three things when addressing the media: the rights of minorities, the rights of women, and free elections.[35] It seemed, therefore, as though Khomeini was solidly harnessed by Nationalists of modernist-religious ideology, and on the surface, Bazargan and the LMI were in a privileged position as far as contacts with Khomeini were concerned. But differences of opinion and personal rivalries separated Khomeini's three advisers, and all of them, albeit to different degrees, from Bazargan.

As Bazargan has put it, the purpose of his trip to Paris was fourfold: to consult with Khomeini, to inform him about the current situation in Iran, to impress him with the need of naming a delegation in Iran which could act on his behalf, and to reestablish contact with the LMI(a). He met Khomeini together with Yazdi on October 30, their first meeting since 1962. Throughout Khomeini was sullen. Bazargan tried to convince him that it was necessary to put some order and method into the revolutionary movement, but Khomeini would have nothing of it. Bazargan got the impression that he had no doubt about his

[35]Cheryl Benard and Zalmay Khalilzad, *The Government of God: Iran's Islamic Republic* (1984), p. 39.

imminent return to Iran, and that his only use for Bazargan was for after that return.

Bazargan's agenda for his talks with Khomeini was the same as his earlier message. When he suggested that the free elections the Shah had finally come to offer would be a good opportunity to penetrate the structures of power and then change the regime legally by means of a constitutional assembly, Khomeini disagreed, arguing that such a course of action would slacken the people's enthusiasm. Khomeini also refused to take any account of the United States. As he saw it, the Americans would not place any direct obstacles into the path of the revolution since its cause was right. At this point Bazargan was so baffled by Khomeini's apparent naiveté that he changed the subject. When Bazargan left the meeting, in response to people who asked how he found Khomeini, he is reported to have responded, "a turbaned Aryamehr."

Khomeini also was not enthusiastic about naming a delegation in Iran. Now we know that by the time a group of clerics loyal to him (Ay. Musavi Ardabili, Ho. Beheshti, Ho. Hashemi Rafsanjani, Ho. Bahonar, Ay. Motahhari, and Ay. Mahdavi Kani) was already functioning inside Iran, but Bazargan probably did not know this. On the other hand, Khomeini did ask Bazargan to prepare him a list of trustworthy and competent Muslims, not only from the LMI, who could form a council to advise him after his return on whom he should endorse as candidates in parliamentary elections and whom he should name to the cabinet.

Two days later Bazargan gave him the following list: Ay. Motahhari, Ay. Abolfazl Zanjani, M. Beheshti, Ho. Hashemi Rafsanjani, and Ho. Mahdavi Kani from the clergy (Ays. Montazeri and Taleqani were not included because they were still in prison); Y. Sahabi, K. Sami, M. Katira'i, N. Minachi, A. Sadr Hajj-Seyyed-Javadi, E. Yazdi and M. Bazargan from among religious Nationalists; Ali Nasab and H. Kazem Haji Tarkhani from the Bazaar; and General Ali-Asghar Mas'udi (one of the LMI's defense lawyers in 1964) and General Valiollah Qarani from among the officers.[36] This list included most of the members of the council already secretly functioning in Teheran, and with few changes it became the Council of the Revolution, whose existence was known but whose composition was at the time shrouded in mystery.

Thus substantive disagreements remained between Bazargan and

[36]This list shows that Bazargan himself excluded all secular politicians from playing any significant role after the revolution. Most striking is the absence on Bazargan's list of Ay. Reza Zanjani. Perhaps Bazargan did not suggest his name and that of his secular allies because he knew that Khomeini would not accept them. In the end not even the more amenable Ay. Abolfazl Zanjani was included in the Council of the Revolution.

Khomeini, and Bazargan was not happy with the result of the talks. In Paris the rivalries between the LMI and the NF and within the LMI also came to the fore. Sanjabi proposed that Khomeini, Bazargan, and he himself sign a tripartite declaration, but Bazargan and Yazdi saw no need for that. In the end Sanjabi published a declaration with his and Khomeini's name (Khomeini had cleared the text, but was reportedly angry at Sanjabi for having juxtaposed their two names on one document[37]) which said that the monarchy did not fulfill the requirements of the law and the Shari'ah because it was tyrannical, corrupt, incapable of resisting foreign pressure, and systematically violated the Constitution, and called for a referendum to establish a national government based on the principles of Islam, democracy, and national sovereignty. Many in the LMI saw in this declaration an attempt to curry favor with Khomeini, and Sanjabi himself did not seem to attach too much importance to it, for in an interview with Le Monde he said that Iran's future government would be Islamic because a representative government in a country whose population was 90 percent Muslim would by definition be Islamic.[38]

Bazargan was also unable to heal the rift between Banisadr on the one hand, and Yazdi and Qotbzadeh on the other. What is more, strong differences of opinion appeared between Bazargan and Banisadr. The latter felt that the severance of all links of dependency between Iran and the United States should be the first priority of the revolution, whereas Bazargan wanted to concentrate on the struggle against dictatorship. At the time Banisadr found more common ground with Sanjabi. Disagreements even surfaced within the LMI. While Bazargan was still in Paris, Qotbzadeh made a statement to the effect that the LMI was finished, that he was forming a new group to succeed it, and that he had the support of Ezzatollah Sahabi and Ay. Taleqani.[39] Both of these men were somewhat more radical than Bazargan, as their collaboration with the Mojahedin had shown, but there is no clear evidence that they had given Qotbzadeh a mandate to make the declaration, especially since both had only recently been released from prison. Yazdi himself was also far more beholden to Khomeini than Bazargan was. He suggested that Bazargan issue a statement acknowledging the paramount leadership of Khomeini over the Iranian revolution, which Bazargan refused to do because he would have to consult with his friends in Teheran first.

On November 5 (Aban 12) Bazargan left for Teheran. One day later violence erupted again on the campus of Teheran University, and

---

[37] Private communication.
[38] Le Monde, November 1, 1978, p. 3.
[39] Abolhasan Banisadr, personal interview, Auvers-sur-Oise, July 1982.

dozens of students were killed by the police. The next day, perhaps under the influence of these killings but certainly as a result of Bazargan's failure to change Khomeini's mind, the LMI issued an official declaration which differed considerably from previous ones.

Titled "Is It Not Time the Ruling Establishment Became Realistic?" the statement said that the events of the last year and a half had clearly shown that (1) the majority of the Iranian people rejected the Shah and his regime and wanted Islamic government, and that (2) the clear majority of the Iranian people had chosen Ay. Khomeini as their leader. And, the statement continued, Ay. Khomeini had constantly repeated that the Shah had to go, that the Pahlavi dynasty had to go, and that the monarchy had to go. The people would not accept anything less than the demands of the clergy. Therefore, the declaration concluded, the Shah should abdicate, if not out of respect for his people then at least out of concern for his personal safety. Foreign governments, especially those who valued stability in Iran, should realize that the Shah's continued presence in Iran was incompatible with stability and order and therefore they should deal with persons who enjoyed the confidence of the Iranian people and its religiopolitical leadership. It warned the officers of the army not to partake in the repression of the revolutionary movement. The declaration was the first LMI to end with a quote from the Qoran.[40]

It is quite obvious that, as a result of his talks with Khomeini, Bazargan completely changed his line and against his better judgment began sounding more intransigent. As noted earlier, his own preferences were far more congruent with those of Ay. Shariatmadari, but realizing Khomeini's charismatic hold on Iranian public emotion, he preferred to remain inside the revolutionary movement and acknowledge Khomeini's leadership. The LMI representatives told the American embassy that as a result of fifteen years of dictatorship the party had lost its independent popular base, and could only hope to be effective if it operated soundly within the revolutionary movement.[41] The tone of the quoted declaration reflects all of this, since Khomeini's leadership and the intransigence of the population are related as empirical facts, not as independently derived policies of the LMI. It was only on December 17 (Azar 26), after the resounding success of the Muharram marches, that all political parties and the ICDFHR issued a joint statement demanding the end of the monarchy in Iran.

The events of early November inaugurated a new, and final phase in the breakdown of the Shah regime. Khomeini was as intractable as

---

[40]*Safehat*, 11, pp. 32–33.
[41]See document dated August 21, 1978, reproduced in *Iran Times*, April 1, 1983.

ever, and the moderate opposition had swung over to his line. The Shah had tried to make a last stand by naming a military government, which in fact included far more civilians than officers. On November 6 the new prime minister, General Gholam-Reza Azhari, proclaimed martial law throughout Iran, but at the same time promised free elections. One day later Khomeini, in an interview with Associated Press, said that since the Shah's government was illegal, any elections it might hold would be devoid of legality too.[42] Azhari's government then proceeded to arrest many opposition leaders, including Bazargan. In prison Bazargan was visited by the head of SAVAK, General Naser Moqaddam, who told him that the Shah had now accepted to reign rather than rule. Bazargan replied that unfortunately it was too late.[43] Subsequently Bazargan and most other political prisoners were released.

In November violence and economic dislocation intensified, and the conditions approached civil war. The new situation was reflected in the contents of U.S. ambassador Sullivan's reports to Washington, as he became convinced that the time had come for America to start seriously thinking about dealing with a post-Shah government. The contacts the U.S. embassy maintained with the LMI have been used by its opponents after the revolution to question the party's loyalty to the revolution. Let us therefore go back to the origins of these contacts.

Negotiating the Transition

It is normal for foreign embassies to maintain contacts with opposition groups.[44] Until the mid-1960s the U.S. embassy had maintained relations with the National Front and opposition figures not affiliated with the NF. After the consolidation of the Shah regime these contacts fizzled out. Describing the situation during his tenure as ambassador, Richard Helms (whose previous position was that of director of the CIA) implies that there were no contacts with the opposition because . . . there was none:

> Let us begin by acknowledging that American policy in Iran was to maintain close relations with the Shah and the government of Iran and to support a country it had regarded under eight presidents as an ally and an important political and military factor in the area of the Persian Gulf. . . . What *was* the opposition in Iran during the period in question? When the two political parties (Iran Novin and Mardom) were disbanded and a one-party system was set up (Rastakhiz), it was even more difficult to find any grouping which was in opposition to the government. Former mem-

[42]Yazdi, *Akharin talashha*, p. 44.
[43]Bazargan, *Enqelab*, p. 57.
[44]On American diplomatic contacts with oppositions see Martin F. Herz, ed., *Contacts with the Opposition: A Symposium* (1980).

bers of the National Front, who had not been coopted by the regime, continued to voice quietly views opposed to the Shah's policies, but the most optimistic revolutionary would hardly have regarded these individuals as a threat to stability.[45]

During William Sullivan's briefings in Washington before he left for Iran, one of his predecessors told him that in Iran he had to "push only one button: the Shah." After his arrival in Iran, in the autumn of 1977, various Iranian individuals claiming to represent the opposition began approaching the American embassy in Teheran. Embassy officials found it difficult to ascertain who was actually representing a significant force and who was not, and who could establish a channel to the militant ulema. Outside Iran, Sadeq Qotbzadeh approached George Griffin, who was the Iran specialist at the State Department Bureau of Intelligence and Research, but he did not achieve much.[46] In June 1978 the U.S. secretary of state, Cyrus Vance gave Sullivan the green light to establish communication with low-level members of the opposition,[47] and consequently embassy officials opened talks with opposition elements. It must be stressed that with the exception of leftists *all* groups were approached: the National Front, the LMI, the Radical Movement, the circle around Ay. Shariatmadari (represented in the talks by Minachi), and the militant Khomeiniite clergy, represented by Beheshti.

The secular National Front representatives at these meetings were "at each other's throats," to quote Ambassador Sullivan,[48] and soon the LMI came to be seen as the most promising avenue. The LMI delegated to these talks Mohammad Tavassoli (Yazdi's brother-in-law, who called himself Tavakkoli to cover his traces) and Abbas Amir-Entezam, who seems to have been chosen because it was thought his *soigné* urbanity would impress the American diplomats favorably. Bazargan himself met a number of times with John Stempel, a political secretary at the U.S. embassy who is fluent in Persian. In September, after Black Friday, Sullivan held a first meeting with Bazargan. It had been arranged by an American business consultant who had connections in the Bazaar.[49] The American embassy's dialogs with oppositional figures greatly annoyed the Shah, who came to the conclusion that the great powers had decided to oust him.[50]

[45]Ibid., pp. 21–22. This text is quite revealing. Notice the surreptitious identification of "Shah" and "country," and of "opposition" and "threat to stability." Because of the first the second became a fact.

[46]William Sullivan, personal communication, August 1984, New York City.

[47]Vance, *Hard Choices*, p. 325.

[48]William Sullivan, personal communication, August 1984, New York City.

[49]William H. Sullivan, *Mission to Iran* (1981), p. 161.

[50]M. R. Pahlavi, *Answer to History* (1980), p. 165.

In all these talks LMI figures gave their reactions and opinions to whatever developments had taken place since the last meeting, and unfailingly told their interlocutors that the Shah had to go. This insistence was interpreted as dogmatic and "ideological." The aim of the U.S. embassy was to persuade the moderate opposition to join a Shah-sponsored coalition government. As late as October 28 Sullivan sent a telegram to Washington urging firm support for the Shah.[51] After the events of early November, however, Sullivan changed his mind. Encouraged by Bazargan and Beheshti, who impressed him with their anti-Soviet sentiments, he began working out a scenario that might assure an orderly transfer of power to a new government in a way that would minimize chaos and safeguard basic, but redefined, American security interests. He outlined his reasons and analyses in a cable titled "Thinking the Unthinkable."[52]

Azhari's government did not manage to bring the situation under control. In December of 1978 the Shah finally resolved to ask a member of the Nationalist opposition to form a government—a month after they had declared the monarchy illegitimate and had put themselves under Khomeini's umbrella. He held talks with Sanjabi and Sadiqi (who had kept somewhat aloof from the National Front), but both men refused to accept the post of prime minister. In the end Shapur Bakhtiar, leader of the Iran party, accepted, and was sworn in on January 6, 1979 (Dey 16, 1357). This put the Nationalist opposition in an awkward position. One of them had defected to the Shah in the last minute; they had to distance themselves from him unequivocally. Bakhtiar's unclear role in the events of January 1962 was recalled,[53] and his acceptance of the premiership was presented as proof that he had been a traitor all along. Both the National Front and the Iran Party expelled him; the IP replaced him with Abolfazl Qasemi, a librarian at Teheran University.

Only one day after Bakhtiar's appointment, Khomeini in a talk to Iranians at his headquarters in Neauphle-le-Château said that he opposed the new prime minister because he had been named by the Shah and would receive the vote of confidence of a parliament that was itself illegal.[54] The LMI members—mainly Bazargan—were less critical. Let us recall that among the secular leaders of the National Front, Bakhtiar's relations with Bazargan had been closest. Despite Bakhtiar's nonreligiosity, Bazargan would sometimes say of him that he was a Muslim without

[51]Jimmy Carter, *Keeping Faith: Memoirs of a President* (1982), p. 439.
[52]Sullivan, *Mission*, pp. 200–203.
[53]See chapter 4, p. 165.
[54]Yazdi, *Akharin talashha*, p. 84.

knowing it. When Bakhtiar decided to accept the premiership, he transferred the management of the company of which he was the director to Bazargan's Yad Company. Throughout his short tenure as prime minister Bakhtiar was in constant contact with Bazargan.[55]

Ambassador Sullivan was skeptical about Bakhtiar's chances of success. He was right, for Bakhtiar had no popular support. Bakhtiar had hoped that if he could be the person who engineered the Shah's departure from Iran, the tide would turn in his favor. Islamic propaganda had become too effective, however, and in the climate of mass mobilization of January and February 1979 he was quickly assimilated by the populace to the Shah regime. Bakhtiar, however, decided to make a last stand and oppose Khomeini's return to Iran, by force, if necessary. In Washington, Brzezinski had taken over the Iranian policy of the Carter administration, and, against the advice of Vance and Sullivan, had come to the conclusion that Bakhtiar had to be supported. Since Sullivan was not trusted anymore, General Robert Huyser, deputy supreme commander of Allied Forces in Europe, was dispatched to Teheran with the mission to persuade the Iranian army to support Bakhtiar and to attempt a coup only if Bakhtiar's government collapsed.[56]

Meanwhile Bazargan, with the approval of the Council of the Revolution and the active participation of Ay. Musavi Ardabili, had begun talks with the military leadership to obtain their neutrality. The two also met with Sullivan to get his approval, and on that occasion the latter was struck by Bazargan's extremely deferential attitude toward Ay. Musavi Ardabili. The LMI had sympathizers in the armed forces and through them knew exactly how things stood in the army.[57] They promised those major figures who had not fled yet that they could leave Iran and take their wealth with them. The talks were conducted with different generals on an individual basis,[58] and had only a very limited effect on the armed forces on the whole. The talks may, however, have encouraged key commanders not to try a coup and to hope for a political settlement instead. Meanwhile the army disintegrated, as more and more units defected and some arms depots were taken by the revolutionaries.

At the same time negotiations also went on between Bazargan and the Council of the Revolution, on the one hand, and Bakhtiar, on the

[55]Shapur Bakhtiar, personal interview, Suresnes, August 12, 1983.

[56]Robert E. Huyser, *Mission to Iran* (1986), p. 88.

[57]William Sullivan, personal communication, August 1984, New York City.

[58]The army's incapacity to negotiate as an institution with the revolutionaries, a reflection of the increased sultanism of the later Shah years, comes out clearly in the memoirs of the Shah's last chief of staff, General Abbas Qarahbaghi. See *E'terafat-e zheneral* (The general's confessions) (1986).

other. In late January Bakhtiar offered to resign, but in Paris Khomeini and Yazdi thought this was premature; it might lead to a military coup and more bloodshed. They therefore instructed the revolutionaries in Teheran to prolong negotiations with Bakhtiar.[59]

The result of these talks was a tentative deal between the Council of the Revolution and Bakhtiar. According to this scenario, which had the approval of Khomeini, Bakhtiar would go to Paris, meet Khomeini, present his resignation to him, and be given some new position by Khomeini, perhaps even as head of an interim administration. A similar arrangement had been worked out for the mayor of Teheran, as a result of which municipal services had kept going. According to Yazdi, the deal fell through when, at the instigation of Ho. Sadeq Khalkhali and Ay. Rabbani Shirazi, Khomeini changed his mind and on January 27, when everything was ready for Bakhtiar's trip, demanded that the prime minister resign before he would receive him.[60] Bakhtiar could not accept this, because if he were to resign before meeting Khomeini, he would have met him only as a private citizen and the meeting would have lacked any political significance.

The difference in attitude between Bazargan and Yazdi, discussed in chapters 2 and 6, comes out in their respective accounts of these last efforts to enact an orderly transfer of power. Whereas Yazdi admits that he and Khomeini opposed Bakhtiar's resignation, and then proceeds to berate Bakhtiar for having tried to hang on to power at all cost, Bazargan seems to have negotiated with Bakhtiar in good faith. He respected Bakhtiar's wish to meet Khomeini as prime minister because otherwise Bakhtiar would have lost face. If the original scenario for a transition had been acted out, "God knows what bloodshed and calamities could have been avoided."[61]

In the last days of the Shah regime Bazargan carried out another important mission for Khomeini. On October 14 (Mehr 2) oil-workers in the south had gone on strike. Now winter was approaching, and on December 29 (Dey 8) Khomeini named Bazargan head of a delegation of five (including Hashemi Rafsanjani) that went to Khuzistan to ensure that enough oil would be pumped to heat Iranian homes. Yadollah Sahabi headed a similar group whose task was to organize domestic distribution of fuel. Cooperating with officials of the Shah regime, Bazargan succeeded, but only after meeting some resistance from leftists. His success demonstrated that the opposition was now organized enough to take over the functions of the government. Bazargan increasingly attracted the attention of foreign journalists and

[59]Yazdi, Akharin Talashha, p. 138.
[60]Ibid., p. 160.
[61]Bazargan, Enqelab, p. 74.

diplomats, and the latter began signifying to him that their governments were ready to recognize a new regime.[62]

Khomeini arrived in Teheran on February 1, 1979 (Bahman 12, 1357) after a fifteen-year exile. An LMI member, Hashem Sabbaghian, headed the committee that prepared for his arrival. The millions of people who greeted Khomeini were a last reminder that Bakhtiar had no chance whatsoever to remain as prime minister. Yet, displaying considerable braggadocio, he clung to his position as "constitutional prime minister." On February 4 (Bahman 15) Khomeini named Bazargan prime minister of the Provisional Government. Fighting broke out on February 9, on February 11 the army declared its neutrality, and soon after Bakhtiar went underground and later fled to Paris.

For a few days Iran had had two prime ministers. Mehdi Bazargan and Shapur Bakhtiar, who over twenty years earlier had driven through the streets of Teheran in the back of a taxi distributing leaflets calling for free elections, now faced each other as rival prime ministers. One had been named by an outgoing dictator, the other by an incoming one. At the dawn of Iran's republican era, the cause of liberal democracy had sunk very low indeed.

Revolutions seem inevitable only after the fact. Until the fall of 1978 few people in the moderate opposition doubted that the Shah would weather the storm. True to their parliamentarian convictions, Bazargan and the LMI hoped for free elections, as a result of which they would be able to establish a legal opposition and advance toward their ultimate goal of democracy. The propensity of the Shah to concede too little too late combined with the charismatic presence of Ay. Khomeini to make a smooth transition to democracy impossible. During the fifteen years since the Shah's other attempt at liberalization much had changed in Iranian society, and the moderates, including Bazargan and the LMI, no longer had a mass base. By staying within the revolutionary camp and trying to occupy positions of responsibility in it, they hoped to continue wielding some influence over Khomeini, realizing that they had no hope of succeeding against his will. Bakhtiar's total failure during the month of his tenure as prime minister proved them right.

The advent of the Carter administration was perceived both by the Shah and the opposition as creating a new flare-up in Iran's long unresolved crisis of sovereignty. This crisis of sovereignty triggered major crises of legitimacy and participation. But unlike the similar complex of crises in 1960–63, the ones in 1977–78 were accompanied by

[62]Ibid., pp. 66–68.

a profound crisis of identity. This crisis of identity had been brought about by the deepening of the gap between the two segments of Iranian society as analyzed in chapter 1, and the challenge to Western sociopolitical models as discussed in chapters 2 and 5. The conjunction of these four crises (to which one might add a minor crisis of distribution) produced an overload which the Iranian polity could not handle. As a result, the liberalization of 1977–78 ended in a revolution that dramatically changed the constellation of forces in Iran. Mehdi Bazargan, who had reluctantly entered politics in 1953, found himself the prime minister of Iran. A man who had always acted in the name of the 1906 Constitution was now called upon to preside over a new regime that represented a clear break with the past.

CHAPTER 7

The Provisional Government

The period from February to November 1979 was of central importance to the LMI. Eighteen years after its founding, its leader, Mehdi
Bazargan, became prime minister of Iran and formed a government in
which men with LMI connections clearly dominated. Provisional governments have not fared well in history, and this one would be no
exception.

In the evening of February 3, 1979 (Bahman 14, 1357), Khomeini
asked the Council of the Revolution (CR) to give him their choice for
the post of prime minister.[1] It chose Mehdi Bazargan. The nominee
asked to be given one day, so that the statutes of the Council of the
Revolution could be written. At ten o'clock on the following morning
the CR met in the presence of Khomeini. Bazargan stated his conditions for accepting the charge.

> First, I would like to express my gratitude and embarrassment for the
> confidence and honor that the Grand Ayatollah and the members of the
> CR are bestowing on me.
>
> Second, now that [we have] the final version of the statutes of the CR, I
> would like to remind everyone that according to that document the
> Council of the Revolution replaces Parliament within the context of the
> existing constitution (minus those aspects that concern the Shah and that

---

[1] The following account of the formation of the Provisional Government is taken from a
series of articles that appeard in *Mizan*, 16, 17, and 18 Bahman, 1359 (February 5, 6, and
7, 1981), and a speech delivered by Bazargan on February 11, 1982 (the third anniversary
of the revolution) and reprinted as *Showra-ye enqelab va dowlat-e movaqqat* (The Council of
the Revolution and the Provisional Government) (1983).

were transferred to the Imam). The leader of the revolution chooses the members of the Council and appoints the prime minister proposed by the Council. He also defines the main lines of government policy so that the government can carry them out under the supervision of the CR.

Third, all you gentlemen know me well and are well aware of my beliefs, my way of thinking, and my record. You know about my services as professor and dean of the Faculty of Engineering, as provisional chairman of the board of the [National Iranian Oil Company], and in the Water Organization of Teheran. You know . . . my temperament. You know that I am a Muslim and that I believe in order, sound management, liberality, consultation, cooperation, and the gradual implementation of plans. I do not intend to change this way of thinking.

Having said this, I wish to ask the worthy leader and the gentlemen to appoint me to this task if their opinion has not changed since yesterday, and to . . . look for somebody else if my conditions and record are not acceptable.

There was a silence and then some whispering, but only S. Ali Khameneh'i seemed to object to Bazargan's conditions. After some deliberation the council unanimously approved Bazargan's nomination. Upon Khomeini's request Ay. Motahhari wrote the decree of appointment:

To His Excellency, Mehdi Bazargan:

At the proposal of the Council of the Revolution and considering the religious and political right that has been conferred upon the [revolutionary] movement's leadership by the widespread demonstrations all over the country, and given my confidence in your faith in the holy doctrine of Islam and my knowledge of your record in the religious and national struggles, I appoint you to form the provisional government independently of your connections to a political party or to any other group, so that you can arrange for the administration of the country, organize a referendum concerning the establishment of an Islamic Republic, call a constitutional assembly composed of the people's elected representatives to ratify the constitution of the new political system, and organize parliamentary elections based on the new constitution. It is incumbent upon you to choose and name the provisional government's members as soon as possible according to the conditions that I have laid down. Government employees, the Army, and the people will fully cooperate with your provisional government and respect the necessary discipline for the attainment of the holy goals of the revolution and the reestablishment of order in the country. I pray to the Almighty for the success of you and the provisional government in this sensitive stage of history.

Ruhollah Al-Musavi Al-Khomeini

As Bazargan would later write, "What this firman significantly does not mention is revolutionary firmness, the propagation of Islam and the imposition of the Shari'ah as a matter of government policy, the export of the revolution and the struggle against infidels, and the saving of the world's dispossessed."[2]

At the time many people believed the CR to have a pluralistic composition reflecting all forces in the anti-Shah coalition, and Bazargan, who knew better, did nothing to set things right. According to an old Persian saying, "Lying is a sin, but telling the truth is not an obligation." The mullas and their lay allies on the CR believed themselves to be the "true" representatives of the nation, hence their claim to replace parliament until the elections. About the government Khomeini said that obedience to it was a religious duty.

Composition of the Government

In choosing his cabinet, Bazargan had a very narrow pool of *ministrables* to consider. They had to be practicing Muslims and they had to possess a record of opposition against the Shah, a good reputation, and technical competency in their area of responsibility. The cabinet that Bazargan put together in the second half of February consisted essentially of members or sympathizers of the LMI, a few National Front figures, and some independents. The most prominent NF leader in the PG was Karim Sanjabi, who took over the Ministry of Foreign Affairs. His brother-in-law Ali Ardalan became minister of the economy. The leader of the PIN, Dariush Foruhar, took charge of the Ministry of Labor. Among prominent secular figures, Ali-Asghar Hajj-Seyyed-Javadi's membership in the PG, proposed by Bazargan, was vetoed by Khomeini, on account of some past anticlerical statements he had made.

Religious modernists dominated the cabinet: among leading LMI figures, Yadollah Sahabi became a minister for revolutionary projects and Sadr Hajj-Seyyed-Javadi minister of the interior.[3] Of the LMI's second generation, Abbas Amir-Entezam was made deputy prime minister for revolutionary affairs. The circle around Ay. Shariatmadari was represented by Naser Minachi, who took over the Ministry for Information and Tourism, whose name was changed to Ministry of National Guidance. Kazem Sami of JAMA became minister of health. Two prominent lay but Islamic revolutionary figures were not included in the cabinet: Abolhasan Banisadr and Sadeq Qotbzadeh. Banisadr's

---

[2]Mehdi Bazargan, *Enqelab-e eslami dar do harekat* (The Islamic revolution in two movements) (1984), p. 78.

[3]Of the remaining leaders of the LMI, Hasan Nazih took charge of the National Iranian Oil Company, and Abbas Sami'i became governor of the Central Province, Iran's most important.

membership had been rejected by Bazargan (despite Khomeini's urging). On the basis of past experience, Bazargan did not believe that Banisadr was capable of working in a team. Qotbzadeh was named director of National Iranian Radio and Television.[4]

Below the cabinet level, candidates for high governmental posts had to have at the minimum no record of involvement with the Shah regime and preferably a history of resistance against it, they had to have some technical qualification, and they had to be Muslims, or at least friendly toward Islam. These conditions excluded large sectors of the Iranian technocratic elite, who, if they were not hostile to the revolution, were apprehensive about its Islamic dimension. Many intellectuals and leaders of the burgeoning professional associations who had started the oppositional movement in 1977 found themselves marginalized by the new government, as did the various leftist groups who had played a role in the final triumph of the revolution. On the opposite end of the revolutionary spectrum one other very important group found itself excluded: the militant ulema who had organized the big demonstrations, and some of whom had a long history of resistance against the Shah. Partly because of Bazargan's anticlericalism, and partly because nobody (including, at that point, they themselves) believed them capable of handling administrative tasks, such ambitious men as Hashemi Rafsanjani, Javad Bahonar, and Sadeq Khalkhali (the leader of the revived Devotees of Islam) remained in the background, where they could engage in intrigue, organize themselves, and criticize the PG's efforts without having to shoulder any direct responsibilities. As a result of these constraints, some groups became disproportionately prominent in the PG and its administration, for example the Islamic Association of Engineers. Bazargan was aware of the problem and admitted that many of his appointees were not qualified.[5]

The composition of the PG changed frequently during the nine months of its existence. The usual pattern was for ministers to resign after failing to gain full authority over their ministry's area of responsibility as a result of interference from fundamentalist forces. Gradually the coloration of the cabinet changed and it became more religiously oriented. First the secular NF members left and were replaced by LMI figures. On April 16 Sanjabi resigned and was replaced by Yazdi. The Ministry of Defense changed hands three times, until it wound up in the hands of Mostafa Chamran.[6] The important Ministry of Justice also

[4]Qotbzadeh lost no time canceling all "vulgar" National Iranian Radio and Television programs and became widely hated in the modern segment of society; meanwhile the clergy lifted its ban against television—leading to a shortage of TV sets on the market.

[5]Abdolali Bazargan, ed., *Masa'el va moshkelat-e nakhostin sal-e enqelab* (The problems and difficulties of the first year of the revolution) (1983), p. 187.

[6]First it was given to the new chief of staff, General V. Qarani, who was assassinated

changed hands when its NF titulary resigned on June 20 and was replaced by Ahmad Sadr Hajj-Seyyed-Javadi. Of all NF ministers, only Ali Ardalan kept his Ministry of the Economy until the end. The religious orientation of the cabinet became even more apparent when in July the PG and the CR agreed to coalesce. Bazargan proposed this to create more solidarity and improve the coordination between the two bodies. Four CR members joined the PG as deputy ministers with full cabinet rank,[7] while Bazargan and three of his colleagues (re)joined the CR. The interference of the fundamentalists in government was not stopped; instead the new clerical government officials gained confidence that they were able to run the country, which made Bazargan and his lay colleagues less indispensable.

The effectiveness of the PG was diminished by its lack of homogeneity. It included Western-educated technocrats who wanted to take over from their prerevolutionary predecessors, and populists who wanted to do away with the "elitist" trappings of the Shah's governments. On March 7 Khomeini chided the government for "showing weakness" and "enjoying luxuries" in the various "palaces" from which it was governing, and after that everybody made an effort to project a populist image.

In spite of all their difficulties, when the Provisional Government resigned in November 1979, most of its members stayed on as caretaker ministers until the new Majles was elected. Khomeini's admonition that the members of the PG disregard their party affiliation was interpreted as meaning that they should resign from all party positions. Among all PG ministers only those belonging to the LMI took this notion seriously, and as a result the LMI had almost no independent presence on the political scene. What was left of the LMI apparatus was in the hands of Ezzatollah Sahabi, who joined the cabinet only in September.

The Tasks of the Provisional Government

Bazargan's administration faced a dilemma typical for many provisional governments: on the one hand it was meant as a transitional

---

shortly thereafter. Two NF figures followed, General Taqi Riahi, and then Admiral Ahmad Madani, who left the post to become governor of Khuzistan.

[7]Hashemi Rafsanjani in the Ministry of the Interior, Khameneh'i in the Ministry of Defense, Bahonar in the Ministry of Education, and Ho. Mohammad-Reza Mahdavi Kani, who was in charge of the revolutionary committees (*komitehs*), became minister of the interior. Beheshti and Musavi Ardabili were asked to join the Ministry of Justice to put the activities of the revolutionary courts within the governmental framework, but they refused.

solution, with no authority to undertake major projects and to take major decisions, and on the other hand it was expected to right all wrongs of the Shah dictatorship and to deliver instant improvements.[8]

Bazargan and his team enjoyed great popularity at the outset, although this popularity was at least partly derivative. There were big demonstrations in early February of 1979, during which Bazargan's name was publicly acclaimed.[9] Bazargan never made a secret of his gradualism; he told an enthusiastic meeting at Teheran University on February 9: "Don't expect me to act in the manner of [Khomeini] who . . . moves like a bulldozer, crushing rocks, roots, and stones in his path. I am a delicate passenger car and must ride on paved and smooth roads, and you must smooth them for me."[10]

Restoring Order

Getting the country organized again proved to be more difficult than anticipated. During the revolution, strike committees and neighborhood committees had been formed, and in the last days before Bakhtiar's flight 300,000 arms had been taken by the people. As a result there was a plethora of armed bands and security committees, while the police and gendarmerie were completely disorganized. At first the CR seemed to agree with Bazargan that these outgrowths of the revolution should be disbanded as early as possible,[11] or absorbed into new state organizations, but they had developed a life of their own. Attempts to bring them under control resulted in their consolidation, and in the end the radical clergy in the Council of the Revolution, sensing the mood of the population and fearing that leftists might be the beneficiaries of the aroused masses' unfulfilled aspirations, threw its weight behind the komitehs, after purging them of undesirable elements.

The second source of irritation for the PG was the proliferation of revolutionary tribunals that now began to convict and shoot real (or imagined) high officials of the Shah regime (including Amir-Abbas Hoveida, on April 7) and what they called corrupt individuals. No doubt many of these executions were quite popular and many political groupings, including the left and the fundamentalists, welcomed them enthusiastically. The PG tried to bring the activities of the revolutionary

---

[8]See Sepehr Zabih, *Iran since the Revolution* (1982), pp. 21–40; and Shaul Bakhash, *The Reign of the Ayatollahs: Iran and the Islamic Revolution* (1984), pp. 52–87. For a day-to-day account, an indispensable source is *Keesing's*, July 27, 1979, pp. 29743–46, and March 21, 1980, pp. 30141–50.

[9]See *Ettela'at*, Bahman 17–19, 1357 (February 6–8, 1979).

[10]A. Bazargan, ed., *Masa'el*, p. 75.

[11]See interview of Hashemi Rafsanjani in Naser Hariri, *Mosahebeh ba tarikhsazan-e Iran* (Interviews with makers of Iranian history) (1979), p. 73.

tribunals under the control of the Ministry of Justice, but failed.[12] Bazargan and his government complained about the interference of these parallel organs of de facto authority, whose activities gave new currency to the word ochlocracy. When pressed about human rights abuses in Iran, Bazargan and his ministers would, rightly, deny any direct responsibility, rather as Amini had done during his brief tenure in 1961–62. But these admissions of impotence contributed even more to the image of weakness that the PG projected.

Finally, the revolutionary guards, or Pasdaran, who were officially established on May 5, 1979, were still operating. Although Chamran and Yazdi at first tried to wield some influence with them, they were soon pushed aside by hard-liners.

In his numerous television appearances Bazargan constantly appealed to the people to be reasonable, patient, and forgiving, but to no avail. He repeatedly stated that until a new constitution was in force, the old one, minus those articles that pertained to the monarchy, would be the basis of government action. He also complained about the mistreatment of those army and government officials who had been maintained in their positions by the PG.[13]

Khomeini, to whom the PG appealed for help, at first did seem willing to grant his hand-picked administration the necessary authority. He retired to Qum in late February and closed his office, referring all matters to the government. But soon he changed his mind, and contented himself with urging everybody to cooperate without taking sides.

While the PG's authority was contested by the fundamentalists in political matters, Bazargan and his ministers also came under attack from the radical left. Militants from the Fada'iyan and various other groups infiltrated both public and private enterprises and urged workers to make demands that the PG could not fulfill. The last prerevolutionary governments had made great concessions to workers in the hope of calming them down, but that had only increased their demands. Unemployment was high, and the PG's policies, aimed at getting production going with the old cadres if necessary, created considerable discontent among the radicals.[14]

All sectors of society wanted rapid improvements and more control over their affairs, as in each enterprise or institution councils formed and claimed authority to run things. When a group was dissatisfied

---

[12]A detailed account of the tribunals' activities can be found in Amnesty International, *Law and Human Rights in the Islamic Republic of Iran* (1980).

[13]A. Bazargan, ed., *Masa'el*, pp. 86 and 169.

[14]For the consequences of this policy, see Joseph Vernoux, *L'Iran des mollah—la revolution introuvable* (1981), pp. 71–84.

with its lot, members would stage demonstrations or sit-ins in ministries. All groups wanted their demands satisfied immediately.

Despite the many difficulties it faced, the economic performance of the Provisional Government was quite impressive. During its tenure, Iran's non-oil exports reached an alltime high: in the Iranian year 1358 (March 1979–March 1980), the percentage of oil in total Iranian exports fell to 39 percent, compared to 96 percent in the last "normal" year under the Shah, and rose again after the fall of Bazargan.[15] The competent management of the Iranian economy during 1979 also helped the country weather the economic embargo declared by Western countries after the seizure of the U.S. embassy hostages.

Nonetheless, the revolutionary mood in the country had little patience for Bazargan's gradualist and methodical approach.[16] Khomeini and the fundamentalists organized in the Islamic Republican party sensed the mounting discontent, and jumped on the anti-PG bandwagon. On July 20, 1980 (Tir 29, 1359), Khomeini asked the Iranian people for forgiveness for having named a weak government that could not act decisively, that had not been young enough.[17]

Provisional Government Relations with Other Groups

By and large, the members of Bazargan's cabinets were middle-class moderates. A few, for example Yazdi and Chamran, tried to act like "revolutionaries." But old conflicts between the NF and the LMI were not forgotten, as the events leading to Sanjabi's resignation demonstrated. While Bazargan and his colleagues in the PG constantly complained about interference from fundamentalists and parallel centers of authority, certain LMI elements who were more closely allied to the fundamentalists complained about NF members of the cabinet. The first foreign minister of the Islamic Republic and leader of the NF, Karim Sanjabi, became the target of such activities. In both 1960–63 and 1977–78, Sanjabi had come in conflict with the LMI, as we saw in earlier chapters. Now a new conflict arose over who would handle U.S.-Iranian relations. Bazargan and his friends maintained their contacts with U.S. embassy officials after the Shah's departure. In Washington, the Iranian embassy was taken over by an "Islamic Committee" under Shahriar Rowhani, a graduate student in physics at Yale Univer-

[15]Markaz-e Amar-e Iran, *Iran dar a'ineh-ye amar* (Iranian statistical yearbook), 1983 (1362), p. 108. It should be noted that these figures were published when the Islamic regime had consolidated itself and sought every opportunity to denounce the Provisional Government.

[16]For telling details, see Vahe Petrossian, "Dilemmas of the Iranian Revolution," *World Today* 36 (1980), 19–25.

[17]Relevant parts of this speech are reproduced in M. Bazargan, *Showra*, p. 71.

sity and son-in-law of Ebrahim Yazdi who had been active in the LMI(a) for quite some time.[18] Sanjabi's personal choice for the diplomatic post, Ha'eri, a reputable Islamic scholar and son of the reviver of the Qum religious establishment, was refused entry to the premises. Sanjabi could not accept that he, as foreign minister, had no control over Iran's relations with the United States and resigned; his replacement by Yazdi compounded the affront. Sanjabi may or may not have been an effective foreign minister, but as former dean of the Faculty of Law at Teheran University and Iranian representative at the International Court of Justice during the oil crisis of 1952, it is understandable that he could not accept lessons in the conduct of foreign policy from a graduate student in physics and an oncologist from Texas, whatever their actual expertise in foreign affairs.[19]

Secular moderate groups such as the NF were disappointed that they had to play second fiddle to Bazargan and the LMI in the PG, but they hoped to salvage their own contacts with Khomeini and therefore did not voice their criticism of the fundamentalists' ascendancy too openly. Faced with the parallel centers of authority, they followed Bazargan, but as heirs to Mosaddeq's secular Nationalism they were still displeased and perhaps resentful at being marginalized by the religious movement. In the eyes of many LMI leaders, the National Front as an organization did not represent much and consisted of a handful of old men living on the memory of their past association with Mosaddeq. Based on this evaluation and the weight of past disagreements and rivalries, the LMI attached no great significance to cooperating with the NF.

Matters were different with secular groups that were not represented in the government, such as professional associations, or the National Democratic Front (NDF) that Mosaddeq's grandson, Hedayatollah Matin-Daftari had founded in March 1979 to fill the space between the NF and the various Marxist groups. These groups came increasingly under attack by violent radical activists who would soon start calling themselves *hezbollahi*, "members of the party of God." Khomeini's prestige as leader of the revolution was still so strong that the secular groups could not name him as the source of the mounting repression. They therefore complained to the government, which was unable to stop *hezbollahi* activities. This inability was then interpreted by the secular forces as an endorsement of repression by the PG. If the PG had explicitly condemned the activities of Islamic militants beyond the

[18]See *Yale Daily News*, April 9, 1980, pp. 1 and 5, for an interesting, if somewhat idealized, account of a student's oppositional activity in exile.

[19]Sanjabi first revealed the background to his resignation in *Ettela'at*, March 18, 1980 (Esfand 27, 1358), p. 8.

routine complaints about the multiplicity of decision-making centers and had sided with the secular groups, it would have undermined its own legitimacy. As Bazargan has put it, "It was not the Nationalists and the intellectuals who appointed the leader of the revolution, it was he who appointed me as head of the Provisional Government."[20] The PG's position seemed to say, "Give us a chance, be patient, for we are your only hope for containing the Islamic radicals," but of course it could not state this so openly. Its task was complicated by the frequent tactical alliances between the moderate secular forces, with whose conceptions of civil rights the PG could agree, and the radical left, whose policy demands were unacceptable.

On the clerical and fundamentalist side, some groups, the Devotees for example, were hostile to the Nationalists, both religious and secular, right from the outset. Their leader, Sadeq Khalkhali, did everything to exacerbate tensions. The role of the fundamentalists in the IRP is more complicated. Islamic Republican party members and LMI figures had worked together as early as the 1960s, and knew each other well. As discussed in chapter 2, there is an affinity between modernism and fundamentalism. In private, somebody like Amir-Entezam could admit that the IRP program would "turn time 1000 years back,"[21] but nobody in the LMI could say so publicly.

The modernists of the LMI did have allies among the clergy. Ay. Abolfazl Zanjani was probably too identified with Mosaddeqism to have any influence on Khomeini. Ay. Taleqani was a charismatic leader in his own right but never challenged Khomeini's leadership openly. He was close to Bazargan, having been one of the founders of the LMI. After his release from prison, however, he decided not to join the LMI again, preferring to remain aloof from organized groups. He maintained contacts with more radical groups, however, such as the Mojahedin, who used these contacts to gain religious legitimacy.

On March 5, 1979, Iranian Nationalists were for the first time able to commemorate the anniversary of Mosaddeq's death openly, and a rally was to be held by his grave in Ahmadabad. Its sponsors were the National Democratic Front, the Mojahedin, the Fada'iyan, and the National Front; all secular groupings. Neither the LMI nor the Provisional Government were involved. A few days before the event, the Council of the Revolution met at the house of Abbas Sheibani and decided that Taleqani should give a long speech, so as to take up all the available time and prevent other speakers from spreading "deviationist

---

[20]*Ba'd az entekhabat-e riasat-e jomhuri cheh shod va cheh bayad kard* (What happened after the presidential elections and what has to be done) (1985), pp. 3–4.

[21]Cheryl Benard and Zalmay Khalilzad, *The Government of God: Iran's Islamic Republic* (1984), p. 112.

words." Secular forces were not to be allowed to "take advantage" of popular feeling for Mosaddeq by posing as his heirs.[22] Taleqani gave a speech before hundreds of thousands of people in Ahmadabad and urged secular Nationalists and the religious movement to maintain their unity. But it was a prefiguration of future developments that he and Ay. Zanjani were the only two clerics to attend the meeting.[23]

Although he had reservations about it, Taleqani time and again reaffirmed his support for the PG. On August 10, 1979 (Mordad 19, 1358), he declared at a Friday congregational prayer meeting: "Mr. Bazargan is Prime Minister and he is a statesman, an academic, an interpreter of the Qoran, and a *faqih* in religion. What other model could we wish for?"[24] Taleqani's early death on September 9 (Shahrivar 18) deprived Bazargan's administration of a valuable outside ally. Taleqani's popularity was immense among all groups, and the radicals would have found it more difficult to attack a cabinet that had his explicit support.

Yet even Taleqani was quite isolated among the clergy. Bazargan's most valuable potential ally was Ay. Motahhari, who was also very close to Khomeini. Motahhari could have played a mediating role between the PG and the CR and the IRP, but he was assassinated in May.

More complicated were the PG's relations with Ay. Shariatmadari and the Muslim People's Republican Party (MPRP) that he had unofficially sponsored. This party seemed to have had a quick and successful start, particularly in Azerbaijan, Shariatmadari's home province, and the Teheran Bazaar, where many merchants are of Azerbaijani origin. The MPRP's moderate program and statements bore great resemblance to the those of the moderates in the PG. In fact, many believed that association with the MPRP could shield them against allegations of opposition to Islam, and groups and personalities such as the National Front, Hasan Nazih, and especially Moqaddam Maragheh'i's Radical Movement, gravitated increasingly toward it.[25] Superficially it seemed logical to seek the backing of a Grand Ayatollah against radical forces that claimed to follow Khomeini. Still, the LMI stayed clear of the Shariatmadari option. Although Bazargan had sought the advice of Shariatmadari in the months preceding the revolution, modernists, with their long history of opposition against the Shah, by and large

---

[22]*Barkhord ba nehzat va pasokh-e ma* (Attitudes to the LMI and our answer) (1983), p. 41.

[23]Bahram Afrasiabi and Sa'id Dehqan, *Taleqani va tarikh* (Taleqani and history) (1981), pp. 412–16.

[24]Quoted in an LMI declaration commemorating the second anniversary of his death, p. 4.

[25]The cooperation of Nazih and Moqaddam Maragheh'i is also explained by their Azerbaijani origin.

had a low opinion of Shariatmadari and regarded him as a typical representative of the type of clergy they had derided in their anticlerical writings. They did not forgive his alleged close relationship with the Shah regime. The tactic paid off in the long run: while the MPRP was crushed in December 1980 and its allies had to go into exile, the LMI is still around.

Summarizing the LMI's relations with other groups and forces during the life of the Provisional Government, one can say that the left united with the secular moderates to fault Bazargan and his colleagues for subservience to Khomeini and the Islamic radicals, that the Islamic radicals joined with the left in denouncing the PG's continuing courteous relations with the West and its lack of revolutionary fervor in general, and that the religious groups all agreed that the PG was too secular. The LMI had seen itself as a bridge between intellectuals and the clergy, but the gaps between the various actors on the Iranian political scene had become so deep that the LMI ended up isolated. It claimed to have the support of the "silent majority," but that can of course not be verified.

The Institutional Question

Shortly after his installation as prime minister, Bazargan declared that his long-term political future depended on his party's showing in the forthcoming elections. Like all members of his generation who had struggled for the respect of the 1906 Constitution, Bazargan's ideal political system was a parliamentary democracy, with or without a monarchy. But the demand for radical change was such that it was out of the question just to do away with those articles of the 1906 Constitution that pertained to the monarchy. In a television address on February 28, 1979, Bazargan spoke of the future "Democratic Islamic Republic."[26]

The first draft of a new constitution had been prepared in Paris by Hasan Habibi and presented to Khomeini. After the return of Khomeini and his entourage more experts worked on it, but it was not publicized until after the plebiscite on a regime change. On March 30 and 31, 1979, Iranians voted to abolish the monarchy. As in all previous plebiscites in Iran, the citizenry had no genuine choice, as they had to respond to the question whether they wanted to see the monarchy replaced by an Islamic republic or not. At that point the concept of Islamic republic lacked any precision. The government announced a

[26] A. Bazargan, ed., *Masa'el*, p. 90.

98.2 percent vote for an Islamic state; the 140,966 "No" votes all came from Teheran. Needless to say, nobody had been able to campaign for a "No" vote.

The final version of the first draft of a new constitution was published on June 18 (Khordad 28). It bore close resemblance to the Constitution of the French Fifth Republic, providing for a semipresidential system. Its Islamic character consisted mainly in a preamble stating the Islamic principles underlying the document, and in the restriction of basic freedoms and civil rights to within the limits of Islamic tenets, a provision that the 1906 Constitution had contained as well. But the draft did not reserve any special authority for the ulema, and therefore was not, strictly speaking, theocratic.

The draft was opposed by secularists for being too religious, and by religious forces for not being Islamic enough. Khomeini had urged the PG to arrange for a plebiscite to ratify the draft, but Bazargan felt bound by his promise to convene a constitutional assembly. As a compromise solution, elections were held to a smaller assembly, in which traditionalist provincial mullas won an overwhelming majority and which they renamed "Assembly of Experts." It did have a handful of secularists, such as Moqaddam Maragheh'i who had been elected in his native Azerbaijan, and two religious modernists topped the list of Teheran deputies: Ay. Taleqani and Abolhasan Banisadr. The LMI members of the PG were not candidates, and the party was thus represented only by Ezzatollah Sahabi, who was not a cabinet member then. The Assembly of Experts convened on August 18, and its proceedings were quickly taken over by Beheshti. Taleqani signified his dissatisfaction by squatting on the floor instead of taking his seat in the hemicycle.

The original mandate of the assembly had been to make a few minor changes in the draft and then approve it, but it proceeded to change the draft almost beyond recognition. The most important change was that it incorporated Khomeini's notion of *velayat-e faqih* into the document, and the Constitution in effect became a dyarchy in which democratic elements (represented by an elected president and an elected parliament) coexisted with a "religious leader" who had ultimate authority and was accountable to nobody. This last change was made only after Taleqani had died, but it is by no means certain that he would have opposed it.

The moderates' and secularists' insistence on proper procedure for the elaboration of the Constitution thus yielded the exact opposite of what they had hoped for. When they saw what was happening in the Assembly of Experts, a majority of PG members, including Bazargan, made an attempt to persuade Khomeini to dissolve the body, but Khomeini would not go along. This move was not made public at the time.

The plebiscite to approve the new Constitution was held after the fall of the PG, on December 2–3. Over 99 percent voted in favor of the new Constitution. The LMI, the NF, and the MPRP had called for a "Yes" vote in spite of their misgivings, while the left called for a "No" vote or an abstention. Participation in the second plebiscite was much lower.[27]

The official results of the two plebiscites that institutionalized the Islamic Republic were similar to Mosaddeq's and the Shah's plebiscites in that the result of all four was a foregone conclusion, but they were different in that the Islamic regime would have won a respectable majority even if it had allowed the citizenry a real choice. Bazargan, who has spent a lifetime struggling for free and fair elections, has cast a shadow on his record by always insisting that the outcomes of these plebiscites legitimize the Islamic Republic and reflect the true preferences of Iranians.

Perhaps it takes a novelist to express the absurd and unnecessary tragedy of a government rigging plebiscites it would have won anyway:

> At this point calm descended on Don Fabrizio, who had finally solved the enigma; now he knew who had been killed at Donnafugata, at a hundred other places, in the course of that night of dirty wind: a new-born babe: good faith; just the very child who should have been cared for most, whose strengthening would have justified all the silly vandalisms. Don Ciccio's negative vote, fifty similar votes at Donnafugata, a hundred thousand "noes" in the whole Kingdom, would have had no effect on the result, would in fact have made it, if anything, more significant; and this maiming of souls would have been avoided.[28]

Policy Dilemmas

Now that we have analyzed the constraints under which the PG had to operate, we can turn to three areas in which Bazargan and his colleagues had to make difficult decisions, decisions that were not uncontested.

---

[27]This is only a very brief outline of the institutionalization of the Islamic Republic. For a detailed account see Bakhash, *Reign,* pp. 71–88, and *Keesing's,* March 21, 1980, pp. 30143–45. For the text of the Constitution and a discussion of it see Gisbert H. Flanz, "A Comparative Analysis of the Constitution of the Islamic Republic of Iran," in *Constitutions of the World: Iran,* ed. Albert P. Blaustein and Gisbert H. Flanz (1980).

[28]Giuseppe [Tomasi] di Lamlpedusa, *The Leopard,* trans. Archibald Colquhoun (1960), p. 134.

The Press

From the very outset the PG and more particularly the LMI were handicapped in that they had no press organs to publicize their views and policies and to defend themselves against attacks from leftist and Islamic radicals. After the long years of censorship under the Shah the written press had developed great dynamism during the liberalization of 1978. In the months after the return of Khomeini the vitality and variety of the Iranian press reached its peak. Journalists and editors took over their publications, as the owners had mostly fled abroad; old periodicals that had been banned under the Shah began to reappear; and new ones sprang up, published by political or special interest groups. In the spring of 1979 more than 360 publications came to the newsstands, some even in the long banned local languages of Kurdish and Azerbaijani Turkish.[29] The journalists and writers belonged mostly to the modern segment of society, many were leftists, and many others had written for the publications of the Shah regime. This was inevitable, since a journalist had nothing else for which to write in the years 1963–77.

The fundamentalists had been irritated by the secular dominance over the press for some time, and gangs of *hezbollahi*s had terrorized editorial offices, newsstands, and bookstores since before Khomeini's return to Iran. The revived press could not take Khomeini to task, because he was still the undisputed leader of the revolution and maintained some pretense of being above the fray. As a result they directed their remonstrances at Bazargan and the PG, "the government." Because of this, Bazargan and his colleagues joined the fundamentalists in denouncing critical publications and journalists as SAVAK agents. The prime minister did not go so far as to condone the *hezbollahi* attacks, but he did not condemn them either. Among all Iranian publications, the newspaper *Ayandegan* had special significance, and its silencing heralded the beginning of repression in Iran.

Ayandegan was a morning newspaper whose editor before the revolution had been Dariush Homayun, one of the most disliked officials of the Shah regime. During the revolution its editors had taken over and turned it into a pluralist forum for all groups, including clerics. Its general tenor was left of center. In May 1979 Khomeini stated publicly that he did not read *Ayandegan*, obviously thinking that this announcement would spell the end of the newspaper. Shortly thereafter Nationalist groups led by the NDF held a meeting to commemorate the 100th anniversary of Mosaddeq's birth. The meeting, which was attacked by

[29]Gholam Hoseyn Sa'edi, "Iran under the Party of God," *Index on Censorship* 1 (1984), 17–18.

hezbollahis, ended with a declaration stating that the participants *did* read *Ayandegan*. As a result efforts got under way to silence the newspaper by "legal" means. On August 7 (Mordad 16), the revolutionary prosecutor of Teheran, Ay. Ahmad Azari Qomi, closed down *Ayandegan*, alleging links with foreign secret services, and arrested most of its staff. The newspaper had been printed on Iran's most modern press, which had also been used for other oppositional publications. By seizing *Ayandegan* the fundamentalists with one blow deprived all other critical mass-circulation newspapers of a printing press (the leftist groups produced their organs in the underground). On August 8 the PG announced a new law that severely regulated the press and that, according to the secular opposition, copied the Shah's press law. The NDF called for mass demonstrations to protest against the curtailment of the freedom of speech, and staged them on August 12–13. *Hezbollahis* attacked the demonstration, and the NDF leader, Hedayatollah Matin-Daftari, became the first Mosaddeqist who had to go underground. On August 14 the International Commission of Jurists denounced the new law as creating a "severe setback for Iranian political life" and introducing the "evil doctrine of guilt by association." One week later, on August 21, the government announced that more than twenty newspapers and magazines had to close down: all were secular and leftist publications except one.[30]

Ayandegan had been the favorite newspaper of the Iranian intelligentsia and the modern segment in general, and its closure confirmed the worst suspicions of those who had never trusted the revolution and it disappointed those who had. The Provisional Government had been without a voice on the press scene, but the LMI could spare no one to start a newspaper or expand the party's monthly "political-ideological organ" *Payam* (Message).

In a country with an illiteracy rate of about 50 percent the PG's lack of control over radio and television was perhaps an even greater handicap than the lack of a sympathetic press. Sadeq Qotbzadeh, who had been appointed head of the National Iranian Radio and Television, purged that institution, one of the most active centers of artistic creativity in Iran, of all leftists. He banned popular entertainment and music from the airwaves, and when fundamentalist criticism of Bazargan mounted, he joined in. Khomeini had discovered the virtues of a radio and television network that was independent of the executive branch, and turned a deaf ear to Bazargan's entreaties to let the PG control the electronic media.

[30]This was the newspaper of Ho. Mohammad Montazeri, Ay. Montazeri's son, who was Colonel Qadhafi's ally in Iran. Because of Imam Musa al-Sadr's disappearance in Libya Montazeri had many enemies among the Shi'ite clergy.

Trouble in the Periphery

Shortly after the installation of the PG, its spokesman, Amir-Entezam, had answered a foreign reporter's question as to the territorial administration of the new regime by stating that Iran would be a federal state, like the United States. Throughout his short tenure as prime minister, Bazargan in his speeches acknowledged the religious and ethnic diversity of Iranians, and tried to reassure all minorities that their rights would be respected in the Islamic Republic.[31] Before a speech in Tabriz, he even went so far as to apologize for not speaking in Azerbaijani Turkish.[32] Nevertheless, postrevolutionary Iran has been almost as centralizing as the Shah regime.

In the chaos that followed the revolutionary take-over of February 1979, autonomist movements sprang up in some peripheral areas of Iran. Fighting broke out in Gorgan province between Turkomans, their Fada'i allies, and the Pasdaran; in Khuzistan the energetic governor, Admiral Ahmad Madani, quickly quelled Arab unrest stirred by Iraq; and most of the areas inhabited by Sunni Kurds were in the hands of Kurdish autonomists.

Kurdistan was shielded from the Islamicization attempts of the fundamentalists. This transformed it into a place of refuge for secularists and leftists, who looked upon it as a possible starting base for the future resecularization of Iran. Plans had been made to hold a Congress of the Peoples of Iran in late August. The *Ayandegan* affair, and the expulsion of the Fada'iyan and the Mojahedin from Teheran University that had closely followed it, lent particular significance to the planned gathering, which many secularist and leftists planned to attend. To crush the momentum of a Kurdistan-based secularist opposition, Pasdaran and military units entered the region, accompanied by Sadeq Khalkhali. Khalkhali started a carnage among Kurdish autonomists and managed to poison relations between Teheran and the Kurds for good. After three weeks Khalkhali was recalled to Teheran and mediation efforts began under the auspices of Taleqani, who had already intervened in March. Negotiations were still going on when the PG fell.

Foreign Relations

At the helm of a country with seriously weakened armed forces, the PG very quickly attempted to reassure other countries that Iran would honor its international agreements. The new Iranian government hastened

[31]A. Bazargan, ed., *Masa'el*, pp. 9, 10, 13, 43, 299, 332, 362.
[32]Ibid., p. 299.

to make up for more than two decades of past alliances with the West. It broke diplomatic relations with Israel (whose diplomatic mission was turned over to the PLO) and South Africa, and Yasir Arafat's triumphant visit elicited a rare smile from Khomeini. But when the PLO proceeded to open an office in Khorramshahr without first obtaining the government's permission, the office was ordered closed, for which the PG was criticized by some hard-liners.

Iran also became a member of the Non-Aligned Movement, and Foreign Minister Yazdi demonstrated Iran's new self-confidence by addressing the United Nations in Persian without providing for simultaneous translation. At Khomeini's personal behest, Iran broke diplomatic relations with Egypt after the Camp David Accords,[33] making a mockery of the PG's pledges not to interfere in other countries' affairs. Meanwhile Taleqani told a visiting Cuban delegation that he considered the Cuban revolution to be Islamic.[34]

Two countries were of particular importance to the PG: Iraq and the United States. Iran had settled its long border dispute with Iraq in 1975; only three years later the Iraqi regime earned the irreconcilable hostility of Khomeini by expelling him from Najaf. After coming to power, Khomeini sent encouraging signals to Iraq's Shi'ites, a majority of the Arab population but politically dominated by Sunnis. Not to be outdone, Iraq began stirring up trouble among the ethnic Arabs in Khuzistan. The Iraqi government even tried to test Iranian defenses by bombing some border villages in March 1979 (Esfand 1357), but the PG defused the crisis by negotiating with the Iraqi government, which agreed to pay compensations.[35]

At the Non-Aligned Nations meeting in Havana in October 1979 Yazdi met with Saddam Husein, the Iraqi president. He was told that Iraqi interference in Iranian affairs in Khuzistan and the Persian Gulf would continue, because the ideology of the Iraqi Ba'th party held that it had to pronounce itself on all Arab issues. To this, Yazdi replied that if a forty-year-old party claimed such a right, by the same logic Ay. Khomeini had an even greater right to interfere in all Shi'ite matters, since Shi'ism and the religious center at Najaf were over 1,000 years old.[36]

Of greater consequence were Iran's relations with the United States. Some American foreign policymakers had advocated an intervention in

[33]*Nameh-ye sargoshadeh be sepah-e pasdaran-e enqelab-e eslami* (Open letter to the Pasdaran forces of the Islamic revolution) (1983), p. 72.

[34]Afrasiabi and Dehqan, *Taleqani*, p. 511.

[35]*Talash-e dowlat-e movaqqat bara-ye jelowgiri az jang-e tahmili-ye Eraq* (The Provisional Government's efforts to prevent the war imposed by Iraq) (n.d.).

[36]*Mosahebeh-ye doktor Yazdi ba mokhber-e nashriye-ye arabi-ye al-majallah* (Dr. Yazdi's interview with the correspondent of the Arab journal *Al-Majallah*) (1985), p. 8.

Iran by inducing the army to carry out a coup,[37] and the members of the PG belonged to a generation that still remembered vividly the coup of 1953. The coming to power of moderate opponents of the Shah was only a second-best outcome for Washington, and in spite of President Carter's assurances that the United States would not interfere in Iranian affairs, CIA agents were sent in quite significant numbers.[38] The U.S. government even tried to continue operating its secret listening post at Kabkan near the Soviet border without informing the PG about this,[39] a clear violation of Iran's sovereignty. When General Qarani, the chief of staff, declared over the Iranian radio that Iran would not tolerate foreign listening posts on its territory, the Iranian employees at Kabkan sequestrated the U.S. military personnel. The incident was solved peacefully in the end.

Nevertheless, the PG tried to maintain normal relations with the United States, partly because of its apprehension about an American intervention, and partly because of the growing Soviet influence in Afghanistan, where pro-Soviet communists had taken power in a violent coup in April 1978. When leftist elements stormed the American embassy on February 14, Yazdi dislodged them with the help of Islamic irregulars.[40] On the crucial question of American arms sales to Iran, the PG tried to continue buying at least some greatly needed spare parts.

American policy toward the PG contributed unwittingly to the growing anti-American sentiment in Iran. Washington considered the PG to be "moderate" and "reasonable," and hoped to strengthen it by cooperating with it. High-ranking members of the PG, including Deputy Prime Minister Amir-Entezam, maintained steady and discreet contact with the American embassy and tried to reassure the U.S. diplomats that things would eventually calm down. On two occasions Bazargan, Yazdi, and Amir-Entezam were briefed by CIA agents.[41] These visible contacts amounted to a "kiss of death" and could only undermine the PG's popularity in Iran. Also, the sudden solicitude of Congress and much of the American media for human rights violations in Iran *after* the revolution struck most people in Iran, even moderate opponents of the revolutionary tribunals' methods, as hypocritical in view of the relatively little attention the Shah's repression had received in the United States.

William Sullivan left his post in April, but his designated successor,

---

[37] Zbigniew Brzezinski, *Power and Principle* (1983), pp. 371, 372, and 393.

[38] See John Kelly, "CIA in Iran," *Counterspy* 3 (April–May 1979), 24–36.

[39] James Bamford, *The Puzzle Palace* (1982), p. 200.

[40] For an eyewitness account, see William H. Sullivan, *Mission to Iran* (1981), pp. 258–66.

[41] James A. Bill, *The Eagle and the Lion: The Tragedy of American-Iranian Relations* (1988), pp. 290–93.

Walter Cutler, was not acceptable to the PG. The American government, miffed, let it be known that henceforth relations would be handled on the level of *chargés d'affaires*. Cutler's rejection was an application of Khomeini's instruction to Yazdi that the United States be treated with circumspect ambiguity.[42]

In late October Bazargan left on his first trip abroad, to attend the anniversary celebrations of Algerian independence on November 1, 1979. The prime minister was accompanied by Yazdi and Chamran, ministers of foreign affairs and defense, respectively. The three LMI leaders used the occasion to meet with Zbigniew Brezezinski. Given Brzezinski's hostility to the Iranian revolution,[43] such a meeting could indeed be viewed with suspicion by people with no confidence in the probity of Bazargan and Yazdi. It appears that news of this meeting was transmitted by Algerian communists within the FLN to their Tudeh comrades in Iran, who relayed the news to the fundamentalists. The latter started a campaign to depict the PG as too beholden to the United States, and Qotbzadeh's radio and television quickly spread this line. Around the same time it was announced in the United States that the Shah would be admitted for medical treatment, and this news precipitated the attack on the U.S. embassy in Teheran, which led to the downfall of the Provisional Government.

Or so it seemed. The attack on the U.S. embassy on November 4, 1979, had actually been planned months before by radical Islamic groups, including one that had originated in the modernist camp. On numerous occasions we have already encountered JAMA, the party that was founded in 1964 by Kazem Sami and Habibollah Peiman. As is so frequent with Iranian political parties, the inevitable occurred and the two leaders split. Sami revived JAMA during the liberalization[44] and remained within the Nationalist camp, participating in the PG. Peiman founded the Jonbesh-e mosalmanan-e mobarez (Movement of Combatant Muslims). On paper this group's ideology was very similar to that of JAMA,[45] but Peiman attached himself to the fundamentalists

---

[42]The terms Khomeini used, *kajdar va mariz*, literally mean "tilt the cup but don't spill its contents." The phrase connotes enticement, accommodation, but ultimate refusal. Khomeini's instruction is reported in *Nameh-ye sargoshadeh*, p. 71.

[43]According to Brzezinski's memoirs the executions of the Shah's generals in March moved him so much that he regretted that the United States had not done more to impose a counterrevolutionary military regime on Iran (*Power and Principle* [1983], p. 393.) His compassion for these generals contrasts starkly with his contempt for the scores of Iranians who had been killed (or tortured) on their orders.

[44]While he kept the acronym, he adapted the actual name to the new times by changing it to Jonbesh-e enqelabi-ye mellat-e mosalman-e Iran (Revolutionary Movement of the Muslim People of Iran).

[45]Rokhsan Manuchehri, "Small but Strong," in *The Iranian* (Teheran), February 16, 1980 (Bahman 27, 1358), p. 4.

(and the Tudeh), and his supporters were prominent in the attack on the American embassy.[46] In addition to discrediting the PG, the radicals also hoped to create a groundswell of enthusiasm in the population which would enable them to crush the moderate MPRP.

After the seizure of the hostages, Bazargan resigned. He had offered his resignation on previous occasions, but only now did Khomeini accept it. In his response to Bazargan's letter, Khomeini thanked him for his ceaseless and exhausting efforts, and reiterated his confidence in Bazargan's religiosity, honesty, and goodwill.[47] In his final television appearance on November 6 and 7, 1979, Bazargan said that he was still an advocate of fraternity, honesty, forgiveness, friendship, and service, and that he was against vengefulness. He defended the record of the Provisional Government and confided that his chief worry for the future was that the sovereignty of the people—as the vice-regent of God—might not be established and in its stead a particular class, such as the ulema, might come to exercise sovereignty.[48]

The fact that Khomeini did not dismiss him in disgrace enabled Bazargan to continue his political activity after the fall of the PG, as we shall see in the next chapter. First, we will consider the LMI as a political party in the first phase of the revolution.

The LMI in 1979

In early 1979 (Dey 1357) the LMI published its new party program. It called for a mixed economy and moral improvement in Iranian society based on three principles: Islam, the 1906 Constitution (to be amended), and the Universal Declaration of Human Rights.[49] On February 6, 1979 (Bahman 17, 1357), the party issued a communiqué to the effect that it would redouble its ideological and organizational efforts now that Ay. Khomeini, exercising his religious and legal rights, had named its leader head of the government.[50]

After most LMI figures joined the PG and refrained from party activity, Ezzatollah Sahabi took over what remained of the LMI. Sahabi had been in touch with various more radical groups, such as the Mojahedin, and was himself to the left of the PG. In the first months after the revolution he used his good personal relations with other

[46]Sepehr Zabih, in his book *Iran since the Revolution* (1982), pp. 43–51, affirms that Peiman's Movement of Combatant Muslims was the main force behind the hostage affair. This thesis does not meet with scholars' unanimity.

[47]A. Bazargan, ed., *Masa'el,* p. 72.

[48]Ibid., pp. 283, 289, and 295.

[49]*Safehat,* 11, pp. 56–69.

[50]Ibid., p. 71.

groups to defuse conflicts and to better the PG's relations with its more revolutionary critics.

On June 17, 1979 (Khordad 27, 1358), Sahabi wrote a lengthy evaluation of the situation in the name of the LMI.[51] At that point a certain degree of disenchantment had already appeared in society, and Sahabi's text was an attempt to define the LMI's position on how things now stood. It began by noting that many of the revolution's problems stemmed from its having been too successful too quickly. The PG had to face five problems: it had no ready programs, it lacked well-known revolutionary figures, the country was in a chaos and difficult to revive, revolutionaries and opportunists were not easily distinguishable, and its leaders were devoid of a common ideological outlook.[52] What follows is a summary of Sahabi's analysis.

The leading forces within the revolutionary movement were Imam Khomeini, the PG, the CR, the ulema, the revolutionary groupings of young people, and the masses of the population. The Islamic revolution was confronted by three forces: the liberal-democratic intellectuals, the Marxists, and the counterrevolution. The primary counterrevolutionaries were the dependent bourgeoisie, which was quietly making a comeback because the revolutionaries lacked the qualified cadres to run things.

The Marxists were only power-hungry, had done nothing constructive since the triumph of the revolution, and stirred up trouble in the provinces and the factories. They were complaining about censorship, yet 85 percent of all newspapers were in their hands or sympathetic to them.

The liberal democrats had to ponder whether their goals and ideas found a favorable echo in the population. The intellectuals were out of tune with the masses, and had to rid themselves of their West-struckness if they hoped to have any impact on society. Nevertheless, the essential demands of these forces were not incompatible with the Islamic revolution, and therefore they should be given a chance to participate in it in recognition of their contribution to the struggle against the Shah.

The PG was weakened not only by the existence of multiple power centers, but also because it was not decisive enough in dealing with problems. It paid too much attention to the antidespotic character of the revolution and not enough to its anti-imperialist dimension. Its

[51]"Bayaniyeh-ye Nehzat-e Azadi-ye Iran: Tahlili az sharayet-e emruzi-ye enqelab-e eslami-ye Iran va naqd-e niruha-ye darun-e enqelab" (LMI declaration: An analysis of the conditions of Iran's Islamic revolution today, and a review of the forces within the revolution), in Safehat, 11, pp. 93–159.

[52]Ibid., p. 110.

outlook was overly bureaucratic and it was not willing to mobilize the young. Its gradualism would pave the way for the counterrevolution to return.

The ulema had been very active during the revolution, but should not seek to monopolize power: that would only increase dissatisfaction.

Sahabi's declaration concluded by arguing that only those members of the original LMI whose outlook on the world had evolved parallel to the growth of the Islamic movement were represented in the new LMI. Concretely, this meant that for Sahabi the LMI was now an unequivocally Islamic party. This text must be seen as an attempt to disassociate the LMI as a party from the PG, which was coming under attack from revolutionary forces. It created a stir among the LMI members of the PG, who objected to its radicalism and bluntness.

The LMI, personified by E. Sahabi, was on the whole more critical of the secular liberals than of the clergy in 1979. On occasions when liberals approached Sahabi for common action or declarations against *hezbollahi* abuses, he did not respond. This attitude came to characterize the LMI in later years: while disagreeing with the Islamic hard-liners and even criticizing them on occasion, the LMI seemed to claim a monopoly on *well-intentioned* criticism, and often went so far as to assimilate any criticism stemming from secular forces to the counter-revolution. In the new political culture of Iran, the LMI wanted to maintain its legitimacy by not associating with secular forces, and by criticizing Islamic forces always from an Islamic viewpoint. But by doing so it also contributed to the consolidation of Islamic hegemony in Iran. For example, in the Assembly of Experts Sahabi spoke out against the principle of *velayat-e faqih*,[53] but once it had passed, he defended it against secular critics.[54]

Ezzatollah Sahabi had spent most of the liberalization of 1977–79 in prison, and he left the LMI in December 1980. The very limited activity of the LMI during the life of the PG can therefore not really be considered typical for the party and what it has stood for.

His tenure as prime minister was a traumatic experience for Mehdi Bazargan. A man who had always insisted on organization, sound management, and rational principles, had presided over one of the more chaotic periods in recent Iranian history. Much as he had tried to communicate with Iranians by being accessible and giving "folksy" television chats, he and his style were out of touch with the situation. It must have saddened Bazargan that the young hostage takers were for the most part engineering and science students. When he resigned,

[53]Bakhash, *Reign*, pp. 84–85.
[54]*The Iranian*, October 3, 1979 (Mehr 11, 1358), pp. 8–11.

Bazargan retreated from public life and remained silent. About one month later he granted an interview to Hamid Algar, in which he articulated his feelings.[55] On his own and Khomeini's relationship with the revolution, Bazargan said:

> It is astonishing that an eighty-year-old man should be much better attuned to the youth than I, who grew up among the young, in the university, and in the revolutionary movement. . . . If you read Khomeini's declarations now, they are very different from what he used to say a year ago, even six months ago. Unconsciously he has adopted the tone of the revolutionaries, and thus he has been able to influence them. I really sense an estrangement and a distance between myself and the people within the revolution, i.e. the young, the *tollab*, the university people, and the [revolutionary] guards. I also consider myself a revolutionary. But what I want is in contradiction with what they want, even though our ultimate aims are perhaps identical.[56]

Commenting on the shift from the early opposition to all superpowers to the later exclusive hostility to the United States, Bazargan said:

> This whole business with the American embassy was probably due to [Khomeini's] influence. It was perhaps four months ago that he began to consider America and Carter as first among our enemies, as ringleaders of this and that, without the slightest proof, just by definition. . . . This had a real effect on the revolutionaries, and they in turn influenced him. He is more of an *entraîneur d'hommes* . . . than Hitler was. Hitler was a genius as an *organisateur de foules*, and Khomeini has the same qualities. That is how he got where he is now.[57]

After the fall of the Provisional Government, Beheshti revealed that Khomeini and the fundamentalists never intended to give Bazargan a chance, and thought of the Nationalist-dominated Provisional Government as a transitional solution. In 1979 Khomeini repeatedly asked Beheshti whether the IRP was ready to form a government. According to Beheshti, it was not.[58]

[55]Bazargan was very blunt in this interview, Algar having led him to believe that he wanted only to collect background information for a book on the revolution that would come out at some point in the not immediate future. But Algar made the interview's text available to *Nasr*, the publication of the MSAs in the United States and Canada, which printed it in its February 1, 1981 (Bahman 12, 1359), issue. By that time Bazargan was under wide attack in Iran, and the interview, accompanied by hostile annotations from the journal's editors, was used against Bazargan. If I use this document, it is only because Bazargan has acknowledged its publication and publicly responded to the accusations contained in the annotations.

[56]Ibid., pp. 13–14.
[57]Ibid., pp. 15–16. The Gallicisms are Bazargan's.
[58]Benard and Khalilzad, *Government of God*, p. 109.

The fate of the Provisional Government revived interest in Crane Brinton's book *Anatomy of Revolution*, and even Bazargan himself ends his own account of the revolutionary movement with a translation of the book's central thesis.[59] Brinton's summary of the dilemma facing moderates in a revolution also applies to the Provisional Government:

> The moderates by definition are not great haters. . . . [They] do not really believe in the big words they have to use. They do not really believe a heavenly perfection is suddenly coming to man on earth. They are all for compromise, common sense, toleration, comfort.[60]

Bazargan and most of his colleagues in the LMI did not believe in the big words, and at least Bazargan himself had the honesty not to use them. Bazargan hoped that by associating with Khomeini, he could gain enough freedom of action to steer a moderate course, for without Khomeini's support he would have no influence on events at all.

The demise of the Provisional Government coincided with the final, spectacular resolution of Iran's crisis of sovereignty. But after that, unlike Crane Brinton's moderates, Bazargan and his associates did not turn to the conservatives, or to foreign powers. This is one reason they were able to survive the period of terror that followed soon after their resignation, and lived to become an opposition party in the Islamic Republic.

[59]Bazargan, *Enqelab*, pp. 225–48.
[60]Crane Brinton, *The Anatomy of Revolution* (1965), p. 146.

CHAPTER 8

The Liberation Movement
of Iran as Loyal Opposition

The fall of the Provisional Government and the hostage crisis were the beginning of the second, more radical phase of the Iranian revolution. From August 1979, when the NDF was neutralized, until 1983, when the Tudeh was outlawed, the Islamic radicals got rid of other parties one by one, until by late 1983 the LMI was the only remaining legal opposition party in Iran. Since the dissolution of the IRP in the spring of 1987, the LMI has been the only political party in Iran. This chapter does not aim at analyzing political developments in Iran since 1980,[1] rather, it focuses on the LMI's efforts to constitute a moderate opposition in a revolutionary country.

After the resignation of the Provisional Government the LMI was slow to reorganize, while the IRP consolidated itself. In the first few months after the seizure of the hostages in November 1979, Bazargan and his friends did not really act as an oppositional group. It was only after the elections of 1980, when the institutions of the Islamic Republic were put in place and Bazargan and a few of his friends became part of the Majles' minority faction, that the LMI became a loyal opposition to the government, although never to the Khomeini regime.

A few weeks after the seizure of the hostages, the students in the U.S. embassy published selected documents to publicize American contacts with Iranian officials. This led to a campaign of what in Iran is called *javv-sazi*, that is, the creation of a hostile atmosphere, in this case directed against the LMI and other moderate forces in Iran. This means

[1] See Shaul Bakhash, *The Reign of the Ayatollahs* (1984), pp. 90ff.

that the LMI has had constantly to reaffirm its loyalty to the revolution and respond to the attacks of its opponents.

The LMI between the Seizure of the Hostages and the Ouster of President Banisadr

After he resigned as prime minister, Bazargan was invited to join the Council of the Revolution, which became the highest organ of the state. He accepted under the condition that he could bring along three of his friends. This was granted and Bazargan chose Hasan Habibi, Ezzatollah Sahabi, and Mostafa Katira'i. Other LMI figures stayed on as ministers in the caretaker government, but Yazdi resigned as foreign minister and was replaced first by Banisadr, and after one week by Sadeq Qotbzadeh. Although the Provisional Government was no more, its LMI members and sympathizers continued working loyally within the transitional structures of government, and Bazargan himself over-saw the work of a number of commissions.[2] Whatever qualms they had in private about the hostage affair, publicly the LMI figures did not condemn it, so as not to lag behind popular enthusiasm.[3] Referring to the act, Yazdi said that "in order to rally the masses this kind of thing should continue."[4] Bazargan, in his interview with Hamid Algar, said, "If I disapprove, God knows what would happen,and if I approve, well, it is possible I wouldn't really believe it."[5]

Dissension in the LMI

As we saw in the previous chapter, differences of opinion within the party had appeared in the spring and summer of 1979, as reflected in Ezzatollah Sahabi's pamphlet. For Sahabi and the left wing of the LMI, anti-imperialism came first. This meant that it was dangerous to weaken the Islamic Movement in the name of freedom, as Bazargan and Yazdi were doing in E. Sahabi's eyes. For Yazdi, by contrast, despotism prepared the ground for imperialism to stage a comeback, and he argued that only a free country, like India, could withstand the pressures of the superpowers.

[2]*Mizan*, February 3, 1981 (Esfand 6, 1359), p. 4.
[3]Even Karim Sanjabi, the leader of the National Front, declared that the action was an understandable reaction to the Shah's entry to the United States, and chided the Provisional Government for not having reacted more firmly to that move. *Ettela'at*, February 16, 1980 (Bahman 27, 1357), p. 2.
[4]*The Iranian*, December 15, 1979 (Azar 24, 1358), p. 8.
[5]*Nasr*, February 1, 1981 (Bahman 12, 1359), p. 12.

On December 21, 1979 (Azar 30, 1358), E. Sahabi and eleven other members presented their resignation to the LMI leadership. The elections were approaching, however, and since the dissidents did not want to add yet another issue to the country's politics, the resignation was kept secret until February 12 (Bahman 23), when the press was informed. The most prominent of the twelve figures to leave the LMI were two sons of party founder Yadollah Sahabi, Ezzatollah and Fereidun Sahabi; Mohammad-Mehdi Ja'fari and Mohammad Bastehnegar (a son-in-law of the late Ay. Taleqani), both of whom had been defendants in the 1963 trials; and Hasan Arabzadeh, who had been active in Mashad. Bazargan released a statement to the effect that the move was an internal affair of the LMI affecting only a few younger members and needed not be given press coverage,[6] and the next day Abbas Radnia attempted to play down the whole matter by pointing out that none of those who had left had been members of the party's Founding Council, and that therefore their move did not constitute a true "split."[7]

The two sides refrained from any kind of public polemics, and both E. Sahabi and Ja'fari continued collaborating with *Mizan*, the LMI's unofficial newspaper after September 1980. Bazargan had tried to minimize the impact of the split by pointing to the "young age" of the dissenters; in fact, however, their youth was precisely what mattered. In the years 1963–77 the LMI had not been able to recruit new blood into the party; the "youngsters" of the years 1960–63 were now middle-aged men. Moreover, they were the only, albeit tenuous, link with the young, revolutionary generation. The defection of Ezzatollah Sahabi, in particular, deprived the party of a widely respected and energetic figure who had good contacts with the Islamic left. Qotbzadeh had gone his own way since the revolution. Among younger men, this left Chamran, Reza Sadr, Yazdi, and Sabbaghian. Chamran was more preoccupied with the armed forces than with politics and, given his past activities in Lebanon, the left and Islamic radicals united in denouncing him as a MOSSAD agent. Reza Sadr became more visible: he had been an effective minister of foreign trade in the PG, and having had a full clerical education, he knew how to deal with meddlesome clerics on their own ground. Yazdi had had his own disagreements with Bazargan[8] and was quite unpopular as a result of the attacks leveled against him, but in the crucial moments after the seizure of the hostages he resisted the temptation to throw in his lot with Khomeini, to whom he was still very close, and remained loyal to Bazargan.

[6]*Ettela'at*, February 12, 1980 (Bahman 23, 1358), pp. 2 and 3.
[7]Ibid., February 13, 1980 (Bahman 24, 1358), p. 3.
[8]*The Iranian*, December 15, 1979 (Azar 24, 1358), p. 8.

The LMI and the Elections of 1980

The two plebiscites of 1979 had set the stage for the elections that would complete the institutionalization of the Islamic Republic. On January 25, 1980 (Bahman 5, 1358), presidential elections were held; the new parliament was chosen in the spring.

The Presidential Elections

The presidential elections gave the Islamic modernists in Iran one more chance to raise their heads. By a series of blunders the IRP was not able to present a candidate of its own.[9] Khomeini had indicated that he did not want a cleric to run, which neutralized the IRP's ambitious leader, Beheshti. The candidacy of the leader of the Mojahedin, Mas'ud Rajavi, had been vetoed because of his merely conditional acceptance of the new Constitution, and therefore the field was open to candidates who had begun their political activity before the rise of fundamentalism.

Abolhasan Banisadr had spent 1979 criss-crossing the country, giving speeches in local mosques, schools, and public places. He had severely criticized the PG's lack of revolutionary and anti-imperialist zeal, and was therefore not associated with the PG. Although Khomeini remained neutral in the presidential campaign, many members of his household, including his son, declared for Banisadr.

The IRP, having failed to present an eligible candidate, threw its support behind Hasan Habibi, the former NF(III) activist in France. Among all the candidates he was closest to the LMI, and a number of Khomeini relatives endorsed him.

Other candidates associated with the Islamic movement were JAMA's Kazem Sami, Sadeq Qotbzadeh, and Sadeq Tabataba'i, who had been the main LMI(a) organizer in Germany, and who had been the administrator of the prime minister's office after Bazargan's resignation. A son-in-law of Khomeini, he was not endorsed by any visible figure.

On the secular side, the chief candidate was Admiral Ahmad Madani, who had been minister of defense and governor of Khuzistan during the PG. Also running were Dariush Foruhar, leader of the PIN, and Mohammad Mokri, Iranian ambassador in Moscow. Neither the LMI nor the NF presented a candidate of their own. Bazargan, who would have been the LMI's obvious candidate, was probably still too shaken by his experience as prime minister to try his luck at the polls, despite public appeals by some of his followers in the

[9]See Bakhash, *Reign*, p. 90.

press. According to another explanation, the accusations leveled against Amir-Entezam, Bazargan's aide in the PG, by the students who seized the American embassy convinced Bazargan not to expose himself to a slander campaign.[10]

The campaign was relatively calm. The candidates all knew each other and concentrated on highlighting their personal merits rather than attacking the others. The religiously oriented candidates benefited from the endorsements from the Khomeini household, by last-minute allegations of the radical students holding the American embassy that Madani had had contacts with the old regime, and by the lowering of the voting age to sixteen. All candidates received equal time on radio and television.

The official results of these elections were as follows:

Abolhasan Banisadr	10,747,345
Ahmad Madani	2,240,160
Hasan Habibi	676,120
Dariush Foruhar	134,132

The four remaining candidates got less then 1 percent each. Inevitably, the counting of the ballots was rigged, but the order of the candidates reflected their popularity at the time. Banisadr was relatively young, and had for over a year manipulated revolutionary symbols and rhetoric adroitly. Many people believed that Khomeini had promised him the presidency in Paris. Madani was the choice of those members of the modern segment who bothered to vote, and an honest counting of the votes would have probably improved his score without getting him elected. Hasan Habibi was less well known, and perhaps hampered by his association with the PG, in which he had served as minister. Foruhar's constituency was limited to the dwindling numbers of Iranian ethno-nationalists. Qotbzadeh had become very unpopular because of his policies at the helm of the radio and television networks, and those who approved of his policies had more serious candidates in Habibi and Banisadr. The remaining candidates were largely unknown.

The presidential elections were the last hurrah of Mosaddeqism in Iran, as all eight presidential candidates had been young National Front activists before 1963 (and after 1963 outside Iran). Only two years later the winner and the runner-up of that election would be opposing the Islamic regime from Europe, one had been executed in Iran, three

[10]Amir-Entezam had continued meeting with American embassy officials, who had a favorable impression of him. In July 1979 he had left Iran to become ambassador to Sweden, but when he was brought to court after the hostage taking, he returned to Iran to defend himself, and was arrested on December 19. During his trial, which began on March 17, 1981, Bazargan obdurately defended his former deputy.

had become politically inactive, and only two continued their careers in a regime that had now officially thrown anathema on Mohammad Mosaddeq.

The Parliamentary Elections

After Banisadr took office, he was appointed head of the CR by Khomeini. Suspicious of political parties, he did not found one. Instead, he and his friends set up an Office for the Cooperation of the People with the President with branches of the "Office" all over the country. These groups presented candidates in Teheran and the provinces.

The IRP had become a highly organized force and put up candidates in most constituencies. Various smaller fundamentalist groups joined it in a grand coalition that dominated the parliamentary campaign, especially in the provinces. Iranian politicians have always neglected the small towns, concentrating their energies either on winning seats in Teheran or in their hometowns where their families were known.[11] In the small provincial towns it was almost by default that local and trusted clerics became the best positioned candidates. Many of them were rallied to the IRP or received its endorsement.

Torn by internal strife, the LMI did not present candidates under its own name. Instead, on February 2 (Bahman 13) it was announced that Bazargan, Y. Sahabi, Ay. Abolfazl Zanjani, and Mohammad-Taqi Shariati had formed a group called Hamnam (Eponym), with the aim of introducing candidates to the public. This was only one of many such groups, and most candidates figured on many different groups. Hamnam declared that it would choose its candidates only on the basis of merit, without regard to party affiliation. The same day Hamnam published a list of twenty-five men as candidates for Teheran, a list that figured veteran LMI leaders such as Bazargan, Y. Sahabi, E. Sahabi, and Yazdi, but also Kazem Sami, Ali-Asghar Hajj-Seyyed-Javadi, and Abdolkarim Lahiji. Two of the founders of the IRP, Hos. Hashemi Rafsanjani and Abdolkarim Musavi Ardabili, were also included, as were a number of sympathetic non-IRP clerics such as Hos. Mohammad-Reza Mahdavi Kani and Ali Golzadeh Ghafuri.[12] After the split in the party, Ja'fari announced that he would seek the seat of Borazjan and Dashtestan (near Bushire, in the south) as an independent. On March 4 (Esfand 13) the group gave candidates in six provincial districts its investiture, including Ho. Hosein Lahuti from Rasht and Mohammad-Javad Raja'ian (a son-in-law of the Nationalist Bazaar leader H. Mahmud Manian) from Zanjan. Finally, on March 13 (Esfand 22) five more candidates

---

[11]Cf. the elections to the twentieth Majles, as analyzed in chapter 4.

[12]For the full list see *Ettela'at*, February 2, 1980 (Bahman 13, 1358), p. 12.

were given Hamnam backing in Teheran, including the future prime minister, Mohammad-Ali Raja'i, and the venerable Manian himself.[13]

The city of Qazvin was the only district where the LMI and the IRP openly competed against each other. Qazvin, a relatively prosperous city only 120 kilometers from Teheran, has a history of political activism and had been a safe Nationalist seat under Mosaddeq. In 1980 the religious establishment of the city, led by Ho. Abutorabi, was opposed to the IRP and its methods, and invited two LMI leaders with roots in the city to contest its two seats: Ahmad Sadr Hajj-Seyyed-Javadi, and Ebrahim Yazdi. The former was a cousin to Ho. Zia'eddin Hajj-Seyyed-Javadi, who had represented the city during the sixteenth and seventeenth Majles (Mosaddeq's tenure as prime minister) and who had sat on the High Council of the National Front until his death in 1961. He accepted, while Yazdi preferred to run for a seat from Teheran. Reluctantly, Abutorabi himself announced his candidacy for the second seat.[14]

Thus, for the 270 seats at stake, Bazargan and his friends fielded or endorsed at most only 40 candidates. This failure to take advantage of the elections is reminiscent of the National Front's failure to put up candidates nationwide in the elections of 1960 and 1961,[15] and was even more inexcusable, given that the elections were far more open than those for the twentieth Majles. In 1980 it was still possible to organize effectively, yet the LMI lost this chance.

The election campaign was marred by widespread violence of *hezbollah* elements against candidates, mainly from the Mojahedin, not fully committed to the new regime. To protest against this state of affairs, two founding members of the LMI, Abbas Radnia and Ahmad Alibaba'i, took back their candidacy in mid-March, while Hasan Habibi and E. Sahabi warned against the danger of "fascism."[16] Bazargan and his friends, however, persevered, and between the two rounds the Hamnam slate of candidates for Teheran even received the endorsement of the IRP-led fundamentalist coalition.

The election law itself did not meet with universal agreement. According to the law devised by the IRP and its allies,

> Members of the National Consultative Assembly will be elected by an absolute majority (50% +) of votes. If in the first round in single or multiple [member] districts such a majority is not obtained, there will be a second round. Thus from among those candidates who do not receive an

[13]For details see *Ettela'at*, March 4, 1980 (Esfand 13, 1358), p. 3; and March 13, 1980 (Esfand 22, 1358), p. 16.
[14]Information on the Qazvin elections were obtained from Ali-Asghar Hajj-Seyyed-Javadi, personal interview, Paris, July 1982.
[15]See chapter 4, pp. 145–53.
[16]*Ettela'at*, February 25, 1980 (Esfand 6, 1358), p. 2.

absolute majority twice as many as the number of representatives in each district will run in the second round, in which a relative majority will suffice.[17]

This law was unfavorable to smaller groups, and all secular forces, the Mojahedin, President Banisadr and his supporters, and also Hamnam opposed it.[18] Candidates were sponsored by many different groups, which makes it impossible to infer anything about the relative strength of political forces from the elections' results.

In the first round of the elections, Abutorabi and A. Sadr Hajj-Seyyed-Javadi soundly defeated the IRP candidates in Qazvin; Ja'fari, unopposed by the IRP, was returned from Borazjan; Raja'ian won a seat from Zanjan; and Ay. Lahuti won in Rasht. The situation in Teheran was complicated by the fact that only fourteen of the city's thirty seats had been filled during the first ballot. The irregularities of the first round, about which even Khomeini's older brother Ay. Pasandideh complained publicly in a letter to Banisadr, were such that the second round was postponed until May. The situation improved somewhat, but it was clear that the IRP and its allies had managed to control the counting of the votes in many places.

In the end Bazargan, Yadollah Sahabi, Yazdi, and Sabbaghian won seats in Teheran, as did Ali-Akbar Mo'infar, the PG's oil minister who has never formally adhered to the LMI but who has been more loyal to it than many a party member. Ezzatollah Sahabi also entered parliament, and Kazem Sami was the only lucky JAMA candidate. One of Ay. Taleqani's daughters, A'zam Taleqani, leader of a Muslim women's organization, also won a Teheran seat.

The Mojahedin had seemed to win a few provincial seats, but the official results did not reflect this. Mas'ud Rajavi had survived the first round, but did not get elected in the end.[19]

Secular Nationalist leaders did not fare well. The MPRP had been disbanded after it had staged a badly organized uprising in the capital of Azerbaijan, Tabriz,[20] and the two secular leaders allied with it, Rahmatollah Moqaddam Maragheh'i and Hasan Nazih, who might have won seats in Azerbaijan, had gone into hiding. The NDF had been driven underground after the *Ayandegan* affair, and the secular

---

[17]Quoted in Sepehr Zabih, *Iran since the Revolution* (1982), p. 65.

[18]Yazdi declared that the group considered the law a "trick." *Ettela'at*, March 4, 1980 (Esfand 13, 1358), p. 3.

[19]Bazargan endorsed Rajavi's candidacy between the ballots, on the grounds that he represented one wing of enthusiastic young believers and that his presence in the Majles would guarantee the rights of the minorities. *Bamdad*, May 7, 1980 (Ordibehesht 17, 1359), p. 3.

[20]For details see Bakhash, *Reign*, pp. 89–90.

democratic left thus lacked a central force. Among NF figures, Karim Sanjabi had been a candidate in his native Kermanshah but withdrew between the two rounds, alleging irregularities. Ahmad Madani won a landslide victory in his native Kerman. The leader of the Iran Party, Abolfazl Qasemi, won in his native Darehgaz. In Fars Province, the leader of the Qashqa'i tribes, Khosrow Khan, won a seat in the first round, but two lesser khans did not make it to the second round.[21] Some of Banisadr's followers also had been NF activists, but they ran as candidates of the "Office" rather than taking the NF label. The most notable successful candidates among these were Ahmad Salamatian, who gained one of the Isfahan seats, and Ahmad Ghazanfarpur, Banisadr's old friend and sometime co-author. In the end, the IRP-led coalition won about 130 seats out of 245, moderates claimed a total of over 50, and the rest were independents most of whom soon gravitated toward the IRP.

The LMI during the Banisadr Presidency

The eighteen months from Banisadr's election to his deposition by Khomeini in June 1981 were characterized by a power struggle between the president and the IRP-led alliance. Fearing a renewed despotism of the executive branch, the Assembly of Experts had drastically curtailed the powers of the presidency. Before the Majles elections Banisadr tried to use his authority as chairman of the Council of the Revolution to name a prime minister, hoping that he would be able to get the new parliament to vote for a prime minister who had the confidence of a president who had Khomeini's confidence. The scheme did not work out, and the formation of a new government was left to the Majles.

Transition to Opposition

Banisadr's followers were a minority in parliament, and thus in effect he became the leader of the opposition. After a long struggle between the president and the IRP, Mohammad-Ali Raja'i finally was sworn in as prime minister in August 1980. Raja'i was a self-made man, having risen from driver to car mechanic to high school mathematics teacher. He had started his political activism in the LMI in the early 1960s, but then became radicalized. A protégé of Ho. Bahonar, he had been imposed on Bazargan's PG as minister of education, and embarrassed the government by announcing the nationalization of all private schools before securing cabinet approval for such a drastic move. Although

---

[21]Lois Beck, *The Qashqa'i of Iran* (1986), pp. 324–26.

Bazargan lists him as an LMI member in his breakdown of the PG's membership,[22] Raja'i can best be characterized as an IRP fellow traveler who maintained cordial relations with Bazargan.

In an interview with *Mizan*, Bazargan defined the LMI's new role as opposition party. He made a distinction between his opposition to the Shah regime and his opposition in the new regime, as the latter enjoyed widespread popular support.[23] Shortly after this, Tavassoli, the last LMI figure in a prominent national position, tendered his resignation as mayor of Teheran, but it was not accepted until December 25 (Dey 4).

In late October 1980 Bazargan wrote a series of four articles in *Mizan* about the new repression and compared it with that of the Shah. He blamed leftists for having misused the freedom under the PG, as a result of which the IRP had obtained the pretext to oppress everybody. He complained about the climate of fear that was reigning over society, and the regime's meddling in people's private lives. He contrasted the tolerance of the Shi'ite Imams with the repression in the Islamic Republic, predicting that if a party misused the sacred realm of religion and the clergy under the pretext that religion and politics were inseparable, oppression would grow. He concluded with the old theme that justice and truth grew better in a climate of freedom, and that no enemy had ever been permanently silenced by repression.[24] As the LMI began to define itself as an opposition party in the autumn of 1980, it never attacked or even criticized Khomeini. At the end of the year, on the first anniversary of the Constitution, the LMI issued a declaration in which it called itself the first party to accept the leadership of Khomeini back in 1963.[25]

Toward the end of 1980 the left began to divide the religious movement into "reactionaries" and "liberals" in its analyses. "Liberal," of course, has a pejorative connotation in Leninist usage, and fundamentalists were quick to adopt the term in reference to the LMI. In response, Yazdi wrote two articles in *Mizan* in which he defined the liberalism of the LMI as being reformist rather than of the secularist tradition established by Voltaire.[26]

In the power struggle between Banisadr and the IRP, the LMI increasingly sided with the former, as Banisadr's experience began

[22]M. Bazargan, *Showra-ye enqelab va dowlat-e movaqqat* (The Revolutionary Council and the Provisional Government) (1983), p. 39.
[23]*Mizan*, September 11, 1980 (Shahriver 20, 1359), p. 2.
[24]Ibid., October 25–30, 1980 (Aban 3–8, 1359).
[25]Ibid., December 10, 1980 (Azar 19, 1359), p. 2.
[26]Ibid., December 20, 1980 (Azar 29, 1359), p. 2, and December 23, 1980 (Dey 2, 1359), p. 2.

more and more to resemble that of the PG. But the LMI always remained friendly with Raja'i. When Bazargan fell ill and had to be hospitalized in December 1980, the prime minister visited him (along with Iranians from all over the country who came in chartered busses), referred to himself as Bazargan's son and pupil, and prayed for Bazargan's recovery because the country would still need him.[27]

The LMI in Parliament

When the new Majles finally convened in early August, Yadollah Sahabi presided over its inaugural session as chairman by seniority. Bazargan became his deputy. The fact that Sahabi and Bazargan were the two oldest members of parliament reflects the generational shift that the revolution had brought about. Subsequently Ho. Hashemi Rafsanjani was elected speaker of parliament, a post he held until he became president in August 1989.

Very soon the distribution of power within the assembly began to change. The IRP began to attract more and more of the independents, and thus formed a solid majority. Opposing this majority was a minority made up of people sharing common roots in the National Movement, that is, LMI members and sympathizers (Mo'infar), Banisadr's personal followers, and isolated members of parliament such as Kazem Sami and Ezzatollah Sahabi; a few erstwhile Shariatmadari supporters who managed to get elected from Azerbaijan; and a few progressive mullas such as Ho. Mohammad-Javad Hojjati Kermani, Sheikh Ali Tehrani, and Ho. Golzadeh Ghafuri. The composition of this opposition changed depending on the issues, but at best it could muster about forty-five votes.

One of the first acts of the new Majles was to change its name from National Consultative Assembly to Islamic Consultative Assembly. The minority voted against, arguing that the Constitution of the Islamic Republic used the former name. This was the first official act deemphasizing Iranian nationhood, and one after the other all institutions whose names had "national" (*melli*) in them changed their names, much to the annoyance of the Mosaddeqists and secularists.

Then the credentials of several members of parliament were contested, most of them secular Nationalists. Madani and Qashqa'i refused to appear before the assembly to defend themselves against charges brought against them on the basis of documents found in the American embassy. The former went first into hiding and then into European exile, while the latter joined his tribe, staged a brief uprising, was caught, tried, and executed on October 8, 1982.[28] Qasemi was arrested,

---

[27]Ibid., December 3, 1980 (Azar 12, 1359), p. 1.
[28]Beck, *The Qashqa'i of Iran*, p. 337.

tried for alleged contacts with the United States and involvement in an aborted coup attempt by pro-Bakhtiar officers and condemned to lifelong prison.[29] Repression also hit the National Front as an organization: on July 20 (Tir 29) the headquarters of both the NF and the IP were attacked, just as Sanjabi was readying himself to give a speech in commemoration of July 21 (Tir 30), the day Mosaddeq had been brought back to power in 1952.[30] The credentials of the Jewish delegate were not accepted because of alleged Zionist connections. Mo'infar faced the credentials committee and won a parliamentary vote. Throughout these proceedings the opposition gave cautious encouragement to the NF deputies-elect, and both Y. Sahabi and Ho. Hojjati Kermani wrote to Madani urging him to come to Teheran and face his accusers. But the LMI deputies did not defend them publicly.

When the Raja'i government sought parliament's vote of confidence, the LMI legislators voted with Banisadr's supporters against Raja'i. They specified that they did not question the prime minister-designate's good intentions, but since they had doubts about his competence it was their Islamic duty to vote against him.

After that, the LMI in fact became an opposition in the Majles, although for a while its members participated fully in all committees. From the start the LMI deputies were attacked, insulted, and ridiculed by radicals in the chamber. Bazargan commented that he was disappointed to see that the Majles was not an assembly of insightful legislators and politicians, but a forum for arousing passions and shouting slogans. He added: "When we are the object of unfounded accusations, we prefer to keep quiet and suffer in silence rather than waste parliament's time with personal matters."[31]

After the first meeting of the Majles, deputies had drawn lots to determine the order in which they could make their first pre-agenda speeches. Nobody was really surprised when Bazargan "drew" one of the last lots, which meant that he got a chance to speak only on February 15, 1981 (Bahman 26, 1359). On that day Bazargan urged Raja'i, Banisadr, and Beheshti, whom Khomeini had named chief justice, to stop feuding. He commended the president for his services as commander of the army, but chided him for claiming more power than the Constitution granted him. He advised Banisadr to carry out his task with more dignity and spend less time on polemics and pamphleteering. But he reserved his sharpest criticism for Beheshti, whom he accused of interfering too much with political matters. At the

---

[29]For details see Bakhash, *Reign*, pp. 117–20.
[30]*Bamdad*, July 21, 1980 (Tir 30, 1359), p. 13.
[31]*Mizan*, September 11, 1980 (Shahrivar 20, 1359), p. 2.

same time he faulted the Raja'i government for its bad management.[32] He also attacked the IRP for trying to set up a one-party state, and added that to prevent such a development the LMI would step up its activities.[33]

When the struggle between the president and the IRP came to a head in the spring of 1981, Bazargan and the LMI continued urging both sides to be more moderate and to try to get along. Banisadr's supporters in the Majles went into hiding in early June; and it was Ali-Akbar Mo'infar who gave a last impassioned speech in defense of the president.

Party Activities

After the fall of the PG and the split caused by the defection of some younger members, it took some time for the LMI to reconstitute itself as a party. Yazdi was the main driving force behind the LMI's revival after the trauma of the hostage crisis. His good contacts with Khomeini's household and inner entourage saved the LMI from the wrath of the more radical elements. As in its first period, 1961–63, the LMI did not make any attempts to become a mass party, or actively to recruit members. The war with Iraq had broken out in September 1980, and after that any attempt to mobilize against the government was represented by the regime as an unpatriotic act. Therefore, the LMI continued its old method of trying to influence people's way of thinking, to gain what it calls hamfekr, "fellow thinkers," rather than members.

The LMI held its first congress after the departure of Ezzatollah Sahabi in July 1980 (Tir 1359). The congress, the LMI's third, ended with a resolution that clearly imitated revolutionary rhetoric. It defined the party's program as resting on three principles: Islam, the Constitution of the Islamic Republic, and the belief in the unity of all Muslims in the world, which necessitated struggling for the liberation of the world's disinherited.[34] A year and a half after the party first presented its new program, its third principle had changed from the Universal Declaration of Human Rights to the unity of all Muslims. This transition from universalism to particularism reflected the new irrelevance of international public opinion to Iranian politics, and the anti-LMI javv-sazi of the Islamic radicals which forced the LMI to bend backward to prove its loyalty to the Islamic Republic.

---

[32]Ibid., February 16, 1981 (Bahman 27, 1359), p. 10.

[33]Christian Science Monitor, March 3, 1981, p. 8.

[34]Mavaze'-e nehzat dar kongrehha-ye seyyom, chaharom, panjom (The Movement's positions in the Third, Fourth, and Fifth Congresses) (1983), p. 11. See Appendix B for a partial translation of the text.

At first the party's activities were low key, centering on talks and seminars at the party's headquarters on Motahhari (Takht-e Tavus) Avenue in Teheran's north in a building owned by Sabbaghian. On these occasions the leaders would speak to party members and sympathizers. After the shock of the PG's demise subsided, Bazargan began his counterattack by defending his record as prime minister and criticizing the methods and policies of the fundamentalists.

On February 24, 1981 (Esfand 5, 1359), the party held its first and last public meeting. Held at the Amjadieh Stadium, it attracted 40,000 people and was billed as a meeting of "the four Teheran deputies." Bazargan, Y. Sahabi, Yazdi, and Sabbaghian addressed the crowd, renewed their allegiance to Mosaddeq, and firmly criticized the government. Yazdi called the IRP's methods "Stalinist." The authorities cooperated by letting regular police handle security instead of the Pasdaran. The success of this meeting raised the hopes of the religious moderates, and *Mizan* proclaimed that the "spell had been broken." The next day the four LMI members of parliament paid a visit to Khomeini, who told them that he suffered from the prevailing lack of unity. Khomeini's brother, Ay. Pasandideh, by contrast, sent a supportive telegram.[35]

On March 5 (Esfand 14) the LMI, invited by President Banisadr, participated in rallies at Teheran University and in Isfahan to commemorate the anniversary of Mosaddeq's death. *Hezbollahi*s appeared on the scene and started roughing up participants when Banisadr began to speak, but for the first time the president's supporters (mainly Mojahedin) fought back. Later the IRP's party organ criticized the LMI for its participation in the meetings.[36] (Bazargan had sat behind Banisadr on the podium.) Nevertheless, when Khomeini made a final effort to reconcile Banisadr and the government by setting up a commission on March 15, Bazargan joined it as mediator.

While the LMI tried to counter the growing anti-Mosaddeq trend in the Islamic Republic, it also strove to maintain its Islamic legitimacy by participating in all marches organized by the regime, be it for religious occasions or the war with Iraq. The party's statements increasingly included Qoranic references.

In the spring of 1981 repression began to hit the LMI. On April 6 the editor of *Mizan*, Reza Sadr, was arrested. In early May Bazargan's weekly television program "Return to the Qoran," which he had aired since December 10, 1980, was canceled.[37] When the party planned to celebrate publicly its twentieth anniversary in mid-May 1981 authorities refused to grant the necessary permission; the LMI instead held a

[35]*Mizan*, February 25, 1981 (Esfand 6, 1359), p. 4.

[36]Ibid., March 8, 1981 (Esfand 17, 1359), p. 10.

[37]Ibid., May 10, 1981 (Ordibehesht 20, 1360), p. 2.

private meeting at the tomb of Taleqani on May 14.[38] The death of Bazargan's brother a few days later gave the LMI an opportunity to demonstrate popular support for Bazargan by publishing hundreds of messages of condolence, including statements by Khomeini and Beheshti, in successive issues of *Mizan*.

Education has always been a high priority for the LMI, and in May 1981 it announced that it would organize three-month afternoon courses at its headquarters for sympathizers and "fellow thinkers." Classes were held on the following subjects:[39]

1. Lessons from the Qoran
2. Readings in the *Nahj ul-Balaghah*
3. History of Early Islam
4. The Bases of Iran's Islamic Revolution
5. Iranian Social and Political History of the Last 200 Years
6. Political Ideologies and Terminologies
7. History of Revolutions
8. Comparative Economics

Mizan

The LMI and the PG had always complained about their insufficient access to the press. For a few months in the summer and autumn of 1980 Yazdi had been given the editorship of *Keyhan*, one of the two major daily newspapers, but it did not become an official organ of the LMI. With the transition and the elections behind them, LMI leaders began publishing their own daily newspaper, *Mizan* (Balance),[40] on September 7, 1980 (Shahrivar 16, 1359). Its editor was Reza Sadr.

The first editorial claimed that the newspaper was not the organ of the LMI, but that it would be open to all Islamic groups. And *Mizan* did publish articles by progressive clerics, former LMI figures, and even an occasional communiqué from the Mojahedin. After only a few issues the paper came under attack from both the fundamentalist press and the Tudeh organ *Mardom*. The regime at that point tolerated Tudeh activities to a considerable degree, and the party was allowed to print and distribute its organ freely. This tolerance worried the LMI, and anti-*Mardom* polemics became a recurrent theme in *Mizan*.

The first violent attacks on *Mizan* came on November 18 (Aban 27) when *hezbollahi* goons ransacked the editorial offices. It is said that on that occasion Khomeini himself ordered the newspaper to be allowed to reappear.

[38]Ibid., May 16, 1981 (Ordibehesht 26, 1360), p. 1.
[39]Ibid., May 11, 1981 (Ordibehesht 21, 1360), p. 1.
[40]The first issue explained that the newspaper wished to be neither left wing nor right wing, but to strike a balance. Yet another neithernorism.

On April 6, 1981, Reza Sadr, the editor of *Mizan*, was arrested and his newspaper closed down. The official reason was that it had engaged in "disrupting the internal security, slander, and insults," charges that stemmed from a *Mizan* editorial that had warned about communist infiltration in the radio and television networks.[41] One week after this incident Bazargan published an appeal in *Enqelab-e Eslami*, Banisadr's newspaper, asking for donations to help pay for the bail. The president's paper joined the campaign in defense of *Mizan*, and the public responded enthusiastically. People lined up at bank counters and contributed five times more than Bazargan had asked for. On April 19 a court ordered the reappearance of *Mizan*, which began publishing the next day. It ceased publication shortly thereafter, however, and was officially banned on June 7.

In late spring of 1981 the conflict between Banisadr, now openly supported by the Mojahedin, and the IRP reached its peak. Banisadr was hampered by the heterogeneity of the coalition supporting him: leftists, moderates, intellectuals, conservative ulema, and certain bazaaris, groups that mistrusted each other. In the person of Banisadr, the modern segment had found a new leader around whom it could rally, and the president increasingly turned to it for support. At this point Khomeini abandoned his neutrality and came out against him. In June matters came to a head: on June 10 the Mojahedin called for a mass meeting, which ended in fighting. On June 15 the National Front made a last stand and called for a demonstration. The meeting never got under way, *hezbollahi* counterdemonstrators having arrived on the scene first. Shortly before it was scheduled to begin, Khomeini went on the radio, charged the NF with apostasy, and called on the LMI to disassociate itself publicly from the meeting. Bazargan immediately obliged.

The LMI thus turned its back on its secular allies of more than two decades, and chose to remain under Khomeini's umbrella. It acted on the principle, enunciated by Yazdi a year and a half earlier, that only association with the Imam conferred legitimacy.[42] Faced with the last liberal effort to stem the tide of a new dictatorship, the LMI sided with the latter. Whether this choice was *right* is an open question; it remains a fact that it allowed the party to survive.

Shortly after these events the LMI lost one of its most important figures. On June 21, Mostafa Chamran, who had been organizing anti-Iraqi guerrilla bands in Kurdistan, was killed at the front. There were rumors that he had been killed by the regime because he had acted as liaison between Banisadr and the army. An estimated 200,000

---

[41]Bill Barker, "Iranian Moderates, Mullahs Clash over Bazargan's Paper," in *Christian Science Monitor*, April 9, 1981, p. 10.

[42]*The Iranian*, December 15, 1979 (Azar 24, 1358), p. 10.

people attended his funeral in Teheran, and it is a sign of the LMI's insufficient sense of publicity that his longtime affiliation with the party went largely unnoticed.

The first elected president of the Islamic Republic was deposed by the Majles on June 21, 1981. On June 28, 1981 (Tir 6, 1359), an explosion at the headquarters of the IRP killed the top leadership of the party, including Beheshti. After Banisadr's ouster Raja'i became president in an election in which the other candidates urged voters to vote for Raja'i. Two months later, on August 30 (Shahrivar 8) a second explosion killed Raja'i and his prime minister, Ho. Bahonar. The deaths of Beheshti and Raja'i affected the relationship between the LMI and the regime in a way similar to what the death of the Mojahedin founders had meant for that organization's links with the LMI. Although political opponents, Bazargan and Beheshti had known each other for a long time. A few months before his death Beheshti said about Bazargan: "I have known him for twenty years, he is a tremendous force. If I have any criticism of him, it is fraternal."[43] Beheshti's death brought younger fundamentalists to the foreground who had no respect for Bazargan whatsoever, which meant that repression would hit the LMI harder in the years to come. Raja'i was replaced by Ho. Ali Khameneh'i, while Bahonar was succeeded first by Ho. Mahdavi Kani and then by Mir Hosein Musavi, who retained his position until the abolition of the post of prime minister in August 1989.

The LMI since 1981

In the summer of 1981 repression intensified in Iran. The Mojahedin and allied leftist groups attempted an armed uprising, and were thoroughly crushed by the regime. Thousands of their militants and sympathizers died at the hands of the security forces in the second half of 1981. In 1982 there was another attempt to oust the regime, this time involving Sadeq Qotbzadeh, who had the tacit support of Ay. Shariatmadari.[44] Qotbzadeh was executed; Shariatmadari, in an unprecedented step, was stripped of his title of *marja'*. The LMI had nothing to do with the plot, and condemned the whole enterprise. Its post-1979 policy of distancing itself from Ay. Shariatmadari now paid off.

In spite of the increased repression in the summer, on August 28 (Shahrivar 6) the Iranian parliament passed a law regulating the activi-

---

[43]*Mizan*, February 19, 1982 (Bahman 30, 1359), p. 2.

[44]For details on this plot see Carole Jerome, *The Man in the Mirror: A True Inside Story of Revolution, Love and Treachery in Iran* (1987), pp. 270–96.

ties of political parties and sent it to the executive branch, but by the summer of 1989 the LMI still had not received official recognition as a political party under the stipulation of this law. The legal uncertainty surrounding the activities of political parties did not prevent the LMI from holding its fourth congress in November 1981, a congress that was dedicated to the memory of Chamran. The resolution issued by the LMI at the congress unambiguously accepted Khomeini's leadership of the country, but on the whole emphasized foreign policy.[45] Two more congresses were held, in March 1983 and March 1984. Oppositional activity became even more difficult than in 1980 and early 1981. Moreover, the LMI lost direct contact with Khomeini after they disagreed with the institutionalization of the law of the talion (*qesas*).

The LMI and the Institutions of the Islamic Republic

After the rout of Banisadr's forces the moderate minority in the Majles had dwindled to a handful: the five LMI deputies, Mo'infar, and Sami. Hasan Habibi, who had been very close to the LMI until 1980, defected to the fundamentalists (and was rewarded with the Ministry of Justice in 1984), as did Mohammad-Javad Raja'ian, the deputy from Zanjan. Ezzatollah Sahabi remained neutral, on the theory that the regime was, if nothing else, anti-imperialist and that it was therefore wrong to weaken it.

The atmosphere in parliament became even more hostile to Bazargan and his friends. The LMI deputies' speeches were interrupted and booed by hecklers, who went so far as to attack the deputies physically, including octogenarian Yadollah Sahabi.[46] On October 7, 1981 (Mehr 15, 1359), Bazargan condemned the daily killings in a speech in parliament that was broadcast live, declaring that those "acts of revenge by the government [would] turn the country into an ocean of blood."[47] This speech resulted in efforts to have the "liberals" expelled from the chamber. Perhaps fearing for their safety, they stayed away voluntarily.

In late 1981 the fundamentalists became so violent that some relative moderates within the regime began to feel threatened. Sometime in December the speaker of parliament, Rafsanjani, tried to visit his imprisoned son-in-law (a son of Ay. Lahuti, the deputy from Rasht who died in prison a bit later), but was prevented from seeing him. To

---

[45]*Mavaze'*, pp. 22–34.

[46]At one point, after even Mohammad-Ali Raja'i's *chador*-clad widow had attacked him in a speech in parliament, Bazargan quoted a Persian verse: "They s—— upon me all but one / The bleeding-bottomed raven's son."

[47]*New York Times*, October 8, 1981, p. 14.

stem the rise of the most radical elements, Rafsanjani proposed an alliance to Bazargan and to Ay. Mohammad-Reza Mahdavi Kani, the overseer of the *komiteh*s and a relative moderate. Subsequently Bazargan and his colleagues returned to the Majles in early January 1982, and there were no more efforts to expel them.[48] After their experience in the PG, however, the LMI members were suspicious of the political clergy, and nothing came of that alliance. As Rafsanjani gradually brought the most radical elements of the IRP under control, he no longer needed the LMI.

The LMI had no newspaper, its activities in the Majles were largely ignored by the official press, and the party came under constant attack during the Friday congregational prayers all over the country. It could only resort to publishing and distributing pamphlets, books, declarations, and open letters to the various turbaned dignitaries of the regime. Bazargan and others gave talks at party headquarters and at the Islamic Association of Engineers, during which they justified the PG's record, criticized the government from an Islamic viewpoint, and attempted to formulate alternatives. Often these meetings would be interrupted by *hezbollahi* thugs, after which, in a recurring pattern, the LMI would call Ay. Mahdavi Kani who would dispatch *komiteh* forces to escort the LMI leaders safely out of the premises while arresting none of the assailants.

New legislative elections had to be held in April 1984. In his last speech in parliament, on August 27, 1983 (Mordad 20, 1362), Bazargan said that it was in the interest of Islam and of the Islamic Republic that there be no pseudo-elections as during the Shah period. If the leaders of Iran deemed electoral competition harmful in times of war, they should hold a plebiscite and ask for the citizens' permission to extend the life of the current parliament or even to rule the country by a new council of the revolution under the general authority of *velayat-e faqih*.

In October, President Ali Khameneh'i said in a newspaper interview that the Iranian elections would be totally free, but that the LMI would not be represented in the new parliament, as nobody would vote for those who are outside the Imam's line. On the basis of Khameneh'i's promise, the LMI announced that it would organize a seminar in its headquarters on the topic of free elections on October 28, 1983 (Aban 6, 1362). But when the authorities refused permission, the LMI canceled the seminar. Yet on that day *hezbollahi*s attacked the party headquarters. When a second seminar was also refused permission by the authorities, the LMI declared that it would boycott the forthcoming elections.

[48]Ralph Joseph, "Iranian Politicians Join Ranks to Curb Fundamentalist Power," in *Christian Science Monitor*, January 11, p. 3.

In the Majles, when on November 1 Hashem Sabbaghian complained about the incidents in a speech, other deputies dragged him away from the rostrum and beat him up.

On May 15, 1984 (Ordibehesht 25, 1363), the LMI published a declaration concerning the elections. It noted that many people had voted for fear of reprisals, and that in general the enthusiasm of the electorate had been less than in 1980. Khomeini had forbidden the Teheran branch of the IRP and the clergy of Teheran and Qum to nominate candidates for provincial seats, as a result of which, the LMI noted, the electoral competition had been somewhat keener outside Teheran: many deputies were not reelected. In Shiraz and Isfahan the election results were invalidated by the government, which alleged rigging by the local authorities.

After the legislative elections of April 1984, the mandate of President Khameneh'i came to a close in the summer of 1985. In November 1984 (Aban 1363) an LMI declaration, "What Is to Be Done," said that a violent minority had cowed the population into submission, and that the people should reassert their sovereignty by participating massively in the election. On February 11, 1985 (Bahman 22, 1363), the LMI held a meeting to commemorate the Islamic revolution at its headquarters. On that occasion, the prosecutor general of Teheran, Mir-Emadi, personally oversaw a *hezbollahi* attack on the building, during which the attackers destroyed furniture and office equipment, took all the cash they could find, and roughed up those present. To punish the LMI for arousing the ire of the "party of God," authorities closed down the headquarters altogether.[49]

Shortly before the presidential elections, relative moderates in the regime had obtained permission for the LMI to reopen its headquarters on Motahhari Avenue. There were some within the regime who wanted the LMI to present a candidate, perhaps to defuse mounting dissatisfaction.

There were long discussions within the LMI as to the advisability of participating in the elections. Yazdi was against, Bazargan for. In the end Bazargan, after some hesitation, registered his candidacy at the Ministry of the Interior. However, the Council of Guardians, which in addition to its veto-power over anti-constitutional and anti-Islamic legislation also screens presidential candidates, rejected Bazargan's candidacy together with forty-seven others, arguing that Bazargan did not believe in *velayat-e faqih*.[50] Only three candidates were given the

---

[49]For a good summary of the LMI's role in Iranian politics after the revolution see Jean Guéyras, "Le Mouvement de libération de l'Iran demeure la dernière opposition légale au régime," *Le Monde*, May 2, 1985, p. 4.

[50]*Keyhan*, August 13, 1985 (Mordad 22, 1364).

green light, all belonging to the economically conservative wing of the IRP. The LMI presented the rejection as proof that freedom did not exist in Iran and called for a boycott of the election.[51]

On November 26, 1985 (Azar 5, 1364), a party statement analyzed the situation. It argued that if things had gone wrong after the revolution, Iranians could blame only themselves and their undemocratic political culture, rather than the British or the Russians. It noted that the LMI had tried to lead popular opposition against the government but that the people by and large had failed to respond favorably to the LMI's invitation, even though the participation rate at the presidential election was lower than on previous occasions.

At this point the LMI reevaluated its strategy and after much internal discussion decided that, mass action having failed, the regime could be weakened only if its legitimacy in the eyes of the Muslim masses were undermined. The long statements in opposition to the war are part of this strategy, and will be discussed later.

The LMI had another chance to question the way the institutions of the Islamic Republic were developing, when on November 10, 1987 (Aban 19, 1366), Khomeini gave a speech in which he considerably expanded the powers of the executive under Islam. Khomeini stated that all prophets had come to establish a just government, and that therefore government was a quintessential part of the religious authorities: if Jesus had not come to reform society, he would not have been crucified.

On December 1, 1987 (Azar 10, 1366), the LMI replied to Khomeini's statements. It noted that the party accepted the primacy of religion and of the Islamic ideology over politics, but that it did not accept the merger of the religious institution with the state, as the two were separate entities. It also gainsaid Khomeini on the political mission of prophets, stating that not all prophets had become rulers (Noah, Abraham, Jesus, Jethro), and that the others (Solomon, Moses, Muhammad) had become rulers because of the needs of their communities, and that their rulership had not been part of their divine mission. It also noted that according to Muslim traditions, Jesus had not been crucified but had ascended to heaven.

In early 1988 the Iranian regime elaborated on Khomeini's statements and declared the validity of *velayat-e motlaqeh-ye faqih*, the absolute rule of the jurisprudent, which in effect gave the government under the *faqih* the authority to bend Islamic tenets in the interest of the common good. In its reaction of January 6, 1988 (Dey 16, 1366), the LMI stated

---

[51]See *Le Monde*, July 31, 1985, p. 4.

that the conferral of absolute powers to the government or to the *faqih* was contrary to Abrahamic monotheism, to Islam, and to the Constitution, and therefore invalid and illegal.

Beginning in the autumn of 1988, there was talk in Teheran about amending the Constitution so as to streamline the functioning of the executive branch. In the spring of 1989, Khomeini appointed a council of twenty-five men to propose changes that would then be submitted for approval by the population in a plebiscite. In a declaration published June 2 (Khordad 12, 1368), the LMI stated that though changing the Constitution was desirable, only a constitutional assembly could do so, and that the council of twenty-five had no legal or constitutional mandate to propose any changes. The LMI proposed abolishing the position of religious leader, since it had been tailor-made for Khomeini and nobody would be able to inherit Khomeini's role as revolutionary leader. The LMI also opposed a presidentialization of the regime, suggesting that the position of prime minister be retained.

The LMI and the Iran-Iraq War

As we saw in the previous chapter, the Provisional Government had tried to keep peace with Iraq. After the Iraqi attack in 1980, however, the LMI loyally supported Iran's war effort. After the expulsion of Iraqi troops from Iranian territory in 1982, however, the LMI made the ending of the war a major axis of its activity. On May 26, 1983 (Khordad 5, 1362), Yadollah Sahabi gave a speech in parliament, in which he called on the government to provide more information on its conduct of the war to the people or at least to parliament. In March 1984 the LMI sent a personal letter regarding the war to Khomeini but was rebuked by him.[52]

In the summer of 1984 the LMI published its first major study on the war, but distribution on a wide scale was prevented by the Ministry of Islamic Guidance. The LMI study maintained that the reconquest of Khorramshahr had had a tremendous political and psychological effect and that Arab countries had offered both peace and reparations at that point: Iran should have seized the opportunity then. The text also revealed that the LMI had privately warned Ho. Hashemi Rafsanjani against pursuing the Iranian offensive beyond Iranian territory because Iran was not equipped for conventional warfare, and if the offensive failed, Iran might have to accept peace on unfavorable terms. But the Speaker of Parliament had responded that Khomeini himself insisted

---

[52]*Towzihati piramun-e mozakereh, atash-bas, solh* (Some explanations regarding negotiations, a truce, and peace) (1985), p. 16.

on the seizure of Basrah.[53] On the ideological side, the LMI wrote that the Qoran not only forbade an aggressive war against unbelievers but even urged moderation in dealing with them. All prophets (including Muhammad) had always waged defensive wars, in support of which assertion both the Qoran and the Jewish bible are quoted.[54]

Concerning the export of the Islamic revolution to Iraq, the document stated that the revolution in Iran had been preceded by forty years of preparatory work in the universities, and that in Iraq the situation was not ripe for a revolution. Moreover, the probability of a popular uprising against Saddam Husein was very low.[55]

In December 1985 the LMI claimed that the document (discussed earlier) had forced the regime to change its rhetoric: because it had no answer to the assertion that an offensive war is un-Islamic, the regime now emphasized its duty to fight evil wherever it was, even beyond Iran's borders.[56] To this argument, the LMI replied that the rationale of fighting against evil until the bitter end was un-Islamic. Like all monotheistic religions, Islam believed in the devil, whom God had authorized to spread corruption in the world. As long as the world existed, therefore, there would be evil and corruption in it, and any attempt to end that state of affairs is by definition doomed to failure.[57]

In September 1986, the LMI published its strongest attack on the war policy of the regime, this time in the form of an open letter to Khomeini himself.[58] The letter stated that the outright and unconditional rejection of peace proposals and negotiations was contrary to God's will, the traditions of the Prophet, and the record of the Imams. It rejected the popular notion that the Third Imam, Husein, had risen in rebellion against the caliph, and averred that until the very end he had tried to avoid conflict.[59] It went on to quote *feqh* sources to the effect that during the occultation of the Twelfth Imam all offensive wars were unlawful. The document then points out that the Prophet had consulted on all political and war-related matters, in spite of his revelations and his innocence. The letter criticized Khomeini for not following that example, and asked him whether he thought that *velayat-e faqih* was above prophethood. It went so far as to ask Khomeini how he would respond to these charges on Judgment Day.[60]

---

[53]*Tahlili piramun-e jang va solh* (An analysis of war and peace) (1984), pp. 51, 52, 54, and 60.

[54]Ibid., pp. 14 and 23.

[55]Ibid., pp. 37–38, and 61.

[56]*Payan-e adelaneh-ye jang-e bi-payan* (The end of the interminable war) (1985), pp. 5–6.

[57]Ibid., p. 9.

[58]*Payam-e nehzat-e azadi beh rahbar-e enqelab-e eslami-ye Iran* (A message of the Liberation Movement to the leader of the Islamic Revolution of Iran) (1986).

[59]Ibid., pp. 13 and 8–9.

[60]Ibid., pp. 14–16.

When the "war of the cities" broke out in February 1988 and Teheran was subjected to daily bombardments, Bazargan sent two telegrams to Khomeini, asking him to receive an LMI delegation to discuss the recent turn of events. Khomeini did not reply, so Bazargan sent him another open letter, which reiterated the LMI's arguments against the war and chided Khomeini for being unreceptive to the advice of others.[61] After the Iranian government's acceptance of the U.N. Security Council's Resolution 598, which called for a cease-fire, the LMI issued a statement on July 23, 1988 (Tir 1, 1367), in which it noted that the decision had been taken during Khomeini's lifetime and with his approval, and warned the government to remain vigilant.

Its principled opposition to the war has earned the LMI new sympathy. Until 1985, the LMI had always acknowledged the leadership of Khomeini while blaming all ills on the government, rather like the National Front's policy vis-à-vis the Shah before 1963. After 1986, it directed its criticism to Khomeini personally, hoping to convince both the Muslim believers who are the social bases of the regime and the traditional ulema of the illegitimacy of the type of rule instituted under the Islamic Republic.

The LMI and the Opposition in Exile

Since the revolution, many Iranian politicians and political groupings have fled the country to work for the overthrow of the fundamentalist regime from abroad. The usual pattern is that those who broke with the revolution at one point accuse those who broke before them of being reactionaries, and in turn accuse those who broke after them of having collaborated with the Khomeini regime. Since the LMI still operates inside Iran, most exiled opposition groups have little sympathy for it. The LMI publicly denounced all foreign-based attempts to overthrow the regime, arguing that if successful such action would reintroduce foreign influence into Iranian politics. Two moderate opposition groups outside Iran, however, view the LMI with sympathy and regularly publish its declarations; these are the *Jebheh* newspaper in London, published by former National Front activists, and Abolhasan Banisadr's Paris-based newspaper *Enqelab-e Eslami dar Hejrat*. Since his break with the Mojahedin in 1984 Banisadr has come to view Bazargan and the LMI much more favorably.

Although it played an important part in the exiled opposition against the Shah, the LMI has refused to take that option under the Islamic Republic. The reason is that its leaders are convinced of the public

---

[61] *Hoshdar piramun-e tadavom-e jang-e khanemansuz* (A warning concerning the continuation of the destructive war) (1988).

support that the Islamic regime still enjoys in Iran, and therefore prefer to work, if at all possible, within the institutions. In spite of all the harassment to which they are subjected, the leaders of the LMI have enjoyed more freedom of action than they had under most of the Shah's dictatorship.

Bazargan has taken only one trip abroad after his fateful journey to Algiers in 1979. In September 1985 he attended the Twenty-Third Congress of German Orientalists in Würzburg, where he read a paper in French: "The Quantification of Qoranic Verses as a New Criterion for Establishing the Chronology of the Qoran." Mojahedin activists were present; they asked him pointedly political questions, and then insulted and roughed him up. Their newspaper later claimed that Mas'ud Rajavi had promised Bazargan logistic help if he joined the exiled opposition.[62] Bazargan, however, in a letter dated September 18, 1985 (Shahrivar 27, 1364), and written during the trip, asked all exiled Iranians to return to Iran, to contribute to the establishment of freedom and democracy.

Society for the Defense of Freedom and the Sovereignty of the Iranian People

In March 1986 the LMI came to the conclusion that those Nationalists who did not share its Islamic ideology had to be involved in its struggle. Relations with those secular members of the Provisional Government who had not left Iran were never broken, and the result of these contacts was the establishment of the Society for the Defense of Freedom and the Sovereignty of the Iranian People (SDFSIP). Begun in March 1986, it includes on its Central Council figures such as Ali Ardalan (former minister of the economy under the PG), Rahim Abedi, Mahmud Manian, and Naser Minachi. It had a total membership of about eighty men and women.[63]

The society's aims are, according to its program, "to struggle against despotism, for political and social freedom, and for the equality of all before the law, and to defend Iran's honor in world public opinion." The division of labor between the SDFSIP and the LMI is therefore that the former limits its activities to the political realm, whereas the latter engages in ideological work too.

In March 1988 the society called for a boycott of the elections to the third Majles, to be held in April 1988, after the LMI was not allowed to run its own candidates. On May 28 (Khordad 9), the revolutionary prosecutor of Teheran had four members of the LMI (including

---

[62]Information on this trip is based on Ahmad Mahrad's account in *Hannoversche Studien über den Mittleren Osten, 1986* (1986), pp. 317–20.
[63]Rahim Abedi, personal interview, May 1989, Boston.

Mohammad Tavassoli and Hashem Sabbaghian) and four members of the SDFSIP (including Ali Ardalan) arrested. The offices of the two organizations were occupied. The LMI's and the SDFSIP's protests did not achieve anything, but the arrested men were released in February 1989, when the regime declared an amnesty to celebrate the tenth anniversary of the Islamic revolution. In March hard-liners in the regime multiplied their attacks on the LMI, and when they succeeded in getting Khomeini to oust Ay. Montazeri from his position as Khomeini's successor, one of the reasons they gave was Montazeri's close contacts with the "liberals."

Khomeini's death on June 3, 1989 did not portend any immediate changes in the LMI's fortunes. The party issued a terse statement that extended its condolences to the relatives, friends, and followers of the deceased, and asked God to grant him mercy and forgiveness. The statement called Khomeini a man whom Iranians had chosen in the darkest moments of imperial despotism to lead them toward freedom, independence, and the rule of Islamic values, and it expressed the hope that the experience of the Islamic revolution would in the future be submitted to wide-ranging evaluation, so that the world might learn from it.[64]

After the death of Khomeini, the Assembly of Experts quickly named President Ail Khameneh'i as his successor. Not being a *marja'*, Khameneh'i did not qualify for the position under the provisions of the 1979 Constitution; but the council of twenty-five proposed to do away with that precondition while simultaneously strengthening the powers of the religious leader. It also suggested the abolition of the post of prime minister. The government announced that on July 2, 1989 (Mordad 6, 1368) Iranians would be asked both to elect a new president and to ratify the proposed constitutional changes. The LMI issued statements criticizing both the contents of the changes and the ways they were implemented, and in effect called for a boycott of both the presidential election and the plebiscite. To nobody's surprise, the constitutional changes were approved and Ali-Akbar Hashemi Rafsanjani was elected president.

Since the elections of 1984 and 1985 the LMI has expanded its activities considerably. The party can now count on a network of sympathizers in the provinces who reprint and distribute its tracts and pamphlets. Moreover, some NF figures who remained in Iran after the outlawing of their movement (H. Manian, Ali Ardalan, Shamseddin Amir-Ala'i) are now cooperating with the party. Ezzatollah Sahabi, whom the regime did not reward with a parliamentary seat for his distancing

---

[64]*Ettela'iyeh-ye nehzat-e azadi-ye Iran be monasebat-e rehlat-e rahbar-e enqelab* (LMI statement on the occasion of the passing away of the leader of the revolution) (1989).

himself from the LMI, has made some moves toward a rapprochement, although he has not rejoined the party.

It is too early to evaluate the role of the LMI as opposition under the Islamic Republic. That regime's Constitution does not provide for a one-party state, thus there is legal ground for the existence of an opposition party. As under the Shah, the LMI has tried to exploit every single legal possibility for its benefit, always stressing that it acts within the bounds of the law. This has the advantage that to silence it, the government has to disregard its own legality.

Given the regime's indifference to its own Constitution and laws in other domains, why has the LMI been tolerated so far? Probably for a combination of reasons. The leaders of the LMI were, after all, the pioneers of the Islamic revival in Iran, and therefore have a genuine constituency in the population. Also, they have maintained courteous relations with some members of the clergy, including Ay. Mahdavi Kani and, more important, Ay. Montazeri, who was Khomeini's designated successor until March 1989, when the Imam dismissed him. Relations with Khomeini himself were maintained indirectly through his brother, Ay. Pasandideh, whose son Reza Pasandideh cooperates with the LMI. Inside the government, many young fundamentalists are former students of Bazargan and still respect him. It is said that pragmatists and radicals inside the government disagree on how to treat Bazargan and the LMI. These contacts have created a certain immunity for Bazargan and his friends.

The party's appeal in the population is very difficult to gauge. As the only legal opposition in Iran after the rout of Banisadr in 1981 and the suppression of the Tudeh in 1983, the LMI's statements and pamphlets are the only oppositional literature available, and therefore widely read and distributed in Iran. When in 1984 Bazargan wrote his account of the revolution,[65] the book sold 100,000 copies, and that in a country where the initial printing of a book is at most 5,000 copies.

But a key sector of the Iranian population, the demoralized remnants of the modern segment, do not forgive Bazargan for having cooperated with Khomeini at the beginning of the revolution. As for the left, its various factions opposed Bazargan's gradualist approach under the Shah, and they have nothing good to say about him now. Whether the LMI has been able to woo back at least some of those Iranians who are inclined toward Islamic fundamentalism but who are disappointed with the regime's record is difficult to tell. It is impossible to know to what extent Iran's triumphant traditional segment considers people like Bazargan and Yazdi as belonging to its collective "us" or to the modern, defeated segment, "them."

[65]M. Bazargan, *Enqelab-e eslami da do harekat* (The Islamic Revolution in two movements) (1984).

Conclusion

More than any other group, the LMI exemplifies the gradual displacement of secularism and the rise of religion in the Iranian polity: one only has to read the party's programs of 1961 and 1980 in succession to get a sense of this development (see Appendices A and B). The founders of the LMI played a leading part in the reintroduction of religion into Iranian politics. Before 1953, their activities were mainly social and religious, as they tried to present an alternative to Marxism to Iranian youth. Between 1953 and 1963 they were active on two fronts: politically they acted as the radical spearhead of the National Movement, and religiously they continued their work as modernists. The two realms remained separate, however, for while their political activism was to some extent motivated by their faith, it was directed toward the mostly secular goals of the National Movement. With the White Revolution of January 1963 all open oppositional activity ceased in Iran, and the leaders of the LMI went to prison. Shortly thereafter the party, or what was left of it, underwent a change: the years 1963–78 saw the gradual elaboration of an ideology explicitly based on Islam. But others were better at this than Bazargan and his friends: in June 1963 Ay. Khomeini raised the banner of revolt and his movement displaced the Nationalists as the main opposition against the Shah. Having been active on behalf of religion since the 1940s, Bazargan and the LMI resented Khomeini's claim that the Islamic movement in Iran started in 1963.[1]

This raises the question of the problematic relationship between the

---

[1]Mehdi Bazargan, *Enqelab-e eslami dar do harekat* (The Islamic Revolution in two movements) (1984), pp. 116–17.

religious modernists and the ulema. Bazargan's and Taleqani's work in the Islamic associations before 1953 stemmed, at least in part, from their dissatisfaction with the official clergy, whose conservatism drove away the youth. This mistrust of the ulema went so far that when Ay. Kashani broke with Mosaddeq in 1953, Bazargan and Taleqani remained loyal to Mosaddeq. The ulema's cordial welcome to the Shah after his return to power in 1953 confirmed their suspicions: the NRM's 1954 letter to Ay. Borujerdi quite bluntly chides him for his support of the Shah. Ay. Khomeini's revolt of 1963 seemed to represent a turning point, and henceforth the modernists, especially their exiled wing, the LMI(a), cooperated closely with Khomeini in a united Islamic movement. This cooperation culminated in the Provisional Government, in which the modernists and the fundamentalists shared power. But the clerical domination over the country since 1981 has once again brought out the anticlericalism of the modernists. While in the 1950s they complained that the clergy did not take enough interest in politics, they now attack it for monopolizing power. Therefore the same people whom some considered religious fanatics in 1953 are now moderates. In 1953–63 they advocated a bigger role for religion in society, whereas now they warn against religious dogmatism and intolerance.

In a way Bazargan and his friends bear a direct responsibility for the emergence of a quasi-theocracy in the last third of the twentieth century. Without their efforts, perhaps Khomeini would not have been able to adopt a style that could bring very different elements in Iranian society together. But just as J. G. Herder cannot be held responsible for the ravages of Nazism, it would be unfair to blame Bazargan and his friends of the LMI for the calamities that have befallen Iran as a result of the Islamic revolution.

The history of the LMI also illustrates the dilemmas facing moderates in polarized societies. Trying to bridge gaps, they end marginalized. Worse, they may be left without any allies, as each side in the conflict criticizes them for their lack of firmness in facing the opposite side. The LMI began as a religiously oriented component of the National Movement, but throughout its life disagreements with the secular elements in the National Front over the proper place of religion in society and politics hampered the effectiveness of the Nationalists. When the LMI leaders were tried in 1963 after the secular Mosaddeqists were freed, the latter did not protest. When the Islamic regime silenced the NF, the LMI did not move.

Politically, the LMI played a pivotal role in both liberalization attempts of the Shah. Both of them failed: in 1963 the Shah reconsolidated his regime, in 1979 he was driven out of the country and lived to witness the collapse of one of the world's oldest monarchies. The different outcomes of the two attempted liberalizations illustrate the internal dynamics of regime changes and crises of participation in regimes with sultanistic tendencies, as analyzed in chapter 1.

In periods of acute crisis institutions crumble and therefore personalities make a great difference. In 1960–63 the Shah had enjoyed personal power for a number of years and was in his prime; by 1977 he was terminally ill and no longer able to act decisively and coherently. In the early 1960s the Shah did not have a strong adversary who could unite the opposition behind him, in 1977–79 the charismatic figure of Ay. Khomeini united all the opposition behind him. Secular oppositional forces in Iran had no comparable leader, which partly explains their rapid slide into irrelevance after the revolution. Bazargan was a reluctant politician in both episodes, more interested in convincing others intellectually than in seizing the initiative and becoming a true leader. Besides, in both cases Bazargan had the thankless task of having to operate under the shadow of charismatic leaders who could not easily be gainsaid: Mosaddeq in 1960–63, and Khomeini in 1977–79.

One level below the leaders, one must compare the differences within the contending forces in 1960–63 as opposed to 1977–79. The Shah regime of the early 1960s was less arbitrary, less sultanistic than fifteen years later. During the first liberalization there had been both a semi-opposition and a pseudo-opposition to fill the space (albeit ineffectively) between the Shah and the Nationalist opposition, and the leader of the semi-opposition, Amini, had afforded the Shah the possibility to ride out the storm by (at least temporarily) satisfying the demands of at least some opposition groups. By 1977 both pseudo-opposition and semi-opposition had disappeared from the scene, and when they raised their heads they were too discredited by their longtime association with the Shah regime to be able to make their presence felt. By 1978 there were simply no independent personalities left in the Shah regime. The sultanism of the Shah's late period is shown by the treatment he reserved for his longtime prime minister Amir-Abbas Hoveida: in return for twelve years of loyal service he had him arrested in November 1978 to "quiet the mob," as he put it. He even instructed the minister of justice to draft extraordinary legislation to bring Hoveida to trial as soon as possible.[2]

Within the opposition attitudes had changed too. As chapter 1 noted, each failure of the Nationalists brought more radical forces to the fore. The radicals of 1953–63, the NRM/LMI, were the moderates in 1977–79. The selfsame people who, in 1957 and 1960, had accused the

---

[2]This episode is recounted in Fereydoun Hoveyda, *The Fall of the Shah*, trans. Roger Liddell (1980), pp. 172–75.

leader of the National Front, Allahyar Saleh, of maintaining too much contact with the American embassy in Teheran now had privileged access to the U.S. ambassador, whom they tried to reassure about American interests. In 1960–63 the National Front had directed all attacks against the prime minister while the more radical NRM/LMI identified the Shah as the main source of corruption and despotism. The LMI still maintained this view in 1977–79, but by now this was a moderate attitude, as the radicals (Khomeini, the Mojahedin, and the left) were not content with getting rid of the Shah and demanded a new type of regime. Duverger's notion of *sinistrisme* applies even more in some nondemocratic settings than in the democracies he studied.

In the masses who made the revolution, the changes are also notable between the early 1960s and late 1970s. One major difference, of course, is simply size: in 1961 or 1963 the opposition to the Shah could draw at most a few tens of thousands demonstrators out into the streets, but by 1978 millions were marching in Teheran. The difference is remarkable, even if we take into account the capital's population growth over the intervening years. Was dissatisfaction so much greater in 1978, after fifteen years of economic growth, than in 1963? Or were appeals to people's religious sensibilities more effective than the call for free elections and the demand that the Shah reign but not rule? The question has no simple answer. What is clear is that the crowds of 1978 were much better organized and more easily manipulated than those of the early 1960s. During the first liberalization the leaders of the Nationalist opposition tried to avoid street confrontations with the Shah's forces; by 1978 an important faction of the clergy, led by Khomeini, was actively organizing them.

While this mass mobilization hastened the departure of the Shah, it also made a transition to democracy more difficult. The Shah regime literally collapsed, as a result of which there was no authority to supervise the transfer of power to the new regime. Bazargan and his friends in the Provisional Government owed their position to the street power of the masses and to Khomeini's personal decision, not to any elections. Their legitimacy was therefore derivative: they were expected to perform momentous tasks without having a proper mandate. Like their moderate predecessors in previous revolutionary movements, they were pushed aside by the radicals who controlled the streets.

Does Shi'ite modernism have a future in Iran? Both modernism and fundamentalism came later to Iran than to other parts of the Islamic world. Yet Iran has also been the first country in which fundamentalism triumphed, where the struggle of modernists to make religion relevant to everyday life succeeded beyond their most optimistic hopes.

Perhaps Iran will also one day be the first country to emerge from fundamentalism.

Modernism grew on the basis of the failures of secularism, and fundamentalists owe at least part of their appeal to the failures of the modernists to effect change in Iran. If Iran's fundamentalist experience does not succeed, the search for an alternative will go on. And if it does succeed, it may, like other revolutions before it, become more moderate as time goes on. In both cases modernists may yet have an important role to play.

The experience of the 1980s has shaken the beliefs of many people in Iran. Monarchists are puzzled by the ease with which the Shah regime crumbled, Nationalists have to ponder why the appeal of liberal constitutionalism was so weak, leftists are wondering why the toiling masses did not follow them, and many religious activists are asking themselves whether their ideals of a moral society are embodied in the Islamic Republic. The disillusionment about ideology has already led to a more genuine acceptance of pluralism among Iran's educated.

This soul-searching affects mainly the intelligentsia, however. At a more popular level, the effects of fundamentalist rule are more difficult to gauge. It may be that by mobilizing the masses and by bringing them into the political process in the name of a this-worldly interpretation of Islam, the revolution has actually provided an added impetus for the process of modernization and secularization in Iran.

Thus, the experience of the Islamic revolution in the end may very well force Muslims in Iran to come to terms with modernity, beyond stating categorically that the problem does not exist because Islam already contains all that is good about modernity. In one sense, the intellectual efforts of Mehdi Bazargan and Ali Shariati have been the beginnings of such an effort. In his own way, Shariati sensed the gap that separated contemporary Iranians from modernity when he wrote that twentieth-century Iran did not have in its past a "Hegel or a Nietzsche; Socialism or Proudhon; Saint-Simon or Marx; Voltaire, Rousseau or the *Encyclopédie*; the Renaissance with the scientific revolutions of Galileo and Copernicus."[3] As one of the most astute observers of the impact of modernity on religion writes, in a modern society, "the religious person is fully aware of living after Darwin, Marx, Freud, Weber and Durkheim. He is also aware of living after Kant, Hegel, Nietzsche, Dostoyevski, and Kierkegaard. If he is committed to a religious tradition that possesses Holy Scriptures, he also knows that he lives after Spinoza's Tractatus and after Wellenhausen. He no longer

[3] Ali Shariati, *Ma va Eqbal* (We and Iqbal) (1978), pp. 92–93.

wastes time on arguing with Wellenhausen, or Freud, or Marx, or Darwin . . . taking them for granted, he asks: where do we go from here?"[4] The fact that all names on this list are Western and that none of them belong to the Islamic tradition does not make the task easier, but neither does it obviate it.

In such an effort, already under way, Islamic modernists have a singular role, for they bring to the task a commitment to Islam as a religion that is genuine. Yet such a task can succeed—if at all—only if there is collaboration with the traditional clergy, which has remained marginal to the Islamic revolution; for only they can lend authority to a rethinking of the role of religion in society. The task also must involve cooperation and cross-fertilization with academic scholars of Islam whose political options have tended to separate them from the Nationalist modernists. And all those involved might benefit from examining the way other religious traditions have coped with modernity, beyond stating that the experience of other religions is irrelevant because they are flawed in a way Islam is not.

Yet, as Michael Fischer put it, "ideologies do not grow and decay through rhetorical competition with other ideologies, nor do social class compositions of polities remain static."[5] The class structure of Iran has been affected by the revolution, not least because of the exodus of a significant part of the modern segment of the population. If the LMI wants to be more than the conscience of the Islamic Republic (or its democratic fig-leaf), the LMI will have to try to build a mass basis for itself, both in Teheran and in the provinces.

The dissolution of the IRP in the spring of 1987 made the LMI the only openly functioning political party in Iran. This situation provided a potential opening for the LMI. But as long as Khomeini was alive, the options of the LMI were limited: it could not take advantage of internal struggles within the regime by making tactical alliances here and there, since Khomeini himself was the ultimate arbiter in these factional struggles. The removal of Ay. Montazeri so shortly before Khomeini's death was a serious blow to the LMI. Had Montazeri been willing to bide his time and moderate his criticism of the Iranian government, he would probably have taken Khomeini's place as religious leader of Iran; and the LMI would certainly have benefited, given the convergence between the religious modernists and Montazeri that has been taking shape since the mid-1980s.

But Montazeri returned to private life in the spring of 1989, and

---

[4]R. J. Zwi Werblowsky, *Beyond Tradition and Modernity: Changing Religions in a Changing World* (1976), p. 19.

[5]M. M. J. Fischer, "Islam and the Revolt of the Petit [sic] Bourgeoisie," *Daedalus* 111 (1982), 115.

power devolved to Ali Khameneh'i and Ali-Akbar Hashemi Rafsanjani after Khomeini's death. Even if these two leaders embark on a more "moderate" course, this moderation will not necessarily involve more democracy for Iran; more likely, it will entail a less confrontational approach to international relations, greater emphasis on economic reconstruction, and a relaxation of state control over mores. Such a policy might conceivably reconcile significant sectors of the Iranian population to the regime, thus weakening the potential bases of LMI support. Should hard-liners regain the upper hand, however, the LMI would face the daunting task of having to provide, under conditions of increased repression, a home for disappointed fundamentalists and a voice for the remnants of the modern segment who would then have nowhere to go.

The Party Program of the Liberation Movement of Iran in 1961

Teheran, Ordibehesht 25, 1340

With the Help of the Great and Almighty God

VERILY, GOD CHANGES NOT WHAT A PEOPLE HAS
UNTIL THEY CHANGE IT THEMSELVES

1. Considering the need to safeguard the rights of the Iranian people, from which, by the will of God, emanate all powers ruling over it
2. Considering the need to [enjoy] the freedom to found National organizations for the purpose of furthering the principle that the Iranian people are at the source of all correct social evolution, and that as long as every Iranian does not feel that he has personal [dignity], freedom, and social value, that as long as he does not feel that he has a say in the conduct of his affairs, and that as long as he is not allowed to engage in social activism, protest, and constructive criticism, then national talents will not flower and the nation will not attain happiness
3. Considering the need to establish social justice, which is of vital importance for maintaining domestic order, for preventing foreign meddling, and for maintaining international peace, especially in the Middle East
4. Considering the country's urgent need for a ruling group deriving its powers from the confidence and support of the people and cognizant of the conditions of the world and our time, which must be determined to enact truly national policies and face every kind of

aggression and provocation to safeguard the people's rights and especially the sacred principles of the National Movement of Iran

5. And finally considering the self-evident truth that the progress of every movement and the survival of every nation are impossible without action, sacrifice, and piety both of society and of the individual:

In compliance with

1. THE HIGH PRINCIPLES OF ISLAM AND IRAN'S CONSTITUTIONAL LAWS
2. THE UNIVERSAL DECLARATION OF HUMAN RIGHTS
3. THE CHARTER OF THE UNITED NATIONS

the Liberation Movement of Iran commences its activities in pursuit of the following goals.

Goals and Points of the Party Program

A. In Domestic Politics

First Point

1. To revive the fundamental rights of the Iranian people and install the rule of law and thereby delimit the powers and responsibilities of the different branches of government for the purpose of establishing the rule of the people by the people.
2. To entrust the government to individuals who are worthy of leading the country in today's developed world among its awoken nations.

Second Point

1. To spread moral, social, and political principles based on the exalted religion of Islam with due attention to the political and cultural conditions of the present age.
2. To encourage honesty and piety and struggle against moral corruption, addictions, and harmful publications.
3. To dispose of the elements of dishonesty and corruption, especially the symbols of foreign dominance, and to discard all those elements which stand in the way of effective, genuine, and quick reforms or which contribute to the weakening of the individual and collective personality of Iranians.
4. To struggle against the enemies of the people's bodily, intellectual, and moral health, that is to say to overcome fear, helplessness, poverty, ignorance, underdevelopment, and disunity.

Third Point

1. To gradually prepare for [the Iranian people's] participation in the running of public affairs, for making good use of democracy, and for claiming their social rights.

Fourth Point

1. To achieve economic independence. To create correct financial, commercial, social, cultural, health, agricultural, and industrial orders.
2. To establish just and peaceful relations between workers and employers, and between peasants and landowners.
3. To develop social security and to create insurance for peasants.
4. To allocate the oil revenues and foreign loans to development projects in agriculture, industry, and infrastructure and to remove said revenues and loans from the country's current budget.
5. To create financial and economic security to encourage the repatriation of private capital held in foreign banks.

Fifth Point

1. To gradually reform the nation's laws by means of creating a central organization for the elaboration of law projects.
2. To comply totally with the independence of the judicial branch, to widen the competencies of general jurisdictions and to abolish special jurisdictions.
3. To reform existing security and judicial apparatuses so as to achieve security and gain for them the confidence and goodwill of the people.

Sixth Point

1. To utilize the manpower of the entire population as the country's main capital, and to create confidence and strong belief in the principle that "A better life results from more useful activity."
2. To combat unemployment and idleness, egoism, self-indulgence, and privileges resulting from discrimination.

Seventh Point

1. To provide for the country's sound administration by
   - stabilizing offices by respecting the independence of officials and encouraging them to seek more expertise and competence,
   - training managers and strengthening offices of management, statistics, and research in all fields,
   - making use of modern methods of management,
   - and by providing for the material and spiritual welfare of government officials.

B. In Foreign Affairs

Eighth Point

1. To strive for the transfer of the right to determine the world's fate from the major powers to the United Nations so as to assure the freedom and independence of small nations. International Justice. World Peace.

Ninth Point

1. To strive for Iran's neutrality.

Tenth Point

1. To base foreign relations on the Charter of the United Nations. To create good understanding between Iran and all nations, especially neighboring countries.

Eleventh Point

1. To strive for unity among peace-loving and neutral nations which share common historical, geographical, cultural, social, or religious interests and to strive for the unity of all Muslim countries so as to facilitate the attainment of these goals.

Twelfth Point

1. To accept responsibility for and to partake in international efforts aimed at solving world problems peacefully.
2. To support genuine national movements and the independence and freedom of all peoples.

The Liberation Movement of Iran Program of July 1980

First Section: Introduction

. . .

Second Section: Principles

The program of the LMI is based on the following three principles:

1. The lofty principles of Islam, the only divine religion ... in the largest sense of the word, [representing] tenets that have been transmitted in their most pristine form by the Shi'ite school ... , and waiting and preparing for the victory at the end of times and for a united world government.

2. The constitution of the Islamic Republic of Iran, which the majority of the Iranian people approved in a referendum held on Azar 11 and Azar 12, 1358, and which is the only valid document and the only firm basis for unity and government.

3. Belief in the worldwide unity of all Muslims [and] continuing struggle for the realization of the *umma*, and the liberation of all the disinherited of the world.

Third Section: Party Program

A. Concerning the preservation of the Islamic revolution and the prevention of its deviation and destruction
   1. To spread the monotheistic world-view and the Islamic ideology.

2. To accept the leadership of the Imam [Khomeini] and to struggle against all acts that might weaken his leadership.

3. To cooperate with the informed, committed, and authentic clergy that [does not wish to monopolize power] and that moves along the path of unity.

4. To identify and expose counterrevolution and to struggle against its various internal and external manifestations.

5. To encourage the population to participate [on all levels] and to struggle against all acts that might result in popular apathy.

6. [To strive for] cultural revolution and to eliminate all traces of despotism, colonialism, and exploitation. (To identify the polytheistic cultural elements of the former order and to struggle against them.)

7. To explain and to establish an Islamic economic order and to cleanse all the country's economic and industrial relationships of the former order's anti-Islamic or non-Islamic values.

8. To struggle for the consolidation of the unity of all strata of the Islamic *umma* and to combat all actions that might sow discord or lead to the control of a particular group.

B. Concerning the establishment of the Islamic Republic

1. To defend the constitution of the Islamic Republic of Iran.

2. To strive for the elimination of the constitution's shortcomings by preparing and ratifying a supplement to it.

3. To struggle for the consolidation of the institutions created by the constitution.

4. To support those responsible in the institutions of the Islamic Republic (the executive, legislative, and judicial branches of government) so long as they act within the bounds of their legal competencies and in the interest of the preservation and continuation of the Islamic revolution.

5. To strive for the strengthening of [Iranian] society's self-reliance in the economic, technical, and scientific realms, and for the severance of the links of dependency with foreign states. To lay the basis of free and independent [foreign] relations that will preserve our people's interests and increase opportunities for the country's resources.

6. To apply the principles enshrined in the constitution precisely and comprehensively so as to build an acceptable Islamic society.

C. Concerning the worldwide spreading of the Islamic revolution

1. To present, both in theory and in practice, the rightness of the monotheistic world-view as the only way to save mankind.

2. To make the experiences and achievements of Iran's Islamic revolution available to the disinherited of the world.

3. To cooperate with and provide material and spiritual help for Islamic and revolutionary movements.

4. To struggle resolutely against all *taghuti* orders in the world (Western and Eastern colonialism).

Liberation Movement of Iran
Tir 1359

Glossary

aref: a person with mystic leanings
ayatollah: lit. "sign of God," title of distinguished *mujtahids*
bast: sanctuary, or place of sanctuary
chaqukesh: knife-wielding thug, often in the service of a politician
emam-e jama'at: the mulla appointed to lead prayers at a mosque
faqih: expert in Islamic jurisprudence
fatva: an authoritative opinion issued by a *mujtahid*
feqh: Islamic jurisprudence
hadith: sayings and deeds of the Prophet or the Imams
hezbollah: "party of God"
hezbollahi: members of the "party of God," fundamentalist activists
hojjat ol-Eslam: clerical title one rank below *ayatollah*
howzeh-ye elmiyeh: center of religious learning and teaching
ijazah: diploma enabling a clergyman to exercise *ijtihad*
ijtihad: independent judgment in the interpretation of Islamic law
javv-sazi: creation of a hostile atmosphere
madrasah: a traditional school of Islamic sciences
Majles: the Iranian parliament
maktab: a traditional elementary school
marja', pl. *maraje':* "source of emulation," highest rank among Shi'i clergy
moballegh: missionary, one who spreads religion
mujtahid: a clergyman entitled to exercise *ijtihad*
mulla: lower-ranking clergyman, also generic term for clergyman
pishnamaz: leader of prayers in a mosque
rowhani: a member of the religious institution
rowzehkhani: the ritual mourning ceremonies for major martyrs

talabeh, pl. *tollab:* students at a *howzeh*

umma: the community of Muslim believers

velayat-e (motlaq-e) faqih: (absolute) rule by the jurisprudent, a cornerstone of Ay. Khomeini's thought.

Bibliography

Primary Sources in Persian

Ba'd az entekhabat-e riasat-e jomhuri cheh shod va cheh bayad kard. Teheran: LMI, 1985.
Bahsi darbareh-ye marja'iyat va rowhaniyat. Teheran: Sazeman-e Enteshar, 1962.
Barkhord ba nehzat va pasokh-e ma. Teheran: LMI, 1983.
Bazargan, Abdolali, ed. *Masa'el va moshkelat-e nakhostin sal-e enqelab.* Teheran: LMI, 1983.
Bazargan, Mehdi. *Mazhab dar Orupa.* Teheran: n.p., 1961.
——. *Modafe'at dar dadgah-e gheir-e saleh-e tajdid-e nazar-e nezami.* N.p.: Entesharat-e Modarres, 1971.
——. *Be'sat va ideolozhi.* Houston, Tex.: Book Distribution Center, 1976.
——. *Marz-e mian-e din va omur-e ejtema'i.* Houston, Tex.: Book Distribution Center, 1976.
——. *Pragmatizm dar Eslam.* Houston, Tex.: Book Distribution Center, 1976.
——. *Azadi-ye Hend.* Teheran: Omid, 1977.
——. *Rah-e teyy shodeh.* Houston, Tex.: Book Distribution Center, 1977.
——. *Serr-e aqab-oftadegi-ye melal-e mosalman.* Houston, Tex.: Book Distribution Center, 1977.
——. *Tabi'at, takamol, towhid.* Houston, Tex.: Book Distribution Center, 1977.
——. *Afat-e towhid.* Houston, Tex.: Book Distribution Center, 1978.
——. *Sazegari-ye Irani.* 2d ed. Houston, Tex.: Book Distribution Center, 1978.
——. Interview given to Hamid Algar. *Nasr,* February 1, 1981.
——. *Bazyabi-ye arzeshha.* Teheran: LMI, 1982.
——. *Showra-ye enqelab va dowlat-e movaqqat.* Teheran: LMI, 1982.
——. *Gomrahan.* Teheran: LMI, 1983.
——. *Enqelab-e eslami dar do harekat.* Teheran: n.p., 1984.
Chegunegi-ye tashkil-e jebhe-ye melli-ye dovvom va naqsh-e nehzat-e moqavemat-e melli-ye Iran. Houston, Tex.: LMI(a), 1977.

Daneshjuyan-e mosalman-e peirow-e khatt-e emam. *Asnad-e laneh-ye jasusi.* Teheran. n.d.

E'terafat-e zheneral. Teheran: Ney, 1986.

Ettela'iyeh-ye nehzat-e azadi-ye Iran be monasebat-e rehlat-e rahbare enqelab. Teheran: 1989.

Goftar-e mah dar namayandan-e rah-e rast-e din, 3 vols. Teheran: Sadduq, n.d.

Hadis-e moqavemat: Asnad-e nehzat-e moqavemat-e melli-ye Iran. Teheran: LMI, 1986.

Hariri, Naser. *Masahebeh ba tarikhasazan-e Iran.* Teheran: 1979.

Hoshdar piramun-e tadavom-e jang-e khanemansuz. Teheran: LMI, 1988.

Markaz-e Amar-e Iran. *Iran dar a'ineh-ye amar.* Teheran: 1983.

Mavaze'-e nehzat dar kongrehha-ye sevvom, chaharom, panjom. Teheran: LMI, 1983.

Mokatebat-e Mosaddeq: Talash baray-e tashkil-e jebhe-ye melli-ye sevvom. Paris: Entesharat-e Mosaddeq, 1975.

Mosahebeh-ye doktor Yazdi ba mokhber-e nashriyeh-ye arabi-ye al-majallah. Teheran: LMI, 1985.

Na'ini, Mirza Mohammad-Hosein. *Tanbih ul-ummah wa tanzih ul-millah: Ya hokumat az nazar-e Eslam.* Teheran: Sherkat-e Sahami-ye Enteshar, 1955.

Nameh-ye sargoshadeh be sepah-e pasdaran-e enqelab-e eslami. Teheran: LMI, 1983.

Payam-e nehzat-e azadi beh rahbar-e enqelab-e eslami-ye Iran. Teheran: LMI, 1986.

Payan-e adelaneh-ye jang-e bipayan. Teheran: LMI, 1985.

Safehati az tarikh-e mo'aser-e Iran: Asnad-e nehzat-e azadi-ye Iran. Vol. 1, 2, and 11. Teheran: LMI, 1982, 1983.

Safehati az tarikh-e mo'aser-e Iran: Asnad-e nehzat-e moqavemat-e melli-ye Iran. Vol. 5. Teheran: LMI, 1984.

Sahabi, Ezzatollah. *Modafe'at-e mohandes Ezzatollah Sahabi dar bidadgah-e tajdid-e nazar-e nezami.* [Springfield, Mo.]: LMI(a), 1976.

Shariati, Ali. *Niayesh.* Mashad, 1948.

——. *Emam va Emamat.* N.p.: MSA reprint, n.d. [1977?].

——. *Fatemeh Fatemeh ast.* Teheran: Shabdiz, 1977.

——. *Ma va Eqbal.* Teheran: Hoseiniyeh Ershad, 1978.

——. *Shi'eh.* Teheran: Hoseiniyeh Ershad, 1979.

Shesh nameh-ye sargoshadeh. Teheran: LMI, 1983.

Tahlili piramun-e jang va solh. Teheran: LMI, 1984.

Talash-e dowlat-e movaqqat bara-ye jelowgiri az jang-e tahmili-ye Eraq. Teheran: LMI, n.d.

Tarikhcheh, jarayan-e kudeta, va khatt-e mashshy-e konuni-ye sazeman-e mojahedin-e khalq-e Iran. N.p.: Entesharat-e Abuzarr, n.d.

Towzihati piramun-e mozakereh, atash-bas, solh. Teheran: LMI, 1984.

Yadnameh-ye bistomin salgard-e nehzat-e azadi-ye Iran. Teheran: LMI, 1981.

Yazdi, Ebrahim. *Akharin talashha dar akharin ruzha.* Teheran: Qalam, 1984.

Zendeginameh-ye sardar-e rashid-e eslam shahid doktor Mostafa Chamran. Teheran: LMI, 1982.

Primary Sources in Other Languages

Abedi, Mahdi, and Gary Legenhausen, eds. *Jihad and Shahadat: Struggle and Martyrdom in Islam.* Houston, Tex.: IRIS, 1986.

Al-e Ahmad, Jalal. *Gharbzadegi (Weststruckness)*. Trans. John Green and Ahmad Alizadeh. Lexington, Ky.: Mazda, 1982.

Alexander, Yonah, and Allan Nanes, eds. *The United States and Iran: A Documentary History*. Frederick, Md.: University Publications of America, 1980.

Amnesty International. *Law and Human Rights in the Islamic Republic of Iran*. London: Amnesty International, 1980.

Arberry, Arthur J. *The Koran Interpreted*. London: Oxford University Press, 1964.

Bakhtiar, Chapour. *Ma fidélité*. Paris: Albin Michel, 1982.

Bazargan, Mehdi. "The Causes of the Decline and Decadence of Islamic Nations." *Islamic Review* 23 (6) (June 1951).

———. *Work in Islam*. Trans. M. Yasfi, Ali A. Behzadnia, and Najpu Denny. Houston, Tex.: Free Islamic Literatures, 1979.

Brzezinski, Zbigniew. *Power and Principle: Memoirs of the National Security Adviser, 1977-1981*. New York: Farrar, Straus and Giroux, 1983.

Carrel, Alexis. *Man the Unknown*. New York: Harper & Brothers, 1935.

———. *Prayer*. Trans. Dulcie de Ste. Croix Wright. New York: Morehouse-Gorham, 1949.

Carter, Jimmy. *Keeping Faith: Memoirs of a President*. New York: Bantam, 1982.

The Documents of Vatican II. New York: Guild Press, 1966.

Donohue, John J., and John L. Esposito, eds. *Islam in Transition: Muslim Perspectives*. New York: Oxford University Press, 1982.

Guénon, René. *The Reign of Quantity and the Signs of the Times*. Trans. Lord Northbourne. London: Luzac, 1953.

Herz, Martin F., ed. *Contacts with the Opposition: A Symposium*. Washington, D.C.: Georgetown University, Institute for the Study of Diplomacy, School of Foreign Service, 1980.

Hoveyda, Fereydoun. *The Fall of the Shah*. Trans. Roger Liddell. New York: Wyndham, 1980.

Khomeini, Ruhollah. *Islam and Revolution: Writings and Declarations of Imam Khomeini*. Trans. and annotated Hamid Algar. Berkeley, Calif.: Mizan, 1981.

La Mennais, Felicité de. *Des progrès de la revolution et de la guerre contre l'église*. Paris: n.p., 1829.

Lecomte de Noüy, Pierre. *Human Destiny*. New York: Longmans, Green, 1947.

Lenin, V. I. *Collected Works*. New York: International Publishers, 1967.

Ministère de l'éducation nationale—Direction des bibliothèques de France. *Catalogue des thèses de doctorat soutenues devant les universités françaises—Année 1963*. Paris: Cercle de la librairie, 1964.

Nobari, Ali-Reza, ed. *Iran Erupts*. Stanford, Calif.: Iran-America Documentation Group, 1978.

Nyerere, Julius K. *Ujamaa—Essays on Socialism*. London: Oxford University Press, 1968.

Pahlavi, Mohammad Reza. *Mission for My Country*. London: Hutchinson, 1960.

———. *Answer to History*. New York: Stein and Day, 1980.

Shariati, Ali. *On the Sociology of Islam.* Trans. Hamid Algar. Berkeley, Calif.: Mizan, 1979.

——. *From Where Shall We Begin?* Trans. Fatollah Marjani. Houston, Tex.: Free Islamic Literatures, 1980.

——. *Marxism and Other Western Fallacies.* Trans. R. Campbell. Berkeley, Calif.: Mizan, 1980.

——. *Man and Islam.* Trans. Fatollah Marjani. Houston, Tex.: Free Islamic Literatures, 1981.

——. *What Is to Be Done: The Enlightened Thinker and an Islamic Renaissance.* Ed. and ann. Farhang Rajaee. Houston, Tex.: IRIS, 1986.

Sullivan, William. "Dateline Iran: The Road Not Taken." *Foreign Policy* 40 (Fall 1980).

——. *Mission to Iran.* New York: W. W. Norton, 1981.

Taleqani, Seyyed Mahmood. *Society and Economics in Islam: Writings and Declarations of Ayatullah Sayyid Mahmud Taleqhani.* Intro. and ed. Hamid Algar, trans. R. Campbell. Berkeley, Calif.: Mizan, 1982.

——. *Islam and Ownership.* Trans. Ahmad Jabbari and Farhang Rajaee. Lexington, Ky.: Mazda, 1983.

U.S. Congress. House. Committee on Government Operations. *United States Aid Operations in Iran.* Report No. 10. 85th Congress, 1st session, 1957.

U.S. Congress. House. Subcommittee on International Organizations of the Committee on International Relations. "Testimony of William J. Butler, chairman of the Executive Committee of the International Committee of Jurists." 95th Congress, October 26, 1977.

Vance, Cyrus. *Hard Choices.* New York: Simon and Schuster, 1983.

Vieille, Paul, and Abol-Hasan Banisadr, eds. *Pétrole et Violence.* Paris: Editions anthropos, 1974.

Secondary Sources in Persian

Afrasiabi, Bahram, and Sa'id Dehqan. *Taleqani va tarikh.* Teheran: Entesharat-e Nilufar, 1981.

Ashraf, Ahmad. *Mavane'-e tarikhi-ye roshd-e sarmayehdari dar Iran: dowreh-ye Qajariyeh.* Teheran: Zamineh, 1980.

Banisadr, Abolhasan. *Vaz'iyat-e Iran va naqsh-e Modarres.* Paris: Entesharat-e Modarres, 1977.

Bastani Parizi, Mohammad-Ebrahim. *Talash-e azadi.* Teheran: Novin, 1977.

Habib, Abdolhayy. "Introduction" to *Faza'el ol-Balkh.* Teheran: Entesharat-e Bonyad-e Farhang-e Iran, 1971.

Jazani, Bizhan. *Tarh-e jame'eh shenasi va mabani-ye estratezhi-ye jonbesh-e enqelabi-ye khalq-e Iran—Tarikh-e si saleh-ye Iran.* Teheran: Entesharat-e Maziar, 1979.

Katouzian, Homa. "Introduction" to Khalil Maleki, *Khaterat-e siasi.* Teheran: Entesharat-e Ravaq, 1979.

Khajehnuri, Ebrahim. *Bazigaran-e asr-e tala'i: Seyyed Hasan-e Modarres.* Teheran: Javidan, 1979.

Madani, S. Jalaleddin. *Tarikh-e siasi-ye mo'aser-e Iran, II.* Teheran: Daftar-e entesharat-e eslami, 1983.

Nuri Ala', Esma'il. *Jame'eh shenasi-ye siasi-ye tashayyo'-e esna-ashari.* Teheran: Qaqnus, 1978.

Secondary Sources in Other Languages

Abrahamian, Ervand. *Iran between Two Revolutions.* Princeton, N.J.: Princeton University Press, 1982.

Ajami, Fouad. *The Vanished Imam: Musa al Sadr and the Shia of Lebanon.* Ithaca, N.Y.: Cornell University Press, 1986.

Akhavi, Shahrough. *Religion and Politics in Contemporary Iran: Clergy-State Relations in the Pahlavi Period.* Albany: State University of New York Press, 1980.

Alfieri, Vittorio. *Of Tyranny.* Trans. Julius A. Molinaro and Beatrice Corrigan. Toronto: University of Toronto Press, 1961.

Algar, Hamid. *The Roots of the Islamic Revolution.* London: The Open Press, 1983.

Amanat, Abbas. "In Between the Madrasa and the Marketplace: The Designation of Clerical Leadership in Modern Shi'ism." In Said Amir Arjomand, ed. *Authority and Political Culture in Shi'ism.* Albany: State University of New York Press, 1988.

Amiralai, Chamseddine. *Les régimes politiques et le consortium de pétrole en Iran (1953-1962).* Aix-en-Provence: La Pensée universelle, 1963.

Amir Arjomand, Said. "Shi'ite Islam and the Revolution in Iran." *Government and Opposition* 16 (1981).

——. "*A la recherche de la conscience collective:* Durkheim's Ideological Impact in Turkey and Iran." *American Sociologist* 17 (1982).

——. *The Shadow of God and the Hidden Imam: Religion, Political Order, and Societal Change in Shi'ite Iran from the Beginnings to 1890.* Chicago: Chicago University Press, 1984.

——, ed. *From Nationalism to Revolutionary Islam.* Albany: State University of New York Press, 1984.

Apter, David E. *The Politics of Modernization.* Chicago: University of Chicago Press, 1965.

Arasteh, A. Reza. *Man and Society in Iran.* Leiden: E. J. Brill, 1964.

——. *Education and Social Awakening in Iran, 1850-1968.* 2d ed. Leiden: E. J. Brill, 1969.

Ashraf, Ahmad. "Historical Obstacles to the Development of a Bourgeoisie in Iran." In M. A. Cook, ed. *Studies in the Economic History of the Middle East from the Rise of Islam to the Present Day.* Oxford: Oxford University Press, 1978.

——. "The Roots of Emerging Dual Class Structure in Nineteenth-Century Iran." *Iranian Studies* 14 (Winter–Spring 1981).

——. "Bazaar and Mosque in Iran's Revolution." Interview given to Ervand Abrahamian. *MERIP Reports* 13 (March–April 1983).

Ashraf, A., and H. Hekmat, "Merchants and Artisans in the Development

Processes of Nineteenth-Century Iran." In A. L. Udovitch, ed. *The Islamic Middle East, 700–1900: Studies in Economic and Social History.* Princeton, N.J.: Darwin Press, 1981.

Avery, Peter. *Modern Iran.* New York: Praeger, 1965.

Bagehot, Walter. *The English Constitution.* Ithaca, N.Y.: Cornell University Press, 1963.

Bakhash, Shaul. *The Reign of the Ayatollahs: Iran and the Islamic Revolution.* New York: Basic Books, 1984.

Bamford, James. *The Puzzle Palace.* Boston: Houghton Mifflin, 1982.

Barthes, Roland. "Le Discours de l'histoire." *Social Science Information* 6 (4) (August 1967).

——. *Mythologies.* Trans. Annette Lavers. New York: Hill and Wang, 1975.

——. *Elements of Semiology.* Trans. Annette Lavers and Colin Smith. New York: Hill and Wang, 1985.

Bayat, Mangol. "A Phoenix too Frequent: The Concept of Historical Continuity in Modern Iranian Thought." *Asian and African Studies* 12 (1978).

——. *Mysticism and Dissent: Socioreligious Thought in Qajar Iran.* Syracuse, N.Y.: Syracuse University Press, 1982.

Bechert, Heinz. *Buddhismus, Staat und Gesellschaft in den Ländern des Theravada Buddhismus.* Vol. 1. Frankfurt: Alfred Metzner, 1966.

——. *Buddhismus, Staat und Gesellschaft in den Ländern des Theravada Buddhismus.* Vol. 2. Wiesbaden: Otto Harrassowitz, 1967.

Beck, Lois. *The Qashqa'i of Iran.* New Haven, Conn.: Yale University Press, 1986.

Benard, Cheryl, and Zalmay Khalilzad. *"The Government of God"—Iran's Islamic Republic.* New York: Columbia University Press, 1984.

Bendix, Reinhard. *Kings or People: Power and the Mandate to Rule.* Berkeley and Los Angeles; University of California Press, 1978.

Bill, James A. *The Eagle and the Lion: The Tragedy of American-Iranian Relations.* New Haven, Conn.: Yale University Press, 1988.

Binder, Leonard. *Iran: Political Development in a Changing Society.* Berkeley and Los Angeles: University of California Press, 1964.

Binder, Leonard; J. S. Coleman; J. LaPalombara; L. W. Pye; S. Verba; and M. Weiner. *Crises and Sequences in Political Development.* Princeton, N.J.: Princeton University Press, 1971.

Blachère, Régis, *Le Problème de Mahomet.* Paris: Presses universitaires de France, 1952.

——. *Introduction au Coran.* Paris: Besson & Chantemerle, 1959.

Borges, Jorge Luis. *Other Inquisitions.* Trans. Ruth L.C. Simms. New York: Simon and Schuster, 1965.

Brinton, Crane. *Anatomy of Revolution.* New York: Random House, 1965.

Burgat, François. "De la difficulté de nommer *intégrisme, fondamentalisme, islamisme.*" *Les Temps Modernes* 43 (March 1988).

Chehabi, Issa. "Kulturelle Beziehungen zwischen Deutschland und Iran." *Die Horen* 26 (123) (Autumn 1981).

Chenu, M.-D. *La "Doctrine sociale" de l'église comme idéologie.* Paris: CERF, 1979.

Chubin, Bahram, and Sepehr Zabih. *The Foreign Relations of Iran.* Berkeley and Los Angeles: University of California Press, 1974.

Corbin, Henri. "La Place de Molla Sadra Shirazi dans la philosophie iranienne." *Studia Islamica* 18 (1963).

Cottam, Richard. *Nationalism in Iran*. Pittsburgh: Pittsburgh University Press, 1978.

Cox, Harvey. *The Secular City: Secularization and Urbanization in Theological Perspective*. New York: Macmillan, 1966.

Dabashi, Hamid. "Early Propagation of *Wilayat-i Faqih* and Mulla Ahmad Naraqi." In Seyyed Hossein Nasr, Hamid Dabashi, and Seyyed Vali Reza Nasr, eds. *Expectation of the Millennium: Shi'ism in History*. Albany: State University of New York Press, 1989.

Dahl, Robert. *Polyarchy*. New Haven, Conn.: Yale University Press, 1971.

Darwin, John. *Britain, Egypt, and the Middle East: Imperial Policy in the Aftermath of War, 1918-1922*. London: Macmillan, 1981.

Dermenghem, Emile. *The Life of Mahomet*. Trans. Arabella Yorke. London: Routledge & Sons, 1930.

Duverger, Maurice. *Political Parties*. Trans. Barbara North and Robert North. New York: John Wiley, 1959.

Edwards, W. Sterling, and Peter D. Edwards. *Alexis Carrel: Visionary Surgeon*. Springfield, Il.: Charles C Thomas, 1974.

Eisenstadt, S. N., ed. *Post-Traditional Societies*. New York: W. W. Norton, 1974. Chapters by Eisenstadt and S. J. Tambiah.

Ekbal, Kamran. "Der politische Einfluss des persischen Kaufmannsstandes in der frühen Kadscharenzeit, dargestellt am Beispiel von Ḩaǧǧi Halil Khan Qazwini Maliku't-Tuǧǧar." *Der Islam* 57 (1980).

Eliade, Mircea. *The Sacred and the Profane*. New York: Harcourt, Brace, World, 1959.

———. *Myth and Reality*. Trans. W. R. Trask. New York: Harper & Row, 1963.

Enayat, Hamid. *Modern Islamic Political Thought*. Austin: University of Texas Press, 1982.

Encyclopaedia of Islam. Leiden: E. J. Brill, 1978. Article on "Islah."

Fischer, Michael M. J. "Persian Society: Transformation and Strain." In Hossein Amirsadeghi, ed. *Twentieth Century Iran*. London: Heinemann, 1977.

———. *Iran: From Religious Dispute to Revolution*. Cambridge, Mass.: Harvard University Press, 1980.

———. "Islam and the Revolt of the Petit [sic] Bourgeoisie." *Daedalus* 111 (1982).

Fisher, David Hackett. *Historians' Fallacies: Towards a Logic of Historical Thought*. New York: Harper & Row, 1970.

Flanz, Gisbert H. "A Comparative Analysis of the Constitution of the Islamic Republic of Iran." In Albert P. Blaustein and Gisbert H. Flanz, eds. *Constitutions of the World, Iran*. Dobbs Ferry, N.Y.: Oceana Publications, 1980.

Floor, Willem M. "The Guilds in Iran: An Overview from the Earliest Beginnings till 1972." *Zeitschrift der Deutschen Morgenländischen Gesellschaft* 125 (1975).

Gasiorowski, Mark. "The 1953 *Coup d'Etat* in Iran." *International Journal of Middle East Studies* 19 (1987).

Geertz, Clifford. *The Interpretation of Cultures*. New York: Basic Books, 1973.

Geiger, Theodor. *Die soziale Schichtung des deutschen Volkes.* Stuttgart: Ferdinand Enke, 1932.

Gibb, H. A. R. *Modern Trends in Islam.* New York: Octagon Press, 1972.

Graham, Robert. *Iran: The Illusion of Power.* New York: St. Martin's Press, 1980.

Gray, Asa. *Darwiniana: Essays and Reviews Pertaining to Darwinism.* Ed. A. H. Dupree. Cambridge, Mass.: Belknap Press of Harvard University Press, 1963.

Greussing, Kurt, ed. *Revolution in Iran und Afghanistan.* Frankfurt: Syndikat, 1980. Article by Ahmad Mahrad.

——, ed. *Religion und Politik im Iran.* Frankfurt: Syndikat, 1981. Article by H. G. Kippenberg.

Grew, Raymond, ed. *Crises of Political Development in Europe and the United States.* Princeton, N.J.: Princeton University Press, 1978.

Grousset, René. *La Face de l'Asie.* Paris: Payot, 1955.

Guiraud, Pierre. *La Sémiologie.* Paris: Presses universitaires de France, 1971.

Haim, Sylvia. "Alfieri and al-Kawakibi." *Oriente Moderno* 34 (1954).

Hairi, Abdul-Hadi. *Shi'ism and Constitutionalism in Iran.* Leiden: E. J. Brill, 1977.

Halliday, Fred. *Iran: Dictatorship and Development.* New York: Penguin, 1979.

Halpern, Manfred. *The Politics of Social Change in the Middle East and North Africa.* Princeton, N.J.: Princeton University Press, 1963.

Hendershot, Clarence. *Politics, Polemics, and Pedagogs.* New York: Vantage Press, 1975.

Hintze, Otto. *The Historical Essays of Otto Hintze.* Ed. Felix Gilbert. New York: Oxford University Press, 1975.

Hourani, Albert. *Arabic Thought in the Liberal Age.* Cambridge: Cambridge University Press, 1983.

Huntington, Samuel P. *Political Order in Changing Societies.* New Haven, Conn.: Yale University Press, 1968.

Huyser, Robert E. *Mission to Iran.* New York: Harper & Row, 1986.

Ibrahim, Saad Eddin. "Anatomy of Egypt's Militant Islamic Groups." *International Journal of Middle East Studies* 12 (1980).

Irani, Ali Reza. "Grundzüge der islamischen Ideologie im Iran." *Politische Studien,* Sonderheft 3/1980.

Irnberger, Harald. *SAVAK oder der Folterfreund des Westens.* Reinbeck bei Hamburg: Rowohlt, 1977.

Jerome, Carole. *The Man in the Mirror: A True Inside Story of Revolution, Love and Treachery in Iran.* London: Unwin Hyman, 1987.

Katouzian, Homa. *The Political Economy of Modern Iran: Despotism and Pseudo-Modernism, 1926-1979.* New York: New York University Press, 1981.

Kazemi, Farhad. *Poverty and Revolution in Iran.* New York: New York University Press, 1980.

Kazemzadeh, Firuz. *Russia and Britain in Persia, 1864-1914.* New Haven, Conn.: Yale University Press, 1968.

——. "The Terror Facing the Bahais." *New York Review of Books,* May 13, 1982.

Keddie, Nikki R. "The Origins of the Religious-Radical Alliance in Iran." *Past and Present* 34 (1966).

——. *Roots of Revolution.* New Haven, Conn.: Yale University Press, 1981.

——. *An Islamic Response to Imperialism: The Political and Religious Writings of Jamal-al-Din "al-Afghani."* Berkeley and Los Angeles: University of California Press, 1983.

——, ed. *Scholars, Saints, and Sufis.* Berkeley and Los Angeles: University of California Press, 1972. Articles by H. Algar, R. L. Chambers, and G. Thaiss.

——, ed. *Religion and Politics in Iran.* New Haven, Conn.: Yale University Press, 1982. Articles by M. Hegland, H. Katouzian, and Yann Richard.

Keddie, Nikki R., and Michael E. Bonine, eds. *Continuity and Change in Modern Iran.* Albany: State University of New York Press, 1981.

Kedourie, Elie. *Afghani and 'Abduh.* London: Frank Cass, 1966.

Kedourie, Elie, and Sylvia G. Haim. *Towards a Modern Iran.* London: Frank Cass, 1980. Articles by E. Abrahamian and M. Bayat.

Kelly, John. "CIA in Iran." *Counterspy* 3 (4) (April-May 1979).

Kolakowsksi, Leszek, *Marxism and Beyond: On Historical Understanding and Individual Responsibility.* Trans. Jane Zielonko Peel. London: Pall Mall Press, 1969.

Ladjevardi, Habib. *Labor Unions and Autocracy in Iran.* Syracuse, N.Y.: Syracuse University Press, 1985.

Lambton, A. K. S. "A Reconsideration of the Position of the *Marja Al-Taqlid* and the Religious Institution." *Studia Islamica* 20 (1964).

Lampedusa, Giuseppe Tomasi di. *The Leopard.* Trans. Archibald Colquhoun. New York: Pantheon Books, 1960.

LaPalombara, Joseph. "Macrotheories and Microapplications in Comparative Politics." *Comparative Politics* 1 (October 1968).

Lecomte de Noüy, Marie. *The Road to "Human Destiny": A Life of Pierre Lecomte de Noüy.* New York: Longmans, Green, 1955.

Lepsius, Rainer. "Zur Strategie des Regimewechsels." In Hans Albert, ed. *Sozialtheorie and soziale Praxis. Eduard Baumgarten zum 70. Geburtstag.* Meisenheim am Glan: Anton Hain, 1971.

Letamendia, Pierre. *La Démocratie chrétienne.* Paris: Presses universitaires de France, 1979.

Lewy, Guenther. "Historical Data in Comparative Political Analysis." *Comparative Politics* 1 (October 1968).

Linz, Juan J. "Opposition in an Authoritarian Regime: The Case of Spain." In Robert Dahl, ed. *Regimes and Oppositions.* New Haven, Conn.: Yale University Press, 1973.

——. "Totalitarian and Authoritarian Regimes." In Nelson Polsby and Fred Greenstein, eds. *Handbook of Political Science.* Vol. 3. Reading, Mass.: Addison Wesley, 1975.

——. "Some Notes toward a Comparative Study of Fascism in Sociological Historical Perspective." In W. Laqueur, ed. *Fascism: A Reader's Guide.* Berkeley and Los Angeles: University of California Press, 1976.

Lipset, Seymour M., and Stein Rokkan. "Cleavage Structures, Party Systems, and Voter Alignments: An Introduction." In S. M. Lipset, and S. Rokkan, eds. *Party Systems and Voter Alignments: Cross-National Perspectives.* New York: Free Press, 1967.

Lorwin, V. R. "Segmented Pluralism: Ideological Cleavages and Political Cohesion in the Smaller European Democracies." *Comparative Politics* 3 (January 1971).

Mahrad, Ahmad. *Iran unter der Herrschaft Reza Schahs*. Frankfurt: Campus, 1977.

Mazlish, Bruce. *The Revolutionary Ascetic: Evolution of a Political Type*. New York: McGraw-Hill, 1976.

Merad, Ali. "The Ideologization of Islam in the Contemporary Muslim World." In Alexander S. Cudsi and Ali E. Hillal Dessouki, eds. *Islam and Power*. London: Croom Helm, 1981.

Merton, Robert. *Social Theory and Social Structure*. Glencoe, Il.: Free Press, 1963.

Millward, William G. "Aspects of Modernism in Shi'a Islam." *Studia Islamica* 37 (1973).

Momen, Moojan. *An Introduction to Shi'i Islam*. New Haven, Conn.: Yale University Press, 1985.

Mottahedeh, Roy P. "The Shu'ubiyah Controversy and the Social History of Early Islamic Iran." *International Journal of Middle East Studies* 7 (1976).

Mozaffari, Mehdi. *L'Iran*. Paris: Librairie générale de droit et de jurisprudence R. Pichon et R. Durand-Auzias, 1978.

Norton, Augustus Richard. *Amal and the Shi'a: Struggle For the Soul of Lebanon*. Austin: University of Texas Press, 1987.

Peters, F. E. *Aristoteles Arabus*. Leiden: E. J. Brill, 1968.

Petrossian, Vahe. "Dilemmas of the Iranian Revolution." *The World Today* 36 (1980).

Petrushevsky, I. P. *Islam in Iran*. Albany: State University of New York Press, 1985.

Popper, Karl R. *The Poverty of Historicism*. New York: Harper, 1964.

Rahman, Fazlur. "Islam: Legacy and Contemporary Challenge." In C. K. Pullapilly, ed. *Islam in the Contemporary World*. Notre Dame, Indiana: Cross Roads Books, 1980.

——. *Islam and Modernity: Transformation of an Intellectual Tradition*. Chicago: University of Chicago Press, 1982.

Ramazani, Rouhollah K. "The Autonomous Republics of Azerbaijan and Kurdistan: Their Rise and Fall." In Thomas T. Hammond, ed. *The Anatomy of Communist Takeovers*. New Haven, Conn.: Yale University Press, 1975.

——. *Iran's Foreign Policy: A Study of Foreign Policy in Modernizing Nations*. Charlottesville: University Press of Virginia, 1975.

——. *The United States and Iran: The Pattern of Influence*. New York: Praeger, 1982.

Reppa, Robert B. *Israel and Iran: Bilateral Relationship and Effect on the Indian Ocean Basin*. New York: Praeger, 1974.

Rodinson, Maxime. *Islam and Capitalism*. Trans. Brian Pearce. Austin: University of Texas Press, 1978.

Rousseau, Jean-Jacques. "Essay on the Origin of Languages. In *On the Origin of Languages*, Trans. with afterword John H. Moran and Alexander Gode. Chicago: University of Chicago Press, 1986.

Rubin, Barry. *Paved with Good Intentions*. London and New York: Penguin, 1981.

Sa'edi, Gholam Hoseyn. "Iran under the Party of God." *Index on Censorship* 1 (1984).

Salehi-Isfahani, Djavad. "The Political Economy of Credit Subsidy in Iran, 1973-1978." *International Journal of Middle East Studies* 21 (1989).

Scheler, Max. *Ressentiment*. Ed. and intro. L. A. Coser, trans. W. W. Holdheim. New York: Schocken, 1972.

Seger, Martin. *Teheran: Eine stadtgeographische Studie*. Vienna: Springer Verlag, 1978.

Shayegan, Daryush. *Qu'est-ce qu'une revolution religieuse?* Paris: Les Presses d'aujourd'hui, 1982.

Le Shi'isme Imamite: Colloque de Strasbourg. Paris: Presses universitaires de France. Article by J. Aubin.

Shils, Edward. "Tradition." *Comparative Studies in Society and History* 13 (1971).

Siegfried, André. *L'Ame des peuples*. Paris: Hachette, 1950.

Stepan, Alfred. "Paths towards Redemocratization: Theoretical and Comparative Considerations." In Guillermo O'Donnell, Philippe Schmitter, and Lawrence Whitehead, eds. *Transitions from Authoritarian Rule: Comparative Perspectives*. Baltimore: Johns Hopkins University Press, 1986.

——. *Rethinking Military Politics: Brazil and the Southern Cone*. Princeton, N.J.: Princeton University Press, 1988.

Thaiss, Gustav. "The Bazaar as a Case Study of Religious and Social Change." In Ehsan Yar-Shater, ed. *Iran Faces the Seventies*. New York: Praeger, 1971.

Toynbee, Arnold. *Civilization on Trial*. New York: Oxford University Press, 1948.

Verba, Sidney. "Some Dilemmas in Comparative Research." *World Politics* 20 (October 1967).

Vernoux, Joseph. *L'Iran des mollah—la revolution introuvable*. Paris: Anthropos, 1981.

Watt, W. Montgomery. *Muhammad: Prophet and Statesman*. London: Oxford University Press, 1974.

Watt, W. M. *Islamic Political Thought*. Edinburgh: Edinburgh University Press, 1980.

Weber, Max. *Economy and Society*. Trans. and ed. Guenther Roth and Claus Wittich. Berkeley and Los Angeles: University of California Press, 1978.

Werblowsky, R. J. Zwi. *Beyond Tradition and Modernity: Changing Religions in a Changing World*. London: Athlone Press, 1976.

Zabih, Sepehr. *The Communist Movement of Iran*. Berkeley and Los Angeles: University of California Press, 1966.

——. *Iran since the Revolution*. London: Croom Helm, 1982.

Zonis, Marvin. *The Political Elite of Iran*. Princeton: N.J.: Princeton University Press, 1971.

Index

335